# Q & A SERIES
# CIVIL LIBERTIES
# AND HUMAN RIGHTS

## SECOND EDITION

Cavendish
Publishing
Limited

London • Sydney

# TITLES IN THE Q&A SERIES

# Q & A SERIES
# CIVIL LIBERTIES AND HUMAN RIGHTS

**SECOND EDITION**

Helen Fenwick, BA, LLB
Reader in Law
University of Durham

Cavendish
Publishing
Limited

London • Sydney

Second edition first published 2001 by Cavendish Publishing Limited, The Glass House, Wharton Street, London WC1X 9PX, United Kingdom

Telephone: +44 (0)20 7278 8000
Facsimile:  +44 (0)20 7278 8080
Email: info@cavendishpublishing.com
Website: www.cavendishpublishing.com

© Fenwick, H          2001
First edition         1995
Second edition        2001

British Library Cataloguing in Publication Data

Fenwick, Helen
Civil liberties and human rights – 2nd ed – (Q & A)
1 Civil rights – England – Examinations, questions, etc
2 Civil rights – Wales – Examinations, questions, etc
I Title
342.4'2'085

ISBN 1 85941 276 9

Printed and bound in Great Britain

A004573
£12·95
6/6/3
323

# PREFACE

These are exciting and confusing times in which to study civil liberties or, as it is becoming more commonly known, domestic human rights. Since the first edition of this book, there has been a rapid acceleration of development of this field of law, which has become almost all-pervasive. There are many new statutes and cases which have been incorporated into the questions in this edition, most notably the Human Rights Act 1998, which has finally incorporated the European Convention on Human Rights and Fundamental Freedoms into domestic law. This is such a significant change that it will affect every civil liberties and human rights course and so the new law and its likely scope forms the focus of many of the questions in this edition. Students will be expected to have a thorough knowledge of the 1998 Act, its implications and the relevant existing case authority on the ECHR as it relates to each and every area of their course, and so these topics have been addressed in depth. The speed of change in this field and the sheer volume of new human rights-related statutes requires some selectivity in the topics chosen for discussion here, but the core areas of any human rights/civil liberties course are examined. New questions have also been included on topics of current and likely future interest, such as privacy, freedom of information, immigration and asylum provisions and discrimination law.

This book is intended for students studying civil liberties who feel that they have a acquired a body of knowledge, but don't feel confident about using it effectively in exams. This book sets out to demonstrate how to apply the knowledge to the question and how to structure the answer. Students often find the technique of answering problem questions particularly hard to grasp, so this book contains a large number of answers to such questions. Such technique is rarely taught in law schools and the student who comes from studying science or Maths 'A' level may find it particularly tricky. Equally, a student who has studied English literature may find it difficult to adapt to the impersonal, logical, concise style which problem answers demand. It is hoped that this book will be particularly useful at exam time, but may also prove useful throughout the year too.

The book provides examples of the kind of questions which are usually asked in end of year examinations, along with suggested solutions. Each chapter deals with one of the main topics covered in civil liberties courses and contains typical questions on that area. The aim is not to include questions covering every aspect of a course, but to pick out the areas which tend to be examined because they are particularly contentious or topical. Many courses contain a certain amount of material which tends not to be examined, although it is important as background.

Some areas tend to be examined only by essays, some mainly, although not invariably, by problems and some by both. The questions chosen reflect this mix and the introductions at the beginning of each chapter discuss the type of question usually asked. It is important not to choose a topic and then assume that it will appear on the exam paper in essay form unless it is in an area where a problem question is never set. If an area might appear as an essay or a problem, revision should be geared to either possibility; a very thorough knowledge of the area should be acquired, but also an awareness of critical opinion in relation to it.

The answers in this book are about the length of an essay that a good student would be expected to write in an exam; some are slightly longer. There are a number of reasons for this: some students can write long answers – about 1,800 words – under exam conditions; some students who can't, nevertheless write two very good and lengthy essays and two reasonable, but shorter ones. Such students tend to do very well, although it must be emphasised that it is always better to aim to spread the time evenly between the four essays. Therefore, some answers indicate what might be done if very thorough coverage of a topic was undertaken.

Each essay also provides notes exploring some areas of the answer in more depth, which should be of value to the student who wants to do more than cover the main points. Some answers provide a number of notes; it would not be expected that any one student would have time to make all the points they contain, but they demonstrate that it is possible to choose to explore, say, two interesting areas in more depth in an answer once the main points have been covered. It can't be emphasised enough that the main points have to be covered before interesting, but less obvious issues can be explored.

Civil liberties' exam papers normally include one question on each of the main areas. For example, a typical paper might include problem questions on: public order, police powers, contempt of court, and essay questions on: the Human Rights Act, freedom of expression, 'open' government, privacy of information, prisoners' rights. Therefore, the questions have to be fairly wide ranging in order to cover a reasonable amount of ground on each topic. Some answers in this book therefore have to cover some of the same material especially where it is particularly central to the topic in question.

The law is stated as at 1 March 2001.

*Helen Fenwick*
*University of Durham*

# CONTENTS

# TABLE OF CASES

# TABLE OF STATUTORY INSTRUMENTS

# TABLE OF EUROPEAN LEGISLATION

# CHAPTER 1

# FREEDOM OF EXPRESSION

## Introduction

This area is obviously a key element in a civil liberties course and therefore may arise in two or possibly more questions on the exam paper. Examiners tend to set general essays in this area; the emphasis is usually on the degree to which a balance is struck between freedom of expression and a variety of other interests such as protecting the administration of justice. However, problem questions are sometimes set, particularly in the area of contempt of court.

There is a large amount of overlap between this area and that of freedom of information, since freedom of information may broadly be viewed as one aspect of freedom of expression. Therefore, what may be termed 'freedom of information issues' may well be treated as aspects of freedom of expression. However, the overlap is not complete: in some circumstances, information may be sought where there is no speaker willing to disclose it and, therefore, such instances tend to fall only within the area of freedom of information. The current interest in further media regulation to protect privacy may well be reflected in civil liberties examinations; therefore, you may well be called upon to consider the conflict between freedom of expression and privacy. In this book, that issue is covered in the chapter on privacy but, of course, the freedom of expression dimension is taken into account.

Students should be familiar with the following areas:

- the Contempt of Court Act 1981 and common law contempt;
- breach of confidence;
- the Broadcasting Act 1990;
- the Obscene Publications Act 1959 and related common law;
- statutory and common law indecency;
- the Cinemas Act 1985;
- the Official Secrets Act 1989;

- blasphemy;
- basic principles of defamation;
- Art 10 of the European Convention on Human Rights (the Convention).

# Question 1

'The Broadcasting Act 1990, the Obscene Publications Act 1959 and the Cinemas Act 1985 between them strike a reasonable balance between freedom of expression and protecting other interests, such as the need to maintain proper standards of taste and decency.' Discuss.

## Answer plan

This is a reasonably straightforward essay question. It is important to consider these statutes only and not the common law in this area, except where there is some particular relationship between the common law and the statute in question when the common law could be considered. Obviously, the question could be 'attacked', in the sense that you might argue that no balance at all should be struck between, for example, freedom of expression on the one hand and the protection of morality on the other; freedom of expression should entirely outweigh the other value, since it is too broad and vague to justify restrictions. Alternatively, it might be argued that the balance to be struck should differ from medium to medium. Essentially, the following areas should be considered:

- subsequent restraints under the Obscene Publications Act 1959;
- censorship on grounds of taste and decency under the Broadcasting Act 1990;
- political censorship under the Broadcasting Act 1990 and the duty of impartiality;
- prior restraints under the Cinemas Act 1985;
- Art 10 of the Convention and the Human Rights Act (HRA) 1998.

# Answer

In attempting to determine how far the statutes in question afford any recognition to freedom of expression, it must be remembered that they were framed by a Parliament which had no legal brake upon its powers; it still does not have to have regard to a written constitution forcing it to take freedom of speech into account. Thus, until recently, it was prepared to frame laws which, if fully enforced, would severely damage freedom of expression. However, such laws are not always fully enforced; if they were, the consequent clash between the media and the Government would tend to bring the law into disrepute. Thus, although by examining the provisions of these statutes, an indication of the 'balance' Parliament had in mind may be gained, other more nebulous factors, including public concern for media freedom, must also be taken into account. But, now, it is not only possible, but also necessary for Parliament, public authorities and the courts to take a stronger stance in favour of freedom of expression, since the HRA 1998 has created a duty to have regard to the guarantee of freedom of expression under Art 10 of the Convention. Legislation must be read by the courts in a manner which gives effect, so far as possible, to Convention rights (s 3 of the HRA 1998); and, if this is not possible, a declaration of incompatibility may be issued (s 4). Further, the Human Rights Act 1998 gives special regard to the importance of freedom of expression (s 12) and forbids restraint of publication before a full trial, unless the court is satisfied that the applicant will win at trial. Thus, it is submitted that both statutory and common law restrictions on freedom of expression will undergo fresh scrutiny, with a possible change in the balance against decency.

While the Cinemas Act 1985 and the Broadcasting Act 1990 are specifically aimed at two particular media, the Obscene Publications Act covers all media under s 1(2), now that the Broadcasting Act 1990 has brought radio and television within its ambit. It does not, however, cover live performances, which fall within the similarly worded Theatres Act 1968. The Broadcasting Acts and the Cinemas Act were passed because it was thought that, due to their particular impact on audiences, films and television required a system of prior restraints, whereas books and

3

other printed material did not. It is very unlikely, therefore, that a film or broadcast could attract liability under the Obscene Publications Act; nevertheless, it provides a further possibility of restraint and can also be used as a guide to the standards censorship will observe.

Of the three statutes, the Obscene Publications Act is the only one which could be said to make a specific attempt at creating a balance between protecting morality on the one hand and safeguarding freedom of speech on the other. The provisions aimed at achieving this balance are s 1(1) and s 4. Section 1(1) prohibits publication of material which tends to deprave and corrupt its likely audience. The meaning of this test has caused the courts some difficulty: the House of Lords held in *Knuller v DPP* (1973) that it did not connote something which might lead to social evil in the sense that the material in question would be likely to cause a person to act in an anti-social fashion. The House of Lords found that such a test would be too narrow and would fail to catch a great deal of material. On the other hand, it was held in *Anderson* (1972) that 'deprave and corrupt' implied something more than 'loathsome, filthy or repulsive'. In any event, it seems clear that a court will take into account contemporary standards of morality in applying this test.[1] Further, it is balanced by the 'public good' defence contained in s 4. This defence requires a jury to ask first whether an article is obscene and, if so, to consider whether its merits outweigh its obscenity. This test was included as a means of giving protection to freedom of expression in relation to publications of artistic merit. However, it has been criticised by Robertson as requiring a jury to embark on the very difficult task of weighing an intrinsic quality against a predicted change for the worse in the minds of the group of persons likely to encounter the article. Further, the defence can be avoided by bringing a charge of indecency at common law; as *Gibson* (1990) demonstrated, the merits of an obscene object may, paradoxically, prevent its suppression while the merits of less offensive objects will not.

However, the application of these tests at the present time, as seen in the trial for obscenity of the book *Inside Linda Lovelace* in 1976, suggests that no book of any conceivable literary merit will be prosecuted for obscenity. Other publications, however, are a different matter: under s 3 of the Act, magazines and other material such as videos can be seized in forfeiture proceedings, which may mean that the full safeguards provided by the Act can be bypassed: full consideration may not be given to the possible literary merits of such material. It seems, therefore, that the protection afforded by the Act to freedom of speech depends more on the willingness of the prosecuting authorities to refrain from bringing prosecutions or on the tolerance of magistrates, rather than on the law itself.

The Williams Committee recommended in 1979 that the printed word should not be subject to any restraint and that other material should be restrained on the basis of two specific tests: first, material which might shock should be available only through restricted outlets; and, secondly, material should not be prohibited unless it could be shown to cause specific harm. Clearly, these proposals would give greater weight to freedom of speech than the protection of morals, in that they would allow greater differentiation between the kind of harm which might be caused by the various media. These proposals have not been implemented and, therefore, the uncertain 'deprave and corrupt' test remains as an arguably unacceptable restraint on artistic freedom.

The Broadcasting Act 1990 is only partly concerned with restraining freedom of expression, but its effect in that area is far more wide ranging than that of the Obscene Publications Act, which can be seen as setting a minimum standard. As part of the 'de-regulation' of television, the Act sets up the Independent Television Commission (ITC) to replace the Independent Broadcasting Authority (IBA) as a public body charged with licensing and regulating non-BBC television services. Under s 6(1)(a), the ITC must attempt to ensure that every licensed television service ensures that nothing is included in its programmes 'which offends against good taste and decency'. The ITC published an updated Programme Code dealing with those matters in 2000. It attempts to strike a balance between preserving good taste and decency on the one hand and avoiding too great a restraint on freedom of speech on the other. It therefore allows sexual scenes, so long as they are presented with tact and discretion. As far as films are concerned it follows the guidelines laid down by the British Board of Film Classification (BBFC) (see below); '18' rated films may be shown, but only after 'the watershed', which varies according to the channel. Furthermore, the BBFC standards are to be regarded as minimum ones; the mere fact that a film has an '18' certificate is not to be taken as implying that it would be proper to broadcast it. The role of the ITC in this respect was, to an extent, duplicated by the Broadcasting Standards Council, set up in 1988 to monitor the standards being maintained in programmes.

The Broadcasting Act 1996 replaced the Council with the Broadcasting Standards Commission (BSC), an independent body to which appointments are made by the Home Secretary. The BSC is placed under a duty to create and implement a Code of Guidance for broadcasters which deals with matters of decency, with particular attention to the depiction of sex and violence (s 108). The BSC is also under a duty to deal with complaints about indecency, sex or violence in broadcasts, and it may have a hearing to enable it to reach a decision (ss 110 and 116). However, its only sanction is to force the broadcaster against whom the complaint has been made to publish its findings. The BBC has similar duties under its Royal Charter and Licence.

In some respects, the new arrangements could be said to represent a slackening of restraint on what may be broadcast, in the sense that the television companies will no longer have to submit their controversial programmes to an outside body for preview and censorship. As the Annan Committee pointed out in 1977, the old system meant that programmes might be subject to dual censorship in being considered first by the IBA and then by the company concerned. However, although such censorship is now solely in the hands of the companies themselves, the ITC has a number of sanctions to use against a company which fails to abide by the Programming Code, ranging from a requirement to broadcast an apology to the power to revoke its licence. The financial penalties available are very severe and may deter the companies from taking risks in their interpretation of what is allowed by the Code.

Further, censorship of television programmes may be based on political grounds, not only on those of taste and decency. A new impartiality clause was introduced by s 6 of the Broadcasting Act 1990, requiring the ITC to set up a Code to require that politically sensitive programmes must be balanced to ensure impartiality.

Such programmes can be balanced by means of a series of programmes; it is not necessary that any one programme should be followed by one specific balancing programme. However, the requirement may mean that some politically controversial programmes are not made, since the expense and difficulty of setting up balancing programmes may prove to have a deterrent effect. The ITC Code makes it clear that a company cannot use the argument that a programme which might be said to have an anti-government bias may be balanced by programmes broadcast by other companies; the company has to achieve impartiality in its own programming. In interpreting this Code, the companies may again act cautiously and may interpret what is meant by 'bias' broadly. Thus, although this provision may seek to balance a need for impartiality against the need to protect freedom of expression, it may not achieve that balance in practice.

Apart from the restraints already mentioned, the Government obtained the widest possible power to censor television under the Broadcasting Act 1981 and this was continued in the 1990 Act. This power was challenged in *Secretary of State for the Home Department ex p Brind and Others* (1990). The Secretary of State issued directives under s 29(3) of the Broadcasting Act 1981 and cl 13(4) of the BBC's Licence and Agreement, requiring the BBC and IBA to refrain from broadcasting words spoken by persons representing certain extremist groups or words spoken supporting or inviting support for those groups. The applicants, broadcasters, sought judicial review of this decision. They submitted that in curtailing freedom of expression where there was no pressing social need to do so, the directives contravened Art 10 of the Convention. This ground of appeal failed, as it was held that the primary legislation in question was not ambiguous; therefore, the Convention need not be taken into account as an aid to its construction. It may therefore be said after this decision that broadcasters' freedom of expression was largely unprotected and appears to depend more on the forbearance of the Home Secretary than on the law. It remains to be seen to what extent the courts' attitude will now differ, but it is arguable that such censorship powers will be extremely difficult to use in future, save where a true national security or prevention of crime justification is arguable under Art 10(2) of the Convention.

The Cinemas Act 1985 does not directly provide for prior restraint on films in the way that the Broadcasting Act does for television; instead, it continues an old power belonging to local authorities to grant licences in respect of the films to be shown in their particular area. The BBFC, a self-censoring body set up by the film industry, may insist on cuts before issuing a certificate allowing the film to be screened or may refuse to issue a certificate at all. The local authority will usually follow the Board's advice, but may choose not to grant a licence to a film regardless of its decision. This means that a dual system of control is set up which may be driven largely by commercial motives: the Board may make quite stringent cuts in order to ensure that a film receives a '15' certificate and so reaches a wider audience.

To what extent will the European Court of Human Rights (ECHR) case law provide a fairer balance between freedom of speech and protection of morality? In *Otto-Preminger Institute v Austria*, the Court found that a State may restrict expressions which may offend a particular population, although otherwise freedom of expression includes freedom to disseminate unpopular, shocking and disturbing information and ideas. Although there is no universal concept of morality (*Handyside* (1976)), the ECHR does give high value to public interest arguments in favour of publication, as demonstrated in recent cases. In *The Observer and The Guardian v UK* (1991) (*'Spycatcher'*), the Commission considered that a strict test of necessity must be applied where the Government seeks to restrict journalistic freedom; and in *Goodwin v UK* (1996), the Court stated that it will tip the balance of competing interests in favour of the interest of democratic society in securing a free press. According to the Court in *Jersild v Denmark* (1994), it is for the media, not the Courts, to decide which reporting techniques are appropriate to their task in acting as a public watchdog. If a broadcast, taken as a whole, raises issues of public concern or public interest, then interference by the State or the courts is not justified. Thus, these cases appear to show that freedom of expression will in future be given greater guarantees in English courts.

Thus, it does appear that English means of protecting freedom of speech are weak; its protection depends largely on the discretion of the Government and prosecuting authorities, rather than the law. Therefore, there is a strong argument that the HRA 1998 will provide such protection. Domestic judges may find some sections of the statutes considered here unsustainable once freedom of speech is given primacy.

## Note

1    This an important point which could be pursued further – the test is known as 'the contemporary standards' test – it derives from *Calder and Boyers* (1969). Because juries will apply this test, the concept of obscenity is, at least theoretically, able to keep up to date.

# Question 2

In the light of developments in this area over the last 15 years, how far would you say that the law successfully balances competing interests in the area of freedom of expression?

## Answer plan

This is clearly a much more general and wide ranging essay than the previous one, although, obviously, the need to consider recent developments does limit its scope.

The following recent legal developments should be considered in the light of the issue raised by the question:

- the Official Secrets Act 1989;
- breach of confidence (*The Observer and The Guardian v UK; The Sunday Times v UK* (1991)); *AG v Blake* (2000);
- common law contempt (*AG v Newspaper Publishing plc* (1990));
- the Broadcasting Acts 1990 and 1996;
- common law on indecency (*Gibson* (1990)); *Muller v Switzerland* (1991);
- blasphemy (*Chief Metropolitan Magistrates' Court ex p Choudhury* (1991)); *Otto-Preminger Institute v Austria* (1994);

- defamation (*Kaye v Robertson and Another* (1991); *Derbyshire County Council v Times Newspaper* (1993));
- the Public Interest Disclosure Act 1998.

## Answer

Freedom of expression tends to come into conflict with other interests to a greater extent than any other liberty. It has come particularly under threat recently, largely, but not exclusively, through common law developments. In considering how far the 'balance' between freedom of expression and other interests has been affected by recent developments, it should be remembered that freedom of expression is not affected only by changes in domestic law. Article 10 of the European Convention on Human Rights (the Convention) guarantees freedom of expression to citizens of Member States and is having increasing influence on the law in this area. Article 10, unlike the previous domestic law, provides a means of attempting to consider the extent to which the 'balance' in question is maintained, since its starting point is the primacy of freedom of expression. Indeed, s 12 of the Human Rights Act (HRA) 1998 both recognises this primacy and the balance which might be made against privacy; freedom of expression is given slightly higher priority. But it can be seen from existing case law, both domestic and relating to the European Court of Human Rights (ECHR), that freedom of expression may be restricted legitimately in the interests of national security, the reputation of others, public morality, confidentiality or prevention of crime.

The Official Secrets Act 1989 represents a highly significant development which is arguably likely to prove more effective in preventing disclosure and publication of information than its predecessor. The Act was supposed to bring about an increase in the information which could be disclosed to the public without incurring criminal liability by introducing a test which took into account the substance of the information. However, it is apparent that there is no test for harm at all in certain of the categories of information covered, including s 1, which prevents members of the Security Services disclosing anything at all, however trivial, about the operation of those services. In the categories covered by s 3(1)(b), although there appears to be a test for harm, it may in fact be satisfied merely by establishing the nature of the information. In other words, once it is shown that the information is of a certain nature it is accepted that harm may automatically flow from its disclosure.

The 1989 Act contained no explicit public interest defence and it follows from the nature of the harm test that one cannot be implied into it; any good flowing from disclosure of the information cannot be considered, merely any harm that might be caused. Thus, the Act was unlikely to have a liberalising impact on the publication of information allowing the public to scrutinise the workings of government.

However, the Public Interest Disclosure Act 1998 is, in theory, of aid to 'whistleblowers' who disclose that a crime, a breach of duty, environmental damage, a miscarriage of justice or a cover-up has occurred. In practice, however, it is feared that the Act's effect will be minimal, since the 'right to disclose' is extremely limited, protecting only disclosure to an employer or equivalent and still leaving much discretion to the courts as to whether liability will still exist for breach of confidence. It remains to be seen whether, and within which boundaries, the 'public interest' disclosure defence will be used successfully by government employees facing disciplinary proceedings.

Developments in those areas have been counterbalanced by the use of the common law as a means of preventing disclosure of information and it may be argued that the common law has not created a satisfactory balance between the need to preserve freedom of expression and the need to maintain confidentiality of information. In *AG v Guardian Newspapers Ltd* (1987), the House of Lords decided (relying on *American Cyanamid Co v Ethicon Ltd* (1975)) that certain newspapers should be prevented from publishing material from *Spycatcher* by Peter Wright after the book had been published in the US. The book included allegations of illegal activity engaged in by MI5. The injunctions continued until, in the hearing of the permanent injunctions, the House of Lords rejected the Attorney General's claim on the basis that the interest in maintaining confidentiality was outweighed by the public interest in knowing about the allegations in *Spycatcher*. Moreover, it was impossible to sustain a restriction based on confidentiality when the worldwide publication of the book meant that the information it contained was clearly in the 'public domain'.

Clearly, the infringement of freedom of speech represented by the temporary injunctions was not as serious as that which would have been caused had the permanent injunctions been granted. Nevertheless, it was significant and suggested that the House of Lords had not given enough weight to the freedom of expression interest in the case. When the ECHR considered the case (*The Observer and The Guardian v UK* (1991); *The Sunday Times v UK* (1991)), it found that, although the temporary injunctions granted after publication of the book in the US had an aim recognised by two of the exceptions to Art 10 – maintaining the authority of the judiciary and protecting national security – they had an effect disproportionate to that aim and therefore constituted a violation of Art 10. The failure of common law to give proper weight to freedom of speech was arguably reflected in the issue of contempt of court which also arose from the *Spycatcher* litigation.

While the temporary injunctions were in force *The Independent* and two other papers published material covered by them. It was determined in the Court of Appeal (*AG v Newspaper Publishing plc* (1990)) that such publication constituted the *actus reus* of contempt on the basis that publication of confidential material, the subject matter of a pending action, damaging its confidentiality and thereby probably rendering the action pointless, created an interference with the administration of justice. Even if publication of such material was in the public interest, that could not justify an interference with the administration of justice. The case therefore affirmed the principle that once an interlocutory injunction has been obtained restraining one organ of the media from publication of allegedly confidential material, the rest of the media may be in contempt if they publish that material, even if their intention in doing so is to bring alleged iniquity to public attention. In other words, the decision allowed the laws of confidence and contempt to operate together as a significant prior restraint on media freedom and this principle was upheld by the House of Lords (*Times Newspapers and Another v AG* (1991)).[1] However, now, s 12 of the HRA 1998 will prevent prior restraint unless the court is satisfied that the applicant is likely to win at trial.

A different approach to restraining disclosures by former members of the security services was adopted in *AG v Blake* (2000).

The defendant, a former security services operative, was, in 1966, sentenced to 42 years' imprisonment for spying. He subsequently escaped to Moscow and, some 30 years later, published his memoirs. The Attorney General did not seek to restrain publication on the basis of confidentiality – presumably because the lapse of time meant that such an argument would have been difficult to sustain – but rather to stop Blake from benefiting from the publication. An injunction was refused at first instance, but was granted by the Court of Appeal on the basis that Blake could be made to disgorge the profits of a criminal action (his disclosures amounting to an offence under the Official Secrets Act 1989). The House of Lords rejected this basis of the Court of Appeal's ruling, because it said that recovery of the profits of criminal activity was an area governed by statute (for example, in relation to drug trafficking) and the court should not extend its scope. They held instead that Blake was in breach of a contractual obligation dating from the time when he was employed by the secret services not to disclose any information about his work. Exceptionally, it was appropriate as a remedy in breach of contract to require Blake to make an account of profits resulting from such a breach to his employer (that is, the government). All royalties from the book were therefore payable to the Attorney General.

In other respects too, recent developments have not made easier the task of those attempting to allow the public to scrutinise the workings of government. The Broadcasting Act 1990 may deter some broadcasters from broadcasting programmes critical of government actions due to its introduction of new impartiality requirements. The Independent Television Commission (ITC) is now under a duty to set up a code to require that politically sensitive programmes be balanced, although such programmes can be balanced by means of a series of programmes, rather than by one specific balancing programme. However, such a requirement may mean that some politically controversial programmes are not made, as the expense and difficulty of setting up balancing programmes may prove to have a deterrent effect.[2]

Government also retains the widest possible power to censor broadcasting under the 1990 Act. This power was challenged in *Secretary of State for the Home Department ex p Brind and Others* (1990) by means of judicial review. The Secretary of State issued directives under s 29(3) of the Broadcasting Act 1981, requiring the

BBC and Independent Broadcasting Authority (IBA) to refrain from broadcasting words spoken by persons representing certain extremist groups. The applicants submitted that in curtailing freedom of expression where there was no pressing social need to do so, the directives contravened Art 10 of the Convention. This ground of appeal failed, as it was held that the primary legislation in question was not ambiguous; therefore, the Convention need not be taken into account as an aid to its construction. Had this ground succeeded, it would have been possible to ensure that decisions taken under these provisions did not disturb the balance between freedom of expression and other interests created by Art 10. However, now, Art 10 must be taken into account and it is submitted that the answer would be different.

The Broadcasting Act also allows potentially wide ranging restraints on freedom of expression if they are thought necessary in order to ensure standards of taste and decency. The Act sets up the ITC, charged under s 6(1)(a) with attempting to ensure that every licensed television service excludes from its programmes that 'which offends against good taste and decency'. The ITC published its first Programme Code dealing with these matters in 1991. It attempted to strike a balance between preserving good taste and decency on the one hand and avoiding too great a restraint on freedom of speech on the other. It therefore allows sexual scenes, so long as they are presented with tact and discretion. The role of the ITC in this respect is to an extent duplicated by the Broadcasting Standards Commission (BSC), set up in 1996 to monitor standards being maintained in programmes. Under s 108 of the Act, the BSC must draw up a Code relating to broadcasting standards. It also deals with complaints about indecency, sex and violence in broadcasting (ss 110 and 116). Thus, it seems that a dual and overlapping system is in place placing an onerous burden on the companies.[3] However, the BSC has been criticised on the basis of being 'toothless', since its only sanction is to force a broadcaster to publish its findings.

The possible wide ranging restraint on television in this respect goes much further than is necessary under the Obscene Publications Act 1959 and, in this sense, is echoed by certain developments in the common law of indecency brought about by *Gibson* (1990). The defendants were convicted of the common law offence of outraging public decency after displaying a model of a human head with earrings made out of human foetuses. On appeal, it was argued that prosecution at common law was barred, due to s 2(4) of the Obscene Publications Act 1959, which provides that where a prosecution is brought in respect of an obscene article, it must be considered within the Act, not at common law. 'Obscene' could mean something which disgusted the public or something which had a tendency to corrupt. Lord Lane held, however, that 'obscene' carried the second meaning, and so the facts remained outside the scope of the Act, with the result that the convictions were upheld. If the defence argument on the meaning of obscene had been accepted, explicit objects could have fallen within s 2(4) – although not within s 1 – and could have benefited from the s 4 defence. As it is, the anomaly has been continued that the artistic merit of objects which more seriously breach normal moral standards – objects which may corrupt – can prevent their suppression, while the merits of less offensive objects cannot. However, the ECHR has been of little help here. In *Muller v Switzerland* (1991), the applicant argued that his conviction for displaying paintings of sexual acts involving animals was a violation of Art 10. However, the Court found that, although Art 10 does protect freedom of artistic expression, morality is a question for domestic determination and so a State may set its own standards, so long as there is a pressing social need for any restriction imposed on artistic expression.

In all the instances considered so far, the interests of the State or the agents of the State in keeping sensitive information secret, in curbing broadcasting on the grounds of national security or in determining what is needed for the protection of taste and decency have tended to prevail over free speech interests. However, it is not suggested that the judiciary are unconcerned with the need to protect freedom of speech; rather, it is suggested that they will wish to provide such protection, but will be most confident in doing so when faced with a competing public interest lying in the less politically sensitive areas of the executive.

Thus, in *Derbyshire County Council v Times Newspaper* (1993), the House of Lords found that the importance attached to free speech by the common law was such that defamation could not be available as an action to local (or central) government. A similar stance was taken in *Chief Metropolitan Magistrates' Court ex p Choudhury* (1991); the applicants applied for judicial review of the refusal of a magistrates' court to grant summonses against Salman Rushdie and his publishers for the common law offence of blasphemous libel. The main issue before the Court of Appeal was whether the offence of blasphemy extended beyond Christianity. The Court reviewed the relevant decisions and concluded that the offence of blasphemy was clearly confined only to publications offensive to Christians. Extending the offence would, it was determined, create great difficulties, as it would be virtually impossible to define the term 'religion' sufficiently clearly. Freedom of expression would be curtailed, as authors would have to try to avoid offending members of many different sects. Clearly, even without extension, the offence of blasphemy poses a serious threat to freedom of expression and therefore it may be argued that, rather than extending the offence, it should be redefined within stricter limits. The ECHR upheld a similar requirement. In *Otto-Preminger Institute v Austria* (1994), the ECHR found that blasphemy must be considered in relation to the society against whose standards it is being judged. Gratuitously causing religious offence would breach Art 9 and so may legitimately be restricted. Further, in *Wingrove v UK* (1997), the Court agreed with the British Board of Film Classification (BBFC) that a certificate should not be given to a film or video which infringes criminal law, whether or not any prosecution is likely. Thus, there is an inherent balancing of rights before film is 'published'.

In contrast, in *Kaye v Robertson and Another* (1990), the Court of Appeal was prepared to curtail freedom of speech not in the interests of the State, but to benefit a private individual, but found no leeway in the common law to allow it to do so. Mr Kaye attempted to prevent publication of an interview with him which had been obtained while he was ill and dazed in hospital after a car accident. He was granted an injunction against the newspaper on the basis of malicious falsehood, but it was held that his claim could not have been based simply on a right to privacy, since such a right was unknown to English law. There was much debate at the time of the passing of the HRA 1998 as to whether this would lead to the development of such a right. It seems that it may well do so. The Court of Appeal in *Douglas v Hello!* (2001) held that the unauthorised publication of photographs of the claimant's wedding could amount to an actionable breach of privacy, as a development of the law of breach of confidence. An injunction restraining publication was not appropriate, however, either because of s 12 of the HRA, or because the normal test of the 'balance of convenience' which applies to interim injunctions came down in favour of the defendants.[4] Now that the courts have taken the step towards recognising a privacy right which may override freedom of expression, it will be important that the law develops in a way which that does not hamper investigative journalism, but catches reporters who are prying into matters of no public interest. Otherwise, the Art 10 freedoms may not be given sufficient weight.

In conclusion, it appears that while most recent developments in UK law are unlikely to ensure that protection of freedom of speech is enhanced where it comes into conflict with the interests of the State, especially the interest of national security, the judiciary do show an awareness of the need to afford such protection. The HRA 1998 requires judges to take an activist stance in this area and it is hoped that Art 10 will be used to create clearer, fairer boundaries to restrictions on freedom of expression. However, judicial determination to create a proper balance between freedom of speech and other interests may find expression only where it is not countered by judicial reluctance to allow the needs (or apparent needs) of national security to be abrogated.

## Notes

1   This judgment could be considered further: it found that *The Sunday Times* should have refrained from publishing material freely available abroad for a period of over a year until after the trial of the permanent injunctions. It seems that the House of Lords did not give enough weight to the free speech interest involved in the case. In this instance, that interest was very strong, as the allegations made in *Spycatcher* concerned matters of great public interest and therefore should arguably have outweighed the possibility that publication of the allegations would constitute an interference with the administration of justice.

2   It could also be noted that the section of the ITC Code which deals with impartiality makes it clear that a company cannot argue that a programme which might be said to have an anti-

government bias could be balanced by programmes broadcast by other companies: the company has to achieve impartiality in its own programming. In interpreting this Code, the companies may play safe and interpret what is meant by 'bias' broadly.

3   In some respects, the new arrangements may represent a slackening of restraint on what may be broadcast, in the sense that the television companies will no longer have to submit their controversial programmes to an outside body for preview and censorship. As the Annan Committee pointed out, the old system meant that programmes might be subject to dual censorship, being considered first by the IBA and then by the company concerned. However, although such censorship is now solely in the hands of the companies themselves, the ITC has a number of sanctions to use against a company which fails to abide by the Programming Code, ranging from a requirement to broadcast an apology to the power to revoke its licence. The financial penalties available are very severe and may deter the companies from taking risks in their interpretation of what is allowed by the Code.

4   The members of the Court of Appeal were divided on the precise basis on which an injunction was refused. It might also be noted here that the approach in *Douglas* was subsequently used in *Venables v News Group Newspapers* (2001) to impose an injunction preventing the publication of the new identities of two men convicted when they were children of murdering a toddler.

# Question 3

(a) There has been an extensive bombing campaign in shopping centres on the British mainland for which the IRA has claimed responsibility. Michael O'Donovan has been arrested, has made a confession to the police and has been charged with conspiring to cause explosions. He intends to plead not guilty, alleging that his confession was extracted after prolonged questioning and physical violence against him. He is due to stand trial in one month. At this point, the following article appears on the 'Issues' page of the *Daily Argus*, a national newspaper:

'THE PROBLEM OF CONFESSIONS

The dangers of relying heavily on confessions in the criminal process are well known. Cases have occurred in which a conviction based on a false confession has had to be overturned. Are suspects really so likely to give in to an uncontrollable urge to confess in police custody as the police appear at times to suggest? An interesting instance of apparent sudden penitence has occurred recently in the shop bombing case. The urge to confess apparently experienced by one of the suspects has now dissipated itself and, apparently, departed, with the result that he now repudiates the confession. We are merely left to speculate as to the true source of the desire to confess. It has not been unknown in previous cases to find that source in a degree of police coercion, rather than in a sudden overwhelming feeling of guilt.'

Advise the Attorney General whether contempt proceedings in respect of this article would be likely to succeed.

(b) After Michael O'Donovan is convicted, the *Daily Argus* publishes the following article:

'SHOP BOMBING CASE: THE SAGA CONTINUES

Michael O'Donovan, the main suspect in this case, has now been convicted and will serve 15 years in prison. He and his family are, of course, utterly astonished and devastated by his conviction. In an exclusive interview with the *Argus* yesterday, his wife told us that he intends to issue writs against two of the police officers at Howton police station, alleging assault and battery. It certainly seems that some sort of inquiry should be made into the somewhat peculiar methods used by certain Howton officers. The rotten apples in the barrel must be dealt with in order to restore public confidence in our police. The *Argus* intends to support the O'Donovan family in any way it can in their search for justice.'

Advise the Attorney General whether contempt proceedings in respect of this article would be likely to succeed.

## Answer plan

Contempt of court is an area that lends itself very readily to setting problem questions and they are therefore sometimes set, although it is more likely that contempt will be dealt with in an essay question dealing generally with restraints on freedom of expression (see above). Such a problem question should not be attempted unless a student is very familiar with the area and, crucially, can determine when proceedings are 'active'. Students should be familiar with the following areas:

- creation of a substantial risk of serious prejudice under s 2(2) of the Contempt of Court Act 1981;
- the concept of 'active' proceedings under s 2(3) and Sched 1 of the Act;
- discussions in good faith under s 5;
- intention to prejudice the administration of justice;
- the concept of imminence in common law contempt;
- creating 'a real risk of prejudice' under the common law doctrine;
- the possibility of establishing a 'trial by newspaper'.

# Answer

This question concerns the rules governing contempt of court arising under the Contempt of Court Act 1981 (hereafter 'the Act') and at common law. The two articles will be considered separately.

Liability in respect of article (a) may arise under the Act. The first question to be determined is whether the publication in question could have an effect on any 'particular proceedings' under s 1 of the Act. The article makes reference to 'the shop bombing case'. The strict liability rule under s 1 of the Act may therefore apply if the following three tests are satisfied.

First, proceedings must be active under s 2(3) and Sched 1 of the Act. O'Donovan (hereinafter 'D') has been arrested and proceedings are therefore active under Sched 1, para 4(a).

Secondly, it must be shown that the article creates a substantial risk of serious prejudice to D's trial (s 2(2) of the Act). According to the Court of Appeal in *AG v News Group Newspapers* (1987), both limbs of this test must be satisfied; showing a slight risk of serious prejudice or a substantial risk of slight prejudice would not be sufficient. As regards the first limb, can it be argued that there is a substantial risk that a person involved in D's trial, such as a juror, would: (a) encounter the article; (b) remember it; and (c) be affected by it so that he or she could not put it out of his or her mind during the trial? As this is a national newspaper, it is possible that jurors and others may encounter the article; however, if the *Argus* has a very small circulation, this risk might be seen as too remote. This point was made in *AG v Independent Television News Ltd* (1994). Following *AG v News Group Newspapers*, the proximity of the article to the trial will clearly be relevant. The Court of Appeal held that a gap of 10 months between the two could not create the substantial risk in question. In contrast, in *AG v Hislop and Pressdram* (1991), a gap of three months did create such a risk. So far, it may be argued that jurors and others would be likely to remember the article. It is not given front page prominence but, on the other hand, the series of bombing attacks will have generated publicity; the case will therefore be very much in the public eye and, like the article in the *Hislop* case concerning Sonia Sutcliffe (wife of the Yorkshire Ripper), the article is therefore more likely to make an impact.

In *AG v Times Newspapers* (1983), it was found that jurors were able to ignore possibly prejudicial comment in newspapers; however, there is a difference between the two cases: the instant case does not concern a relatively trivial incident which happens to attract publicity due to the fame of one of the persons involved, but, rather, a number of very serious incidents. It is, therefore, argued that there is a risk that a juror might see and remember the article. Nevertheless, it is of a relatively mild nature; might it not therefore be blotted out by the immediacy of the trial? It is not couched in particularly vitriolic language; however, it might be expected to convey two ideas to the jury: first, that D did make a confession; and, secondly, that it was probably obtained by the use of oppression. It is arguable that these two very specific pieces of information soberly conveyed might make more impact on jurors than a forceful opinion couched in more emotive language.

Assuming then that the first limb of s 2(2) is fulfilled, can it be argued that the effect of this article would be seriously prejudicial? It is not yet known what will occur at the trial. The defence may argue for the exclusion of the confession under s 76(2)(a) of the Police and Criminal Evidence Act 1984. If such an argument is successful, the jury will never know that the confession was made. However, a member of the jury who has read the article will be aware that the confession was made and may be prejudiced against the defendant, because he or she may wonder why it is being kept secret. Alternatively, if the confession is admitted, the defence may not try to discredit the police evidence for fear that D will have to put his character in issue. In that case, a juror might be prejudiced in favour of D by the article.

It appears then possible to put forward a reasonable argument to the effect that s 2(2) is fulfilled. It must next be established that s 5 does not apply. Following *AG v English* (1983), the test to be applied seems to be – looking at the actual words present (as opposed to considering what could have been omitted), is the article written in good faith and concerned with a question of general legitimate public interest which creates an incidental risk of prejudice to a particular case? This test will cover direct references to the particular case according to *AG v Times Newspapers* (1983). It is possible on this basis to argue that s 5 does apply, on the basis that the validity of confession evidence is clearly a matter of genuine public interest, the article appears to be written in good faith and seems merely to be using the shop bombing case as an example of the problem it is concerned with. It therefore bears comparison with the articles which escaped liability in the two cases mentioned. Given that the HRA 1998 should have the effect of encouraging the courts to apply s 5 in favour of freedom of expression, it is likely that this will be the approach adopted here. On this argument, liability cannot be established under the Act.

There is the alternative possibility of establishing liability at common law, although it should be noted that in the only case in which such liability was established when proceedings were active, the *Hislop* case, the tests under the Act *and* at common law were satisfied. It might be said that the Act would be undermined if liability could be established at common law in an instance where proceedings were active, but the Act did not establish liability. Again, it may be expected that the HRA 1998 will act to inhibit the courts from using common law contempt in situations clearly falling within the scope of the 1981 Act. In any event, a finding that the article was written in good faith under s 5 might seem to preclude a finding that the editor of the paper in question intended to prejudice proceedings. Nevertheless, the possibility of establishing liability at common law will be explored briefly.[1]

Section 6(c) of the Act preserves liability for contempt at common law if intention to prejudice the administration of justice can be established. 'Prejudice (to) the administration of justice' clearly includes prejudice to particular proceedings; therefore, the instant case will fall within s 6(c) if the following test can be satisfied. An intention to prejudice the proceedings against D must be established. The test for intention established in the following cases must be considered (*AG v Newspaper Publishing plc* (1987); *AG v The Observer and Guardian Newspapers Ltd* (1989); *AG v News Group Newspapers* (1988); *AG v Hislop and Pressdram* (1991); *AG v Sport Newspapers Ltd* (1991)). The test is – did the defendant either wish to prejudice proceedings or foresee that such prejudice was a virtually inevitable consequence of publishing the material in question?[2] Note, however, the dilution of this test which appeared to occur in *AG v Newspaper Publishing plc* (1987): the test used appeared to be whether or not the consequences were 'foreseeable', suggesting not that the editor in question should actually have foreseen them, but that an objective observer would have done so. This would, of course, be an easier test to satisfy. However, since, in practice, it will be necessary to infer that the editor foresaw such a consequence, the difference between the two tests may be of only theoretical importance.

In the instant case, given the lack of any particular involvement that the *Daily Argus* has in the case, it would be hard to show a desire to prejudice D's trial. It would also be difficult to establish that an objective observer would have foreseen that such prejudice would be a virtually inevitable consequence of the publication. Such an observer might consider such a result to be probable (see the argument as to the substantial risk of serious prejudice above), but *AG v Sport* established that that is not sufficient.[3]

The argument above tends towards the conclusion that liability cannot be established either under the Act or at common law.

Turning to article (b), it may first be asked whether or not it could affect any particular proceedings. It could be argued that no proceedings can be discerned in the problem question (or such a faint possibility that it can be discounted) or, alternatively, that there will probably be civil proceedings eventually for assault and battery. The latter alternative will be pursued in some depth but some consideration will be given to the former.[4]

The article could affect the civil action D intends to bring against the police for assault and battery, and, therefore, s 1 of the Act might apply. However, those proceedings are not yet active under s 2(3) and Sched 1, as the case has not yet been set down for trial or a date for the hearing fixed (see Sched 1, s 13(a) and (b)). Section 1 of the Act cannot, therefore, apply.

The area of liability at common law preserved by s 6(c) may nevertheless apply if the following three tests are satisfied. First, an intention to interfere in the administration of justice in the assault and battery action must be established. The argument on intention has been considered above and need not be repeated in detail. The question is whether the test for intention already considered can be fulfilled. It could be argued that this case resembles that of *AG v News Group Newspapers* (1988); the *Argus* is involving itself in a campaign to support the O'Donovan family through its pages and possibly through funding. On this basis, a desire to prejudice proceedings, or at least a recognition that this is a highly probable consequence of the publication of this article, may be established.

Secondly, the issue of imminence must be considered (the concept comes from *Savundranayagan* (1968)). It may no longer be necessary to show that proceedings are imminent according to *obiter dicta* in *AG v News Group Newspapers* (1988) and according to one of the judges in *AG v Sport Newspapers* (1991). It is arguable that proceedings are so far off (writs have not yet been issued and may never be) that proceedings cannot be said to be imminent. It is uncertain what the alternative test is. It was said in *AG v News Group Newspapers* that if intention to prejudice proceedings could be shown, it was unnecessary to prove imminence; nevertheless, there cannot be an intention to prejudice something which cannot even be identified as a possibility. Thus, the test must be that proceedings can be identified as a possibility. This test appears to be satisfied in the instant case.

Thirdly, it must be shown that the publication amounts to conduct which creates a real risk of prejudice to the administration of justice in the particular proceedings. There seem to be two possible methods of satisfying this test in the instant case:

(a) the publication places pressure on the police to settle the assault and battery action rather than allow it to go to court where their actions will be inquired into. There is some resemblance between this case and *Hislop and Pressdram* (1991), in which it was found that *Private Eye* had placed pressure on Sonia Sutcliffe to drop the libel action. Temperate pressure, it was found, would be acceptable. It is arguable that this short article, which makes only one reference to an inquiry, would not place immoderate pressure on the police;

(b) the other possibility is that this article, which comes very close to alleging that the officers in question did assault D, could prejudice witnesses or, conceivably, the judge involved in the eventual assault action. It must create a real risk of prejudice. There will be no jury to be prejudiced, as juries do not hear civil actions for assault and battery. Given the length of time likely to elapse before this action, which will probably be greater than the 10 months in question in *AG v News Group Newspapers* (1987) (see above in respect of article (a)), and given the fact that no jury is involved, it will be hard to establish that the action may be prejudiced. Thus, it appears that no liability can be established at common law in respect of the possibility that the possible civil action for assault and battery will be affected by article (b).

In conclusion, on article (b), it appears that it will be difficult to establish an intentional interference with the administration of justice in the assault and battery action, as a definitional element of this form of liability is absent. The argument that the article could affect those involved in the action is very flimsy. As an alternative argument, there is the controversial possibility that a form of strict liability contempt still exists at common law, arising from *AG v Times Newspapers* (1974), which may offer a chance of establishing liability on the argument that article (b) may be said to amount to a 'trial by newspaper', but there can be no certainty on this point. However, the decision of the ECHR in *Sunday Times v UK* (1979) (which reviewed the *AG v Times Newspapers* (1974) decision) required that the public interest should be taken into account in dealing with this type of contempt. Since the HRA 1998 obliges the English courts to take account of that decision, it is unlikely that the publication of the second article would in the end result in a finding of contempt on this basis.[5]

## Notes

1 This point is open to argument. It could be said that in the majority of cases, a finding of good faith under s 5 would preclude a finding of intention to prejudice proceedings, but, in two instances, it might not. First, it might be determined that although the newspaper acted in good faith, one of the other ingredients of s 5 was missing, such as the incidental nature of the prejudice caused to proceedings. Secondly, it might be shown that where a newspaper recognised a strong risk that proceedings would be prejudiced, but did not desire such prejudice (as may have been the case in *AG v The Observer and Guardian Newspapers Ltd* (1989)), a finding of good faith may not be precluded. This might more readily be determined, given the watering down of the test for intention which occurred in that case.

2 Further, although this issue has not yet arisen and may be unlikely to arise, it is necessary to show that the almost inevitable effect of the article would also have been obvious to an objective observer. The defence could conceivably argue that the editor in question did foresee (not desire) that the article would almost certainly have the effect in question, but that an objective observer would *not* have come to that conclusion.

3 Had the first test been satisfied, it would have been necessary to establish that proceedings were imminent (see argument on this point below). This test would, of course, be readily satisfied, as proceedings are active. It would also have been

necessary to establish that a real risk of prejudice to proceedings existed (*Thompson Newspapers* (1968)). Again, this has already been considered under s 2(2) and unless it is proposed to establish at this point that the article prejudiced proceedings in a further alternative manner (as in *Hislop and Pressdram* (1991)), there seems to be no need to consider this question again.

4   This further possibility depends on finding that article (b) could amount to a 'trial by newspaper'. Bearing in mind the argument as to imminence, it could be said that, at this stage, no proceedings can be discerned. However, even if, therefore, the article does not present a risk to particular proceedings, it could be said to represent a trial by newspaper, because it comes close to making a judgment on the liability of the police officers. *AG v Times Newspapers* (1974) could be relied upon as authority. However, there are difficulties with this argument. First, it may be that s 6(c) will apply to this form of liability at common law. This argument could equally have been considered above as part of the discussion on s 6(c); an article amounting to a 'trial by newspaper' could represent an alternative means of fulfilling the *actus reus* of the area of liability preserved by s 6(c). In support of this contention, it could be argued that s 6(c) is intended to affect all liability at common law because, otherwise, the intention of the ECHR in the *Sunday Times* case (1979) would not be given full effect. This would mean that 'scandalising the court' would presumably also require *mens rea*; intention to interfere with the course of justice generally would have to be shown. If this argument is correct, it would be necessary to go on to show that the *Argus* recognised that the article would almost inevitably usurp the function of the court. This might be possible, but such an argument must at present be put forward tentatively.

5   It could be argued that the words 'administration of justice' used in s 6(c) could be interpreted to mean 'in particular proceedings only', in which case, a form of strict liability contempt may still exist at common law. This point is not settled; there is no post-Act authority on it. It would be much easier to establish liability using this argument, as it would

only be necessary to establish that the article usurped the function of the courts, not that the *Argus* recognised that fact.

# Question 4

'The Diceyan view of the judges' role as guardians of freedom of speech through their application of the common law may be revived as a result of recent developments.' Discuss.

## Answer plan

Obviously, it is necessary in this answer to cover both recent common law and statutory developments. The question does not mention Art 10 of the European Convention on Human Rights (the Convention), but both its existing influence and likely future developments should be considered; it could be argued that it has, to an extent, taken over the role the judges may once have had as the guardians of freedom of speech.

The following matters should be considered:

- breach of confidence – the judgment in the European Court of Human Rights (ECHR) (*The Observer and The Guardian v UK* (1991); *The Sunday Times v UK* (1991));
- common law contempt in conjunction with breach of confidence (*AG v Newspaper Publishing plc* (1990));
- common law contempt – the concept of imminence;
- comparison between common law contempt and common law indecency;
- the common law on indecency (*Gibson* (1990));
- blasphemy (*Chief Metropolitan Magistrates' Court ex p Choudhury* (1991));
- *Derbyshire County Council v Times Newspaper* (1993)) and the Human Rights Act (HRA) 1998;
- conclusion – the judges' failure as guardians of freedom of speech – Art 10 of the Convention.

# Answer

It will be argued that, although, as the *Derbyshire County Council* case (1993) demonstrated, it is a fundamental common law principle that freedom of speech should be upheld, that principle has been inconsistently applied in judicial decisions. Indeed, it will be suggested that common law developments have, until now, tended to undermine statutory guarantees of freedom of expression. Furthermore, it will be suggested that the protection of freedom of speech offered by Art 10 of the Convention is, in general, a more influential force in this area than judicial decisions, especially now that the Convention is directly applicable in our courts. Article 10, unlike previous domestic law, provides a better method of attempting to consider competing interests, in that its starting point is the primacy of freedom of expression. Now that the HRA echoes this primacy, the courts' previous approach may be untenable.

The failure of the common law in balancing the need to preserve freedom of expression against the need to maintain confidentiality of information was seen in *AG v Guardian Newspapers* (1987). In 1986, *The Guardian* and *The Observer* published some material from *Spycatcher* by Peter Wright. The book included allegations of illegal activity engaged in by MI5. The Attorney General obtained temporary *ex parte* injunctions, preventing them from further disclosure of such material. In 1987, the book was published in the US and many copies were brought into the UK. After that point in 1987, the House of Lords decided (relying on *American Cyanamid Co v Ethicon Ltd* (1975)) to continue the injunctions against the newspapers on the basis that the Attorney General still had an arguable case for permanent injunctions. It should be noted that there was a three to two majority in making this decision. Lord Bridge delivered a powerful dissenting speech, making the point that his confidence in the ability of the common law to safeguard freedom of speech had been undermined by the majority decision and implying that he had therefore become convinced of the need to enact the Convention into UK law.

The injunctions continued until, in the hearing of the permanent injunctions, the House of Lords rejected the Attorney

General's claim on the basis that the interest in maintaining confidentiality was outweighed by the public interest in knowing of the allegations in *Spycatcher*. Moreover, it was impossible to sustain a restriction based on confidentiality when the worldwide publication of the book meant that the information it contained was clearly in the 'public domain'. Clearly, the infringement of freedom of speech represented by the temporary injunctions was not as serious as that which would have been caused had the permanent injunctions been granted. Nevertheless, it was significant and suggested that the House of Lords had not given enough weight to the freedom of expression interest in the case.

When the ECHR considered the case (*The Observer and The Guardian v UK; The Sunday Times v UK*), it found that although the temporary injunctions granted after publication of the book in the US had an aim recognised by two of the exceptions to Art 10 – maintaining the authority of the judiciary and protecting national security – they had an effect disproportionate to that aim and therefore constituted a violation of Art 10. Section 12 of the HRA 1998 requires courts to have particular regard in civil proceedings to freedom of expression and makes prior restraint by injunction dependent upon evidence that the applicant will win at trial. Further, s 12(4) requires that, before any civil remedy is granted which would restrict freedom of expression, the court must consider whether it would be in the public interest for the material to be published and whether the material is or is about to be in the public domain. Thus, the publication of journalistic, artistic and literary material seems less likely to be restrained by future courts, although only future case law will determine to what extent freedom of expression is strengthened.

The failure of the law of confidence to give proper weight to freedom of speech was arguably also reflected in the issue of contempt of court which also arose from the publication of *Spycatcher*. While the temporary injunctions were in force, *The Independent* and two other papers published material covered by them. It was determined in the Court of Appeal (*AG v Newspaper Publishing plc*) that such publication constituted the *actus reus* of common law contempt, on the basis that publication of confidential material, the subject matter of a pending action, damaging its confidentiality and thereby probably rendering the action pointless created an interference with the administration of justice.[1] The case therefore affirmed the principle that once an interlocutory injunction has been obtained restraining one organ of the media from publication of allegedly confidential material, the rest of the media may be in contempt if they publish that material, even if their intention in doing so is to bring alleged iniquity to public attention. In other words, it allowed the laws of confidence and contempt to operate together as a significant prior restraint on media freedom, and this principle was upheld by the House of Lords (*Times Newspapers and Another v AG* (1991)).[2] However, the above qualifications as to the extent to which the information is already in the public domain and whether there is a public interest reason for publication will apply.

Further recent developments in common law contempt may have a significant impact on press freedom, particularly the uncertainty as to the *sub judice* period arising partly from *AG v Sport Newspapers Ltd and Others* (1991). A newspaper which publishes a story concerning occurrences which may lead to criminal proceedings may commit a contempt of court if publication falls within a certain period of time before proceedings commence. Under the Contempt of Court Act 1981, this period will clearly begin once a warrant for arrest is issued or an arrest is made, but, at common law, it may begin substantially earlier than that. The test as to when the period begins is very uncertain: the prosecution argued, relying on *AG v News Group Newspapers plc* (1988), that proceedings need not even be imminent and this argument was accepted by Bingham LJ, although not by Hodgson J. In *AG v BBC* (1996), it was held that even humorous and satirical broadcasts are covered by contempt law. *Have I Got News For You* was found to have created contempt by appearing to regard the Maxwell brothers as guilty of fraud charges made against them, even though the trial date was six months away. This case can be criticised for its assumption that juries are uncritical and do not understand humour.

Common law contempt has the potential to operate as a significant restraint on the media. If it is not to do so, it is essential to define, as clearly as possible, the period during which publication of matter relevant to criminal proceedings will be risky. If proceedings need not even be imminent, it appears that reporting of matters which may give rise to criminal proceedings at some point in the future will be severely circumscribed. The test of imminence is itself too wide, but would be preferable to the uncertainty on this point which was exacerbated by this case. Moreover, there is no defence of public interest at common law, although s 5 of the Contempt of Court Act 1981 contains such a provision (which was brought in to take account of the ruling in the ECHR that UK contempt law breached the Art 10 guarantee of freedom of speech). Thus, common law contempt clearly has the ability to undermine the statutory protection for freedom of speech and a public interest defence will have to be implied in future by courts in order to uphold Convention rights and the HRA 1998.

The wide ranging and flexible doctrine of common law contempt bears some resemblance to the common law of indecency: both doctrines work in tandem with statutes which create a narrower and more precise area of liability. In both instances, therefore, the common law tends to undermine the statute. This relationship between common law indecency and the Obscene Publications Act 1959 was emphasised in *Gibson and Sylveire* (1990). The defendants were convicted of the common law offence of outraging public decency after displaying a model of a human head with earrings made out of human foetuses. On appeal, it was argued that prosecution at common law was barred, due to s 2(4) of the Obscene Publications Act 1959, which provides that a prosecution at common law will not be pursued 'where it is of the essence of the offence that the matter is obscene'. 'Obscene' could mean something which disgusted the public or something which had a tendency to corrupt. If 'obscene' carried the first meaning, a conviction under the common law could not be sustained, as there was no suggestion that the exhibition of the earrings had a tendency to corrupt. Lord Lane held, however, that it was plain from s 1(1) of the Act that 'obscene' carried the second meaning. It was argued that to restrict the meaning of 'obscene' in that way would undermine the defence contained in s 4 of the Act, which could be invoked if the material in question was, *inter alia*, of artistic worth. However, Lord Lane held that the words of s 1(1) were plain and clearly indicated that the restricted meaning of 'obscene' applied throughout the Act; he refused to depart from the normal canons of statutory construction.

If the Court of Appeal had accepted the defence argument on the meaning of obscene, any explicit article which could be called a 'publication' would have fallen within the Obscene Publications Act and could have benefited from the s 4 defence. Alternatively, the court could have found that the common law offence was subject to a defence based on the public good. As it is, the anomaly has been continued that the artistic merit of objects which more seriously breach normal moral standards – objects which may corrupt – can prevent their suppression, while the merits of less offensive objects cannot.

Just as common law contempt undermines the safeguard for freedom of speech contained in s 5 of the Contempt of Court Act, so common law indecency undermines the similar safeguard of s 4 of the Obscene Publications Act. The suggestion is that the judiciary are, too often, reluctant to weigh up freedom of speech against other values; they tend to make decisions on technical grounds, without considering the full implications of the decision. However, where the threat to freedom of speech is very clear and where the State interest asserted lies in one of the less contentious areas of the executive, the judiciary have sometimes evinced a determination to rely on common law principles to protect free speech. Such a determination seemed to underly the decision of the House of Lords in *Derbyshire County Council v Times Newspaper* (1993) that defamation would not be available as an action to local (or central) government.

The new requirement, however, under the HRA 1998 that the courts take account of Art 10 should lead to greater and more consistent consideration of public interest arguments in favour of publication. This is not to deny that the courts have not in some cases looked to the ECHR even before the HRA 1998 came into force, as, for example, the Court of Appeal did in the *Derbyshire* case. This also occurred in *Bow Street Magistrates' Court ex p Choudhury* (1990); the applicants applied for judicial review of the refusal of a magistrates' court to grant summonses against Salman Rushdie and his publishers for the common law offence of blasphemous libel. The main issue before the Court of Appeal was whether the offence of blasphemy should extend beyond Christianity. The court reviewed the relevant decisions and concluded that the offence of blasphemy was clearly confined only to publications offensive to Christians. Extending the offence would, it was determined, create great difficulties, as it would be virtually impossible to define the term 'religion' sufficiently clearly. Freedom of expression would be curtailed, as authors would have to try to avoid offending members of many different sects.

The applicant's argument that discrimination in the exercise of freedom of religion breached Arts 9 and 14 of the Convention failed on the ground that the exception in respect of the rights and freedoms of others in Art 9(2) applied: the envisaged extension of UK law to protect Islam would involve a violation of Art 10, which guarantees freedom of expression. Such an extension was not, therefore, warranted. Clearly, even without extension the offence of blasphemy poses a serious threat to freedom of expression and, therefore, it may be argued that rather than extending the offence, it should be redefined within stricter limits. In *Otto-Preminger Institute v Austria* (1994), the Court referred to the necessity to balance freedom of expression against religious freedom (Art 9) and stated that blasphemy must be judged against the population of the area in which publication or speech takes place. However, the definition of the offence itself falls within the State's margin of appreciation and so reform is unlikely.

In conclusion, it appears then that the common law cannot always be relied upon to protect freedom of speech where it comes into conflict with the interests of the State. The flexibility of the common law may be used to undermine statutes containing provisions specifically intended to protect freedom of speech. It is also arguable – bearing developments in the laws of confidence and contempt in mind – that judges are sometimes prepared to be creative in applying the common law when the result would favour the interests of the State. On the other hand, the House of Lords, in applying the common law in the *Derbyshire* case, showed an awareness that freedom of speech needs protection, and that such protection can be sought from the common law. Once Art 10 of the Convention finds full expression in domestic courts through the HRA 1998, it is likely that the existing common law protection of free speech will be strengthened and developed into a less contradictory body of case law; perhaps then, judges will truly take on the role envisaged by Dicey and develop a coherent, enforceable right.

## Notes

1 It could be pointed out that even if publication of such material was in the public interest, that could not justify an interference with the administration of justice.

2 This important judgment could be looked at in more detail: it found that *The Sunday Times* should have refrained from publishing material freely available abroad for a period of over a year until after the trial of the permanent injunctions. It seems that the House of Lords did not give enough weight to the free speech interest involved in the case. In this instance, that interest was very strong, since the allegations made in *Spycatcher* concerned matters of great public interest and should, therefore, arguably have outweighed the possibility that publication of the allegations would constitute an interference with the administration of justice.

# Question 5

'Blasphemy law is in urgent need of reform.' Discuss.

## Answer plan

A reasonably straightforward essay question if you are familiar with this particular area. You need to consider whether reform means complete abolition or whether the function of blasphemy law (if you think it has a legitimate one) can be taken over by changes to another area of law, or whether blasphemy law requires extension to cover all religions. Bear in mind the need to create a balance between freedom of expression on the one hand and protection for religious sensibilities on the other. Essentially, the following matters should be considered:

- ambit of blasphemy law (the *Lemon* rulings);
- The Law Commission's 1985 Report;
- *Chief Metropolitan Magistrates' Court ex p Choudhury* (1991);
- Art 9 of the European Convention on Human Rights (the Convention) and its implications for domestic law;
- incitement to racial hatred under the Public Order Act 1986.

# Answer

The basis of the offence of blasphemous libel which derived from *Taylor's* case (1676) was that the defendant had aspersed the Christian religion, and, more particularly, Anglicanism. By the middle of the 19th century, and, in particular, after the case of *Ramsay and Foote* (1883), it became clear that the basis of blasphemy had changed: it required a scurrilous attack on Christianity, rather than merely reasoned and sober arguments against it.

It was thought by 1950 that the offence no longer existed, but it was resurrected in *Lemon* (1979). *Gay News* published a poem 'The love that dares to speak its name', by a Professor of English Literature, James Kirkup. It expressed religious sentiment in describing a homosexual's conversion to Christianity and, in developing its theme, it metaphorically attributed homosexual acts to Jesus. A private prosecution was brought against *Gay News* and the editor and publishing company were convicted of the offence of blasphemous libel.

The Court of Appeal held that the intention or motive of the defendants was irrelevant, since blasphemy was a crime of strict liability and the Lords confirmed that mere intention to publish the material constituted the *mens rea* of the offence. Moreover, it could be committed by a Christian, as there was no need to show that the material had mounted a fundamental attack on Christianity (as had been thought). There was no defence of publication in the public interest; serious literature could therefore be caught. The work in question need not be considered as a whole. All that needed to be shown was that the material in question, which was published with the defendant's knowledge, had crossed the borderline between moderate criticism on the one hand and immoderate treatment of objects sacred to Christians on the other. There was no need to show indecent or offensive treatment of such objects, nor was it necessary to show that resentment would be likely to be aroused. Neither was the past requirement to show that a breach of the peace might be occasioned by publication of the material necessary.

This decision has been much criticised, since it inhibits juxtaposition of sexuality with aspects of the Anglican religion by writers and broadcasters. In common with other parts of the common law, it allows the Obscene Publications Act 1959 to be circumvented, because it admits of no public good defence. Moreover, there are already various areas of liability arising at common law and under statute which could be used to prevent offence being caused to Christians.

*Gay News* applied to the European Court of Human Rights (ECHR) on a number of grounds, including that of a breach of Art 10. This application was ruled inadmissible in a cautious judgment. It was found that the Art 10 guarantee of freedom of expression had been interfered with, but that the interference fell within the 'rights of others' exception of Art 10(2). Was the interference necessary in a democratic society? It was found that once it was accepted that the religious feelings of citizens may deserve protection if attacks reach a certain level of savagery, it seemed to follow that the domestic authorities were best placed to determine when that level was reached. The argument used in the *Handyside* case (1976) seemed to underlie the decision: a very wide margin of appreciation is required in sensitive areas linked closely to national culture. A similar stance was taken in *Otto-Preminger Institute v Austria* (1994), which concerned suppression of a film which was deemed to be an abusive attack on Catholicism. The ECHR found that no breach of Art 10 had occurred because the rights of others exception applied. It seems, therefore, that UK blasphemy law, despite its width, is compatible with Art 10. This is implicitly recognised in *Wingrove v UK* (1997), which allows restraint of publication of any item which would infringe criminal law.

It seems fairly clear that this offence will not be extended beyond Anglicanism. The Law Commission, in their 1985 Report, concluded that an offence of wounding the feelings of adherents of any religious group would be impossible to construct, because the term 'religion' could not be defined with sufficient precision. The argument in favour of extension of the offence was put and rejected in *Chief Metropolitan Magistrates' Court ex p Choudhury* (1991), a case which arose out of the publication of Salman Rushdie's *The Satanic Verses*. The applicants applied for judicial review of the refusal of a magistrates' court to grant summonses against Salman Rushdie and his publishers for, *inter alia*, the common law offence of blasphemous libel. The Court of Appeal determined, after reviewing the relevant decisions, that the offence of blasphemy was clearly confined only to publications offensive to Christians. Extending the offence would, it was determined, create great difficulties as it would be virtually impossible to define the term 'religion' sufficiently clearly. Freedom of expression would be curtailed, as authors would have to try to avoid offending members of many different sects.

The applicants did not, however, rely only on domestic law; during argument that the offence should be extended, it was said that UK law must contain a provision to give effect to the Convention guarantee of freedom of religion under Art 9. In response, it was argued and accepted by the Court of Appeal that the Convention need not be considered, because the common law on the point is not uncertain. However, the respondents nevertheless accepted that, in this particular instance, the Convention should be considered.

It was found that the UK was not in breach of the Convention, because extending the offence of blasphemy would breach Arts 10 and 7; the exceptions of Art 10(2) could not be invoked, as nothing in the book would support a pressing social need for its suppression. Furthermore, it was uncertain that Art 9 was applicable; it would be infringed if Muslims were prevented from exercising their religion, but such restrictions were not in question. Moreover, Art 9(2) contains a number of exceptions, including that of protection for the rights of others, which would be relevant.

The applicants put forward the further argument that UK blasphemy law discriminated against Muslims and, therefore, a violation of Art 14 read in conjunction with Art 9 had occurred. This interpretation of Art 9, read alongside Art 14, had been rejected by the European Commission in the *Gay News* case (1982). In this case, it also failed on the ground that the envisaged extension of UK law to protect Islam would involve a violation of Art 10, which guarantees freedom of expression. Such an extension was not, therefore, warranted. It seems clear from this ruling and from statements made by Lord Scarman in the House of Lords in *Lemon*, which were relied upon in the *Choudhury* case, that the judiciary are not minded to extend this offence.

It is clear that some change is needed in the current law for at least two reasons. First, from a pragmatic point of view, the present situation, since it is perceived by Muslims as unfair, is a considerable source of racial tension; it both engenders feelings of anger and alienation in the Muslim community and, when these feelings are expressed through such activities as book-burning and attacks on booksellers stocking *The Satanic Verses*, increased feelings of hostility towards Muslims in certain sections of the non-Muslim population. Secondly, it is indefensible that the State should single out one group of citizens and protect their religious feelings while others are without such protection. Since extension of the law does not seem a realistic alternative due to the difficulty of defining 'religion', it would appear that abolition of blasphemy as an offence would be the simplest way of remedying the current unfairness of the law in this area. However, it is arguable that abolition should be coupled with creation of a new offence of incitement to religious hatred, and this is the argument we will now turn to.

The International Covenant on Civil and Political Rights, of which the UK is a signatory, requires contracting States to prohibit the advocacy of 'national, racial or *religious* hatred that constitutes incitement to discrimination, hostility or violence' (Art 20). In practical terms, it would be fairly straightforward to amend ss 17, 18, 19 and 23 of Pt III of the Public Order Act 1986, which prohibit incitement to racial hatred, to include religious groups. This would remedy the present situation, which permits the advocacy of hatred against Muslims, while Sikhs and Jews (as racial groups) are protected from such speech. The problem of defining religion of course still remains; however, since such incitement represents a far narrower area of liability than blasphemy, the danger that a wide interpretation of 'religion' would lead to the courts being overrun by claims from obscure groups is accordingly less great. Furthermore, prosecutions in this area can only be brought with the consent of the DPP, so the possibility of frivolous prosecutions being brought would be slight. There appears, therefore, to be an arguable case for extending the offence of incitement to racial hatred to cover religious groups.

The acceptability of the proposal to create such a new offence is dependant on the assumption that the prohibition of incitement to racial hatred under the Public Order Act does not already create an unacceptable infringement of freedom of speech. The ECHR has previously stated that race-hate speech is outside the protection of Art 10 (*Glimmerveen and Haagenback v Netherlands*

(1999)) or that prosecution is necessary in a democratic society. It may be argued, however, that the offences as currently conceived go beyond the mischief they are intended to prevent. There is an argument that some provision should be available to prevent racist speech due to its special propensity to lead to disorder and that such protection should be extended to religious groups, but it is suggested that one could comfortably support the addition of incitement to religious hatred to Public Order Act offences only once they had been reformed to encompass a much narrower area of liability.

# Question 6

Relatives of old people in the Sunnymede Old Peoples' Home become suspicious after a number of the residents become ill. Evidence of neglect comes to light and certain of the relatives decide to sue the home. The owners of the Home enter into negotiations with the relatives' legal representatives, with a view to settling out of court. Meanwhile, the *Daily Argus*, a national newspaper, publishes the following article (article (a)) on its 'Personal Lives' page:

'CARING FOR OLD PEOPLE IN THE 90s

Joan Smith set out one day last June to visit her mother in the Sunnymede Old Peoples' Home in Southton. It was a lovely day and she was looking forward to the visit. But when she arrived, she was appalled by the state of the Home. Some of the residents were sitting around unwashed in night clothes, others were still in bed, although it was midday and they were able to get up. They all looked bored, listless and passive. The floors were filthy, as were the beds. For lunch, Joan's mother was offered a small bowl of soup. Joan was absolutely devastated and is now desperately trying to get her mother into another Home. But how can these conditions exist? Do we want to neglect our old people in this way? It is time the government woke up to this problem and instituted a rigorous system of inspection for these Homes. Otherwise, people like Joan's mother will continue to suffer.'

A year later, criminal charges are brought against the officer in charge of the Sunnymede Home, Mrs Sly, for assaults allegedly committed by her on a resident of the Home. At this point, the *Daily Screech*, a national newspaper, publishes the following article (article (b)):

'"CARE" WORKERS?

How do you get a job in an Old Peoples' Home? Does your background have to be investigated? Do you have to have good qualifications? The answer to both these questions appears to be 'no' if the case of Mrs Sly, a 'care' worker who has just been charged with assaulting an old person, is anything to go by. Mrs Sly has had four posts in Old Peoples' Homes in the last five years. She was dismissed from the second one after a disciplinary hearing, which found that she had neglected old people in her charge. How is it that she went on to obtain two more posts? It is time that the appointment of workers to these Homes was looked into carefully; their background should be fully investigated. At present, there seems to be no control at all: this is a scandal which the *Daily Screech* is determined to root out.'

Advise the Attorney General whether contempt proceedings in respect of either of these articles would be likely to succeed.

## Answer plan

As noted above, contempt of court is an area that lends itself very readily to setting problem questions. A problem question should not be attempted unless a student is very familiar with the area and, crucially, can determine when proceedings are 'active'. Students should be familiar with the following areas:

- creation of a substantial risk of serious prejudice under s 2(2) of the Contempt of Court Act 1981;
- the concept of 'active' proceedings under s 2(3) and Sched 1 of the Act;
- discussions in good faith under s 5;
- intention to prejudice the administration of justice;

- creating a 'real risk of prejudice';
- the concept of imminence in common law contempt;
- the possibility of establishing 'trial by newspaper'.

# Answer

This question concerns the rules governing contempt of court arising under the Contempt of Court Act 1981 (hereafter 'the Act') and at common law. The two newspaper articles will be considered separately.

Liability in respect of article (a) will not arise under the Act, since the proceedings are not 'active'. This test arises under s 2(3) and the starting and ending points for civil proceedings are defined in Sched 1. The starting point for civil proceedings occurs when the case is set down for a hearing in the High Court or a date for the hearing fixed (Sched 1, ss 12 and 13). Since the civil proceedings in question are only at the negotiating stage, this starting point has not yet arisen.

However, liability may arise at common law in respect of article (a). Section 6(c) of the Act preserves liability for contempt at common law if intention to prejudice the administration of justice can be shown. 'Prejudice (to) the administration of justice' clearly includes prejudice to particular proceedings. Once the requirement of intent is satisfied, it is easier to establish contempt at common law, rather than under the Act, as it is only necessary to show 'a real risk of prejudice' and proceedings need only be imminent, not 'active'.

The test for intention to prejudice the administration of justice was established in *AG v Newspaper Publishing plc* (1990) and *AG v News Group Newspapers* (1988). It was made clear that 'intention' connotes specific intent and therefore cannot include recklessness. The test may be summed up as follows: did the defendant either wish to prejudice proceedings or foresee that such prejudice was a virtually inevitable consequence of publishing the material in question? Thus, it is not necessary to show a desire to prejudice proceedings or that where there was such a desire, it was the sole desire. This test is based on the meaning of intent arising from two rulings on the *mens rea* for murder from *Hancock and Shankland* (1986) and *Nedrick* (1986).

This is a subjective test, but the Court of Appeal in *AG v Newspaper Publishing plc* (1987) (the '*Spycatcher*' case) appeared to be asking whether or not the consequences in question were 'foreseeable', suggesting not that the defendant should actually have foreseen them, but that an objective observer would have done so. This would, of course, be an easier test to satisfy, although since, in practice, it will be necessary to infer that the defendant foresaw the consequences, the difference between the two tests may be of only theoretical importance.

A number of circumstances may allow the inference of intention to prejudice the proceedings to be made. In *AG v News Group Newspapers plc* (1988), the newspaper's support for the prosecution in its columns and in funding a private prosecution allowed the inference to be made. The *Sun* case may be contrasted with *AG v Sport Newspapers Ltd and Others* (1991), in which the test for intention was more strictly interpreted. One David Evans, who had previous convictions for rape, was suspected of abducting Anna Humphries. He was on the run when the *Sport* published his convictions; the proceedings were not therefore active and so the case arose at common law. Could it be said to be foreseeable as a virtual certainty that prejudice to Evans' trial would occur as a result of the publication? It was held that there was a risk of such prejudice, of which the editor of the *Sport* was aware, but that such awareness of risk was not sufficient. Clearly, had the *mens rea* of common law contempt included recklessness, it would have been established. Similarly, article (a) may create a risk of prejudice to the future proceedings, but even if the editor of the *Argus* recognises this risk (which is unclear), it cannot be said that prejudice is virtually certain to be created, since the proceedings are such a long way off.

Further, it is also suggested that the *actus reus* of common law contempt cannot be established; the proceedings in question are probably *sub judice* (see *AG v News Group Newspapers*), but the risk of prejudice is very uncertain, since the proceedings will not occur for some time and the article may therefore be forgotten by those involved in the case.[1] Moreover, no jury will be involved, since the action seems to be either in tort (for negligence) or in contract and, although a judge or witnesses might be prejudiced by this article, it is suggested that this is less likely.

In *Hislop and Pressdram* (1991), it was found that the defendants, who were one party in an action for defamation, had interfered with the administration of justice because they had brought improper pressure to bear on the other party, Sonia Sutcliffe, by publishing material in *Private Eye* intended to deter her from pursuing the action. There was a substantial risk that the articles might have succeeded in their aim; had they done so, the course of justice in Mrs Sutcliffe's action would have been seriously prejudiced, as she would have been deterred from having her claim decided in a court. However, the pressure placed on the Home as a litigant is less immoderate than that brought to bear in the *Hislop* case; it is therefore argued that a real risk of prejudice does not arise on this argument either. Thus, on this reasoning, no liability will arise in respect of article (a), since intention has not been shown and, further, a real risk of prejudice is unlikely to arise.

One further possibility may be considered. Could article (a) amount to a 'trial by newspaper'? Even if the article does not present a risk to particular proceedings it could be said to represent a trial by newspaper because it comes close to making a judgment on the liability of the Home. *AG v Times Newspapers* (1974) could be relied upon as authority. However, there are difficulties with this argument. It is probable that s 6(c) will apply to this form of liability at common law (assuming that it exists at all). This argument could equally have been considered above as part of the discussion on s 6(c); an article amounting to a trial by newspaper could represent an alternative means of fulfilling the *actus reus* of the area of liability preserved by s 6(c). In support of this contention, it could be argued that s 6(c) should affect all liability at common law because, otherwise, the intention of the European Court of Human Rights (ECHR) in the *Sunday Times* case (1979) will not be given full effect. This would mean that 'scandalising the court' would presumably also require *mens rea*: intention to interfere with the course of justice generally would have to be shown. If this argument is correct, it would be necessary to go on to show that the *Argus* recognised that the article would almost inevitably usurp the function of the court or desired that it should do so. However, given the requirement under the HRA 1998 to respect freedom of expression unless restriction is 'necessary', it is unlikely that the courts will be looking to extend the scope of contempt in this way. Therefore, the argument for liability on this basis can only be put forward very tentatively.[2]

Liability in respect of article (b) may arise under the Act. The first question to be determined is whether the publication in question could have an effect on any 'particular proceedings' under s 1 of the Act. The article makes reference to Mrs Sly; therefore, the strict liability rule under s 1 of the Act may apply if the following three tests are satisfied.

First, proceedings must be active under s 2(3) and Sched 1 of the Act. Mrs Sly (hereinafter 'D') has been charged and proceedings are therefore active under Sched 1, s 4(a).

Secondly, it must be shown that the article creates a substantial risk of serious prejudice to D's trial (s 2(2) of the Act). According to the Court of Appeal in *AG v News Group Newspapers*, both limbs of this test must be satisfied; showing a slight risk of serious prejudice or a substantial risk of slight prejudice would not be sufficient. As regards the first limb, can it be argued that there is a substantial risk that a person involved in D's trial, such as a juror, would: (a) encounter the article; (b) remember it; and (c) be affected by it so that he or she could not put it out of his or her mind during the trial? As this is a national newspaper, it is possible that jurors and others may encounter the article; however, if the *Screech* has a very small circulation, this risk might be seen as too remote. It was found in *AG v Independent Television News Ltd* (1994) that a small circulation would clearly be one factor predisposing a court to determine that prejudice to proceedings did not occur. The principles to be applied were comprehensively reviewed by the Court of Appeal in *AG v Mirror Group Newspapers* (1997). It was emphasised that the prosecution must prove the risk beyond reasonable doubt. Relevant factors will include the prominence of the article and the novelty of its content (which will affect its impact on the reader). The length of time between publication and trial is also very significant. In *AG v News Group Newspapers* (1986), a gap of 10 months was held to obviate the risk of prejudice. On the other hand, in *AG v BBC* (1996), a risk was held to exist despite a gap of six months.

It is unclear what interval of time will elapse between charging Mrs Sly and the trial. This is clearly a crucial point, since, as indicated above, the longer the period, the less likely it is that a substantial risk of prejudice will be proved. If it is more than nine months, it is unlikely that the article will be held to be prejudicial. Moreover, the Court of Appeal in *AG v Mirror Group Newspapers* noted that the residual impact of a prejudicial article could be reduced by the effects of the jury's listening to evidence over a prolonged period, and the judge's directions. In this case, therefore, it could be argued that, although there is a risk that a juror might see and remember the article, it is of a relatively mild nature and might therefore be blotted out by the immediacy of the trial. The article is not couched in particularly vitriolic language, although it does convey information about Mrs Sly which is likely to create an unfavourable impression.

The stronger argument appears to be to the effect that s 2(2) is not fulfilled. However, since this is not absolutely certain it must next be established that s 5 does not apply. Following *AG v English* (1983), the test to be applied seems to be – looking at the actual words written (as opposed to considering what could have been omitted), is the article written in good faith and concerned with a question of general legitimate public interest which creates an incidental risk of prejudice to a particular case? This test will cover direct references to the particular case according to *AG v Times Newspapers*. It is possible on this basis to argue that s 5 does apply on the basis that the conditions in Old Peoples' Homes are clearly a matter of genuine public interest, the article appears to be written in good faith and seems merely to be using Mrs Sly as an example of the problem it is concerned with. It therefore bears comparison with the articles which escaped liability in the two cases mentioned. On this argument, liability cannot be established under the Act.

There is the alternative possibility of establishing liability at common law if intention to prejudice proceedings is present, although it should be noted that in the only case in which such liability was established when proceedings were active, the *Hislop* case, the tests under the Act and at common law were satisfied. It might be said that the Act would be undermined if liability could be established at common law in an instance where proceedings were active, but the Act did not establish liability. This argument is reinforced by the obligation under the HRA 1998 to give proper weight to the right to freedom of expression under Art 10 of the Convention. In any event, a finding that the article was written in good faith under s 5 might seem to preclude a finding that the editor of the paper in question intended to prejudice proceedings (a necessary ingredient of liability at common law). This would seem to be the end of the matter, but it will further be argued that, in any event, intention to prejudice proceedings cannot be shown.

Section 6(c) of the Act preserves liability for contempt at common law if intention to prejudice the administration of justice can be established. 'Prejudice (to) the administration of justice' clearly includes prejudice to particular proceedings; therefore, the instant case will fall within s 6(c) if the following three tests can be satisfied. First, an intention to prejudice the proceedings against D must be established. The test for intention established in the following cases should be considered (*AG v Newspaper Publishing plc*; *AG v The Observer and The Guardian Newspapers Ltd* (1989); *AG v News Group Newspapers*; *AG v Hislop and Pressdram*; *AG v Sport Newspapers Ltd*). The test is – did the defendant either wish to prejudice proceedings or foresee that such prejudice was a virtually inevitable consequence of publishing the material in question?

In the instant case, given the lack of any particular involvement that the *Screech* has in the case, it would be hard to show a desire to prejudice D's trial. It would also be difficult to establish that an objective observer would have foreseen that such prejudice would be a virtually inevitable consequence of the publication. Such an observer might consider such a result to be probable (see the argument as to the substantial risk of serious prejudice above), but that is not sufficient.

The argument above tends towards the conclusion that liability cannot be established under either the Act or at common law.

## Notes

1   Had it appeared that the article might well create a real risk of prejudice and had the first test for intention been satisfied, it would have been necessary to consider in more detail the question whether proceedings were 'imminent'. This test would, probably, be readily satisfied as *dicta* in *AG v*

*Newspapers* and, in the *Sport* case, suggested that even 'imminence' need not be established once the *mens rea* is shown.

2   On the other hand, it could be argued that the words 'administration of justice' used in s 6(c) could be interpreted to mean 'in particular proceedings only', in which case, a form of strict liability contempt may still exist at common law. This point is not settled: there is no post-Act authority on it. It would be much easier to establish liability using this argument, as it would only be necessary to establish that the article usurped the function of the courts, not that the *Argus* recognised that fact.

# Question 7

'The head of contempt known as "scandalising the court" should be abolished, since it represents a failure to give sufficient weight to the interest in freedom of speech and now has no legitimate function.' Discuss.

## Answer plan

This question, of course, relates to a narrow and specialised area of contempt of law; therefore, you need to be very familiar with this particular area of contempt and to have encountered some ideas as to its reform in order to attempt this question.

The following matters should be considered:

• *mens rea* under this head of common law contempt;
• *actus reus* under this head;
• impact on freedom of speech;
• reform – abolition or curtailment of this area of law?

# Answer

This type of contempt arose to protect the judicial system from media attacks. The idea behind it is that it would be against the public interest if the media could attack judges and cast doubt on their decisions – suggesting, for example, that a judge has shown bias – because the public confidence in the administration of justice would be undermined. It has not been affected by the Contempt of Court Act 1981 (hereafter 'the Act'), because there are normally no proceedings which could be affected; any relevant proceedings will usually be concluded. If an attack on a judge occurred during the 'active' period, it would probably fall outside the Act, as any risk it created would be to the course of justice as a continuing process, rather than to the particular proceeding. Prosecutions are rare (and, in recent times, unheard of in the UK), but Lord Hailsham said in *Baldry v DPP of Mauritius* (1982), a Privy Council decision, that though it was likely that only the most serious or intolerable instances would be taken notice of by courts or Attorney Generals, nothing had happened in the intervening 80 years to invalidate the analysis of this branch of contempt put forward in *Gray* (1900). Thus, this branch of contempt law is still alive and cannot merely be disregarded by the media.

The concern here is with publications interfering with the course of justice as a continuing process, as opposed to publications affecting particular proceedings. The first issue to be considered concerns the mental element under this form of contempt. Such publications must fall outside the Act, which, according to s 1, is concerned only with publications which may affect particular proceedings. They must therefore arise at common law; the question is whether *mens rea* must be shown. It could be argued that the words 'administration of justice' used in s 6(c) could be interpreted to mean 'in particular proceedings only', in which case, forms of strict liability contempt may still exist at common law. Support could be found for such an interpretation, on the basis that s 6(c) is concerned to demonstrate that where intention can be shown, nothing prevents liability arising at common law. Given the context in which this statement is made (appearing to present a contrast to the strict liability rule), it might seem that the area of liability preserved by s 6(c) would cover the same ground as s 1, but only in instances in which *mens rea* could be shown. This point is not settled: there is no post-Act authority on it.

If, on the other hand, s 6(c) covers all interferences with the administration of justice at common law, whether of a long term nature or not, it would appear to cover 'scandalising the court', which would run counter to the ruling of the Divisional Court in *Editor of New Statesman* (1928) and to persuasive authority from other jurisdictions. However, requiring a need to show *mens rea* may be the more satisfactory approach, as it would be more likely to be in line with the HRA 1998 obligation to give proper weight to Art 10 of the Convention. Otherwise, common law contempt might have too wide a potential and the intention of the European Court of Human Rights (ECHR) in the *Sunday Times* case (1979) would not be given full effect. This would mean that liability for 'scandalising the court' would arise only where intention to interfere with the course of justice generally was shown. If, on the other hand, the view taken in *Editor of New Statesman* (1928) is correct, there would be no need to show an intention to lower the repute of the judge or court in question, merely an intention to publish.

The *actus reus* of this form of contempt consists of the publication of material calculated to lower the reputation of a court or judge, thereby creating a real risk of undermining public confidence in the due administration of justice. There are two main means of fulfilling this *actus reus*. First, a publication which is held to be scurrilously abusive of a court or judge may provide the classic example of scandalising the court. The leading case is *Gray* (1900), which arose from the trial of one Wells on a charge of obscene libel, in which Darling J warned the press not to publish a full account of court proceedings (because details of obscene matter would have been included). After they were over, the *Birmingham Daily Argus* published an article attacking him and referring to him as an 'impudent little man in horsehair' and 'a microcosm of conceit and empty-headedness' (who) 'would do well to master the duties of his own profession before undertaking the regulation of another'. This article was held by the Divisional Court to be a grave contempt, as it was 'not moderate criticism; it amounted to personal, scurrilous abuse of the judge in his capacity of judge'.

On the other hand, in *Ambard v AG for Trinidad and Tobago* (1936) reasoned criticism of certain sentences was held by the Privy Council not to constitute contempt on the basis that 'Justice is not a cloistered virtue: she must be allowed to suffer the scrutiny and respectful, even though outspoken, comments of ordinary men'. In a more recent case, *Metropolitan Police Commissioner ex p Blackburn* (1968), the Court of Appeal re-affirmed this position.

Secondly, a publication may scandalise a court if it imputes bias to a judge – even if it does so in a moderate way – on the basis that allegations of partiality will undermine confidence in the basic function of a judge. The leading case in this area is *Editor of New Statesman* (1928). The pioneer of birth control, Dr Marie Stopes, lost a libel action and an article commenting on the case stated: '... the verdict represents a substantial miscarriage of justice ... we are not in sympathy with Dr Stopes, but prejudice against her aims should not be allowed to influence a Court of Justice as it appeared to influence Mr Justice Avory in his summing up. Such views as those of Dr Stopes cannot get a fair hearing in a court presided over by Mr Justice Avory.' The editor was found to be in contempt because, although the article was serious and seemingly respectful, it imputed unfairness and lack of impartiality to the judge in the discharge of his judicial duties.

The high water mark of this variety of scandalising the court occurred in *Colsey* (1931). A moderate article had imputed unconscious bias to a judge because, in making a determination as to the meaning of a statute, he might have been influenced by the fact that he had himself earlier, as Solicitor General, steered it through Parliament. This was the last successful prosecution for this form of contempt on the UK. Prosecutions may have been discouraged due to the attacks on the *Colsey* ruling, which clearly laid itself open to the charge of amounting to an unjustified encroachment on the free speech principle.

Some critics argue that the offence of scandalising the court should be abolished altogether on the grounds that the rationale of the offence – undermining public confidence in the administration of justice – is too vague to justify imposing restrictions on freedom of speech. They argue that a system of justice should not be so lacking in self-confidence that it must suppress attacks on itself and, further, that the significance of the judicial function *supports* the need to allow untramelled speech on the subject. Harold Laski has written:

> To argue that the expression of doubt ... as to judicial impartiality is an interference in the course of justice because the result is to undermine public confidence in the judiciary is to forget that public confidence is undermined not so much by the comment as by the habit which leads to the comment.

It may be argued that the public will have *more* confidence in the judiciary if it can be freely discussed. Moreover, because no jury sits in such cases, the judicial system is, in a sense, claimant and judge in the same case, thereby giving rise to a suggestion of bias. It may be asked why only judges and not, for example, politicians or members of the clergy, should receive this special protection from criticism? Why single out judges for such insulation? The position may be compared to that in the US, where this form of contempt has withered away due to the ruling in *Bridges v California* (1941); it was held that the evil of displaying disrespect for the judiciary should not be averted by restricting freedom of expression, as enforced silence on a subject is more likely to engender resent, suspicion and contempt.

On the other hand, it might be said that allowing certain sections of the press complete *carte blanche* to attack judicial decisions and perhaps impute bias does create a risk of undermining public confidence, and that an action for defamation is not a sufficient remedy, because it would place a judge in an invidious position while the action was being held. It might also be argued that the singling out of judges can be justified on the basis that, unlike other public figures, judges have no forum from which to reply to criticism.

In conclusion, it is suggested that a compromise between these two positions is needed, which would allow protection for judges where it was genuinely needed, but would rid the law of the uncertainties of this form of contempt which, on the face of it, affords little respect to the free speech principle. The compromise could be effected by adopting the course advocated by the Law Commission – replacement of this form of liability with a narrowly drawn offence covering the distribution of false matter with intent that it should be taken as true and knowing or being reckless as to its falsity when it imputes corrupt conduct to any judge.

# Question 8

Do you consider that the Contempt of Court Act 1981 has succeeded in creating a fairer balance between freedom of speech and the administration of justice?

## Answer plan

A reasonably straightforward essay question if you are familiar with the reforms in this area undertaken after the *Sunday Times* decision by means of the Contempt of Court Act 1981. The following matters should be discussed:

- the need to show a substantial risk of serious prejudice under s 2(2) of the Contempt of Court Act 1981;
- the concept of 'active' proceedings under s 2(3) and Sched 1 of the 1981 Act;
- discussions in good faith under s 5;
- the survival of common law contempt and its relationship with the 1981 Act;
- intention to prejudice the administration of justice;
- the concept of imminence in common law contempt;
- the possibility of establishing a 'trial by newspaper'.

## Answer

The Contempt of Court Act 1981 brought about various reforms which were intended to give greater weight to freedom of speech in order to bring about harmonisation between UK contempt law and Art 10 of the European Convention on Human Rights (the Convention). In particular, it created a stricter test for risk of prejudice which gave less weight to the administration of justice, it created a shorter *sub judice* period and it allowed discussions in good faith of public affairs to escape liability.

The new test for risk of prejudice arises under s 2(2) and requires that a substantial risk of serious prejudice must be shown. According to the Court of Appeal in *AG v News Group Newspapers* (1987), both limbs of this test must be satisfied; showing a slight

53

risk of serious prejudice or a substantial risk of slight prejudice would not be sufficient. However, it should be noted that Lord Diplock has interpreted 'substantial risk' as excluding a 'risk which is only remote' (*AG v English* (1983)). If this should be taken to mean that fairly slight risks are sufficient, it is open to question as seeming not to further the policy of the Act which is to narrow down the area of liability covered by criminal contempt. However, it seems to have been interpreted in later cases as excluding such risks, creating in effect a test, it is submitted, of fairly or reasonably substantial risk. It is therefore suggested that it has moved the balance somewhat away from the administration of justice towards freedom of speech.

Orders postponing reporting of certain matters may be made under s 4(2) of the 1981 Act,[1] which provides that during any legal proceeding held in public a judge may make an order postponing reporting of the proceedings if such action 'appears necessary for avoiding a substantial risk of prejudice to the administration of justice in those proceedings'. This is quite a wide provision which on its face provides little protection for media freedom. However, s 4(2) is receiving a strict interpretation by the courts. In *Ex p The Telegraph plc* (1993), the Court of Appeal found that even where a substantial risk to proceedings might arise this need not mean that an order must be made. The court based this finding on the need to consider the two limbs of s 4(2) separately: first, a substantial risk of serious prejudice to the administration of justice should be identified flowing from publication of matters relating to the trial; and, secondly, it should be asked whether it was necessary to make an order in order to avoid the risk. In making a determination as to the second limb, a judge should consider whether, in the light of the interest in open justice, the order should be made at all and, if so, with all or any of the restrictions sought.[2]

The test for the *sub judice* period which arises under s 2(3) is more clearly defined than the test at common law and, therefore, proceedings are 'active' (or *sub judice*) for shorter periods. Thus, the test is intended to have a liberalising effect. Further, even where a publication is published in the active period and satisfies s 2(2), it may still escape liability if the prosecution cannot show that it does not amount to 'a discussion in good faith of public affairs or other matters of general public interest' or that 'the risk of impediment or prejudice to particular legal proceedings is not merely incidental to the discussion' (s 5). In other words, media discussions of various issues are less stifled under the Act than they were previously under the common law.

*AG v English* (1983) is the leading case on s 5 and is generally considered to provide a good example of the kind of case for which s 5 was framed. After the trial had begun of a consultant who was charged with the murder of a Down's syndrome baby, an article was published in the *Daily Mail*, which made no direct reference to him, but was written in support of a pro-life candidate, Mrs Carr, who was standing in a by-election. Mrs Carr had no arms; the article referred to this fact and continued: '... today the chances of such a baby surviving are very small; someone would surely recommend letting her die of starvation. Are babies who are not up to scratch to be destroyed before or after birth?'

Lord Diplock adopted a two-stage approach in determining the s 5 issue. First, could the article be called a 'discussion'? The Divisional Court had held that a discussion must mean the general airing of views and debating of principles. However, Lord Diplock considered that the term 'discussion' could not be confined merely to abstract discussions, but could include consideration of examples drawn from real life. Applying this test, he found that a discussion could include accusations without which the article would have been emasculated and would have lost its main point. Without the implied accusations, it would have become a contribution to a purely hypothetical issue. It was about Mrs Carr's election and also the general topic of mercy killing. The main point of her candidature was that killing of sub-standard babies did happen and should be stopped; if it had not asserted that babies were allowed to die, she would have been depicted as tilting at imaginary windmills. Thus, the term 'discussion' could include implied accusations.

Secondly, was the risk of prejudice to Dr Arthur's trial merely an incidental consequence of expounding the main theme of the article? Lord Diplock held that in answering this, the Divisional Court had applied the wrong test in considering whether the article could have been written without including the offending words. Instead, the Court should have looked at the actual words written. The main theme of the article was Mrs Carr's election policy; Dr Arthur was not mentioned. Therefore, this article was the antithesis of the one considered in the *Sunday Times* case (1979), which was concerned entirely with the actions of distillers. Clearly, Dr Arthur's trial could be prejudiced by the article, but that prejudice could properly be described as incidental to its main theme. Thus, s 5 applied; the article did not therefore fall within the strict liability rule. This ruling was generally seen as giving a liberal interpretation to s 5. Had the narrow interpretation of the Divisional Court prevailed, it would have meant that all debate in the media on the topic of mercy killing would have been prevented for almost a year – the time during which the proceedings in Dr Arthur's case were active from charge to acquittal.

This ruling gave an emphasis to freedom of speech which tended to bring the strict liability rule into harmony with Art 10 as interpreted by the European Court of Human Rights (ECHR) ruling in the *Sunday Times* case. However, despite this broad interpretation of s 5, the media obviously does not have *carte blanche* to discuss issues arising from or relating to any particular case during the 'active' period.

Due largely to the operation of s 5, the strict liability rule seems to have created a fairer balance than was the case at common law between freedom of speech and protection for the administration of justice. However, the uncertainty as to the application of s 5 where the article focuses on the case itself means that s 5 will allow some legitimate debate in the press to be stifled and, therefore, it might be argued that further relaxation is needed, such as a general public interest defence. However, the experience of the US, where the existence of the First Amendment has meant that there is far less restraint, has demonstrated that a very liberal approach can give rise to problems. Witnesses' statements may be obtained pre-trial, while assertions of guilt or confessions may all be made public. In *Nebraska Press Association v Stuart* (1976), the Supreme Court held that adverse publicity before a trial would not necessarily have a prejudicial effect on it and, therefore, a prior restraint would not be granted. Barendt argues further that a conviction would not be obtained in respect of an already published article which created a risk of prejudicial effect. In response to this stance, procedural devices such as delaying the trial or changing its venue have been adopted, but they are not always very effective, leaving open the possibility that defendants may appeal against conviction and obtain an acquittal due to the publicity. Thus, there may be an argument for simplifying the s 5 test, but not for relaxing it too far.

It may be argued, then, that the tests under the 1981 Act, especially the s 5 test, have tended to afford recognition to the free speech principle, but the possibility of escaping from the 'balance' created by the Act by using the common law has been preserved by s 6(c). Common law contempt presents not only an alternative, but also, where proceedings are active, an additional possibility of establishing liability. It presents such an alternative in all instances in which proceedings are not active, assuming, of course, that the *mens rea* requirement can be satisfied, and it has proved to be of great significance in this context, due to the readiness with which it is sometimes accepted that the common law tests have been fulfilled.

The doctrine has therefore attracted criticism as circumventing the 1981 Act, but it may also, even more controversially, present an alternative in instances where proceedings are active, but liability under the Act could not be established, thus opening up the possibility that the Act and, in particular, the provisions of s 5, could be undermined. This is of particular significance given that s 5 was the main means adopted to take account of the ruling in the ECHR that UK contempt law breached the Art 10 guarantee of freedom of speech.

Common law contempt was established in the *Hislop* case (1991) in an instance where proceedings were active and therefore the relationship between the concept of good faith under s 5 and the question of intention under s 6(c) came under consideration. It appeared that a finding of intention to prejudice the administration of justice necessary to found liability for contempt at common law would probably preclude a finding of good faith under s 5. This finding seemed to obviate the possibility of proceeding at common law in appropriate instances in order to avoid the operation of s 5, which would have undermined the policy of the Act as intending to provide some safeguards for media freedom. However, the point is open to argument. It could be said that in the majority of cases a finding of good faith under s 5 would indeed preclude a finding of intention to prejudice proceedings, but, in one instance, it might not.

It might be shown that where a newspaper recognised a strong risk that proceedings would be prejudiced, but did not desire such prejudice (as may have been the case in *AG v Newspaper Publishing plc* (1990)), a finding of good faith might not be precluded. A publisher might argue that his or her recognition of the risk to proceedings was outweighed (in his or her own mind) by the need to bring iniquity to public attention. Section 5 might cover such a situation, thereby preventing liability under statute, although it might still arise at common law. In other words, the principle arising from *AG v Newspaper Publishing plc* might apply even where proceedings were active and where publication of material covered by an injunction fell within s 5. Thus, in this sense, common law contempt clearly has the ability to undermine the statutory protection for freedom of speech.

This possibility may be unlikely to arise. However, this does not mean that a prosecution at common law could never succeed in an instance in which proceedings were active, but prosecution under the Act failed. For example, s 5 might be irrelevant, because it might be clear that the article did not concern a discussion in good faith of public affairs. However, s 2(2) might not be satisfied on the basis that, although some risk of prejudice arose, it could not be termed serious enough. In such an instance, there appears to be no reason why the common law could not be used instead, on the basis that the test of showing 'a real risk of prejudice' is less difficult to satisfy. If so, it would be possible to circumvent the more stringent s 2(2) requirement. Of course, it would be necessary to prove an intention to prejudice the administration of justice.

It may be concluded that some broadening of s 5, development of a public interest defence at common law and tightening up parts of the common law test, especially the test for imminence, might be desirable. Scope for such changes is clearly given by the HRA 1998, which obliges the courts to develop the common law in line with the requirements of Art 10 of the Convention, and thus to give greater weight than in the past to freedom of expression. This would mean that the media would be more clearly allowed to discuss matters of public interest focusing mainly on the particular case. Miller favours the Australian approach, which allows a balancing exercise between the public interest in publication and the interest in a fair trial to be carried out, and which does allow suppression of material where the risk it creates to a fair trial is very clear.

## Notes

1   It could be pointed out that, at common law, a judge could order postponement of a publication in order to prevent, for example, the disclosure of the identity of a witness. The leading authority is *AG v Leveller Magazine Ltd* (1979), in which it was accepted that if, in the course of regulating its own proceedings, a court made an order designed to protect the administration of justice, then it would be incumbent on those who knew of it not to do anything which might frustrate its object.

2   The point might be made that the position of the media when a s 4(2) order is made in respect of reporting a summary trial is less clear; however, it was established in *Clerkenwell Metropolitan Stipendiary Magistrate ex p The Telegraph and Others* (1993) that, in such circumstances, the media have a right to be heard and must be allowed to put forward the case for discharging the order.

# Question 9

'The Obscene Publications Act 1959 strikes a reasonable balance between freedom of expression and the protection of morals.' Do you agree?

## Answer plan

Quite a straightforward essay question. It is important to bear in mind that argument should concentrate on the Act, except where there is some particular relationship between the common law and the statute in question when the common law could be considered. Obviously, the question could be 'attacked', in the sense that it could be argued that no 'balance' at all should be struck between freedom of expression on the one hand and the protection of morality on the other: freedom of expression should entirely prevail, since 'the protection of morals' is too vague a concept to justify restricting it.

Essentially, the following matters should be considered:

- ambit of liability under the Obscene Publications Act 1959;
- the public good defence;
- relationship with the common law;
- forfeiture proceedings;
- compatibility with Art 10 of the European Convention on Human Rights (the Convention).

# Answer

Obscenity law operates as a subsequent restraint and, in practice, is aimed mainly at books, magazines and other printed material, although, theoretically, it could be used against broadcasts, films or videos, each of which have their own regulatory frameworks. The harm sought to be prevented is a corrupting effect on an individual. In other words, it is thought that an individual will undergo a change for the worse after encountering the material in question. The rationale of the law is thus overtly paternalistic. Of course, if all material which could corrupt were suppressed, a severe infringement of freedom of speech would occur. Thus, the statute which largely governs this area – the Obscene Publications Act 1959 – takes the stance that in preventing material which may deprave and corrupt, a line must be drawn between erotic literature and the truly obscene, on the basis that hardcore pornography does not deserve special protection. This echoes the approach in the US, where hardcore pornography is not defined as 'speech', because it is thought that the justification for the constitutional protection for freedom of speech does not apply. In fact, oddly enough, this seems to mean that pornography receives less protection in the US than in the UK.

The idea of preventing corruption had informed the common law long before the 1959 Act; it sprang from the ruling in *Hicklin*

(1868). Determining whether material would 'deprave and corrupt' was problematic, especially since it was unclear to whom the test should be applied. Two cases in 1954 showed the uncertainty of the law. In *Martin Secker and Warburg* (1954), it was determined that the test applied to persons who might encounter the material in question. But, at the same time, in *Hutchinson* (1954), it was determined that the test should be applied to the most vulnerable person who might conceivably encounter the material and that the jury could therefore look at the effect it might have on a teenage girl. Moreover, the jury could find that something which could merely be termed shocking could deprave and corrupt.

The 1959 Act was passed in an attempt to clear up some of this uncertainty, although it failed to lay down a clear test for the meaning of the term 'deprave and corrupt'. The *actus reus* of the offence involves the publication of an article which tends, taken as a whole (or where it comprises two or more distinct items the effect of one of the items), to deprave and corrupt[1] a significant proportion of those likely to see or hear it (s 1(1)). This is a crime of strict liability: there is no need to show an intention to deprave and corrupt, merely an intention to publish. Once it is shown that an article is obscene within the meaning of the Act, it will be irrelevant, following the ruling of the Court of Appeal in *Calder and Boyars* (1969), that the defendant's motivation could be characterised as pure or noble.

This test is hard to explain to a jury and uncertain of meaning, with the result that, as Robertson notes, directions such as the following have been given: '... obscenity, members of jury, is like an elephant; you can't define it, but you know it when you see it.' However, it is clear from the ruling of the Court of Appeal in *Anderson* (1972) that the effect in question must be more than mere shock. The trial judge had directed the jury that the test connoted that which was repulsive, loathsome or filthy. This explanation was clearly defective, as it would have merged the concepts of indecency and obscenity, and it was rejected by the Court of Appeal on the basis that it would dilute the test for obscenity which, it was said, must connote the prospect of moral harm, not just shock. The conviction under the Act therefore had to be overturned due to the misdirection.

The House of Lords in *Knuller v DPP* (1972) considered the word 'corrupt' and found that it denoted a publication which produced 'real social evil' – going beyond immoral suggestions or persuasion. This was quite a strict test, but it was qualified by the House of Lords in *DPP v Whyte* (1973). The owners of a bookshop which sold pornographic material were prosecuted. Most of the customers were old men who had encountered the material on previous occasions and this gave rise to two difficulties. First, the old men were unlikely to engage in anti-social sexual behaviour and therefore the meaning of 'corrupt' had to be modified if it was to extend to cover the effect on them of the material: it was found that it meant creating a depraved effect on the mind which need not actually issue forth in any particular sexual behaviour. Secondly, it was suggested that the old men were already corrupt and, therefore, would not be affected by the material. However, it was held that corruption did not connote a once-only process: persons could be 're-corrupted' and, on this basis, a conviction was obtained.

The 'deprave and corrupt' test must be applied to those likely to see or hear the material in question and therefore the concept of relative obscenity is imported into the Act. In other words, the obscenity or otherwise of material cannot be determined merely by consideration or analysis of the material in question. It will depend on the character of the consumer and, in this sense, presents a contrast with German obscenity law which absolutely prohibits hard core pornography although soft core material is quite freely available. It was determined in *DPP v Whyte* (1972) that, in order to make a determination as to the type of person in question, the court could receive information as to the nature of the relevant area, the type of shop and the class of people who go there. The jury must consider the likely reader in order to determine whether the material would deprave and corrupt him or her rather than considering the most vulnerable conceivable reader.[2]

The jury has to consider whether the article would be likely to deprave and corrupt a significant proportion of those likely to encounter it, and its effect as a whole on persons likely to encounter it should be considered, not merely the effect of specific passages of a particularly explicit nature.[3] However, in *Anderson* (1972), it was made clear that where the article consists of a number of items, each item must be considered in isolation from the others. Thus, a magazine which is, on the whole, innocuous, but contains one obscene item can be suppressed, although a novel could not be. Further, in *O'Sullivan* (1995), it was held that it is not necessary to prove that any person was depraved and corrupted by reading or seeing the article: 'The fact that the article in question is sold in premises frequented only by persons who are already depraved and who go there for the purpose of feeding their depravity is not in itself sufficient to negative obscenity.' This appears to contradict some earlier cases.

It seems clear that a court will take into account changing standards of morality (the 'contemporary standards' test from *Calder and Boyars*) in considering what will deprave and corrupt. Therefore, the concept of obscenity is, at least theoretically, able to keep up to date. The application of these tests at the present time was seen in the trial for obscenity of the book *Inside Linda Lovelace* in 1976, which suggested that a prosecution brought against a book of any conceivable literary merit would be unlikely to succeed.[4]

The defence of public good which arises under the s 4 of the 1959 Act was intended to afford recognition to artistic merit and thus may be seen as a highly significant step in the direction of freedom of speech. Under the 1959 Act, it is a defence to a finding that a publication is obscene if it can be shown that 'the publication of the article in question is justified as for the public good, in that it is in the interests of science, literature, art, learning or of other objects of general concern'. Expert evidence will be admissible to prove that one of these possibilities can be established and it may include considering other works. It was determined in *Penguin Books* (1961) in respect of *Lady Chatterley's Lover* that the jury should adopt a two-stage approach, asking, first, whether the article in question is obscene and, if so, going on to consider whether the defendant has established the probability that its merits are so high as to outbalance its obscenity, so that its publication is for the public good. The failure of the prosecution was seen as a turning point for literary freedom. In *DPP v Jordan* (1977), the House of Lords approved this two-stage approach and the balancing of obscenity against literary or other merit.[5]

Although the test of public good has clearly afforded protection to freedom of expression in relation to publications of artistic merit, it has been criticised: it requires a jury to embark on the very difficult task of weighing a predicted change for the worse in the minds of the group of persons likely to encounter the article against literary or other merit. Thus, an effect or process must be imagined which, once established, must be measured against an intrinsic quality. Geoffrey Robertson has written: '... the balancing act is a logical nonsense [because it is not] logically possible to weigh such disparate concepts as "corruption" an "literary merit".' The test seems to create an almost complete paradox: it assumes that an individual can be corrupted, which suggests a stultifying effect on the mind, and yet can also experience an elevating effect due to the merit of an article.

However, such criticisms of the test are open to two objections. First, a person could experience corruption in the sense that his or her moral standards might be lowered, but he or she might retain a sense of literary or artistic appreciation. Secondly, and this might seem the more satisfactory interpretation, the message of the article and its general artistic impact (through, for example, its influence on other works which followed it) might be for the public good, although some individuals who encountered it were corrupted. Thus, the term 'publication' in s 4 must mean publication to the public at large, not only to those who encounter the article, if the test is to be workable.

It should be noted that the defence can be avoided by bringing a charge of indecency at common law; as *Gibson* (1990) demonstrated, the merits of an obscene object may, paradoxically, prevent its suppression, while the merits of less offensive objects cannot. The House of Lords confirmed the existence of the substantive offence of outraging public decency and conspiring to commit it in *Knuller v DPP* (1972). This offence was preserved in the s 5(3) of the Criminal Law Act 1977 and, in *Gibson* (1990), the Court of Appeal re-affirmed the ruling of the House of Lords in *Knuller* as to its ingredients. The defendants were convicted of the offence after displaying in an art gallery a model of a human head with earrings made out of freeze-dried human foetuses of three to four months' gestation. It may be noted that, at first instance, the jury was directed that they were entirely free to use their own standards in deciding whether the model was indecent.

Argument on appeal centred on s 2(4) of the 1959 Act which provides that where a prosecution is brought in respect of an obscene article, it must be considered within the Act, not at common law: '... where it is of the essence of the offence that the matter is obscene.' 'Obscene' could denote something which disgusted the public or something which had a tendency to corrupt; if it carried the first meaning, the prosecution failed, as there was no suggestion that the exhibition of the earrings had a tendency to corrupt. Moreover, if the second, more restricted, meaning were accepted, that would undermine the defence contained in s 4 of the 1959 Act which could be invoked if the material in question was, *inter alia*, of artistic worth.

However, Lord Lane held that the words of s 1(1) were plain and clearly indicated that the restricted meaning of 'obscene' applied throughout the Act; he refused to depart from the normal canons of statutory construction. If the defence argument on the meaning of obscene had been accepted, any explicit article which could be called a 'publication' would have fallen within s 2(4) of the 1959 Act and could have benefited from the s 4 defence. Alternatively, in order to avoid the complexities of this approach, the Court of Appeal could have found that, although indecent objects fell within the common law, they must be subject to a public good defence, echoing that provided by s 4. As it is, the anomaly has been continued that the artistic merit of objects which more seriously breach normal moral standards – objects which may corrupt – can prevent their suppression, while the merits of less offensive objects cannot. It is clear, therefore, that this offence allows escape from the statutory safeguards.

Under s 3 of the Act, magazines and other material, such as videos, can be seized in forfeiture proceedings if they are obscene and have been kept for gain. No conviction is obtained; the material is merely destroyed and no other punishment is imposed; therefore, s 3 may operate at a low level of visibility. These proceedings may mean that the safeguards provided by the Act can be, to an extent, bypassed: full consideration may not be given to the possible literary merits of such material when signing a seizure order.

There is not much evidence that magistrates take a very rigorous approach to making a determination as to forfeiture. They do not need to read every item, but need only look at samples selected by the police and seem, in any event, more ready than a jury to find that an item is obscene. It seems, therefore, that the protection afforded by the 1959 Act to freedom of speech may depend more on the exercise of discretion by the police as to the enforcement of s 3, or on the tolerance of magistrates, rather than on the law itself. However, s 3 can be used only in respect of material which may be obscene, rather than in relation to *any* form of pornography; it was held in *Darbo v DPP* (1992) that a warrant issued under s 3, allowing officers to search for 'sexually explicit material', was bad on its face, as such articles would fall within a much wider category of articles than those which could be called obscene.

Despite the inadequacies and anomalies indicated here, it may be that UK law on obscenity is in harmony with Art 10 of the Convention. In the *Handyside* case (1976), the European Court of Human Rights (ECHR) had to consider the test of 'deprave and corrupt'. A book called *The Little Red Schoolbook*, which contained chapters on masturbation, sexual intercourse and abortion, was prosecuted under the 1959 Act on the basis that it appeared to encourage early sexual intercourse. It was determined that the book fell within Art 10(1). The Court then considered the protection of morals provision under Art 10(2); it found that the requirements of morals vary from time to time and from place to place, and that the domestic State authorities were therefore best placed to judge what was needed. The fact that the book was circulating freely in the rest of Europe was adjudged irrelevant to this issue. In finding that para 2 applied, the judgment accepted that domestic legislators would be allowed a wide margin of appreciation[6] in attempting to secure the freedoms guaranteed under the Convention in this area, although this was not to be taken as implying that an unlimited discretion was granted. This stance was again taken in *Muller v Switzerland* (1991) in respect of a conviction arising from the exhibition of explicit paintings: the fact that the paintings had been exhibited in other parts of Switzerland and abroad did not mean that their suppression could not answer to a pressing social need. But, in *Scherer v Switzerland* (1994), a violation of Art 10 was found where the obscene material had been shown to a small audience of consenting adults, since there can be no pressing social need to protect the public in these circumstances and so interference with freedom of expression is unjustified. Hence, in future, much will depend on the degree of public access to the material and any security measures taken to prevent the material reaching those who do not wish to see it.

In conclusion, it may be said that the 1959 Act succeeds in striking a balance between the protection of morals and freedom of speech, which seems to be in harmony with the balance created by Art 10, bearing the margin of appreciation in mind. However, it is suggested that use of the common law disturbs this balance, since the public good defence – a key element in it – can be circumvented. It remains to be seen whether the Human Rights Act 1998 will spark an extension of the public good defence to the common law offences, but such a development would be in line with the obligation imposed on the courts to develop the common law in line with the requirements of Art 10, and thus to give greater weight than previously to freedom of expression.

## Notes

1   It might be pointed out that the 1959 Act is not only concerned with the protection of morals. The test as to depravity and corruption could be applied to any material which might corrupt; it is clear from the ruling in *John Calder Pub v Powell* (1965) that it is not confined to descriptions or representations of sexual matters and it could, therefore, be applied to a disturbing book on the drug-taking life of a junkie. This ruling was followed in *Skirving* (1985), which concerned a pamphlet on the means of taking cocaine in order to obtain maximum effect. In all instances, the test for obscenity should not be applied to the type of behaviour advocated or described in the article in question, but to the article itself. Thus, in *Skirving*, the question to be asked was not whether taking cocaine would deprave and corrupt, but whether the pamphlet itself would.

2   In *Penguin Books* (1961), which concerned the prosecution of *Lady Chatterley's Lover*, the selling price of the book and the fact that, being in paperback, it would reach a mass audience was taken into account.

3   It may be reasonably straightforward to identify a group of whom a significant proportion might encounter the material, but it is unclear how it can then be determined that they would

be likely to experience depravity and corruption as a result. The ruling in *Anderson* (1972) was to the effect that in sexual obscenity cases, and normally in other obscenity cases, the defence cannot call expert evidence as to the effect that an article may have on its likely audience. Thus, generally, the jury will receive little help in applying the test.

4 Thus, in December 1991, the DPP refused to prosecute the Marquis de Sade's *Juliette*, even though it is concerned (fictionally) with the torture, rape and murder of women and children.

5 In *DPP v Jordan*, the attempt was made to widen the test. The main question was whether the articles in question – hardcore pornography – could be justified under s 4 as being of psychotherapeutic value for persons of deviant sexuality, in that the material might help to relieve their sexual tensions by way of sexual fantasies. It was argued that such material might provide a safety valve for such persons, which would divert them from anti-social activities, and that such benefit could fall within the words 'other objects of general concern' deriving from s 4. The House of Lords, however, held that these words must be construed *ejusdem generis* with the preceding words: 'Art, literature learning, science'. Since these words were unrelated to sexual benefit, the general words which followed them could not be construed in the manner suggested. It was ruled that the jury must be satisfied that the matter in question made a contribution to a recognised field of culture or learning, which could be assessed irrespective of the persons to whom it was distributed.

6 It might be noted that the scope of the domestic margin of appreciation is not the same in respect of all the aims listed in Art 10(2). The protection of morals would appear to be viewed as requiring a wide margin due to its subjective nature, in contrast with the protection of the authority of the judiciary which is seen as a more objective notion. The uncertainty of the notion of the protection of morals appears in the lack of a discernible common European standard.

# CHAPTER 2

# FREEDOM OF INFORMATION

## Introduction

Freedom of information and freedom of expression are very closely linked, if not, in some respects, indistinguishable, since some speech is dependent on access to information which is in turn a form of speech. Therefore, what may be termed 'freedom of information' issues could also be treated as aspects of freedom of expression. However, the overlap is not complete: in some circumstances, information may be sought where there is no speaker willing to disclose it. Such a situation would tend to be considered purely as a freedom of information issue.

Examiners tend to set general essays in this area; the emphasis is usually on the degree to which a balance is struck between the interest of the individual in acquiring government information and the interest of the State in withholding it. The balance between what may be termed State interests, such as defence or national security and the individual entitlement to freedom of information is largely struck by the Official Secrets Act 1989 and various common law provisions.

Students should be familiar with the following areas:

- the Official Secrets Act 1989;

- the Security Services Act 1989, the Intelligence Services Act 1994, the Interception of Communications Act 1985 and the Police Act 1997;

- DA Notices;

- the Public Records Act 1958 and data protection legislation, particularly the 1998 Act;

- freedom of information measures in other countries, particularly Canada and the US, and the UK Act;

- common law contempt;

- breach of confidence;

- the voluntary Government Code on access to information;
- the Public Interest Disclosure Act 1998.

# Question 10

Critically evaluate the means available to the Government in order to prevent disclosure of information, with a view to assessing the effectiveness of freedom of information legislation.

## Answer plan

This is clearly quite a general and wide ranging essay which requires knowledge of a number of different areas. It is concerned both with methods of ensuring that information cannot fall into the hands of those who might place it in the public domain and with methods of preventing or deterring persons from publication when a leak has occurred. Both issues are aspects of freedom of expression and are touched on in Chapter 1, but the first is given greater prominence here. The question asks you, in essence, to present a critical analysis of the current scheme preventing disclosure of certain information and to consider whether the right of access to information recently introduced will dramatically improve the public's access to information. Essentially, the following areas should be considered:

- the impact of the Official Secrets Act 1989: 'harm tests' and the Public Interest Disclosure Act 1998;
- the relationship between the Official Secrets Act, the Security Services Act 1989, the Intelligence Services Act 1994 and the Interception of Communications Act 1985;
- use of the common law as a means of preventing disclosure of information – common law contempt and breach of confidence;
- comparison with the DA Notice system – criticism of the system as currently operated;
- freedom of information measures in other countries;
- efficacy of the previous voluntary Code and likely effect of the Freedom of Information Act 2000;

- comparison with the operation of the Public Records Acts 1958 and 1967, as amended, and the Data Protection Act 1998, as amended.

# Answer

It has often been said that the UK is more obsessed with keeping government information secret than any other Western democracy. It is clearly advantageous for the party in power to control the flow of information in order to ensure that citizens are unable to scrutinise some official decisions. The justification for this climate of secrecy is that freedom of information would adversely affect 'ministerial accountability'. In other words, ministers are responsible for the actions of civil servants in their departments and must therefore be able to control the flow of information emanating from the department in question. However, this doctrine is not easy to defend in a democracy; it might be thought that ministers would be made more accountable, not less, if the workings of officials were made fully open to public scrutiny. However, s 2 of the Official Secrets Act 1911 created a climate of secrecy in the civil service which greatly hampered the efforts of those who wished to obtain and publish information about the workings of government.

The Official Secrets Act 1989, which de-criminalised disclosure of some official information, was therefore heralded as amounting to a move away from obsessive secrecy. However, since it is in no sense a freedom of information measure, it will not allow the release of any official documents into the public domain, although it will mean that if certain pieces of information are disclosed, the official concerned will not face criminal sanctions. (He or she might, of course, face an action for breach of confidence as well as disciplinary proceedings.)

Narrowing down of the official information covered by the new Act was supposed to be achieved by introducing a 'harm test', which took into account the substance of the information. Clearly, such a test is to be preferred to the width of s 2 of the Official Secrets Act 1911, which covered all official information, however trivial. However, there is no test for harm at all in the category of information covered by s 1(1) of the 1989 Act, which prevents members or former members of the security services disclosing anything at all about the operation of those services. All such members come under a lifelong duty to keep silent, even though their information might reveal serious abuse of power in the security services or some operational weakness. Equally, there is no test for harm under s 4(3) of the Act which covers information obtained by or relating to the issue of a warrant under the Interception of Communications Act 1985 or the Security Services Act 1989.

The harm tests under the Act are further diluted in various ways. Under s 3(1)(b), which covers confidential information obtained abroad, the mere fact that the information is confidential 'may' be sufficient to establish the likelihood that its disclosure would cause harm. In other words, a fiction is created that harm may automatically flow from such disclosure. The Act contains no explicit public interest defence and it follows from the nature of the harm test that one cannot be implied into it; any good flowing from disclosure of the information cannot be considered, merely any harm that might be caused. Moreover, no express defence of prior publication is provided; the only means of putting forward such argument would arise in one of the categories in which it was necessary to prove the likelihood that harm would flow from the disclosure; the prosecution might find it hard to establish such a likelihood where there had already been a great deal of prior publication. Thus, the Act was unlikely to have a liberalising impact on the publication of information allowing the public to scrutinise the workings of government. The Public Interest Disclosure Act 1998 is also far from being a likely source of greater freedom of information; although, in principle, it would give a defence of 'public interest' disclosure to those facing Official Secrets Act disciplinary proceedings, full protection only exists where the disclosure is made in good faith to an employer or regulatory body. Thus, disclosure to the media is still a risky method and will be justified only where the malpractice is exceptionally serious or the whistleblower acts to avoid victimisation or a cover-up or an inept official investigation has occurred.

The Official Secrets Act 1989 works in tandem with other measures designed to ensure secrecy. Sections 1 and 4(3) work in conjunction with the provisions of the Security Services Act 1989 to prevent almost all scrutiny of the operation of the security service. Even where a member of the public has a grievance concerning the operation of the service, it will not be possible to use a court action as a means of bringing such operations to the notice of the public – under s 5 of the Security Services Act, complaint can only be made to a tribunal and, under s 5(4), the decisions of the tribunal are not questionable in any court of law. Furthermore, the Act provides for no real form of parliamentary oversight of the security service, but this has, to some extent, been remedied by s 10 of the Intelligence Services Act 1994, which set up for the first time a Parliamentary Committee to oversee the operation of MI5, MI6 and Government Communications Headquarters (GCHQ). However, since the Committee is not a Select Committee, its powers are limited.

In a similar manner, s 4(3) of the Official Secrets Act, which prevents disclosure of information about telephone tapping, works in tandem with the Interception of Communications Act 1985. Under the 1985 Act, complaints can be made only to a tribunal (set up under the Act), with no possibility of scrutiny by a court. Furthermore, tribunal decisions are not published and although an annual report must be made available, giving some information on the number of intercept warrants issued, it is first subject to censorship by the Prime Minister.

Developments in the use of the common law doctrine of confidence as a means of preventing disclosure of information provide a further means of ensuring secrecy where information falls outside the categories covered by the Official Secrets Act, or where it falls within one of them, but a prosecution is not undertaken. *AG v Guardian Newspapers* (1987), which concerned publication of material from *Spycatcher* by Peter Wright, demonstrated that temporary injunctions could be obtained to prevent disclosure of official information, even where prior publication has ensured that there is little confidentiality left to be protected. The House of Lords decided (relying on *American Cyanamid Co v Ethicon Ltd* (1975)) that temporary injunctions could be continued where there was still an arguable case for permanent injunctions. However, the House of Lords eventually rejected the claim for permanent injunctions on the basis that the interest in maintaining confidentiality was outweighed by the public interest in knowing of the allegations in *Spycatcher*. Moreover, it was impossible to sustain a restriction based on confidentiality when the worldwide publication of the book meant that the information it contained was clearly in the 'public domain'.

When the European Court of Human Rights (ECHR) considered the case (*The Observer and The Guardian v UK* (1991); *The Sunday Times v UK* (1991)), it found that although the temporary injunctions granted after publication of the book in the US had aims recognised by two of the exceptions to Art 10 – maintaining the authority of the judiciary and protecting national security – they had an effect disproportionate to those aims and therefore constituted a violation of Art 10. The injunctions obtained before publication in the US were not found to breach Art 10; therefore, this decision will not discourage use of such injunctions in many instances where a disclosure of official information is threatened. Use of such injunctions may have a wide ranging impact due to the decision as to the issue of contempt of court which also arose from the publication of *Spycatcher*. However, the Human Rights Act (HRA) 1998 aims to prevent this situation recurring; s 12 requires a real likelihood of success at trial before prior restraint will be allowed. It remains to be seen how this measure will be interpreted.

The Court of Appeal in *AG v Newspaper Publishing plc* (1990) affirmed the principle that once an interlocutory injunction has been obtained restraining one organ of the media from publication of allegedly confidential material, the rest of the media may be in contempt if they publish that material, even if their intention in doing so is to bring alleged iniquity to public attention. Such publication must be accompanied by an intention to prejudice the eventual trial of the permanent injunctions, but only in the sense that it was foreseen that such prejudice, while undesired, was very likely to occur. Thus, the laws of confidence and contempt were allowed to operate together as a significant prior restraint on media freedom and this principle was upheld by the House of Lords (*Times Newspapers and Another v AG* (1991)).

It may be argued that the House of Lords did not give enough weight to the public interest in knowing of the allegations made in *Spycatcher* which should have outweighed the possibility that publication of the allegations would constitute an interference with the administration of justice. It is now arguable that an action for breach of confidence may be a very useful tool where it is thought that an action under the Official Secrets Act 1989 might fail. The information concerned must retain its quality of confidentiality, however. For example, in *AG v Blake* (2000), a former security services operative published his memoirs. The Attorney General did not seek to stop this on the basis of breach of confidence, because the information concerned was at least 30 years old, and did not in itself prejudice national security. The House of Lords, however, held that the Attorney General was entitled to an account of any profits from the publication of the memoirs, because such publication involved a breach of a contractual on the part of the operative, dating from his employment by the security services, not to disclose any information about his work.

A further restraint over obtaining an injunction or damages for breach of confidence is to be found in s 12 of the HRA 1998. This requires any court considering such relief not to grant any interim injunction unless it is satisfied that the claimant is likely to be successful at trial. Moreover, it must have particular regard to the importance of freedom of expression, and in relation to journalistic, literary or artistic material, consider both the public interest and the extent to which the relevant information is, or is about to be, in the public domain. It therefore appears that, in future, courts will apply existing statutory and common law rules with a far greater focus upon the public right to know.

Government and the media may normally avoid such head-on confrontation as court action by means of a curious institution known as the 'DA' Notice system. This system, which effectively means that the media censor themselves in respect of publication of official information, may preclude the need to seek injunctions to prevent publication. The DA Notice Committee was set up with the object of letting the press know which information could be printed: it was intended that if sensitive political information was covered by a 'DA' Notice, an editor would decide against printing it.[1]

The value and purpose of the system was called into question, due to an incident in 1987. The BBC, which wished to broadcast a programme to be entitled *My Country Right or Wrong* concerning issues raised by the *Spycatcher* litigation, consulted the 'DA' Notice

Committee before broadcasting and were told that the programme did not affect national security. However, the Attorney General then obtained an injunction preventing transmission on the ground of breach of confidence (*AG v BBC* (1987)), thereby disregarding the 'DA' Notice Committee. According to the Attorney General, the injunction then affected every organ of the media because of the July ruling of the Court of Appeal in *AG v Newspaper Publishing plc* (1987) (this was a preliminary ruling on the *actus reus* of common law contempt, which was affirmed as noted above). This case demonstrated the wide ranging constraint on the media which the laws of confidence and contempt could have when acting in concert.[2]

It may appear that although the 'DA' Notice System is itself objectionable in some respects, it is to be preferred to this heavy-handed use of injunctions which leaves the media with very little guidance as to what to publish or broadcast. Of course, it may be argued that the sanctions available to deter the media from publication, either on the ground of breach of confidence or under the Official Secrets Act 1989, are too wide ranging and are at the root of media fears as to what may be published and it is therefore these measures, and particularly the Act itself, which demand reform. Such arguments, as suggested above, have validity. However, given the width and complexity of the Act, it is probably better that the media should have guidance as to what may safely be published; if such guidance is not available, the Act may have an even more 'chilling' effect than its provisions warrant, due to uncertainty as to which information it covers. Thus, it may be argued that decisions of the 'DA' Notice Committee should be accepted and should preclude prosecutions or the use of injunctions.

All these measures may be contrasted with the situation where there is effective freedom of information legislation. Canada introduced its Access to Information Act in 1982.[3] The US has had such legislation since 1966. Its Freedom of Information Act applies to all parts of the Federal Government unless an exemption applies. Exempted categories include information concerning defence, law enforcement and foreign policy. The exemptions can be challenged in court and the onus of proof will be on the agency withholding the information to prove that disclosure could bring about the harm the exemption was intended to prevent.[4] This attitude to secrecy, with its presumption that information must be disclosed unless specifically exempted, can be contrasted with that in the UK, which takes the opposite stance: no general, statutory provision is made for such disclosure – the starting point is to criminalise disclosure in certain categories.

American freedom of information provision can, in particular, be contrasted with the UK Public Records Act 1958, as amended by the Public Records Act 1967, which provided that public records in the Public Records Office were not available for inspection until the expiration of 30 years, and longer periods can be prescribed for sensitive information. Some information can be withheld for 100 years or forever and there is no means of challenging such decisions. For example, at the end of 1987, a great deal of information about the Windscale fire in 1957 was disclosed, although some items are still held back.

However, for the past decade, there has been a slow but progressive movement towards freedom of information legislation for the UK, culminating in the Freedom of Information Act 2000.

The Government published a White Paper in July 1993 setting out its intentions in relation to freedom of information, which included the means of allowing citizens access to some government information, and reform of the Official Secrets Act 1989, so that disclosure of a specific document would be criminalised, as opposed to disclosure of a document belonging to a class of documents which might cause harm. A voluntary Code allowing the citizen access to information in certain specified areas was put in place in 1994.

It is suggested that a voluntary Code cannot replace a statutory right of access. The promise to release information only related to 'useful' or 'useable information'. However, in countries which have freedom of information, the usefulness of the information is determined by the person who seeks it, rather than by government ministers or civil servants. Usefulness is not an objective quality, but depends on the purposes of the seeker which only he or she can appreciate, and, therefore, it may be argued that this is an unwarranted limitation on the principle of 'openness'. Challenge through an ombudsman is unlikely to be as effective as challenge in a court. A voluntary Code cannot be used to challenge existing measures preventing access to information.

Voluntary open government asks the citizen to trust the government to act against its own interests. Clearly, the government may be prepared voluntarily to release some information which is out of date or of a general, discursive nature or innocuous for some other reason, but this may be less likely where the information will cause political embarrassment and may enable the opposition to make a more informed and therefore more damaging attack on government. A statutory basis began to look more likely in 1997 when a further White Paper proposed a Freedom of Information Act. This has now taken shape in the form of the Freedom of Information Act 2000, which will be brought into force over the next few years (with a final deadline of 2005). Once in force, the Act will have a number of important consequences. Primarily, it will create a general right of access to information, instead of the voluntary Code, and the Data Protection Act 1998 and Public Records Act 1958 will be amended accordingly. The new right will allow the public access to information held by a wide definition of public authorities, including local government, the NHS, schools and college, and the police. An Information Commissioner will be appointed to supervise the new scheme and the public will be able to contact him directly. Public authorities must, on request, indicate whether they hold information required by an individual and, if so, communicate that information to him within 20 working days. However, some forms of information will be exempt, including that relating to security matters or which might affect national security, defence or the economy. Most controversially, information may be withheld if it is believed to be likely to inhibit the free and frank provision of advice or exchange of views, or might 'prejudice the effective conduct of public affairs'. Such vague terms could allow the Government to exempt from the disclosure provisions any information which is merely embarrassing or damaging to reputation. However, a right to appeal is granted by the Act and much will depend upon future interpretations of the statute. Thus, it remains to be seen whether the new Act will be a substantial step towards greater openness and democracy in public authorities.

## Notes

1   It could be pointed out that the system is entirely voluntary and in theory the fact that a 'DA' Notice has not been issued does not mean that a prosecution under the Official Secrets Act 1989 is precluded, although, in practice, it is very unlikely. Press representatives sit on the committee as well as civil servants and officers of the armed forces.

2   Criticism levelled at the system could be considered at this point: in the Third Report from the Defence Committee (1980), the 'DA' Notice System was examined and it was concluded that it was failing to fulfil its role. It was found that major newspapers did not consult their 'DA' Notices to see what was covered by them and that the wording of 'DA' Notices was so wide as to render them meaningless. The system conveyed an appearance of censorship which had provoked strong criticism. It was determined that the machinery for the administration of 'DA' Notices and the 'DA' Notices themselves needed revision. The review which followed this reduced the number of Notices and confined them to specific areas.

3   It might be pointed out that the Canadian model was a strong one for the UK freedom of information legislation, because the Canadian constitution has many features of the Westminster model of government: ministerial responsibility and parliamentary government.

4   In order to balance this argument, it could be pointed out that although the principle of freedom of information in the US has attracted praise, its application in practice has often been criticised. In particular, the business community in the US considers that the system is being abused by persons who have a particular financial interest in uncovering commercial information. A number of reforms have been suggested since 1980 and, in 1986, a major Freedom of Information Act reform was passed, which extended the exemption available to law enforcement practices.

# Question 11

Douglas Hurd (the then Home Secretary) called the Official Secrets Act 1989 'a great liberalising measure'. Do you agree with his view?

## Answer plan

This essay clearly demands close analysis of the provisions of the new Act; however, the context in which it must be placed should also be considered. The following matters should be discussed:

- s 2 of the Official Secrets Act 1911 compared with the 1989 Act;
- categories of information covered by the Official Secrets Act 1989; harm tests in different categories – lack of a harm test in s 1(1);
- defences under the 1989 Act – actual and potential – 'reversed' *mens rea*;
- other measures creating liability in respect of the disclosure of official information;
- conclusion: lack of liberalising effect.

# Answer

The Official Secrets Act 1989 was brought into being largely in response to the failure of the government to secure a conviction under s 2 of the Official Secrets Act 1911 in *Ponting* (1985). However, it had been recognised for some time even before the *Ponting* case that s 2 was becoming discredited due to its width: it criminalised the unauthorised disclosure of any official information at all.

Once the decision to reform the area of official secrecy had been made, an opportunity was created for radical change which could have included freedom of information legislation along the lines of the instruments in the US and Canada. However, it was made clear from the outset that the legislation was unconcerned with freedom of information; it did not allow the release of any official documents into the public domain.[1] Thus, any claim that it is a liberalising measure must rest on other aspects of the Act. The aspects which are usually considered in this context include the introduction of tests for harm, the need to establish *mens rea*, the defences available and de-criminalisation of the receiver of information. In all these respects, the Act differs from its predecessor. However, the extent to which these differences will bring about any real change, any real liberalisation, is open to question.

Clearly, if only to avoid bringing the criminal law into disrepute, a 'harm test' which takes into account the substance of information is to be preferred to the width of s 2 of the Official Secrets Act 1911, which covered all official information, however trivial. However, will the harm tests have a liberalising effect in other respects? There is no test for harm at all under s 1(1) which is intended to prevent members or former members of the security services disclosing anything at all about the operation of those services. All such members come under a lifelong duty to keep silent, even though their information might reveal serious abuse of power in the security service or some operational weakness. These provisions also apply to anyone who is notified that he or she is subject to the provisions of the sub-section. Equally, there is no test for harm under s 4(3) which covers information obtained by or relating to the issue of a warrant under the Interception of Communications Act 1985 or the Security Services Act 1989.

The harm tests under the Official Secrets Act are further diluted in various ways. Under s 3(1)(b), which covers confidential information obtained abroad, the mere fact that the information is confidential 'may' be sufficient to establish the likelihood that its disclosure would cause harm. In other words, a fiction is created that harm may automatically flow from such disclosure. Under s 1(3), which criminalises disclosure of information relating to the security services by a crown servant as opposed to a member of MI5, it is not necessary to show that disclosure of the actual document in question would be likely to cause harm, merely that the document belongs to a class of documents disclosure of which would be likely to have that effect. Even in categories where it is necessary to show that the actual document in question would be likely to cause harm, such as s 2(1) or s 4(1), the task of doing so is made easy in two ways: first, it is not necessary to show that any damage actually occurred; and, secondly, the tests for harm themselves are very wide. Under s 2(2), for example, a disclosure of information relating to defence will be damaging if it is likely to obstruct seriously the interests of the UK abroad. The tests for harm are not made any more stringent in instances where a non-Crown servant discloses information. Under s 5, if anyone discloses information which falls into one of the categories covered, the test for harm will be determined by reference to that category.

The Act contains no explicit public interest defence and it follows from the nature of the harm test that one cannot be implied into it; any good flowing from disclosure of the information cannot be considered, merely any harm that might be caused. Moreover, no express defence of prior publication is provided; the only means of putting forward such argument would arise in one of the categories in which it was necessary to prove the likelihood that harm would flow from the disclosure; the prosecution might find it hard to establish such a likelihood where there had been a great deal of prior publication. Section 6 expressly provides that information which has already been leaked abroad can still cause harm if disclosed in the UK. The test for harm will depend on the category the information falls into. If the information fell within s 1(3), the test for harm might be satisfied even where newspapers all over the world were repeating the information in question, on the basis that although no further harm could be caused by disclosure of the particular document, it nevertheless belonged to a class of documents disclosure of which was likely to cause harm. Thus, the harm tests under the Act are deceptive; the readiness with which they may be satisfied suggests that the Act is unlikely to have a liberalising impact on the publication of official information.

One of the objections to the old s 2 of the 1911 Act was the failure to include a requirement to prove *mens rea*. The new Act includes such a requirement only in two instances – in all the others, it creates a reversed *mens rea*: the defence can attempt to prove that the defendant did not know (or have reasonable cause to know) of the nature of the information or that its disclosure would be damaging. However, because the defence is tied in to the harm tests, it does not operate in the same way in every category. Under ss 1(1) and 4(3), only the first part of the defence is relevant. Under s 3(1), although it appears that both parts are relevant, in fact, where the information falls within s 3(1)(b), the defence may have no opportunity to prove that there was no reasonable cause to believe that disclosure of the document would be damaging. However, under ss 5 and 6, the prosecution must prove *mens rea*, in the sense that it must be shown that the disclosure was made in the knowledge that it would be damaging. This is a step in the right direction and a clear improvement on the 1911 Act; nevertheless, the burden of proof on the prosecution would be very easy to discharge if the information fell within s 1(3) or s 3(1)(b) due to the nature of the tests for damage included in those sections.

The other clear improvement is the de-criminalisation of the receiver of information. The receiver will often be a journalist; if he or she refrains from publishing the information, no liability will be incurred. Of course, this advantage might be said to be more theoretical than real, in that it was perhaps unlikely that the mere receiver would be prosecuted under the 1911 Act, even though that possibility did exist. Similarly, although the tests for harm are to be welcomed, it must be remembered that prosecution under the 1911 Act, theoretically possible in respect of extremely trivial disclosures, was not in practice undertaken; therefore, given the width of the harm tests, it could be said that very little has changed. Furthermore, the fact that journalists were included at all in the net of criminal liability under s 5 has been greatly criticised on the basis that some recognition should be given to the important role of the press in informing the public about government actions.[2]

Finally, in making a determination as to the liberalising impact of the Act, it must be borne in mind that other sanctions for the unauthorised disclosure of information exist. A very large number of statutes already invoke criminal sanctions to enforce secrecy on civil servants in the particular areas they cover.[3] For example, s 11 of the Atomic Energy Act 1946 makes it an offence to communicate to an unauthorised person information relating to atomic energy plant. Further, s 1 of the Official Secrets Act 1911 is still available to punish spies. The government also made it clear that actions for breach of confidence would be used against civil servants in instances falling outside the protected categories.

Thus, while it may be accepted that the Act at least allows argument as to a defendant's state of knowledge in making a disclosure to be led before a jury, it does not allow for argument as to the good intentions of the persons concerned, who may believe with reason that no other effective means of exposing iniquity exists. Of course, good intentions are normally irrelevant in criminal trials; not many would argue that a robber should be able to adduce evidence that he intended to use the proceeds of his robbery to help the poor. However, it is arguable that an exception to this rule should be made in respect of the Official Secrets Act 1989: a statute aimed specifically at those best placed to know of corruption or malpractice in government, should, in a democracy, contain such a defence. The fact that it does not argues strongly against the likelihood that it will have a liberalising impact.

## Notes

1   Steps towards far greater freedom of information were taken by the Public Interest Disclosure Act 1998 and the Freedom of Information Act 2000, both of which could be considered briefly here.

2   This point could be considered further: a comparison could be drawn with the constitutional role of the press recognised in the US by the Pentagon Papers case (*New York Times Co v US* (1971)). The Supreme Court determined that no restraining order on the press could be made so that the press would remain free to censure the Government.

3   The overlap between the Official Secrets Act, the Security Services Act 1989 and the Interception of Communications Act 1985 could be considered here: see ss 1 and 4 of the Official Secrets Act 1989.

# Question 12

'In recent years, there has been a significant movement towards more open government which is largely, but not wholly, attributable to decisions under the European Convention on Human Rights.' Critically evaluate this statement.

## Answer plan

This is clearly a less general and wide ranging question than Question 11, since the need to consider recent developments limits its scope. It should be borne in mind that the statement makes a number of separate assertions, each of which must be evaluated. Essentially, the following issues should be considered:

- possible movement towards openness in government – the Official Secrets Act 1989, the Security Services Act 1989, the Intelligence Services Act 1994 and the Interception of Communications Act 1985, as well as the influence of the European Convention on Human Rights (the Convention) in bringing about changes in the area of official secrecy;
- features of the Security Services Act, the Intelligence Services Act 1994 and the Interception of Communications Act – ousting of the jurisdiction of the courts – secrecy as to tribunal decisions;
- use of the common law as a means of preventing disclosure of information– common law contempt – breach of confidence – response of the European Court of Human Rights (ECHR);
- the Official Secrets Act 1989 – 'harm tests' – lack of a public interest defence – the Public Interest Disclosure Act 1998;
- limitations of the Convention;
- the Freedom of Information Act 2000.

# Answer

A general survey of certain recent developments might indeed suggest that a movement towards more open government has been taking place over the last 15 years. Scrutiny of interception of communications was apparently made possible under the Interception of Communications Act 1985; M15 was acknowledged to exist and placed for the first time on a statutory basis in 1989; disclosure of a range of information was decriminalised under the 1989 Official Secrets Act; MI6 and GCHQ were placed on a statutory basis under the Intelligence Services Act 1994, which also set up a Parliamentary Committee to oversee the work of the security and intelligence services. The voluntary Code on access to government information put in place in 1994 seemed to indicate a clear desire to move towards more open government. However, a closer look at some of these developments reveals, it will be argued, that they did not arise due to a sudden perception of the value of freedom of information, but were imposed on the government. It will further be argued that, in general, these changes have not had a very clear or significant liberalising impact.

The Interception of Communications Act 1985 came into being after the decision of the ECHR in the *Malone* case (1984), which found that the tapping of Mr Malone's telephone constituted a breach of Art 8 of the Convention, which protects the right to privacy. However, the decision only required the UK Government to introduce legislation to regulate the circumstances in which the power to tap could be used, rather than giving guidance as to what would be acceptable limits on the right to privacy.

The response of the Government in the Interception of Communications Act was to provide that complaints can be made only to a tribunal set up under the Act, with no possibility of scrutiny by a court. Furthermore, tribunal decisions are not published and, although an annual report giving some information on the number of intercept warrants issued must be made available, it is first subject to censorship by the Prime Minister. Interestingly, in 1986, CND brought a High Court action challenging the decision to tap phones of its members (*Secretary of State for Home Affairs ex p Ruddock* (1987)) on the ground that the Government had aroused a legitimate expectation through published statements that it would not use tapping for party political purposes. The action failed, but did establish the principle that the courts were entitled to review unfair actions by government arising from failure to live up to legitimate expectations created in this way. The judge, Taylor J, also stated that the jurisdiction of the court to look into such a complaint against a minister should not be totally ousted. That case was the last time such statements would be heard publicly in respect of telephone tapping: s 9 of the Act then (in intention) precluded the possibility of their repetition.

Similarly, the Security Services Act 1989 came into being largely as a response to the finding of the ECHR that a complaint against MI5 was admissible (*Harman and Hewitt v UK* (1986)). The case was brought by two former NCCL officers, Patricia Hewitt and Harriet Harman, who were complaining of their classification as 'subversive' by MI5 which had placed them under surveillance. Part of their complaint concerned a breach of Art 13 of the European Convention on the basis that no effective remedy for complainants existed. The Security Services Act places MI5 on a statutory basis, but prevents almost all effective scrutiny of its operation. Even where a member of the public has a grievance concerning its operation, it will not be possible to use a court action as a means of scrutinising such operation: under s 5, complaint can only be made to a tribunal and, under s 5(4), the decisions of the tribunal are not questionable in any court of law.

Possibly it would not be true to say that this measure came into being solely due to the operation of the ECHR. Its inception was probably also influenced by the challenge to the legality of the tapping of the phones of CND members already mentioned in *Secretary of State for the Home Department ex p Ruddock*, which proved embarrassing to the Government, although it failed. In any event, it does not appear that these statutes will open up the workings of internal security to greater scrutiny. They suggest a perception that no breach of the Convention will occur so long as a mechanism is in place that is able to consider the claims of aggrieved citizens, however ineffective that mechanism might be.

The two statutes mentioned will work in tandem with the Official Secrets Act 1989, which was not brought into being in response to pressure from Europe, but largely due to pressure from other sources. In particular, the failure of the Government to secure a conviction under s 2 of the Official Secrets Act 1911 in *Ponting* (1985) probably had a significant effect. It had been recognised for some time even before the *Ponting* case that s 2 was becoming discredited due to its width. Obviously, the criminal law is brought into disrepute if liability is possible in respect of extremely trivial actions. The 1911 Act had no test of substance and although obtaining a conviction should therefore have been relatively straightforward, the decisions in *Aitken* (1971) and *Ponting* suggested that the very width of the section was undermining its credibility.

The decision to reform the area of official secrecy opened an opportunity for radical change which could have included freedom of information legislation along the lines of the instruments in the US and Canada. However, it was made clear from the outset that the legislation was unconcerned with freedom of information. Thus, one must be cautious in heralding the Official Secrets Act 1989 as amounting to a move away from obsessive secrecy; it does not allow the release of any official documents into the public domain, although it does mean that if certain pieces of information are released, the official concerned will not face criminal sanctions. (He or she might, of course, face an action for breach of confidence as well as disciplinary proceedings.)

It is, however, fair to accept that the 1989 Act covers much less information than its predecessor did due to its introduction of a 'harm test', which takes into account the substance of the information. Clearly, such a test is to be preferred to the width of s 2 of the Official Secrets Act 1911, which covered all official information, however trivial. However, there is no test for harm at all under s 1(1), which prevents members or former members of the security services disclosing anything at all about the operation of those services. All such members come under a lifelong duty to keep silent, even though their information might reveal serious abuse of power in the security services or some operational weakness. These provisions also apply to anyone who is notified that he or she is subject to the provisions of the sub-section. Equally, there is no test for harm under s 4(3) which covers information obtained by, or relating to, the issue of a warrant under the Interception of Communications Act 1985 or the Security Services Act 1989.[1]

The Act contains no explicit public interest defence and it follows from the nature of the harm test that one cannot be implied into it; any good flowing from disclosure of the information cannot be considered, merely any harm that might be caused. Moreover, no express defence of prior publication is provided; the only means of putting forward argument along such lines would arise in one of the categories in which it was necessary to prove the likelihood that harm would flow from the disclosure; the prosecution might find it hard to establish such a likelihood where there had been a great deal of prior publication. Thus, although it may be said that some features of the Act suggest a move towards some liberalisation of official secrecy law, it was clearly intended that this move should not be fully carried through. Both public interest and prior publication defences are available, although in limited circumstances, under the Public Interest Disclosure Act 1998.

On the other hand, the Act may prove more effective than the 1911 Act in deterring the press from publishing the revelations of a future Peter Wright in respect of the workings of the security service. After publication of the book *Spycatcher* in the US in 1987, the Attorney General succeeded in arguing that publication of *Spycatcher* material by the newspapers should be prevented.The House of Lords decided (relying on *American Cyanamid Co v Ethicon Ltd* (1975)) to continue the injunctions against the newspapers on the basis that the Attorney General still had an arguable case for permanent injunctions (*AG v Guardian Newspapers Ltd* (1987)). The injunctions continued until, in the hearing of the permanent injunctions, the House of Lords rejected the Attorney General's claim on the basis that the interest in maintaining confidentiality was outweighed by the public interest in knowing of the allegations in *Spycatcher*. Moreover, it was impossible to sustain a restriction based on confidentiality when the worldwide publication of the book meant that the information it contained was clearly in the 'public domain'.

Clearly, the Government's argument as to the need to maintain secrecy had been pressed too far. Nevertheless, the House of Lords had very readily accepted such argument in respect of the temporary injunctions. When the ECHR considered the case (*The Observer and The Guardian v UK* (1991); *The Sunday Times v UK* (1991)), it found that although the temporary injunctions granted after publication of the book in the US had an aim recognised by two of the exceptions to Art 10 – maintaining the authority of the judiciary and protecting national security – they had an effect disproportionate to that aim and therefore constituted a violation of Art 10. The injunctions obtained before publication in the US were not found to breach Art 10; therefore, this ruling will do nothing to discourage use of such injunctions in many instances where a disclosure of official information is threatened. Use of such injunctions will have a wide ranging impact due to the decision (*AG v Newspaper Publishing plc* (1990)) as to the issue of contempt of court which also arose from the publication of *Spycatcher*.[2]

A Government White Paper in 1993 led to the setting up of a voluntary Code of Practice on Access to Government Information in 1994. This Code was revised in 1997 and 1998. It commits government departments to publishing the facts and analysis behind government decisions. It is subject to many exceptions, however, including information relating to international relations, defence, national security, law enforcement, legal proceedings and Whitehall 'internal discussions and advice'. A much more significant development is the passing of the Freedom of Information Act 2000, which will be brought into force over the next few years. This will require public bodies to disclose information. Although there are still many exceptions under the Act, it is major step forward, in that under it, access to information will now become a statutory right (subject to exceptions), rather than a discretionary privilege.

It may be concluded that claims under the Convention have led to some breaking down of the tradition of secrecy in government. The failings of the Security Services Act, the Interception of Communications Act and the caution of the European Court judgment in the *Spycatcher* case do not, however, support the suggestion that radical change has occurred, or can occur, by this means. The ECHR appears to have contented itself with half measures, with the result that the impact of its decisions in this area has been, and almost certainly will be, minimal. It is probably fair to say that a movement towards open government has occurred, although it has until recently been far from radical and, to an extent, perhaps, it is more apparent than real. The Freedom of Information Act will be a welcome radical addition to this field of law and the timing of the 1997 White Paper upon which it is based does strongly suggest that the Human Rights Act 1998 and the consequent necessity of compliance with the Convention was a driving force behind the new statute. Although there are exceptions to the right of access to information held by public authorities which the new Act creates, it is at least an important symbolic commitment towards far more open government and should have real practical impact on individual rights.

## Notes

1   It could be argued that the harm tests under the Official Secrets
    Act are further diluted in various ways. Under s 3(1)(b), which
    covers confidential information obtained abroad, the mere fact
    that the information is confidential 'may' be sufficient to
    establish the likelihood that its disclosure would cause harm.
    In other words, a fiction is created that harm may
    automatically flow from such disclosure. Under s 1(3) which
    applies to civil servants who disclose matters relating to
    security, the test for damage may be fulfilled merely by
    proving that the document belongs to a class of documents
    likely to cause harm. Thus, not only need there be no proof
    that disclosure of the document itself actually caused harm,
    but there need not even be proof that it was likely to do so.

2   The basis of this decision and its full implications could be
    explained. While the temporary injunctions were in force, *The
    Independent* and two other papers published material covered
    by them. It was determined in the Court of Appeal (*AG v
    Newspaper Publishing plc* (1990)) that such publication
    constituted the *actus reus* of contempt. The case therefore
    affirmed the principle that once an interlocutory injunction has
    been obtained restraining one organ of the media from
    publication of allegedly confidential material, the rest of the
    media may be in contempt if they publish that material, even if
    their intention in doing so is to bring alleged iniquity to public
    attention. In other words, it allowed the laws of confidence
    and contempt to operate together as a significant prior
    restraint on media freedom, and this principle was upheld by
    the House of Lords (*Times Newspapers and Another v AG* (1991)).
    This decision suggests that the House of Lords did not fully
    appreciate the extent to which this decision, in combination
    with the possibility of obtaining a temporary injunction where
    an arguable case for breach of confidence had been made out,
    would hand the Government an effective and wide ranging
    means of silencing the media when publication of sensitive
    information was threatened.

# Question 13

To what extent will freedom of information legislation have a radical effect on government in the UK? Discuss with reference to recent developments.

## Answer plan

This is clearly quite a specific topic which calls for an answer confined to the recent developments, rather than a general and wide ranging answer looking at the whole area of government secrecy. Obviously, a substantial part of the essay must be devoted to differences between the voluntary Code and the new statute. Essentially, the following areas should be considered:

- freedom of information measures in other countries, specifically Canada and the US;
- the Security Services Act 1989, the Official Secrets Act 1989, the Intelligence Services Act 1994 and the Interception of Communications Act 1985;
- the voluntary Code on access to information;
- comparison between the Code and a statutory right of access;
- the Freedom of Information Act 2000.

## Answer

In order to answer this question, it is necessary to consider briefly the measures introduced in other countries which recognise the principle of open government. Relevant UK developments will be considered and the argument put forward that, until recently, they fell short of the models in place abroad. It will be argued that although the principle of 'open' government has been steadily gaining some recognition in the UK, it will not make an impact in practice until the new statutory right to know is established and allows challenge to all currently excluded categories of information.

Most democracies have introduced freedom of information legislation within the last 10 or 20 years. Canada introduced its

Access to Information Act in 1982, while the US has had such legislation since 1966. Its Freedom of Information Act applies to all parts of the Federal Government, unless an exemption applies. Exempted categories include information concerning defence, law enforcement and foreign policy. The exemptions can be challenged in court and the onus of proof will be on the agency withholding the information to prove that disclosure could bring about the harm the exemption was intended to prevent. It should be noted that although the principle of freedom of information in the US has attracted praise, its application in practice has often been criticised. In particular, the American business community considers that the system is being abused by persons who have a particular financial interest in uncovering commercial information. A number of reforms have been suggested since 1980 and, in 1986, a major Freedom of Information Act reform was passed, which extended the exemption available to law enforcement practices.

Until very recently, the attitude to secrecy exemplified by the many democracies which have freedom of information legislation, such as that in Canada or the US with its presumption that information must be disclosed unless specifically exempted, could be contrasted with the Official Secrets Act 1989 in the UK, which takes the opposite stance: no general statutory provision was made for such disclosure; the starting point is to criminalise disclosure in certain categories. American freedom of information provision can, in particular, be contrasted with the former provisions under the UK Public Records Act 1958. Considering all the various and overlapping methods of preventing disclosure of official information in the UK and bearing in mind the contrasting attitude to this issue evinced in other democracies, it may seem that the UK had become increasingly isolated in its stance as a resister of freedom of information legislation. The current Government has now, however, brought about the enactment of the Freedom of Information Act 2000, which will be brought into force over the next few years (with a deadline of 2005). Once in force, it will give individuals a statutory right of access to government information, and will mean that pressure groups such as the UK Freedom of Information Campaign will be able to get to grips with issues which are pre-occupying other democracies, rather than constantly having to attempt to penetrate the secrecy surrounding central government.

With hindsight, recent developments might suggest that a significant movement towards more open government has been taking place in the UK over the last 20 years and increased rapidly throughout the 1990s. The Data Protection Act 1984 (now replaced by the Data Protection Act 1998) established access rights to personal information on computerised files. Following this inroad into the principle of non-disclosure, the Campaign for Freedom of Information supported private members' bills which brought about acceptance of the principle of access rights to manual files in some areas, including local government. Scrutiny of interception of communications was apparently made possible under the Interception of Communications Act 1985; MI5 was acknowledged to exist and placed for the first time on a statutory basis in 1989, while disclosure of a range of information was decriminalised under the 1989 Official Secrets Act. The Intelligence Services Act 1994 placed MI6 and GCHQ on a statutory basis, and also set up a Parliamentary Committee to oversee the work of the security and intelligence services. The Environmental Protection Regulations 1992 mean that the UK now has environmental freedom of information, although subject to wide ranging exceptions. The Public Interest Disclosure Act 1998 may, in time, create a culture of greater openness and restrict the scope of official secrecy by allowing limited public interest disclosure.

After the 1992 election, the Prime Minister promised a review of secrecy in Whitehall to be conducted by William Waldegrave, the Minister with responsibility for the Citizen's Charter, which would concentrate on the large number of statutory instruments which prevent public disclosure of government information in various areas, with a view to removing those which did not appear to fulfil a pressing need. It was also promised that a list of secret Cabinet Committees with their terms of reference and their ministerial membership would be published.

The Government published a White Paper in July 1993 which set out its intentions in relation to freedom of information and led to the setting up of a voluntary Code of Practice in April 1994, allowing citizens access to some specific categories of government information. The Code applied to relevant 'background' information and was subject to a large number of exemptions, including information relating to international relations, defence, national security, law enforcement, legal proceedings and Whitehall 'internal discussions and advice'.

But issue-based statutes and voluntary Codes have serious weaknesses when compared to statutory rights of access to information. After the Official Secrets Act 1989, a large amount of information was shifted outside the ambit of official secrecy, yet no means of access to this information was granted. The Parliamentary Committee set up under the 1994 Act is not a Select Committee and so has limited powers to subject the security services to scrutiny. Anomalies and inconsistencies became obvious; for example, if access to environmental information is available, why not consumer protection information? The Government's commitment to greater openness could be seen in the development of its extensive website and databases, with free internet access. But there was still a difference between the voluntary Code and a binding statutory right of access: the former permitted access, allowing citizens denied such access the right to appeal to an ombudsman; the latter promises full freedom of information except in specific and narrow protected categories, with a right to challenge the denial of access through the courts.

The case for voluntary open government as opposed to a general right of access was not a strong one, for three main reasons. First, William Waldegrave's promise to release information only related to 'useful' or 'useable information'. However, in countries which have freedom of information, the usefulness of the information is determined by the person who seeks it, rather than by government ministers or civil servants. Usefulness is not an objective quality, but depends on the purposes of the seeker, which only he or she can appreciate, and, therefore, it may be argued that this is an unwarranted limitation on the principle of 'openness'. Challenge through an ombudsman is very unlikely to be as effective as challenge in a court.

Secondly, voluntary open government asks the citizen to trust government to act against its own interests. Clearly, government may be prepared voluntarily to release some information which is out of date or innocuous for some other reason, but this may be less likely where the information will cause political embarrassment and may enable opposition to make a more informed and therefore more damaging attack on government. The change in language from permissive to compulsory is thus an important one, since governments will find it harder to suppress information entirely. Thirdly, once the value of the open government principle is accepted the argument against enshrining it in legislation begins to look unconvincing. The new Freedom of Information Act 2000 should therefore only clarify and make more certain a process which under voluntary open government was already supposedly in being; it will not mean that matters which might be damaging to the public interest will be disclosed as they will fall within the exception clauses. Therefore, government might be hard pressed to identify the nature of the material it wishes to seek to suppress under a voluntary system, which it would have to disclose under the new legislation. So, the new Act is most significant for creating a right to access, whatever its limitations and exceptions. The Act follows the American legislation's pattern with similar exempted information categories. However, where a public interest argument can be made for disclosure, the exemptions may be overridden; and appeals to a tribunal and ultimately to a court provide a far more satisfactory framework than was at first expected. The Freedom of Information Act will allow any citizen access to the majority of government information without any need to justify his or her wish to access it, and the exceptions for defence, national security, law enforcement, effective government and so on allow enough similarity between the old and new systems to minimise the impact on existing official secrecy and confidentiality laws. So, once the Act is brought into force, its impact will be an important if largely symbolic one for British citizens.

# Question 14

Critically evaluate recent developments in the law of confidence and their likely impact on freedom of information and government secrecy.

## Answer plan

This topic might obviously appear as part of a general and wide ranging essay or, as here, in its own right. It is concerned with the use of prior restraint under the doctrine of breach of confidence as a means of preventing publication of information and, of course, will mainly involve consideration of the *Spycatcher* case. Essentially, the following matters should be considered:

- breach of confidence – balancing public interest in disclosure of information against the interest in keeping it confidential;
- the nature of the public interest defence (*Lion Laboratories v Evans and Express Newspapers* (1985));
- duty of confidence can bind third parties – use of interim injunctions (*AG v Guardian Newspapers Ltd* (1987));
- the judgment of the European Court of Human Rights (ECHR) on the Art 10 issue (*The Observer and The Guardian v UK* (1991); *The Sunday Times v UK* (1991));
- common law contempt in conjunction with the law of confidence;
- s 12 of the Human Rights Act (HRA) 1998;
- *AG v Blake* (2000).

# Answer

Breach of confidence is a civil remedy affording protection against the disclosure or use of information which is not generally known, and which has been entrusted in circumstances imposing an obligation not to disclose it without authorisation from the person who originally imparted it. This area of law developed as a means of protecting secret information belonging to individuals and organisations. However, it can also be used by government to prevent disclosure of sensitive information and is, in that sense, a back up to the other measures available to government, including the Official Secrets Act 1989. In some respects, it may be more valuable than the criminal sanction provided by the Act. It may attract less publicity than a criminal trial, it offers the possibility of quickly obtaining an interim injunction and no jury will be involved. The possibility of obtaining an interim injunction is very valuable since, in many instances, the other party (usually a newspaper) will not pursue the case to a trial of the permanent injunctions, since the secret will probably no longer be newsworthy by that time.

However, where government, as opposed to a private individual, is concerned, the courts will not merely accept that it is in the public interest that the information should be kept confidential. Government will have to show that the public interest in keeping it confidential, due to the harm its disclosure would cause, is not outweighed by the public interest in disclosure. Thus, in *AG v Jonathan Cape* (1976), when the Attorney General invoked the law of confidence to try to stop publication of Richard Crossman's memoirs on the ground that they concerned Cabinet discussions, the Lord Chief Justice accepted that such public secrets could be restrained, but only on the basis that the balance of the public interest came down in favour of suppression. Since the discussions had taken place 10 years previously, it was not possible to show that harm would flow from their disclosure; the public interest in publication therefore prevailed.

The nature of the public interest defence – the interest in disclosure – was clarified in *Lion Laboratories v Evans and Express Newspapers* (1985). The Court of Appeal held that the defence extended beyond situations in which there had been serious wrongdoing by the plaintiff. Even where the plaintiff was blameless, publication would be excusable where it was possible to show a serious and legitimate interest in the revelation. Thus, the *Daily Express* was allowed to publish information extracted from the manufacturer of the intoximeter, even though it did not reveal iniquity on the part of the manufacturer. It did, however, reveal a matter of genuine public interest: that wrongful convictions might have been obtained in drink driving cases due to possible deficiencies of the intoximeter.

The leading case in this area is now the House of Lords' decision in *AG v Guardian Newspapers Ltd (No 2)* (1990), which confirmed that the *Lion Laboratories Ltd v Evans* approach to the public interest defence was the correct one, and also clarified certain other aspects of this area of the law. In 1985, the Attorney General commenced proceedings in Australia in an attempt to restrain publication of *Spycatcher* by Peter Wright. The book included allegations of illegal activity engaged in by MI5. In 1986, after *The Guardian* and *The Observer* published reports of the forthcoming hearing which included some *Spycatcher* material, the Attorney General obtained temporary *ex parte* injunctions preventing them from further disclosure of such material.

In 1987, the book was published in the US and many copies were brought into the UK. After that point, the House of Lords decided (relying on *American Cyanamid Co v Ethicon Ltd* (1975)) to continue the injunctions against the newspapers on the basis that the Attorney General still had an arguable case for permanent injunctions. In making this decision, the House of Lords were obviously influenced by the fact that publication of the information was an irreversible step. This is the usual approach at the interim stage: the court considers the balance of convenience between the two parties and will tend to come down on the side of the claimant, because of the irrevocable nature of publication. However, as an interim injunction represents a prior restraint and as it is often the most crucial, and, indeed, sometimes the only stage in the whole action, it may be argued that a presumption in favour of freedom of expression should be more readily allowed to tip the balance in favour of the defendant. This may especially be argued where publication from other sources has already occurred, which will be likely to increase, and where the public interest in the information is very strong. The House of Lords' decision was eventually found to be in breach of Art 10 of the Convention; the effect of that decision will be considered below.

In the trial of the permanent injunctions (*AG v Guardian (No 2)* (1988)), the Crown argued that confidential information disclosed to third parties does not thereby lose its confidential character if the third parties know that the disclosure has been made in breach of a duty of confidence. A further reason for maintaining confidentiality in the particular instance was that the unauthorised disclosure of the information was thought likely to damage the trust which members of the service have in each other and might encourage others to follow suit. These factors established the public interest in keeping the information confidential. On the other hand, some of the information in *Spycatcher*, if true, disclosed that members of MI5 in their operations in England had committed serious breaches of domestic law in, for example, bugging foreign embassies or effecting unlawful entry into private premises. Most seriously, the book included the allegations that members of MI5 attempted to destabilise the administration of Mr Harold Wilson, and that the Director General or deputy Director General of MI5 was a spy. The newspapers contended that the duty of non-disclosure, to which newspapers coming into the unauthorised possession of confidential state secrets may be subject, does not extend to allegations of serious iniquity of this character.

It was determined that whether or not the newspapers would have had a duty to refrain from publishing *Spycatcher* material in June 1986 before its publication elsewhere, any such duty had now lapsed. Thus, the mere making of allegations of iniquity was insufficient, of itself, to justify overriding the duty of confidentiality, but the articles in question published in June 1986 had not contained information going beyond what the public was reasonably entitled to know and, in so far as they went beyond what had been previously published, no detriment to national security had been shown that could outweigh the public interest in free speech, given the publication of *Spycatcher* that had already taken place. Thus, balancing the public interest in freedom of speech and the right to receive information against the countervailing interest of the Crown in national security, continuation of the injunctions was not necessary.[1]

It appears likely that the permanent injunctions would have been granted but for the massive publication of *Spycatcher* abroad. That factor seems to have tipped the balance in favour of the newspapers. It appears that the operation of the public interest defence may tend to involve a value judgment by the judge, rather than application of a clear legal rule. Until s 12 of the HRA 1998 gave primacy to freedom of speech and brought the Convention's protection into domestic courts, it was thought that judges may sometimes be too prone to be swayed by establishment arguments. The *Spycatcher* judgment also made it clear that once the information has become available from other sources, even though the plaintiff played no part in its dissemination and indeed tried to prevent it, an injunction is unlikely to be granted. This principle was affirmed in *Lord Advocate v Scotsman Publications Ltd* (1989).

The judgment in the ECHR on the temporary injunctions granted in the *Spycatcher* case (*The Observer and The Guardian v UK*; *The Sunday Times v UK*) did not really have a clear liberalising influence on this area of law. The court found that the injunctions clearly constituted an interference with the newspapers' freedom of expression, but that the interference fell within two of the exceptions provided for by para 2 of Art 10: maintaining the authority of the judiciary and protecting national security. Those exceptions could be invoked only if the injunctions were necessary in a democratic society, in the sense that they corresponded to a pressing social need and were proportionate to the aims pursued. The injunctions in force before publication of the book in the US had the aim of preventing publication of material which, according to evidence presented by the Attorney General, might have created a risk of detriment to MI5. The nature of the risk was uncertain, because the exact contents of the book were not known at that time, as it was still only available in manuscript form.[2] Were the actual restraints imposed proportionate to these aims? The injunctions did not prevent the papers pursuing a campaign for an inquiry into the operation of the security services and, though preventing publication for a long time – over a year – the material in question could not be classified as urgent news. Thus, the interference complained of was proportionate to the ends in view.

However, the court took the view that, after publication of the book in the US, the aim of the injunctions was no longer to keep secret information secret; it was to attempt to preserve the reputation of MI5 and to deter others who might be tempted to follow Peter Wright's example. It was uncertain whether the injunctions could achieve those aims and it was not clear that the newspapers who had not been concerned with the publication of *Spycatcher* should be enjoined as an example to others.[3] Thus, a breach of Art 10 had occurred, but only in relation to the injunctions granted after publication in the US.

It is arguable that this was a very cautious and pragmatic judgment, resting as it does only on the fact that the book was published in the US before the House of Lords' decision to uphold the temporary injunctions. The court seems to have been readily persuaded by the Attorney General's argument that a widely framed injunction was needed in July 1986, but it is arguable that it was wider than it needed to be to prevent a risk to national security.[4]

This judgment did nothing to curb the use of 'gagging injunctions' in actions for breach of confidence where there has not been prior publication of the material. In any such action, even if the claim was of little merit, it was always possible to argue that its subject matter should be preserved intact until the merits of the claim can be considered. Even if the claimant then decides to drop the action before that point, publication of the material in question would have been prevented for some substantial period of time.

It must further be borne in mind that there have been recent developments which will allow breach of confidence a greater potential than it previously possessed to prevent dissemination of government information. While the temporary injunctions were in force, *The Independent* and two other papers published material covered by them. It was determined in the Court of Appeal (*AG v Newspaper Publishing plc* (1990)) that such publication constituted the *actus reus* of contempt. The case therefore affirmed the principle that once an interlocutory injunction has been obtained restraining one organ of the media from publication of allegedly confidential material, the rest of the media may be in contempt if they publish that material, even if their intention in doing so is to bring alleged iniquity to public attention. Such publication must be accompanied by an intention to prejudice the eventual trial of the permanent injunctions, but only in the sense that it was foreseen that such prejudice, while undesired, was very likely to occur. Thus, the laws of confidence and contempt were allowed to operate together as a significant prior restraint on media freedom, and this principle was upheld by the House of Lords (*Times Newspapers and Another v AG* (1991)).

It may be that the House of Lords did not appreciate the extent to which this decision, in combination with the possibility of obtaining a temporary injunction where an arguable case for breach of confidence had been made out, would hand government an effective and wide ranging means of silencing the media when publication of sensitive information was threatened. However, the potential of this method should already have been apparent. In 1987, the BBC wished to broadcast a programme to be entitled *My Country Right or Wrong*, which was to examine issues raised by the *Spycatcher* litigation. The Attorney General obtained an injunction preventing transmission on the ground of breach of confidence (*AG v BBC* (1987)). According to the Attorney General, the injunction then affected every organ of the media, because of the July ruling of the Court of Appeal in *AG v Newspaper Publishing plc*

(1987) (this was a preliminary ruling on the *actus reus* of common law contempt which was affirmed as noted above).

It seems fairly clear that although the Government eventually lost in the *Spycatcher* case, the decision did not have any liberalising impact as far as enhancing the ability of newspapers to publish information about government is concerned. The most pernicious aspect of breach of confidence – the ease with which interim injunctions may be obtained – will remain unaffected by this case, except in instances where a great deal of prior publication has occurred. Where such an injunction is obtained, it will affect all of the media, in the sense that they will not wish to risk criminal liability for contempt of court.

Case law since *Spycatcher* has, however, indicated that there are limits to the scope of breach of confidence. In *Lord Advocate v The Scotsman Publications Ltd* (1990), a former member of MI6 published privately a book of memoirs dealing with the years 1948–53. A total of 279 copies were distributed. The Lord Advocate sought an injunction restraining any publication of extracts from the book in *The Scotsman*. He conceded that the publication of the contents of the book would in no way prejudice national security, but argued that any publication by a former member of the security services would be contrary to the public interest. The House of Lords, however, refused to grant an injunction. In the light of the Lord Advocate's concession and the fact that the book had already received some circulation (albeit limited), there was no reason to restrain publication by the press. More recently, in *AG v Blake* (2000), the courts considered the publication of the memoirs of a notorious spy, who had worked for the British intelligence services in the 1960s, had been convicted and imprisoned, and had then escaped to Russia. The Attorney General did not even seek to base his case on breach of confidence in this instance, since the events described took place more than 30 years previously. The House of Lords, however, while not restraining publication, ordered that all royalties otherwise payable to Blake should be forfeited to the Attorney General. This was on the basis that Blake was in breach of a contractual obligation dating from his employment by the security services not to disclose any information about his work, and this was a case where exceptionally an account of profits was the appropriate remedy for a breach of contract.

In the area of statutory provisions which affect the liability for breach of confidence, there has been the Public Interest Disclosure Act 1998. This aims to protect 'whistleblowers' by providing a defence of public interest, and overriding the law of confidence. It renders such whistleblowers vulnerable, however, if they disclose the information to a person other than an employer or a relevant regulatory body. It remains to be seen how effective this legislation will be in restricting actions based on breach of confidence.

Finally, as noted earlier, the HRA 1998, and in particular s 12, will require courts considering the award of damages or the issue of injunctions for breach of confidence to give proper consideration to the countervailing freedom of speech issues. So, although breach of confidence remains an important weapon in the government's armoury, it is likely to be of more limited effect in the future than may have seemed likely at the time of the *Spycatcher* litigation.

## Notes

1   It was further determined that an injunction to restrain future publication of matters connected with the operations of the security service would amount to a comprehensive ban on publication and would undermine the operation of determining the balance of public interest in deciding whether such publication was to be prevented; accordingly, an injunction to prevent future publication which had not yet been threatened was not granted.

2   It could be pointed out that the House of Lords wanted to preserve the Attorney General's right to be granted a permanent injunction; if *Spycatcher* material had been published before that claim could be heard, the subject matter of the action would have been damaged or destroyed. In the court's view, these factors established the existence of a pressing social need.

3   It could be noted further that, after publication in the US, it was not possible to maintain the Attorney General's rights as a litigant, since the substance of his claim had already been destroyed; had permanent injunctions been obtained against

the papers, that would not have preserved the confidentiality of the material in question.

4   This point could be pursued further: the injunction could have required the newspapers to refrain from publishing Wright material which had not been previously published by others until (and if) the action to prevent publication of the book was lost. Such wording would have taken care of any national security interest; therefore, wording going beyond that was disproportionate to that aim The judgment could also have set itself against the narrow view that the authority of the judiciary is best preserved by allowing a claim of confidentiality set up in the face of a strong competing public interest to found an infringement of freedom of speech for over a year.

# CHAPTER 3

# FREEDOM OF ASSEMBLY AND ASSOCIATION

## Introduction

Freedom of assembly is a subject which almost invariably appears on examination papers in civil liberties, often, but not always, in the form of a problem question. The concern in such questions is with the conflict between the need on the one hand to maintain public order and, on the other, to protect freedom of assembly. Whether problem questions or essays are set, the concern in either case will be with those provisions of the criminal law most applicable in the context of demonstrations, marches or meetings. Freedom of association tends to be considered in an essay question which also covers freedom of assembly, but it sometimes arises as an independent essay topic.

Problem questions sometimes call on the student to discuss *any* issues which may arise, as opposed to considering criminal liability only, in which case, any tortious liability incurred by members of an assembly or by police officers may arise, as well as questions of criminal liability. The possibility of judicial review of police decisions may also arise.

Students should have general knowledge of the background to the Public Order Act 1986 and, in particular, should be familiar with the following areas:

- notice requirements under s 11 of the Public Order Act 1986;
- conditions which can be imposed under ss 12 and 14 of the Act on processions and assemblies;
- banning power under s 13 of the Act;
- liability under ss 5, 4, 4A and 3 of the Act;
- liability for obstruction of a police officer under s 89(1) of the Police Act 1996;

- common law power to prevent a breach of the peace;
- public nuisance;
- obstruction of the highway under s 137 of the Highways Act 1980;
- public order provisions of Pt V and s 154 of the Criminal Justice and Public Order Act 1994;
- Arts 10 and 11 of the European Convention on Human Rights (the Convention).

# Question 15

Citizens of Southton are very concerned about plans to build a nuclear power station on the outskirts of Southton. On Saturday morning, Brenda, a citizen of Southton, holds a meeting in Southton Town Hall in order to discuss the matter, which is attended by 100 Southton residents. The meeting becomes heated and Brenda suggests that they should all march at once to the town square (half a mile away at the head of the main road through the town, which leads to the shopping centre) in order to gain more publicity for their cause. The group sets off, Brenda leading. Brenda asks Philip to bring up the rear of the procession.

As the group moves down the main road and nears the town square, two police officers, Elaine and George, approach Brenda and tell her that she must disperse part of the group because it is holding up traffic and may cause other pedestrians to move off the pavement into the road. Brenda does not comply with the request. The procession arrives at the town square and Brenda begins to address the meeting. George again asks Brenda to disperse half the group and, further, to re-site the meeting on the outskirts of the town. She refuses, and George then informs her that he is arresting her for failing to comply with his orders. Brenda calls on Philip to continue the meeting and he moves towards the front of the group.

Seeing the arrest of Brenda, the group becomes angry. Encouraged by Philip, the group spreads out across the road, largely blocking the road and the pavement. Philip, with some of its members, calls on shoppers entering the main road not to go on, but to join the demonstration. George calls on Philip to disperse part of the group, but is ignored. Some shoppers join in, but others attempt to push past the demonstrators. One of the demonstrators, Roger, shouts and swears at the shoppers who are attempting to push past. He waves his fists threateningly at them and calls on other members of the group not to allow them to pass. Elaine and George move to arrest Philip and Roger.

Consider the criminal liability (if any) incurred by Brenda, Philip and Roger.

### Answer plan

This question is confined to criminal liability incurred by members of the assembly; therefore, other possible issues, such as the lawfulness of any of the arrests and the question of breach of the peace, need not be considered. This question raises a large number of issues which typically appear on exam papers.

The essential matters to be discussed are:

- notice requirements under s 11 of the Public Order Act 1986;
- 'triggers' under ss 12 and 14 of the Act;
- conditions which can be imposed under ss 12 and 14 on processions and assemblies;
- liability which may arise under ss 5 and 4 as amended;
- public nuisance;
- obstruction of the highway under s 137 of the Highways Act 1980.

## Answer

Liability in this case arises mainly under the Public Order Act 1986 (hereinafter 'the Act'), but common law provisions will also be highly relevant. The possible criminal liability incurred by Brenda, Philip and Roger will be considered in turn.

Under s 11 of the Act, advance notice of a procession must be given if it falls within one of three categories. The march from the town hall falls within s 11(1)(a), as it is intended to demonstrate opposition to the building of the power station. As no notice of the march was given, Brenda may have committed an offence under s 11(7)(a) of the Act, as she is the organiser of the march. However, the notice requirement does not apply under s 11(1) if it was not reasonably practicable to give any advance notice. This provision was intended to exempt spontaneous demonstrations such as this one from the notice requirements, but is defective due to the use of the word 'any'. This word would suggest that a phone call made five minutes before the march sets off would fulfil the requirements, thereby exempting very few marches. Although the march sets off suddenly, it is possible that Brenda had time to make such a phone call; on a strict interpretation of s 11, she is therefore in breach of the notice requirements, as it was reasonably practicable for her to fulfil them.

However, it can be argued that the word 'any' should not be interpreted so strictly as to exclude spontaneous processions where a few minutes was available to give notice, because to do so would defeat the intention behind including the provision. If read in combination with the requirements as to giving notice by hand or in writing, it should be interpreted to mean any written notice. If it were not so interpreted, it might be argued that s 11 breaches the guarantee of freedom of expression or freedom of assembly under Art 10 or 11 of the Convention. Since s 3 of the HRA 1998 requires that, where statutes are ambiguous, they should be interpreted so as to conform with the UK's Convention obligations, s 11 should be interpreted in so far as it is ambiguous in accordance with Art 10 or 11. Following this argument, liability will not arise under s 11.

Brenda may further incur liability under s 12(4) of the Act, as she was the organiser of a public procession, but failed to comply with the condition imposed by Elaine to disperse part of the group. Elaine can impose conditions on the procession only if one of the four 'triggers' under s 12(1) is present. The third of these, that the police officer in question must reasonably believe that 'serious disruption to the life of the community' may be caused by the procession, may arguably arise. The group of 100 citizens were marching down the main street of the town; Elaine's fear that traffic may be obstructed or passers by forced into the road may found a reasonable apprehension that the life of the community will be disrupted and it is arguable that such disruption may be termed serious. On this argument, Elaine is entitled to impose conditions on the march.

The condition imposed must relate to the disruption apprehended. This may be said of the requirement to disperse half the group; Brenda will therefore incur liability under s 12(4), unless she can show that the failure arose due to circumstances outside her control. Although the powers of an organiser to disperse members of a march are limited, it is clear that Brenda made no effort at all to fulfil the condition. It is therefore argued that she has committed the offence under s 12(4).

Brenda may further incur liability under s 14(4) of the Act, as she was the organiser of a public assembly, but failed to comply with the condition imposed by the most senior police officer present at the scene (who can be a constable) to re-site the assembly and disperse part of the group. It should be noted that as the group was in a public place and comprised more than 20 persons, it constituted a public assembly under s 16 of the Act. George can impose conditions on the assembly only if one of four 'triggers' under s 14(1) is present. These are identical to those arising under s 12(1) and the third of these will again be considered as the easiest to satisfy in the circumstances. It will be argued that, at the point of imposing the condition, the behaviour of the assembly did not fulfil the terms of the 'trigger', although it may have done so at a later stage. Unlike the march, there is no evidence that, at this stage, the assembly held up traffic. In the case of *Reid* (1987), it was determined that the 'triggers' should be strictly interpreted: the words used should not be diluted. In the instant case, a group of 100 citizens were gathered on the street in the morning on a Saturday; although it could be argued that such a circumstance might cause some disruption in the community (in terms of blockage of the pavement), it is less clear that a reasonable person would expect the disruption to be serious. On this argument, George had no power to impose conditions on the assembly; no liability therefore arises under s 14(4). The question of whether the failure to comply with the condition imposed arose due to circumstances beyond Brenda's control need not, therefore, be addressed.[1]

Brenda may, however, have incurred liability under s 137 of the Highways Act 1980, which provides that a person will be guilty of an offence if he 'without lawful authority or excuse in any way wilfully obstructs the free passage of the highway'. In *Nagy v Weston* (1966), it was held that a reasonable user of the highway will constitute a lawful excuse and that, in order to determine its reasonableness or otherwise, the length of the obstruction must be considered, its purpose, the place where it occurred and whether an actual or potential obstruction took place. In *Arrowsmith v Jenkins* (1963), it was determined that minor obstruction of traffic can lead to liability under the Highways Act. The assembly in question was held in a certain street which linked up two main roads, with the result that the street was completely blocked for five minutes and partly blocked for 15 minutes. The organiser was convicted. However, the question of the purpose of the obstruction, mentioned in *Nagy v Weston*, was given greater prominence in *Hirst and Agu v Chief Constable of West Yorkshire* (1986) – it was said that courts should have regard to the freedom to demonstrate. On that basis, the purpose of an assembly as a means of legitimate protest may suggest that it can amount to a reasonable user of the highway.[2] Some support for this approach is to be found in the House of Lords' decision in *DPP v Jones* (1999), where two members of the majority specifically held that there is a right of peaceful assembly on the public highway, provided it does not obstruct the public's primary right of passage. The level of obstruction caused by Brenda's procession may well, therefore, be the crucial factor in deciding on her liability.

Brenda may also have incited the group to commit a public nuisance by blocking the highway. However, according to *Clarke* (1964), the disruption caused must amount to an unreasonable use of the highway in order to found liability for public nuisance. Thus, once obstruction has been shown, the question of reasonableness arises. However, as has already been pointed out, it is arguable that to cause a minor disruption for a legitimate purpose does not constitute an unreasonable use of the highway. It is unlikely that a user of the highway could be reasonable under the Highways Act but, nevertheless, able to amount to a public nuisance. This seemed to be accepted in *Gillingham Borough Council v Medway Dock Co* (1992). On this argument, liability for public nuisance will not arise.

Philip's possible criminal liability will now be considered. He may incur liability under s 12(4) in respect of his part in organising the march. The Act does not define the term 'organiser' and there is no post-Act case law on the issue; therefore, the issue as to the meaning of the term cannot be settled with certainty. However, it is submitted that, on the dictionary definition of the term, Philip is an organiser. This contention is supported by the ruling from *Flockhart v Robinson* (1950) that a person who indicated the route to be followed should be designated an organiser as well as the person who planned the route. Thus, it appears likely that the term includes stewards. (If, in the alternative, it could be argued that Philip's role is too uncertain to allow him to fall within the term 'organiser', he could nevertheless incur liability under s 12(5) as a member of the march, subject to the argument below.) Therefore, the argument for liability on Brenda's part under s 12(4) will also apply to Philip, unless he was unaware of the condition imposed. It appears that Philip was at the back of the group when the condition was imposed and, therefore, it seems possible that he may have been unaware of it, in which case, he will not attract liability under s 12(4) of the Act.

On the assumption that Philip is a co-organiser, the above arguments as to Brenda's liability arising under s 137 of the Highways Act 1980 or for public nuisance will be relevant, but it is argued that they will fail to establish liability on the basis that although the demonstration does partly block the road and shoppers are impeded, the demonstration may still be termed legitimate and, therefore, not unreasonable. Philip's actions in trying to persuade shoppers to join the demonstration may be viewed as in keeping with the aims of a legitimate protest.

Philip may incur liability under s 14(4) as an organiser of an assembly which is in breach of a condition imposed. When Philip took over leadership of the assembly, the situation changed; he encouraged the group to block the street and stop passers by. It is arguable that the fourth 'trigger', arising under s 14(1)(b), may have been fulfilled. It consists of an evaluation of the purpose of the assembly rather than an apprehension that a particular state of affairs may arise. The senior police officer present must reasonably believe that the purpose of the assembly is 'the intimidation of others with a view to compelling them not to do an act they have a right to do or to do an act they have a right not to do'.

Possibly the third 'trigger' could also apply to this situation, but that point need not be considered, because the fourth 'trigger' seems to be most clearly indicated: the group are trying to prevent some persons entering the road leading to the shopping centre and are therefore trying to prevent persons doing something they have a right to do (presumably in the sense that there is a right to pass along the highway); the question is whether their actions have gone beyond what might be acceptable as part of a legitimate demonstration and could suggest an intention to intimidate. As noted above, it was determined in *Reid* (1987) that the 'triggers' should be strictly interpreted. In *Reid*, the defendants shouted, raised their arms and waved their fingers; it was determined that such behaviour might cause discomfort, but not intimidation, and that the two concepts could not be equated. In *News Group Newspapers Ltd v SOGAT* (1982), it was held that mere abuse and shouting did not amount to a threat of violence for the purposes of intimidation under s 7 of the Conspiracy and Protection of Property Act 1875. In the instant case, it could be argued that the groups' behaviour in merely shouting at the shoppers could not amount to intimidation, but that in attempting to impede their passage, the behaviour crossed the boundary between discomfort and intimidation. On that basis, it appears that George had the power to impose conditions on the assembly.

Philip made no effort to comply with the condition imposed and will therefore incur liability under s 14(4). He may also incur liability under s 14(6) as inciting others to commit the offence under s 14(5) of taking part in a public assembly and knowingly failing to comply with the condition imposed. However, this point cannot be settled, as it is unclear from the facts whether or not other members of the group were aware of the condition imposed.

Following the above argument, Roger may incur liability under s 14(5). Moreover, he may incur liability under s 14(6) as an organiser, in that he calls on other members of the group to impede shoppers. He may be said to have taken on the role of organiser at this point. However, these points cannot be settled, as it is unclear from the facts whether or not Roger was aware of the condition imposed.

Roger may further incur liability under s 5(1) of the Act in respect of his behaviour towards the shoppers. In order to show this, his behaviour must amount to 'threatening, abusive or insulting words or behaviour or disorderly behaviour' which takes place in the hearing or sight of a person likely to be caused harassment, alarm or distress thereby. The three terms used must be given their ordinary meaning (*Brutus v Cozens* (1973)). The word 'likely' imports an objective test into the section: it is necessary to show that a person was present at the scene, but not that he or she actually experienced the feelings in question. Had Roger confined himself to abuse, it could be argued that his behaviour would be likely merely to irritate the shoppers. However, his use of threatening gestures might be likely to cause the stronger emotion connoted by the concept of harassment. Moreover, Roger appears to satisfy the *mens rea* requirement under s 6(4); it appears probable that he is aware or intends that his words or behaviour are threatening, although possibly not abusive or insulting.

However, a defence under s 5(3)(c) is available to Roger if it can be argued that his behaviour was reasonable. An argument for giving a wide interpretation to the term 'reasonable' can be supported on the basis that in so far as s 5 is ambiguous, it should be interpreted in accordance with Art 11 of the Convention. As already noted, if a statute is ambiguous, it should be interpreted in conformity with the Convention (see s 3 of the HRA 1998). Whether a forceful demonstration which included some disorderly behaviour could fall within the terms of Art 11, which extend only to peaceful protest, is, however, debatable. Thus, even if the term 'reasonable' is widely interpreted, it would not appear wide enough to encompass the behaviour in question which, it seems, went beyond persuasion and became coercion. It is submitted that this defence would fail. It appears, then, that Roger may incur liability under s 5.

It might be argued that Philip will also incur liability under s 5, but this argument would probably fail; his behaviour may cause discomfort or inconvenience to the shoppers, but it is argued that the words of s 5 connote a higher level of distress.

Roger's behaviour may also support an argument that he has committed an offence under s 4, which is couched in the same terms as s 5, except for the omission of 'disorderly behaviour' and with the added need to show that somebody was likely to apprehend the use of immediate violence by Roger or another, or that he intended to arouse such an apprehension. Both these possibilities may be present. The behaviour in question must be specifically directed towards another person. Following *Ambrose* (1973), rude or offensive words or behaviour may not necessarily be insulting, while mere swearing may not fall within the meaning of 'abusive'. However, Roger's behaviour in waving his fists may fall within the meaning of the term 'threatening'. Possibly, in the circumstances – two police officers were present and Roger does not seem directly to approach the shoppers – they might be unlikely to apprehend immediate violence. However, it seems that Roger intended his words to provoke the rest of the group into using some force against the shoppers. Following the ruling in *Horseferry Road Metropolitan Stipendiary Magistrate ex p Siadatan* (1991), 'violence' in this context must mean immediate and unlawful violence. This was confirmed in *Winn v DPP* (1992). It is concluded that Roger's behaviour does not satisfy this strict test,[3] although it may fall within s 4A (inserted by s 154 of the Criminal Justice and Public Order Act 1994), which creates liability for intentionally causing harassment, alarm or distress.

## Notes

1   Had the argument under s 14(4) been resolved differently, Brenda might have fallen within the provision under s 14(6), as she called on Philip to take over as leader, thereby arguably inciting him to commit the offence under s 14(5) of taking part in an assembly and knowingly failing to comply with a condition imposed.

2   This argument is supported by the provisions of the Public Order Act; Pt II of the Act recognises the existence of marches and processions and therefore by necessary implication permits them so long as its provisions are complied with. On this basis, the brevity of the obstruction and its purpose as part of a legitimate protest suggest that the march amounted to a reasonable use of the highway.

3   It may be worth considering whether members of the group, including Philip and Roger, may incur liability in respect of the offence of affray under s 3 of the Act. In order to establish an affray, it must first be shown that the defendant used or threatened unlawful violence towards another and, secondly, that his conduct was such as would cause a person of reasonable firmness present at the scene to fear for his personal

safety. As Roger uses threatening gestures, it may be argued that the first limb of s 3(1) is fulfilled, but a strong argument can be advanced that the second is not; due to the fact that the gestures are part of a demonstration, it is probable that a person of reasonable firmness would not fear unlawful violence, even though such a person might feel somewhat distressed. In *Taylor v DPP* (1973), Lord Hailsham, speaking of the common law offence, said 'the degree of violence ... must be such as to be calculated to terrify a person of reasonably firm character'. The Act of course refers to 'fear', as opposed to terror, but this ruling suggests that 'fear' should be interpreted restrictively. On this argument, no liability will arise in respect of s 3.

# Question 16

How far would it be fair to say that the Public Order Act 1986 and Criminal Justice and Public Order Act 1994 create a reasonable balance between the public interest in freedom of assembly and the need to maintain order?

### Answer plan

A very common essay question on the Public Order Act. It requires a sound knowledge of the key provisions of the Act, but also the related measures at common law and in other statutes. Such measures create the context within which the Act operates, and so they should play some part in your answer. A distinction should initially be drawn between prior and subsequent restraints contained in the Act. Essentially, the following matters should be considered:

- legal recognition of freedom of assembly – the Human Rights Act (HRA) 1998;
- background to the Public Order Act and the Criminal Justice and Public Order Act (CJPOA) 1994;
- provisions aimed specifically at processions and assemblies under ss 11, 12, 13, 14 (as amended by s 70 of the CJPOA);
- prior and subsequent restraints under ss 11–14;

- low level public order offences under ss 4, 4A and 5;
- other statutory or common law public order offences.

# Answer

Until the HRA 1998 came into force, the law afforded virtually no recognition to the right to meet and march, apart from a very limited right to hold meetings, which applies only to parliamentary candidates before a general election, and arises under ss 95 and 96 of the Representation of the People Act 1983. Further, there are certain specific statutory prohibitions on meetings in certain places or at certain times. Under the Seditious Meetings Act 1817, meetings of 50 or more are prohibited in the vicinity of the Westminster during a parliamentary session. Aside from these specific provisions, freedom of assembly must operate within a legal framework intended to maintain public order. The difficulty is clearly that in seeking to maintain public order, the constitutional need to allow freedom of assembly in a democracy may be obscured. In order to determine how far the Public Order Act 1986 allows a balance to be maintained between these two interests, this essay will focus on certain of its provisions, particularly those creating prior restraints, which appear most likely to affect freedom of assembly. However, in future, it is likely that freedom of assembly will be given greater priority by the courts in their interpretation of the European Convention on Human Rights through the HRA. Demonstrations are a form of expression falling within Art 10 of the Convention (as confirmed by *Steel v UK* (1999)), so that s 12 of the HRA will require the courts to give particular consideration to that Article in deciding to grant relief in civil proceedings. Where the proceedings are criminal, s 12 of the HRA does not apply, but there will still be an obligation under s 3 of the HRA to interpret the legislation compatibly with Art 10 wherever possible. The same will apply to Art 11, which guarantees the right to peaceable assembly and demonstration, subject to restrictions in so far only as they are necessary for one of the stipulated reasons, such as national security, safety, prevention of disorder, etc. Restrictions must be proportionate to their legitimate aim (*Ezelin v France* (1991)) and peaceable demonstrators must be protected from reprisal

(*Plattform 'Arzte für das Leben' v Austria* (1988)). Thus, UK law remains vulnerable to Art 10 or 11 challenges on these points.

The Public Order Act 1986 contains various prior restraints on assemblies, which may mean that they cannot take place at all or can take place only under various limitations. These restraints are contained in ss 12, 13 and 14 of the Act. Sections 12 and 13 are underpinned by s 11, which provides that the organisers of a march (not a meeting) must give advance notice of it to the police. This statutory national notice requirement was an entirely new measure, although, in some districts, a notice requirement was already imposed under local provisions. The notice must specify the date, time and proposed route of the procession, and give the name and address of the person proposing to organise it. Under s 11(7), the organisers may be guilty of an offence if the notice requirement has not been satisfied or if the march deviates from the date, time or route specified. Clearly, s 11 may prove of some deterrence value to organisers; such persons obviously bear a heavy responsibility in ensuring that any deviation does not occur. If it does occur, an organiser may have a defence under s 11(8) or (9) that he or she either had no reason to suspect that it had occurred or that it arose due to circumstances outside his or her control. Obviously, it may be difficult for an organiser to discharge this burden. Section 11 therefore criminalises what may be trivial administrative errors. Clearly, police officers may use a discretion in initiating prosecutions under the section, but it can be argued that this leaves the power open to abuse and means that s 11 is available to be more rigidly enforced against marchers espousing unpopular causes.[1]

Sections 12 and 13 grew out of the power under s 3 of the Public Order Act 1936, allowing the Chief Officer of Police to impose conditions on a procession or apply for a banning order if he apprehended serious public disorder. The power to impose conditions on public assemblies under s 14 is an entirely new power. The power to impose conditions on processions under s 12 is much wider than the old power, as it may be exercised in a much wider range of situations. It is identical to the power under s 14 and can be exercised in one of four situations: the senior police officer in question must reasonably believe that serious public disorder, serious damage to property or serious disruption to the life of the community may be caused by the procession. The fourth 'trigger' condition, arising under ss 12 and 14(1)(b), consists of an evaluation of the purpose of the assembly, rather than an apprehension that a particular state of affairs may arise. The senior police officer must reasonably believe that the purpose of the assembly is 'the intimidation of others with a view to compelling them not to do an act they have a right to do or to do an act they have a right not to do'.

'Serious disruption to the life of the community' is a very wide phrase and clearly offers the police wide scope for interpretation. It might be interpreted widely if police officers wished to cut down the cost of the policing requirement for an assembly, because the conditions then imposed, such as requiring a limit on the numbers participating might lead to a reduction in the number of officers who had to be present. The fourth 'trigger' requires a police officer to make a political judgment as to the purpose of the group in question. It must be determined whether the purpose is coercive or merely persuasive. Asking police officers to make such a judgment clearly lays them open to claims of partiality in instances where they are perceived as out of sympathy with the aims of the group in question.

The conditions that can be imposed if one of the above 'triggers' is thought to be present are very wide in the case of processions: any condition may be imposed which appears necessary to the senior police officer in order to prevent the mischief envisaged occurring. Obviously, they are not completely unlimited; if the condition imposed bears no relationship to the mischief it was intended to avert, it may be open to challenge. The conditions which may be imposed under s 14 are much more limited in scope, presumably because it was thought that marches presented more of a threat to public order than meetings. However, the scope for challenging the conditions is very limited: there is no method of appealing from them; it is only possible to have them reviewed for procedural errors or unreasonableness in the High Court. It was made clear in *Secretary of State for the Home Department ex p Northumbria Police Authority* (1987) that such a challenge would succeed only where a senior officer had evinced a belief in the existence of a 'trigger' which no reasonable officer could entertain: no presumption in favour of freedom of assembly would be imported.

Under s 13, a ban must be imposed on a march if it is thought that it may result in serious public disorder. This reproduces the old power under s 3 of the Public Order Act 1936. Assuming that a power was needed to ban marches expected to be violent, this power was nevertheless open to criticism, in that once a banning order had been imposed, it prevented all marches in the area it covered for its duration. Thus, a projected march likely to be of an entirely peaceful character would be caught by a ban aimed at a violent march. The campaign for nuclear disarmament attempted to challenge such a ban after it had had to cancel a number of its marches (*Kent v Metropolitan Police Commissioner* (1981)), but failed, due to the finding that an order quashing the ban could be made only if there were no reasons for imposing it at all. It is arguable that the 1986 Act should have limited the banning power to the particular marches giving rise to fear of serious public disorder, but this possibility was rejected by the Government on the ground that it could be subverted by organisers of marches who might attempt to march under another name. It would therefore, it was thought, have placed too great a burden on the police, who would have had to determine whether or not this had occurred. However, in making this decision, it is arguable that too great a weight was given to the possible administrative burden placed on the police and too little to the need to uphold freedom of assembly.

The banning power is greatly extended by the provisions of s 14A of the 1986 Act (inserted into it by s 70 of the CJPOA 1994). Section 14A allows for the banning of assemblies, whereas s 13 applies only to marches, and it is dependent on a less stringent test than 'serious public disorder'; it provides in summary that a chief officer of police may apply for a banning order if he reasonably believes that an assembly is likely to be trespassory and may result in 'serious disruption to the life of the Community'. If the local council makes the order, it will apply to all trespassory assemblies for a period of four days and within a radius of five miles from a specified centre. This provision is clearly aimed at certain groups of demonstrators such as hunt saboteurs or 'tree people' and others protesting against road building. It represents a significant new restriction on freedom of assembly which, it is suggested, is insufficiently tempered by the limiting provisions. In the leading case on the power, however,

*DPP v Jones* (1999), the House of Lords found in favour of the demonstrators. The ban had been imposed around Stonehenge to prevent midsummer assemblies at the monument. The defendants, who were protesting at the lack of access, had gathered on the grass verge beside a road on the perimeter of Stonehenge. There were about 20 people present, and some of them, having refused to move, were arrested and charged. Two questions arose for consideration. First, whether the prosecution had to prove that all 20 people were trespassing in order to obtain a conviction of any one of them. The answer to this was no – providing an assembly as a whole falls within the scope of a ban, anyone participating will commit an offence. The second question was whether on the facts the assembly was 'trespassory'. This depended on whether it exceeded the rights of those concerned to use the highway. The Divisional Court had held that since what was concerned was a static demonstration, this had nothing to do with the right to pass along the highway, and was therefore trespassory. The majority of the House of Lords disagreed, holding that provided the rights of other citizens to use the highway were not unduly restricted, a demonstration of this kind did not constitute a trespass. The decision of the Crown Court to allow the demonstrators appeal against conviction was upheld. In arriving at their conclusion, two members of the House made reference to Art 11. It is to be expected that post-HRA 1998, if similar issues arise under these provisions, greater reliance will be placed on Art 11. In addition, since a demonstration is a form of expression (as confirmed by *Steel v UK* (1999)), defence arguments could also be based on Art 10.

So far, only prior restraints on assemblies have been considered; these are particularly pernicious, as they attract less publicity than restraints imposed once an assembly is in being and may, in the case of a ban, mean that the whole purpose of the march – to gain support for a cause – is lost. Where conditions are imposed on a march limiting the number of participants and re-routing it, its impact may be almost entirely lost, but that fact will not be apparent to the public. This is not, of course, to argue that the subsequent restraints available do not represent a restriction on freedom of assembly. It is merely to note that use of such restraints may at least receive publicity.

When considering the subsequent restraints imposed by the Public Order Act 1986, it is important to bear in mind that it merely operates in the context of a very wide range of public order powers arising under a variety of statutes and under various common law powers. These restraints are not aimed specifically at assemblies, but generally at keeping the peace. However, freedom of assembly is affected by them and, as it has no special constitutional protection, is in a very vulnerable position due to their number and width. These restraints derive from the common law power to arrest in order to prevent a breach of the peace, the offence of public nuisance, liability for obstruction of a police officer under s 51(3) of the Police Act 1964, for obstructing the highway under s 137 of the Highways Act 1980 and for the offence of aggravated trespass under s 68 of the CJPOA 1994. There is clearly some overlap between these forms of liability and those arising under ss 12 and 14 of the Public Order Act. Everything that has already been said as to ss 12 and 14 also applies *during* the assembly: the senior police officer present, who may, of course, be a constable, can impose the conditions mentioned if, after the assembly is in being, it is apparent that one of the 'trigger' conditions is in being or is about to come into being. These powers can be used as an alternative or in addition to the other available powers.

There is also some overlap between the lower level public order offences arising under ss 4, 4A and 5 of the Public Order Act and the other forms of liability mentioned. Section 5 is the lowest level offence contained in the Act and the most contentious. It creates liability in respect of threatening, abusive or insulting words or behaviour, or disorderly behaviour which take place in the hearing of someone likely to be caused distress, alarm or harassment; there is no need to aim the words or behaviour at a specific individual, nor need anyone actually experience the feelings mentioned. Thus, taken at its lowest level, s 5 criminalises disorderly behaviour, which may cause a person to experience harassment. Section 5 was included as a measure aimed at anti-social behaviour generally, but its breadth and vagueness have given rise to the criticism that the police have been handed too broad a power. Section 5 requires *mens rea* in respect of the conduct in question, but not in respect of the feelings likely to be experienced by another (s 6(4)). Had it required an intention to create a likelihood that others would experience harassment, alarm or distress due to the behaviour in question, it might have been less likely to catch persons participating in forceful demonstrations; such persons might have been able to argue that behaviour which could be termed disorderly and which might be capable of causing harassment to others was intended only to make a point; and that it had not been realised that harassment might be caused. As things stand, it would be open to the defence in such circumstances to show that such behaviour was 'reasonable' (s 5(3)(c)), but the Act gives no guidance as to the meaning of the term. Recent cases have further extended s 5's scope. In *Vigon v DPP* (1997), D was convicted under s 5 for installing a video camera to take films of women trying on swimsuits at his clothing stall. It was held that turning on the camera was 'insulting behaviour' within s 5. In *DPP v Orum* (1988), D repeatedly used foul language in the street during an argument and threatened to hit police who tried to arrest him. Since the only other persons present were police officers, the magistrates dismissed the charge,s as no one was 'likely to be caused harassment, alarm or distress'. But, on appeal, the court found that the police officers were 'persons' for the purposes of s 5.

It may be concluded that while the Act confers on the police greater powers to keep the peace, it affords, by implication, virtually no recognition to freedom of assembly. In so far as such a freedom exists, it largely relies for its protection on police discretion in using these extensive powers. The Act fails to differentiate between groups of hooligans and legitimate demonstrations. Finding the right balance in this area will in future depend on the extent to which the courts feel able to use the HRA 1998 and Arts 10 and 11 of the Convention to interpret the law so as to recognise a right to demonstrate, while still protecting the public from unruly and disruptive behaviour.

## Note

1 Argument as to the effect of s 11 could be pursued further. Section 11 makes a gesture towards freedom of assembly in its attempt to exempt spontaneous demonstrations from its provisions. The notice requirement does not apply under

s 11(1) if it was not reasonably practicable to give any advance notice. This provision is defective, due to the use of the word 'any'. This word would suggest that a phone call made five minutes before a march sets off would fulfil the requirements, thereby exempting very few marches. However, it can be argued that the term 'reasonably practicable' should not be interpreted so strictly as to exclude spontaneous processions where a few minutes was available to give notice, as that was not the intention behind including the provision. If such processions were not exempted, it might be argued that s 11 breaches the guarantee of freedom of assembly under Art 11 of the Convention. The effect of s 3 of the HRA 1998 is that, where statutes are ambiguous, they should be interpreted so as to conform with the UK's Convention obligations, s 11 should be interpreted in so far as it is ambiguous in accordance with Art 11.

# Question 17

Abel and Clare are members of the City youth club. They and 40 other teenagers attend the youth club on Friday evening and are told that it has to close down that night. All the teenagers immediately walk out of the club in protest and assemble on the pavement outside it. While they are angrily discussing the closure of the club, Edwin and Fred, two police officers in uniform, approach the group. Clare begins to address the group, telling them that they must remain peaceful in order to air their grievances more effectively. Edwin tells her that she must disperse part of the group if she wants to hold a meeting. She asks some of the teenagers to leave, but takes no action when they make no attempt to do so. The meeting continues and becomes more heated. Abel then suggests that they should march through the town.

The group sets off, Clare leading. She asks Abel to help her to keep the group in order. Abel moves to the back of the group in order to do so. Traffic is held up for 10 minutes as the group enters the town. Edwin again asks Clare to disperse half the group. She approaches Abel and asks him to help her to get some of them to leave. He refuses, telling her that it is her problem, for she is the leader. Clare asks two of the teenagers to leave, but takes no further action when they fail to comply with her request. Edwin then says that she will have to give him the names and addresses of the members of the group. She refuses and Edwin then informs Clare that he is arresting her for failing to comply with his orders. Clare calls on Abel to continue the march and he moves towards the front of the group.

Consider the criminal liability (if any) incurred by Abel and Clare.

### Answer plan

This is a fairly typical problem question dealing with issues which arise mainly, but not entirely under the Public Order Act 1986 in respect of marches and assemblies. It should be noted that the answer is confined to the question of possible criminal liability incurred by Clare and Abel; possible tortious liability incurred by Clare, Abel or the police officers is therefore irrelevant, as is the possibility that Clare or Abel could seek to challenge the police decisions by way of judicial review. The essential matters to be discussed are:

- notice requirements under s 11 of the Public Order Act 1986;
- 'triggers' under ss 12 and 14 of the Act;
- conditions which can be imposed under ss 12 and 14 of the Act on processions and assemblies;
- liability which may arise under ss 12 and 14;
- public nuisance;
- obstruction of the highway under s 137 of the Highways Act 1980.

## Answer

Liability in this case arises mainly, but not exclusively under the Public Order Act 1986 (hereinafter 'the Act'). The liability of both possible defendants will be considered in turn, beginning with Clare.

Under s 11 of the Act, advance notice of a procession must be given if it falls within one of three categories. This march falls within s 11(1)(a), as it is intended to demonstrate opposition to the action of the local authority in closing the youth club. As no notice of the march was given, Clare may have committed an offence under s 11(7)(a) of the Act, as she is the organiser of the march. However, the notice requirement does not apply under s 11(1) if it was not reasonably practicable to give any advance notice. This provision was intended to exempt spontaneous demonstrations such as this one from the notice requirements, but is defective, due to the use of the word 'any'. This word would suggest that a phone call made five minutes before the march sets off would fulfil the requirements, thereby exempting very few marches. Although the march sets off suddenly, it is possible that Clare had time to make such a phone call; on a strict interpretation of s 11, she is therefore in breach of the notice requirements, as it was reasonably practicable for her to fulfil them. However, it can be argued that notice was informally and impliedly given to the police officers already on the scene, or, alternatively, that the term 'reasonably practicable' should not be interpreted so strictly as to exclude spontaneous processions where a few minutes was available to give notice, because to do so would defeat the intention behind including the provision. Thus, on either argument, liability will not arise under s 11.

Clare may be liable under s 14(4) of the Act, since she was the organiser of a public assembly, but failed to comply with the condition imposed by the most senior police officer present at the scene (Edwin) to disperse part of the group. It should be noted that as the group was in a public place and comprised more than 20 persons, it constituted a public assembly under s 16 of the Act. Edwin can impose conditions on the assembly only if one of four 'triggers' under s 14(1) is present. The third of these, and arguably the easiest to satisfy, provides that the police officer in question must reasonably believe that 'serious disruption to the life of the community' may be caused by the assembly. In the case of *Reid* (1987), it was determined that the 'triggers' should be strictly interpreted: the words used should not be diluted. In the instant case, a group of 42 teenagers were gathered on the street in the evening; even if it could be argued that such a circumstance might cause some disruption in the community (in terms of noise or blockage of the pavement), it is less clear that a reasonable person would expect the disruption to be serious. On this argument,

Edwin had no power to impose conditions on the assembly; no liability therefore arises under s 14(4). The question whether the failure to comply with the condition imposed arose due to circumstances beyond Clare's control need not, therefore, be addressed.

Will Clare be liable under s 12(4) of the Act, as she was the organiser of a public procession, but failed to comply with the conditions imposed by Edwin to provide the names and addresses of the group or to disperse part of it? Edwin can impose conditions on the procession only if one of the four 'triggers' under s 12(1) is present. The triggers are identical to those under s 14(1). The third of these may possibly arise. The group of teenagers were marching through the town; in such circumstances, it may be more readily argued that serious disruption to the life of the community may reasonably be apprehended. Such disruption could be argued for either, on the basis that passers by may be jostled by the group, especially if it has grown more excitable, or on the basis that traffic may be seriously disrupted. The fact that traffic has already been held up for 10 minutes may support a reasonable belief that such disruption may occur. Serious obstruction of the traffic might arguably amount to some disruption of the life of the community. Both possibilities taken together could found a reasonable apprehension that the life of the community will be seriously disrupted. Following this argument, Edwin is entitled to impose conditions on the march.

The conditions imposed must relate to the disruption apprehended; this may be said of the requirement to disperse half the group, but not of the order that Clare should disclose the names and addresses of the group. Thus, liability may arise only in respect of the failure to comply with the former condition. Clare made some attempt to comply with it, but did not succeed; she will therefore be liable under s 12(4), unless she can show that the failure arose due to circumstances outside her control. Although the powers of an organiser to disperse members of a march are limited, it may be argued that, in approaching only two members of the group, Clare made, in any event, a token effort only; it is therefore argued that she has committed an offence under s 12(4).

Clare may also fall within the provision under s 12(6) as she called on Abel to lead the march, thereby arguably inciting him to commit the offence under s 12(5) of taking part in a procession and knowingly failing to comply with a condition imposed. According to the Court of Appeal in *Hendrickson v Tichner* (1977), incitement requires an element of persuasion or encouragement; moreover, following *Krause* (1902), the solicitation must actually come to the notice of the person intended to act on it. Both conditions appear to be fulfilled: Clare asks Abel to continue the march as opposed to merely expressing the hope that he will do so; it is clear from his actions that Abel hears her request. It will be argued below that, at this point, Abel was aware of the failure to comply with the condition.

Clare may further have incurred liability under s 137 of the Highways Act 1980, which provides that a person will be guilty of an offence if he 'without lawful authority or excuse in any way wilfully obstructs the free passage of the highway'. In *Nagy v Weston* (1965), it was held that a reasonable user of the highway will constitute a lawful excuse, and that in order to determine its reasonableness or otherwise, the length of the obstruction must be considered, its purpose, the place where it occurs and whether an actual or potential obstruction took place. There is no evidence to suggest that the group assembled outside the youth club caused obstruction; however, the march did cause a brief obstruction of the highway. In *Arrowsmith v Jenkins* (1963), it was held that a minor obstruction of traffic can lead to liability under the Highways Act. However, the question of the purpose of the obstruction, mentioned in *Nagy*, was given greater prominence in *Hirst and Agu v Chief Constable of West Yorkshire* (1986): it was said that courts should have regard to the freedom to demonstrate. This approach was confirmed by *DPP v Jones* (1999), where the House of Lords recognised that a demonstration should not be treated as an improper use of the highway unless it causes undue disruption to other users. Such an approach is, of course, given added weight by the need for the courts to give appropriate weight, by virtue of the HRA 1998, to the rights of freedom of expression and assembly in Arts 10 and 11 of the Convention. On this basis, the brevity of the obstruction and its purpose as part of a legitimate protest suggest that the march amounted to a reasonable user of the highway. The stronger argument seems to be that liability under the Highways Act for inciting the group to obstruct the highway will not be established.[1]

Clare may also have incited the group to commit a public nuisance by blocking the highway;[2] however, according to *Clarke* (1964), the disruption caused must amount to an unreasonable use of the highway in order to found liability for public nuisance. Thus, once obstruction has been shown the question of reasonableness arises. In this instance, there has been some obstruction of the highway for 10 minutes. However, as has already been pointed out, it is arguable that to cause such a minor disruption for a legitimate purpose does not constitute an unreasonable user of the highway. It is unlikely that a user of the highway could be reasonable under the Highways Act, but nevertheless able to amount to a public nuisance. This seemed to be accepted in *Gillingham Borough Council v Medway Dock Co* (1992). On this argument, liability for public nuisance will not arise.

Abel's possible criminal liability will now be considered. It is not argued that Abel will attract liability as an organiser of the assembly under s 14(4) of the Act as, at the point when the group constituted an assembly, he was merely a member of it. Further, as such a member, he will not attract liability under s 14(5), even if he was aware of the condition imposed at that point by Edwin, on the basis of the argument already put forward under s 14(4) in respect of Clare.

It is not argued that Abel will attract liability under s 12(4) on the basis that it was his suggestion which set the march in motion. It is submitted that such action is not sufficient to warrant designating Abel an organiser. However, Abel may attract such liability as an organiser on the ground that Clare has, in effect, asked him to act as a steward of the march. The Act does not define the term 'organiser' and there is no post-Act case law on the issue; therefore the issue as to the meaning of the term cannot be settled with certainty. However, it is submitted that, on the dictionary definition of the term, Abel is an organiser. This contention is supported by the ruling from *Flockhart v Robinson* (1950) that a person who indicated the route to be followed should be designated an organiser, as well as the person who planned the route. Thus, it appears likely that the term includes stewards. Therefore, the argument for liability on Clare's part under s 12(4) will also apply to Abel, unless he was unaware of the condition imposed. The burden of proof is on the prosecution to prove that he was so aware and, as it appears that Abel was at the back of the group when the condition was imposed, it may be difficult to discharge that burden.[3]

If, in the alternative, it could be argued that Abel's role is too uncertain to allow him to fall within the term 'organiser', he could nevertheless be liable under s 12(5) as a member of the march. However, against that, it could be argued that although the requisite *mens rea* under s 12(5) may have been established in respect of Abel, part of the *actus reus* is missing, in that one individual who merely remains with the march does not suggest non-compliance with an order to disperse half the march.

On the assumption that Abel is a co-organiser, and bearing in mind that it was his suggestion which set the march in motion, the above arguments as to Clare's liability arising under s 137 of the Highways Act 1980 or for public nuisance will be relevant but, as in her case, will fail to establish liability.

Thus, in conclusion, Clare is most likely to attract liability under s 12(4) and (6) of the Act. Abel may attract liability under s 12(4) of the Act. (This last point depends on which of the two alternative arguments are put forward: see Note 3.)

## Notes

1   It could be argued further that Clare's conduct could not be described as 'wilful', in the sense that, at the point when obstruction is caused, Edwin appears to be giving some sanction to the march and Clare may be relying on his official connivance.

2   It could be noted at this point that Clare did not suggest that the group should march through the town and that, although she assumes the position of leader, this is not sufficient to amount to incitement. The question could be addressed as to whether her implied encouragement to the group could amount to incitement.

3   An alternative argument could be pursued at this point. Following *Ross v Moss* (1965), 'knowledge' appears to include wilful blindness. Abel is presumably aware that Clare has been arrested and is aware that she wished to disperse part of the group. It could be argued that he deliberately shut his eyes to what was occurring. On this basis, it appears that Abel may incur liability under s 12(4); as he made no attempt to disperse

part of the group, he seems to have no grounds for arguing that failure to comply with the condition arose from circumstances outside his control.

# Question 18

The Asian community in Northton become increasingly concerned about Northton City Council employment practices. A number of council workers have recently been made redundant; a disproportionate number of them are Asians. A group of 25 Asians decide to hold a demonstration outside the Civic Centre on the courtyard in front of it. On the day appointed, they assemble, appoint Ali as their leader and shout at workers going in to the Centre, telling them not to go in, but to join the demonstration. When the workers do not respond, the Asians, including Ali, become angrier; they wave their fists threateningly at some of the workers.

Three police officers arrive on the scene; one of them, Belinda, asks Ali to move the group away from the front of the Centre. Ali angrily refuses and Belinda arrests him for refusing to comply with her order. One of the other Asians, Rashid, jumps onto a box and shouts and swears at Belinda to release Ali. He waves his fists threateningly at her.

Discuss the criminal liability, if any, of Ali and Rashid.

## Answer plan

This question is partly concerned with liability which may arise in respect of assemblies under the Public Order Act 1986 and partly with various general public order offences, of which some, but not all arise under the Act. It should be borne in mind that the problem concerns an assembly only, and not a march. Further, the assembly is not taking place on the highway. Therefore, liability particularly associated with marches and with assemblies on the highway will not arise.

Essentially, the following matters should be discussed:

- 'triggers' under s 14 of the Act;
- conditions which may be imposed under s 14;

- liability under ss 5, 4, 4A and 3 of the Act;
- liability under ss 68 and 69 of the Criminal Justice and Public Order Act 1994;
- liability for obstruction of a police officer under the s 51(3) of the Police Act 1964.

# Answer

Liability in this case may arise mainly but not exclusively under the Public Order Act 1986 (hereafter 'the Act').

Ali may attract liability under s 14(4), as he was the organiser of a public assembly, but failed to comply with the condition imposed by the most senior police officer present at the scene (where the officers are of equal rank, this condition will be fulfilled when one of them issues an order) to disperse part of the group. It should be noted that as the group was in a public place and comprised more than 20 persons, it constituted a public assembly under s 16 of the Act. Belinda can impose conditions on the assembly only if one of four 'triggers' under s 14(1) is present. Under s 14(1)(a), the police officer in question must reasonably believe that serious public disorder, serious damage to property or serious disruption to the life of the community may be caused by the assembly. The fourth 'trigger', arising under s 14(1)(b), consists of an evaluation of the purpose of the assembly rather than an apprehension that a particular state of affairs may arise. The senior police officer present must reasonably believe that the purpose of the assembly is 'the intimidation of others with a view to compelling them not to do an act they have a right to do or to do an act they have a right not to do'.

Possibly the third 'trigger' could apply to this situation, but that point need not be considered, because the fourth 'trigger' seems to be most clearly indicated: the Asians are trying to prevent persons entering the Civic Centre and are therefore trying to prevent persons doing something they have a right to do (presumably in the sense that there is a right to pass along the highway to a place of work); the question is whether their actions have gone beyond what might be acceptable as part of a legitimate demonstration and could suggest an intention to intimidate. In the case of *Reid* (1987), it was determined that the triggers should be strictly interpreted: the words used should not diluted. In *Reid*, the defendants shouted, raised their arms and waved their fingers; it was determined that such behaviour might cause discomfort, but not intimidation and that the two concepts could not be equated. In *News Group Newspapers Ltd v SOGAT* (1982), it was held that mere abuse and shouting did not amount to a threat of violence for the purposes of intimidation under s 7 of the Conspiracy and Protection of Property Act 1875. In the instant case, it could be argued that the Asians' behaviour in merely shouting at the Civic Centre workers could not amount to intimidation, but that in making threatening gestures with their fists, it crossed the boundary between discomfort and intimidation. On that basis, it appears that Belinda had the power to impose conditions on the assembly.

Ali made no effort to comply with the condition imposed. The question of whether the failure to comply with it arose due to circumstances beyond his control need not therefore be addressed. Ali may therefore incur liability under s 14(4). Ali may also incur liability under s 68 of the Criminal Justice and Public Order Act 1994. The section requires first that the defendant has trespassed. This seems to be satisfied, since Ali has probably exceeded the terms of an implied licence to be on the courtyard, and the courtyard is not excluded from s 68, since it is not part of the highway. Secondly, it must be shown that the defendant intended to disrupt or obstruct a lawful activity or intimidated persons so as to deter them from that activity. This last requirement may also be satisfied by Ali's behaviour in shouting at the workers entering the Civic Centre. It may perhaps be inferred that Ali did intend to intimidate the workers since he makes threatening gestures towards them. Ali may also commit the offence under s 69 of failing to leave land after a direction to do so is given founded on a reasonable belief that the offence under s 68 is being committed. Belinda tells Ali to leave the land and he refuses to do so.

Following the above argument, Rashid may be liable under s 14(5) of the 1986 Act for taking part in a public assembly and knowingly failing to comply with the condition imposed. However, this point cannot be settled, as it is unclear from the facts whether or not Rashid was aware of the condition imposed or, following *Vane v Yiannopoullos* (1965), was wilfully blind as to its existence. He may also incur liability under s 68 of the 1994 Act on the same argument as that which applied to Ali.

However, Rashid may incur liability under s 5(1) of the 1986 Act in respect of his remonstration with Belinda. His behaviour must amount to 'threatening, abusive or insulting words or behaviour or disorderly behaviour' which take place in the hearing or sight of a person likely to be caused harassment, alarm or distress thereby. These three terms must be given their ordinary meaning following *Brutus v Cozens* (1973). The word 'likely' imports an objective test into the section: it is necessary to show that a person was present at the scene, but not that he or she actually experienced the feelings in question. It was determined in *DPP v Orum* (1988) that a police officer may be the person mentioned in s 5, but, in such instances, Glidewell LJ thought it might be held that a police officer is less likely to be caused harassment, alarm or distress than an ordinary person. Rashid shouts, swears and gestures aggressively; this behaviour may clearly be termed disorderly or even threatening and it is arguable, given the width of the concept of harassment, that it would be likely to cause feelings of harassment, although probably not of alarm, to Belinda. Had Rashid confined himself to abuse, it could be argued that his behaviour would be likely merely to irritate Belinda. However, his use of threatening gestures might be likely to cause the stronger emotion connoted by the concept of harassment. It appears then that Rashid may incur liability under s 5, subject to argument below as to the *mens rea* requirement under s 6(4). On the same argument, he may incur liability under s 4A assuming that Rashid *intended* to cause harassment, etc, and did cause it.

Rashid's behaviour may also support an argument that he has committed an offence under s 4 of the Act which is couched in the same terms as s 5, except for the omission of 'disorderly behaviour' and with the added need to show that Belinda was likely to apprehend the use of immediate violence by Rashid or another, or that he intended to arouse such an apprehension. Both these possibilities may be present. The behaviour in question must be specifically directed towards another person. Following *Ambrose* (1973), rude or offensive words or behaviour may not necessarily be insulting while mere swearing may not fall within the meaning of 'abusive'. However, Rashid's behaviour may fall within the meaning of the term 'threatening', since he waves his fists threateningly at Belinda. Possibly, in the circumstances – two other police officers were present and Rashid does not directly approach her – Belinda might be unlikely to apprehend immediate violence. However, in jumping onto a box, presumably in order to draw attention to himself, it is possible that Rashid may intend that his words should provoke the rest of the group into using violence against Belinda. Following the ruling in *Horseferry Road Metropolitan Stipendiary Magistrate ex p Siadatan* (1991), 'violence' in this context must mean immediate and unlawful violence. This was confirmed in *Winn v DPP* (1992). Possibly, this strict test is not fulfilled. Rashid, however, does appear to satisfy the *mens rea* requirement under s 6(3): it appears probable that he is aware or intends that his words or behaviour are threatening, although probably not abusive or insulting. Thus, liability may not be established under s 4, but as s 6(4), which determines the *mens rea* required under s 5, is expressed in substantially the same terms as s 6(3), this argument will establish liability under s 5.

It could also be argued that in shouting and waving his fists at the Civic Centre workers, Ali may incur liability under s 5. On the face of it, such behaviour can readily be termed disorderly and may have been likely to cause one of the workers harassment, whether or not any worker actually experienced harassment. However, a defence under s 5(3)(c) is available to Ali if he can prove that his behaviour was reasonable. Possibly, this defence could be invoked on the basis that in the context of the particular demonstration which was aimed at a boycott of the Civic Centre, such behaviour was reasonable.[1] On this argument, Ali will not incur liability under s 5.

Rashid may have obstructed Belinda in the execution of her duty; if so, this will amount to an offence under s 89(1) of the Police Act 1996. Following *Rice v Connolly* (1966), three tests must be satisfied if liability for this offence is to be made out. First, it must be shown that the constable was in the execution of his or her duty. In this instance, Belinda was in the process of effecting a lawful arrest under s 14(7) and so was clearly within the execution of her duty. Secondly, it must be shown that Rashid did an act which made it more difficult for Belinda to carry out her duty. Rashid's behaviour may have amounted to an irritant, but he did not physically attempt to prevent the arrest as the defendant in *Hills v Ellis* (1983) did. This is not to imply that a physical act must occur, but that the police must actually be impeded in some way. In *Lewis v Cox* (1985), a persistent inquiry as to where an arrested friend was being taken was held to amount to obstruction. The defendant opened the door of the police van, clearly preventing it from driving off, in order to make the inquiry after being told to desist. Thus, his actions can be distinguished from Rashid's, in that they did impede the police officers.

However, a finding of obstruction on Rashid's part receives some support from *Ricketts v Cox* (1981): a refusal to answer questions accompanied by abuse was held to amount to obstruction. As, according to *Rice v Connolly*, a refusal to answer questions does not amount to obstruction, the abuse alone must have constituted the obstruction. On that basis, Rashid appears to have obstructed Belinda. Assuming for the moment that this argument is sound, it must finally be shown, following *Lewis v Cox*, that Rashid behaved wilfully, in the sense that he acted deliberately with the knowledge and intention that he would obstruct her. It is clear that he acted deliberately in abusing her and he clearly did intend to prevent the arrest. It appears, therefore, that this test is fulfilled. Nevertheless, the weight of the authorities suggests that the second test is not fulfilled and therefore it appears that, apart from the doubtful authority of *Ricketts and Cox*, Rashid will not be liable for obstruction of a police officer.

In conclusion therefore it appears that Ali will incur liability under s 14 of the 1986 Act and under ss 68 and 69 of the 1994 Act; Rashid will be likely to incur liability under ss 4 and 5 of the 1986 Act and under s 68 of the 1994 Act.[2]

## Notes

1  An argument for giving such a wide interpretation to the term 'reasonable' can be supported on the basis that to criminalise such behaviour could arguably amount to a very far reaching curb on the freedom to protest which might be in breach of Art 11 of the European Convention and so challengeable under the HRA 1998.

2  It might be worth considering the argument that all the Asians, including, of course, Ali and Rashid, also incur liability in

respect of the offence of affray under s 3 of the Act. In order to establish an affray, it must first be shown that the defendant used or threatened unlawful violence towards another and, secondly, that his conduct was such as would cause a person of reasonable firmness present at the scene to fear for his personal safety. As the Asians use threatening gestures, it may be argued that the first limb of s 3(1) is fulfilled, but a strong argument can be advanced that the second is not; due to the fact that the gestures are part of a demonstration, it is probable that a person of reasonable firmness would not fear unlawful violence, even though such a person might feel somewhat distressed. In *Taylor v DPP* (1973), Lord Hailsham, speaking of the common law offence, said 'the degree of violence ... must be such as to be calculated to terrify a person of reasonably firm character'. The Act of course refers to 'fear' as opposed to terror, but this ruling suggests that 'fear' should be interpreted restrictively. On this argument, no liability will arise in respect of s 3.

# Question 19

How far does UK law afford recognition to freedom of association?

## Answer plan

A fairly common and quite straightforward essay question. It requires a sound knowledge of the key provisions in the area and of the influence of Art 11 the European Convention on Human Rights (the Convention).

Essentially, the following matters should be considered:

- lack of legal recognition of freedom of association;
- s 2 of the Public Order Act 1936;
- the Prevention of Terrorism (Temporary Provisions) Act 1989 – proscribed groups – the Terrorism Act 2000;
- Art 11 of the Convention;
- *Council of Civil Service Unions v Minister for the Civil Service* (1984).

# Answer

In general, there are no restrictions under UK law on the freedom to join or form groups which do not constitute conspiracies, although, equally, there is little likelihood of legal redress if a person is excluded from a group or prevented from joining one. However, in two areas, freedom of association is subject to constraints.

A number of specific statutory provisions place limits on the freedom to join or support groups associated with the use of violence for political ends. The most general restriction arises under s 2 of the Public Order Act 1936, which prohibits the formation of military or quasi-military organisations. Under s 2(1)(b), a quasi-military organisation is defined as 'one organised and trained or organised and equipped either for the purpose of enabling them to be employed for the use or display of physical force in promoting any political object' or in such a manner that it could be reasonably apprehended that such was the case. The use of the words 'reasonably apprehended' extends the ambit of this provision and means that it has the potential to catch quite a wide range of groups, assuming that they have, or appear to have, a political objective. However, not many prosecutions have been brought under this provision. The last successful one was in *Jordan and Tyndall* (1963). The defendants were both members of a fascist group called Spearhead. They engaged in various activities which included practising foot drill and storing sodium chloride, with the probable aim of using it to make bombs. It was held that their activities satisfied the test under s 2(1)(b).

Alternatively, under s 2(1)(a), a group organised, trained or equipped in order to allow it to usurp the function of the army or police would fall within this prohibition against quasi-military groups, thus possibly catching vigilante groups, such as the Guardian Angels (a group organised with the object of preventing crime on underground railways).

Certain other provisions which place limits on freedom of association are aimed at a number of specified groups. The latest version of the anti-terrorism legislation, the Terrorism Act 2000, makes it an offence under s 11 to belong to a proscribed organisation. The organisations currently proscribed are listed in Sched 2 to the Act. The Schedule lists various paramilitary organisations, including the IRA, the INLA, the UVF and the UFF. Despite the ceasefire in Northern Ireland, there do not seem to be any current moves to lift proscription.

Further, an organisation need not engage in terrorism itself; it is enough if it promotes or encourages it. The 2000 Act introduces for the first time a right of appeal against the Secretary of State's refusal to 'deproscribe' an organisation. Under s 5 of the Act, appeals will go to a specially constituted Proscribed Organisations Appeal Commission, and from thence on a point of law to the Court of Appeal. There will, therefore, now be some judicial control over this area, in which the courts have in the past shown reluctance to become involved. In *McEldowney v Forde* (1971), for example, an order was made under Statutory Instrument banning republican clubs or any like organisation, thus potentially outlawing all nationalist political parties. Nevertheless, the House of Lords preferred not to intervene, Lord Diplock stating that he would do so only if proscription were extended to bodies obviously distanced from republican views.

Proscription has been seen as providing a means of channelling expressions of outrage at IRA activities, thereby tending to prevent illegitimate expressions of public anger. It may discourage supporters of terrorist organisations and may signal political strength. On the other hand, it has been argued that these benefits are minimal and that it is 'a cosmetic part of the PTA' which is, in fact, 'counter productive, as it impedes criminal investigation and political discussion'. Lord Jellicoe's review of the Operation of the PTA doubted the value of proscription, considering that its value might be outweighed by its detrimental effects in terms of constraining the free expression of views about Northern Ireland outweigh its value. In response, a Home Office Circular was issued, giving guidance to the police as to the proper use of ss 1 and 2, bearing in mind the possible effect on freedom of expression.

Under s 13 of the 2000 Act, it is an offence to wear any item which arouses a reasonable apprehension that a person is a member or supporter of a proscribed organisation. This provision is obviously aimed at preventing such organisations arousing public support. A previous version of this offence was invoked in *DPP v Whelan* (1975) against leaders of a provisional Sinn Fein protest march against internment in Northern Ireland, all of whom wore black berets, while some wore dark glasses, dark clothing and carried Irish flags. It was found that, first, something must be 'worn' as apparel and, secondly, that it must be a uniform. Something might amount to a uniform if it was worn by a number of persons in order to signify their association with each other or it was commonly used by a certain organisation. By this means, the third requirement that the uniform shall signal the wearer's association with a particular political organisation can also be satisfied. Alternatively, it may be satisfied by consideration of the occasion on which the uniform was worn without the need to refer to the past history of the organisation. The justification for retention of these provisions is doubtful as they clearly overlap with those under the s 1 of the Public Order Act 1936 and, moreover, they appear to have been rendered unnecessary by the ceasefire.

Apart from groups associated with violence, restrictions on freedom of association have been at issue in relation to trade union membership. Three issues arise in this context: freedom not to join a trade union; freedom to choose between unions; and the limits of the basic freedom to belong to a union. The first was considered by the ECHR in *Young, James and Webster v UK* (1981). In 1975, British Rail entered a closed shop agreement, which made membership of a certain trade union a condition of employment. The three applicants, who were already employed by British Rail, disagreed with the political activities of trade unions; they therefore refused to join the union and were dismissed. They claimed that their dismissal on this ground constituted an infringement of Art 11 of the European Convention.

The European Court found that the agreement between British Rail and the unions was lawful under the Trade Union and Labour Relations Act 1974, which allowed for dismissal for refusing to join a trade union, unless the refusal was on grounds of religious belief. In determining whether that provision infringed Art 11, the court considered the 'negative aspect' of freedom of association, in other words, the right not to join a group. It found that the negative aspect was not on the same footing as the positive aspects, but that when an individual's freedom of choice in association was so abridged – where there was only one ground on which it was possible to refuse to join a union – then an interference with freedom of association had occurred, because it must necessarily include freedom of choice. This did not mean that all closed shop agreements would infringe Art 11; the court was careful to confine its argument to the facts of the specific case. The drafters of the Convention were aware of closed shop agreements operating in certain of the Member States and therefore deliberately omitted a clause protecting an individual's right not to be compelled to join an association. The court did not find that the agreement was necessary under Art 11(2), but decided the case solely under para 1. In response, UK law was changed by means of a provision inserted into s 58 of the Employment Protection (Consolidation) Act 1978, which widened the exception on grounds of religious belief to include making a dismissal unlawful if the person objected on the grounds of a deeply held conviction to being a member of a trade union. The current position is that dismissal for refusal to join a union will be unlawful whatever the grounds on which the refusal is based (s 152 of the Trade Union and Labour Relations (Consolidation) Act 1992).

The need to show a very clear curtailment of choice where the issue concerned the negative aspect of freedom of association was affirmed in a recent decision of the European Court (*Sibson v UK* (1993)), which concerned a choice between unions rather than a choice as to whether to join one at all. The applicant had resigned from his union, the TGWU, due to dissatisfaction with its decision in respect of a complaint he had made; he had then been ostracised by his workmates, who threatened to go on strike unless he rejoined the union or was employed elsewhere. He joined another union and his employer then sought to employ him at a depot some distance away; he refused this offer, resigned and claimed constructive dismissal. When this claim failed in the domestic courts, he applied to the European Commission, alleging a breach of Art 11. It was found in the court that no breach had occurred: his treatment did not infringe the very substance of his freedom of association, he had not been subject to a closed shop agreement and had had the offer of continuing to work for the company without joining the union. Moreover, he had had no objection to union membership as such.

Possibly, this decision should not be characterised as one entirely concerned with the negative aspect of freedom of association because, in order to rejoin the TGWU, the applicant would have had to resign from the second union. Therefore, the claim could have been characterised as concerning the right of an employee to choose which particular union to join, free from pressure from workmates or the employer. The applicant had been faced with the choice of working elsewhere or resigning from one union and joining another. It might appear that such a situation gives rise to a highly significant issue: freedom of choice in trade union membership, and that, therefore, this decision is unfortunate in leaving such freedom unprotected, so long as the employee retains the basic freedom not to join a union. It is instructive to note that the International Covenant on Economic, Social and Cultural Rights, unlike the European Convention, includes 'the right to join the Trade Union *of his choice'*. *Ahmed v UK* (1999) demonstrated that regulating local government officers in order to maintain their political neutrality is a legitimate aim and so was justified, so long as the officers were allowed to *join* a political party.

During the Conservative Government's period of office from 1979 to 1997, no move was made to outlaw union membership *per se*. Such a move would, of course, have constituted a clear breach of Art 11. However, certain measures have been taken which have curtailed choice of unions or had the effect of reducing the size of the group which retains the right to union membership. The issue of whether to regulate union membership has a wide margin of appreciation (*Gustafsson v Sweden* (1996)).

Certain bodies, such as the army under the Army Act 1955, the police under s 4 of the Police Act 1964 and certain public officials, have traditionally been debarred from union membership, but this group was enlarged when civil servants working at Government Communications Headquarters (GCHQ) were de-unionised. Their challenge to the ban on trade unions was considered in *Council of Civil Service Unions v Minister for the Civil Service* (1984) (the *GCHQ* case). The Minister for the Civil Service, the Prime Minister, Margaret Thatcher, gave an instruction by means of an Order in Council to vary the terms of service of the staff at GCHQ, with the effect that staff would no longer be permitted to join national trade unions. Six members of staff and the union involved applied for judicial review of the Minister's instruction, on the ground that she had been under a duty to act fairly by consulting those concerned before issuing it.

The House of Lords found that the decision making process had, in fact, been conducted unfairly. Usual practice had created a legitimate expectation that there would be prior consultation before the terms of service were altered; therefore, there was a legitimate expectation that that practice would be followed, which had not been fulfilled. However, the Prime Minister argued that national security considerations had outweighed the duty to act fairly; had there been prior consultation, this would have led to strikes which would have affected operations at GCHQ, which was the very reason why union membership had been withdrawn. In her assessment, the requirements of national security outweighed those of fairness.

The appellants argued first that this argument was an afterthought and, secondly, that national security had not been and would not be affected, in part because the unions were offering a no-strike agreement. However, the House of Lords held that the Prime Minister was better placed than the courts to determine what was needed by national security, although it was held that there must be some evidence of danger to national security; a mere assertion that such danger existed would be insufficient. As some evidence of such a danger had been put forward, the challenge to the trade union ban failed.

A group from GCHQ then applied to the European Commission, alleging a breach of both Art 11 and of the Art 13 provision that there must be an effective remedy for violation of a Convention right. They were claiming that judicial review did not afford such a remedy.[1] It was accepted that the ban infringed the applicants' freedom of association; the question was whether it could be justified. The Government argued that it fell within Art 11(2), because it was adopted in furtherance of the interests of national security, and that the margin of appreciation allowed to Member States in that respect should be wider than in respect of the other exceptions, because it should be assumed that only the domestic authorities were competent to make a determination as to the needs of national security. Therefore, once it had made a determination that national security would be affected by industrial disruption and that a no-strike agreement would be inadequate, its decision could not be questioned by an outside body. It followed that the blanket ban imposed was not disproportionate to the end in view, which was to protect national security.

The Commission found that the ban amounted to a clear *prima facie* breach of Art 11; the question was whether it could be justified. The second sentence of Art 11 was considered. The word 'lawful' was interpreted as meaning 'in accordance with national law'. The Civil Service Order in Council which had been made fulfilled that requirement. Could the term 'restriction' mean 'destruction'? It was found that the fact that the ban was complete did not mean that it would not be proportionate to the aim pursued. The application was found to be manifestly ill founded as far as Art 11 was concerned. Those who refused to give up their trade union membership were eventually dismissed.

It may be concluded that UK law has allowed freedom of association to be abrogated too readily, although, given the limitations of judicial review, this is unsurprising. As in many other areas of civil liberties, the need is to be able to consider the merits of a particular infringement of a freedom, not merely the procedure followed in infringing it. Freedom of association is particularly vulnerable to infringement, since it is not always afforded the same significance as other more prominent freedoms, such as freedom of expression. The judges may therefore have been less prepared to find that it may be protected by means of fundamental common law principles. The HRA 1998 should, of course, now encourage them to give proper weight to this freedom, and will, in any case, require them to take full account of the European case law on Art 11.

## Note

1   It may be worth pointing out that in the *GCHQ* case, the House of Lords first had to determine whether the decision was open to judicial review at all. In this instance, the Prime Minister was exercising powers derived from the Royal Prerogative, which were traditionally seen as not open to judicial review, as derived from the common law and not from statute. However, Lord Denning in *Laker Airways v Department of Trade* (1977) seemed to have effected some erosion of that principle and, following his lead, the House of Lords determined that the mere fact of the power deriving from the prerogative as

opposed to statute was not a sufficient reason why it should not be open to review.

# CHAPTER 4

# PRIVACY

## Introduction

Examiners tend to set general essays in this area, rather than problem questions. The emphasis is usually on the degree to which a balance is struck between the interest of the State and other bodies in intruding on the individual, or in obtaining and publishing personal information, and the interest of the individual in maintaining personal privacy and the privacy of personal information. These two areas of privacy can be broken down into bodily and sexual privacy, the privacy of the home, access to personal information and the protection of personal formation.

At present, questions are often asked which concern the balance struck between privacy and freedom of expression; this is a very topical issue. There have, for example, been various government proposals for reform, including the introduction of a tort of privacy. These have been somewhat overshadowed, however, by a debate about the extent to which the HRA 1998 will lead to the courts developing a common law right to privacy. Another important topic concerns the needs of national security and crime control which clearly conflict with privacy in a range of ways arising from the provisions of a certain group of statutes: the Security Services Act 1989, the Interception of Communications Act 1985 and the Intelligence Services Act 1994. The most recent addition to this area is the Regulation of Investigatory Powers Act 2000. Therefore, essay questions may ask you to consider the conflict between those needs and the individual's interest in maintaining personal privacy and the privacy of the home. The HRA 1998 will also be relevant to discussions of this area.

There is some overlap between the areas of freedom of information and privacy, since the principle that citizens should be able to gain access to their own personal information which is held by various bodies may fall under either head. However, the question of how far people should have access to their own personal information may be viewed most readily as a privacy issue, since the access is sought in order to ensure, *inter alia*, that the confidentiality of the information is maintained, not that it should be made freely available.

Students should be familiar with the following areas:

- breach of confidence;
- defamation and malicious falsehood;
- trespass and nuisance;
- proposals for the new tort of invasion of privacy;
- the potential role of the HRA 1998;
- the Data Protection Acts 1984 and 1998 and the Freedom of Information Act 2000;
- the Official Secrets Act 1989, the Security Services Act 1989, the Interception of Communications Act 1985, the Intelligence Services Act 1994, the Police Act 1997 and the Regulation of Investigatory Powers Act 2000.

# Question 20

'The law of confidence has developed so far that it can now confidently be said that it provides adequate protection for personal information; therefore, a statutory tort of invasion of privacy is not needed.' Do you agree?

## Answer plan

A fairly demanding essay question, which requires familiarity with the law of confidence. The statement made in the title should be questioned as follows. First, does confidence provide adequate protection for personal information? Secondly, assuming that it does, is it better, in terms of preserving media freedom, to protect such information through the doctrine of confidence or through a new tort? Essentially, the following points should be considered:

- development of doctrine of confidence – relationship between the parties may be informal;
- obligation of confidentiality may be imposed on third parties;
- the public interest defence;
- ambit of the proposed tort;

- comparison between the proposed tort and breach of confidence: impact on media freedom;
- Arts 8 and 10 of the European Convention on Human Rights (the Convention) and the impact of the HRA 1998.

# Answer

No tort of invasion of privacy exists in the UK as in the US to control the activity of the media in obtaining information regarding an individual's private life and then publishing the details, possibly in exaggerated, lurid terms. However, certain legal controls arising from the law of confidence do exist, although they are not aimed directly at the invasion of privacy and they can be used against the media when private information is published. However, it will be argued that this control is still fairly limited in scope and, to some extent, aimed at the protection of other interests, arguably making it ill suited to the protection of privacy. Further, it will be suggested that extension of confidence with a view to providing greater protection for personal information should be viewed with caution, due to the threat which would be posed to media freedom.

The Younger Committee, which reported on the legal protection of privacy in 1972, considered that confidence was the area of the law which offered most effective protection of privacy. It has a wider ambit than defamation, in that it prevents truthful communications and also appears to protect confidential communications, whether or not their unauthorised disclosure causes detriment to the reputation of any person. It may be that detriment is, in fact, caused to the reputation of the person who is the subject when personal information is disclosed, as in *Woodward v Hutchins* (1977) or *Lennon v News Group Newspapers Ltd* (1978), but the rulings do not appear to rest on the need to demonstrate such detriment. However, it must be remembered that confidence, while quite closely associated with it, is protecting a somewhat different interest from that of privacy; it is concerned with the preservation of confidentiality and therefore is not apt to cover all possible circumstances in which private life is laid bare.

Breach of confidence will be established, according to Lord Greene MR in *Saltman Engineering Co Ltd v Campbell Engineering Co*

*Ltd* (1963), if information which has a quality of confidence about it as it is not in the public domain is transmitted in circumstances importing an obligation of confidence, and there is then unauthorised use of that information. As *Duke of Argyll v Duchess of Argyll* (1965) demonstrated, these ingredients may arise when confidential information is imparted in a relationship of trust not of a contractual nature and, therefore, personal information is clearly covered. However, that ruling was delivered in the context of a formal relationship – marriage – and, combined with other rulings such as that in *Thompson v Stanhope* (1774), suggests that breach of confidence is relevant only where a formal relationship can be identified.

In *Stephens v Avery* (1988), however, which concerned information communicated within a close friendship, it was not found necessary to identify a formal relationship between the parties at the time when the information was communicated, thus suggesting that the confidential nature of the information was the important factor: '... it is unconscionable for a person who has received information on the basis that it is confidential subsequently to reveal that information. No particular pre-existing relationship is needed.' This contention is supported by the ruling in *Francome v Mirror Group Newspapers* (1984).

These comments might appear to cover a communication of confidential information by one complete stranger to another so long as the communicator informed the recipient that the information was confidential. If so, *Stephens v Avery* dramatically points the way to a broader use of breach of confidence as a means of protecting privacy. However, it may be going too far to suggest that this ruling would support the use of confidence in relation to secrets passed between strangers. The ratio of the case would seem to be merely that no pre-existing formal relationship is needed; as the information was passed within a close friendship, it was not necessary for the decision to state that there was no need to identify any relationship at all. The comment to that effect was therefore only *obiter,* and so it is not certain that courts in future would be prepared to accept that confidences passed between slight acquaintances or strangers should be protected. Perhaps they would not, since the betrayal of trust for which the law of confidence has traditionally sought to provide a remedy would be less apparent, or perhaps completely absent, in such instances.

*Stephens v Avery* also demonstrated that a newspaper which was not a party to the original relationship, but was directly involved, in that it had been approached by one of the parties, could have obligations associated with a relationship of trust imposed upon it. *AG v Guardian Newspaper Ltd* (1987) (the *Spycatcher* case) took this a stage further, in making it clear that if an editor of a newspaper is not directly approached, but has merely acquired the information, he or she can be held to be under the same duty of confidence if he or she is aware that the information is confidential. However, it must be possible to identify an obligation of confidentiality (in the *Stephens and Avery* sense) at some point in the transaction. In the *Spycatcher* litigation, the relationship of trust was that originally subsisting between Peter Wright and MI5.

Thus, the need to identify a confidential obligation often associated with a relationship of trust places a limitation on the use of this remedy – it must exist at some point, but, usually, a reporter will investigate and acquire facts without incurring any such obligation. Even where it can be identified and one party then discloses a story to a newspaper, the courts have placed limitations on this remedy which arise from the 'public interest' defence. In *Woodward v Hutchings* (1977), intimate facts about Tom Jones and another pop star were revealed to the *Daily Mirror* by a former agent who had been their confidante. The plaintiffs sought an injunction on the ground of breach of confidence. There had been a relationship of trust and they claimed that the agent should not be able to take unfair advantage of that confidence.

The Court of Appeal failed to uphold the claim on the basis that the plaintiffs had sought to publicise themselves in order to present a certain 'image' and therefore could not complain if the truth were later revealed. This decision has been criticised on the basis that a need to reveal the truth about the plaintiffs was irrelevant to the breach of confidence on the part of the agent, but it has not been overruled. The public interest in knowing the truth about the plaintiffs seemed to rest on a refusal to use the law to protect their attempt to mislead the public and therefore would not usually be in question in relation to the disclosure of personal information. A recent application can be seen in *Barrymore v News Group Newspapers* (1997). B applied for an injunction to restrain publication of an article about his relationship with another man.

The court held that disclosure of the secrets of a relationship could in itself, be a breach of confidence. Thus, the injunction was granted.

The most recent developments in this area have taken place following the coming into force of the HRA 1998. There was much debate at the time that this Act was before Parliament as to whether it would lead to the development of a common law right of privacy. Concern that the courts might adopt such right with too great enthusiasm led to the inclusion of s 12 of the Act, which requires courts to pay due attention to freedom of expression. That the HRA 1998 may lead to significant developments seems to be confirmed by the Court of Appeal decision in *Douglas v Hello!* (2001). It was held that the unauthorised publication of photographs of the claimant's wedding could amount to an actionable breach of privacy, as a development of the law of breach of confidence. This was so, even though the wedding was not 'private', in that the rights to publish photographs had been sold to another magazine. An injunction restraining publication was not appropriate, however, either because of s 12 of the HRA, or because the normal test of the 'balance of convenience' which applies to interim injunctions came down in favour of the defendants. The decision was subsequently relied on in V*enables v News Group Newspapers* (2001) to impose an injunction preventing the publication of the new identities of two men convicted when they were children of murdering a toddler.

Given the way that the law appears to be developing, it is important that any defences which may be available to the media are also given due weight. One possibility is the defence of 'disclosure of iniquity'. In other words, the claimant cannot use this remedy to cover up his or her own wrong doing and therefore the public interest in disclosure will prevail. However, it is uncertain whether this 'public interest defence' is limited to cases of iniquity. The House of Lords considered *obiter* in *British Steel Corp v Granada Television* (1981) that publication of confidential information could legitimately be undertaken only where there was misconduct but, on the other hand, in *Lion Laboratories v Evans* (1985), Stephenson LJ said that he would reject the 'no iniquity, no public interest rule' on the basis that 'some things are required to be disclosed in the public interest in which case no confidence can be prayed in aid to keep them secret and [iniquity] is merely an instance of just cause and excuse for breaking confidence'.

These rulings concerned confidential information held by private companies and seem to leave open the possibility of a broad public interest defence which, it seems from *Woodward*, may also sometimes apply in the case of public figures. Where personal information relating to an ordinary individual is in issue, it would seem from the ruling in *X v Y* (1988) that the public interest defence is confined to cases of iniquity, although a proviso to this principle may arise where the claimant, due to no fault of his or her own, creates a danger to the public. This proviso may be said to arise either as a variant of the public interest defence – although the claimant, due to a particular mental state, is not responsible for it, wrongdoing is likely to arise through his agency if the information is suppressed – or as a specific exception to it. The general principle can be supported on the basis that private persons have a greater interest in maintaining confidentiality of information than have private companies or public figures.

The above discussion should not be taken as assuming that the public interest will always require disclosure of information and will therefore invariably be in competition with the private interest of the plaintiff in suppressing it. In certain circumstances, such as those which arose in *X v Y*, there may be a public interest in maintaining confidentiality. A newspaper wished to publish information deriving from confidential hospital records which showed that certain practising doctors were suffering from the AIDS virus. In granting an injunction preventing publication Rose J took into account the public interest in disclosure, but weighed it against the private interest in confidentiality and the public interest in encouraging AIDS patients to seek help from hospitals, which would not be served if it was thought that confidentiality might not be maintained.

Even where the public interest defence is raised in relation to a private company, the manner in which the information was obtained may be relevant; if the means used to obtain it suggest a gross breach of trust, such as the use of a telephone tap, the law of confidence may be successfully invoked. In *Francome v Mirror Group Newspapers* (1984), reporting of breaches of the race rules might not have attracted a remedy due to the iniquity defence, but the use of telephone tapping in order to obtain the story may have persuaded the Court of Appeal to allow a remedy.

The statutory tort of invasion of privacy which was proposed under the 1993 Green Paper would fill some of the gaps which may still be left by the law of confidence, even taking into account recent developments expanding its scope (for example, *Douglas v Hello!* (2001). The new tort would cover the publication of personal information without authorisation which causes substantial distress. Such information has been defined as those aspects of an individual's personal life which a reasonable person would assume should remain private. Use of the word 'substantial' would limit the ambit of the tort; confidence might sometimes be available, although liability under the new tort would not be. The tort would not be subject to a general defence of public interest.

It would be a defence under the proposals to show that the act was done: for the purpose of preventing, detecting or exposing the commission of a crime; or for the purpose of preventing the public from being misled by some public statement or action of the individual concerned; or for the purpose of informing the public about matters directly affecting the discharge of any public function of the individual concerned; or for the protection of public health or safety; or under any lawful authority. Clearly, these defences are more tightly drawn than the broad public interest defence under the law of confidence.

In conclusion, although it has been argued that there are gaps in the protection offered to privacy by the common law doctrine of confidence, it does not necessarily follow that statutory measures to protect it should be adopted. On the one hand, it could be argued that, rather than an uncontrolled development of confidence, coupled with a vague public interest defence, a tort of invasion of privacy would be preferable as possibly providing clearer protection for freedom of speech. Thus, the ruling in *Stephens v Avery* could be used to support introduction of such a tort, rather than as an argument that it has become unnecessary. On the other hand, the defence under the law of confidence, if more clearly defined, might provide greater protection for the media than the very specific defences under the new tort. At present, it seems that the exposure of seriously anti-social conduct would not fall within the defences under the proposed tort, although it probably would fall within the defence under the law of confidence.

Thus, the development of confidence in order to fill the gap currently left by the lack of a tort of invasion of privacy should be viewed with caution, but it is suggested that under the current arrangements, such development is preferable to the introduction of the new tort. It should be remembered that such a tort would operate alongside confidence to provide a further restraint on freedom of speech. In terms of protection of privacy, confidence has now developed to the point where personal information will be protected in a wide range of situations. Now that the UK has enacted freedom of information legislation, a right to privacy could be enacted without detriment so long as press freedom is separately supported. Courts must now also maintain a delicate balance between Arts 8 and 10 of the Convention. Section 12 of the HRA 1998 clearly puts freedom of expression first where there is a conflict, and this was taken into account in *Douglas v Hello!* (2001). Further cases will be needed, however, before a proper judgment can be made as to whether the balance is being struck in the right place.

# Question 21

'Not one of the various proposals for further press regulation succeeds in creating a proper balance between freedom of the press and privacy.' Discuss.

## Answer plan

A reasonably straightforward essay question. It is important to concentrate on the various proposals, rather than undertaking a general review of the law relating to privacy. Obviously, the question could be 'attacked', in the sense that it could be argued that no balance at all should be struck between freedom of expression on the one hand and the protection of certain forms of private information on the other: freedom of expression should always prevail. This might be argued in relation to private information bearing on the public life of public figures. Alternatively, it might be argued that the balance to be struck should differ depending on the public interest value of the information. Essentially, the following matters should be considered:

- methods of self-regulation and proposals for their improvement;
- a statutory tribunal to regulate the press;
- proposals for a statutory tort of invasion of privacy;
- defences under the new tort;
- proposals to remedy various kinds of intrusion made with the intent to obtain personal material for publication.

## Answer

Given the Human Rights Act (HRA) 1998's enactment, the debate on how best to create a satisfactory right to respect for private and family life (in compliance with Art 8 of the European Convention on Human Rights (the Convention)) has re-opened. Proposals for further press regulation can be divided into three main areas, which will be considered in turn. First, I will consider the various experiments with methods of self-regulation and proposals for their improvement, or for a statutory tribunal to regulate the press; secondly, the proposals for a statutory tort of invasion of privacy; and, thirdly, proposals to remedy various kinds of intrusion made with the intent to obtain personal material for publication.

Until recently, it was thought that the press should regulate itself as regards protection of privacy, rather than using civil or criminal sanctions. Self-discipline was preferred to court regulation in order to preserve press freedom and, to this end, the Press Council was created in 1953. It was supposed to regulate the press and therefore issued guidelines on privacy and adjudicated on complaints. It could censure a newspaper and require its adjudication to be published. In practice, however, a number of deficiencies became apparent; the Council did not issue clear enough guidelines; its decisions were seen as inconsistent; and, in any event, ineffective – it had no power to fine or award an injunction. Moreover, it was seen as too lenient, it would not interfere if the disclosure in question could be said to be in the public interest and what was meant by the public interest was uncertain.

Its inefficacy led the Younger Committee, convened in 1972, to recommend a number of proposals offering greater protection from intrusion by the press. These proposals were not implemented, but, recently, a perception again began to arise, partly influenced by *Kaye v Robertson*, that further measures might be needed to control the tabloid newspapers, although, at the same time, there was concern that they should not prevent legitimate investigative journalism. This perceived need led eventually to the formation of the Committee on Privacy and Related Matters (hereafter 'Calcutt I') in 1990, which considered a number of measures, some relevant to actual publication and some to the means of gathering information. The Committee decided that improved self-regulation should be given one final chance and recommended the creation of the Press Complaints Commission, which was set up in 1991. At the present time, self-regulation is still being tried and may well operate eventually alongside the new forms of liability once they are in place.

The Commission agreed a Code of Practice which the newspapers accepted. It can receive and pronounce on complaints of violation of the Code and can demand an apology for inaccuracy, or that there should be an opportunity for reply. Intrusion into private life is allowed under the Code only if it is in the public interest; this is defined as including 'detecting or exposing seriously anti-social conduct' or 'preventing the public being misled by some statement or action of that individual'. Harassment is not allowed. The Code makes special mention of hospitals and requires that the press must obtain permission in order to interview patients. The Commission does not require the complainant to waive any legal right of action as the Press Council was criticised for doing. However, it has the same limited sanctions as the Press Council.

The Broadcasting Standards Commission took over in 1996 from the Broadcasting Complaints Commission the similar role of trying to ensure that broadcasters avoid the unwarranted infringement of privacy in the making and broadcast of radio and television programmes, and dealing with complaints in this area. It issues a Code with which broadcasters are expected to comply. The term 'privacy' will receive quite a wide interpretation according to the ruling in *Broadcasting Complaints Commission ex p Granada Television Ltd* (1993). Granada television challenged a finding of the BCC that matters already in the public domain could, if re-published, constitute an invasion of privacy. In judicial review proceedings, it was found that privacy differed from confidentiality and went well beyond it, because it was not confined to secrets; the significant issue was not whether material was or was not in the public domain, but whether, by being published, it caused hurt and anguish. There were grounds on which it could be considered that publication of the matters in question had caused distress and, therefore, the BCC had not acted unreasonably in the *Wednesbury* sense in taking the view that an infringement of privacy had occurred.

After self-regulation under the new Code had been in place for a year, Sir David Calcutt (hereafter 'Calcutt II') reviewed its success and determined that the Press Complaints Commission 'does not hold the balance fairly between the press and the individual ... it is in essence a body set up by the industry ... dominated by the industry'. He therefore proposed the introduction of a statutory tribunal which would draw up a Code of Practice for the press and would rule on alleged breaches of the Code; its sanctions would include those already possessed by the Press Complaints Commission and, in addition, the imposition of fines and the award of compensation. When the matter was considered by the National Heritage Select Committee in 1993, it rejected the proposal of a statutory tribunal in favour of the creation of another self-regulatory body to be known as the Press Commission, which would monitor a Press Code and which would have powers to fine and to award compensation.

Support for a statutory tort of invasion of privacy has been far from unanimous in the relevant Committees. Thus, while the Younger Committee recommended the introduction of a tort of disclosure of information unlawfully acquired, Calcutt I decided against recommending a new statutory tort of invasion of privacy relating to publication of personal information, although the Committee considered that it would be possible to define such a tort with sufficient precision. Calcutt II recommended only that the Government should give further consideration to the introduction of such a tort, but the Heritage Select Committee made a more positive recommendation and this view was adopted by Lord Mackay in his Green Paper, published in July 1993. However, the Paper did not suggest that legal aid should be available to those seeking redress under the new civil privacy liability. If the proposal was to be implemented without the provision of legal aid, the new provisions might merely be used – as, arguably, defamation has been – by powerful figures to protect their activities from scrutiny, while the ordinary citizen might be unable in practice to obtain redress for invasions of privacy.

Turning now to the substantive merits of such a tort, it may be noted that the possible definition put forward by Calcutt I was designed to relate only to personal information which was published without authorisation. Such information was defined as those aspects of an individual's personal life which a reasonable person would assume should remain private. The main concern of the Committee was that true information which would not cause lasting harm, was already known to some and was obtained reputably might be caught by its provisions. The Green Paper, however, proposed a broader area of liability: the tort would cover any invasion of privacy causing substantial distress.

The Calcutt Committee did not consider that liability should be subject to a general defence of public interest, although it did favour a tightly drawn defence of justified disclosure. The difficulty here is that it might not always be possible for a journalist trying to investigate corruption in public life to show that there was a clear justification for gathering the relevant information if the investigation was still at an inchoate stage; in order to be effective in protecting worthwhile journalism, any defences would have to require only an honest belief by the journalist that his or her investigations had one of the justificatory purposes. The Green Paper suggested a defence of public interest which would cover the same areas as will be discussed below in relation to criminal liability. In particular, it would be a defence to show that the act in question was done: for the purpose of preventing, detecting or exposing the commission of a crime or other seriously anti-social conduct; or for the purpose of preventing the public from being misled by some public statement or action of the individual concerned. However, under the Green Paper, it was suggested that the defences should be narrowed down to exclude 'seriously anti-social conduct'. If the UK were to enact a right to privacy without including such a defence which would afford protection to the freedom of the press, the detriment caused might outweigh the value of such a right. On the other hand, if the proposed tort were subject to a very wide-ranging defence, it might be emasculated. Thus, in the US, the scope of privacy rights is limited by a general defence of 'newsworthiness', which allows many stories disclosing embarrassing and painful personal facts to be published. This perhaps suggests that there is little value in looking to the US for a model if a UK right to privacy is to have any efficacy.

At present, proposals for reform seem to be faced with two extremes: on the one hand, a claim of invasion of privacy might be met by such a general defence of public interest or newsworthiness that it has, in most instances, very little chance of success, while, on the other, a narrow defence of public interest or 'justified publication' might allow invasion of privacy too much scope. Arguably, an acceptable middle way forward may be to enact very specific and narrowly defined areas of liability relating to particularly intrusive invasions of privacy which differentiate between the lives of ordinary citizens who happen to come into the public eye and the lives of public figures. It is to consideration of proposals for such measures that I will now turn.

The kinds of particularly clear invasions of privacy which arguably require some kind of statutory response are as follows: physical intrusion by reporters both onto the individual's own property or onto other private property where he or she happens to be as in *Kaye*; the taking of photographs for publication without the subject's consent; and the use of bugging devices. The Younger Committee proposed the introduction of a tort and crime of unlawful surveillance by means of a technical device, and both Calcutt Committees recommended the creation of a specific criminal offence providing more extensive protection – a recommendation which was backed by the National Heritage Select Committee when it considered the matter. The clause proposed by Calcutt II creating the offence would also offer the individual whose privacy had been invaded the possibility of obtaining injunctions in the High Court to prevent publication of material gained in contravention of the clause provisions; damages would also be available to hold newspapers to account for any profits gained through publication of such material.

Criminal liability under the clause would be made out if the defendant did any of the following with intent to obtain personal information or photographs, in either case with a view to their publication: entering or remaining on private property without the consent of the lawful occupant; placing a surveillance device on private property without such consent; using a surveillance device whether on private property or elsewhere in relation to an individual who is on private property without his or her consent; and taking a photograph or recording the voice of an individual who is on private property without his or her consent and with intent that the individual should be identifiable. This offence seems to specify the forbidden acts fairly clearly and to be aimed at preventing what would generally be accepted to be undesirable invasions of privacy; it is worth noting that France, Germany, Denmark and the Netherlands all have similar offences on the statute books. It should be noted that the offence would not cover persistent telephoning, or photographing, interviewing or recording the voice of a vulnerable individual, such as a disaster victim or a bereaved relative, in a public place.

It would be a defence to any of the above to show that the act was done: for the purpose of preventing, detecting or exposing the commission of a crime or other seriously anti-social conduct; or for the purpose of preventing the public from being misled by some public statement or action of the individual concerned; or for the purpose of informing the public about matters directly affecting the discharge of any public function of the individual concerned; or for the protection of public health or safety; or under any lawful authority. *Prima facie*, the defences seem to range widely enough to prevent public figures from being able to use the offence to stifle legitimate investigative journalism. The defences relating to anti-social conduct and misleading statements were added by Calcutt II and, it is submitted, are essential to draw a clear distinction between the private citizen and the public figure, and to ensure the accountability of the latter. The interpretation given to the defences would of course be crucial in ensuring that this distinction was maintained,[1] but it is suggested that the proposed offence should be cautiously welcomed as an addition to self-regulation; it provides a remedy against some unjustifiable invasions of privacy, without risking the deterrence of serious journalism and the concomitant loss of public accountability vital to a healthy democracy.

Some of the ground covered by the above proposals has been covered to a limited extent by the Protection from Harassment Act 1997. This makes it an offence to pursue a course of conduct which amounts to harassment of another, where the harasser knows or ought to know that this will be its effect. It also provides for a civil remedy in the form or damages or a restraining order. The primary target of this legislation was 'stalking', however, and it has severe limitations as a weapon against press intrusion on privacy. Most significant is the requirement of a 'course of conduct', which means that a single intrusion would not engage the Act's provisions (see *Sai Lau v DPP* (2000)). Although the Act has been used quite frequently since coming into force, there are no examples of it being applied to press invasions of privacy.

In conclusion, it is by no means certain that the various proposals that have been put forward in this area would achieve the right balance between privacy and press freedom (even assuming that the political will to legislate in this area exists). The prospects for parliamentary reform are, in any case, likely to remain low until it has become clear how the HRA 1998 will impact on the area. Section 12 of the Act requires the courts to give proper weight to freedom of expression in considering restraints on publication. As has been shown, however, by the Court of Appeal decision in *Douglas v Hello!* (2001), the courts may well be prepared to develop the law of breach of confidence into something resembling a fully-fledged right of privacy. In addition, the Press Complaints Commission and the Broadcasting Standards Commission, as public authorities, will have to act compatibly with the Convention in exercising their powers. Will this result in a change in the situation under which the PCC, for example, holds against the press in only 1% of the cases initiated? The way in which these regulatory bodies strike the balance between Arts 8 and 10 may well determine whether there is a need for further statutory control.

**Note**

1   It could be pointed out that the defences would offer reasonable protection to journalists if an honest belief in the factor in question was required. If a reasonable belief was required, this might stifle investigative journalism since, at an early stage in the investigation, such a belief could not be formed.

# Question 22

How far, if at all, does the law protect bodily and sexual privacy? Is reform in this area needed?

### Answer plan

A fairly tricky essay question since, unlike access to personal information, there is no obvious and coherent body of law which is relevant. It is probably a good idea to begin by considering what is meant by bodily and sexual privacy.

Essentially, the following areas should be considered:

*   possible ambit of bodily and sexual privacy;
*   bodily privacy and crime control: police powers in this area;
*   corporal punishment;
*   bodily privacy in the medical context;
*   personal autonomy as to the expression of sexuality – legal restraints;
*   relevant European Court of Human Rights (ECHR) decisions – *Laskey* (1997); *Sutherland* (1998); *Rees* (1987); and *Lustig-Prean* (1999).

# Answer

Bodily and sexual privacy may be seen as encompassing two main interests. First, individuals have an interest in preventing actual physical intrusions on the body. This interest consists of a negative right to be 'left alone' in a physical sense, but may also encompass a positive claim on the state to ensure that bodily integrity is not infringed. However, the main concern here is with the extent to which the State allows such infringement. Secondly, individuals have an interest in retaining autonomy as regards freedom of choice in decisions as to the disposal or control of his or her own body. Usually, the individual is, in effect, asking the State to leave him or her alone to make such decisions in order to preserve autonomy. In some instances, however, the individual will be requiring the assistance of the authorities in ensuring that he or she is able to exercise autonomy. Thus, personal privacy at its simplest level may be defined as the freedom from physical intrusion, but, arguably, the concept may be expanded to encompass individual autonomy, thereby allowing a variety of interests to be considered under this head.

The law determines that, in certain circumstances, bodily privacy may give way to other interests. Thus, s 55 of the Police and Criminal Evidence Act 1984 allows intimate strip searches, but recognises that the violation they represent may occur only in well defined circumstances. Examination may occur only if there is reasonable suspicion that drugs or implements which might be used to harm others may be found. The examination may only be carried out by a nurse (or a medical practitioner in respect of drugs or a weapon) or, if that is not practicable, it can be carried out by a police officer who must be of the same sex as the person to be searched. Customs officers have similar (and slightly stronger) rights.

The question as to how far clothing could be removed for other purposes in police custody was considered in *Lindley v Rutter* (1980) and a general order to remove the bras of all female detainees in the police station was challenged. Justification was put forward for the order on the grounds that the detainees might otherwise injure themselves. However, it was found that such treatment constituted an affront to human dignity and therefore needed a clearer justification which could be derived only from the specific circumstances of the arrestee: something particular about the individual in question must support a suspicion that she might do herself an injury. It was found that, in removing a detainee's bra where such specific justification did not exist, the police officer in question had acted outside her duty. Thus, the court evinced a reluctance to accept a general invasion of privacy.

Certain forms of punishment may be seen as an unjustified intrusion onto bodily integrity. Corporal punishment was outlawed in state schools after the decision of the ECHR in *Campbell and Cosans v UK* (1982), which was determined not on the basis of Arts 3 or 8, but under Art 2 of the First Protocol, which protects the right of parents to have their children educated according to their own philosophical convictions. However, corporal punishment in private schools was not outlawed and, in *Costello-Roberts v UK* (1993), the ECHR found that the UK had a responsibility to ensure that school discipline was compatible with the Convention, even though the treatment in question was administered in an institution independent of the state. However, although the Court considered that there might be circumstances in which Art 8 could be regarded as affording protection to physical integrity which would be broader than that afforded by Art 3, in the particular circumstances, the adverse effect on the complainant was insufficient to amount to an invasion of privacy. In the most recent case to deal with this area, however, *A v UK* (1999), the European Court showed itself willing to interfere in family life in order to protect the rights of a child. A nine year old boy had been repeatedly beaten with a cane by his stepfather. The stepfather was acquitted of assault, having relied on the defence of reasonable chastisement. The European Court held that the failure to protect the boy from ill treatment meant that the UK was in breach of Art 3. To this extent, the Convention will protect bodily integrity, and this raises the possibility of the English courts further developing this area under the HRA 1998.

Personal autonomy has been clearly recognised for some time in the US as a legitimate privacy interest – in *Doe v Bolton* (1973), Douglas J said:

> The right to privacy means freedom of choice in the basic decisions of one's life respecting marriage, divorce, procreation, contraception, education and upbringing of children.

Personal autonomy connotes an interest not in preventing physical intrusion by others, but in the extent to which the law allows an individual a degree of control over his or her own body.

Recognition of the need to allow such self-determination has become more prominent this century. Thus, abortion and suicide are no longer crimes under the Abortion Act 1967 and the Suicide Act 1961. However, limits as to self-determination are represented by the Prohibition of Female Circumcision Act 1985 and the Surrogacy Act 1985 (although it should be noted that surrogacy is only curbed by the Act, not outlawed: it only prevents commercial surrogacy arrangements). Such measures may suggest that the 20th century has placed greater value on bodily self-determination: the presumption is that, in this matter, the individual should apply his or her own moral standards, except when this allows something particularly abhorrent in British society to occur, such as female circumcision. Then, the law will impose the wider social standard on the particular individual.

The question of the ambit of self-determination has arisen most frequently in the context of medical treatment, but the law has not so far made much progress in the direction of granting the concept recognition. This question has been particularly pertinent in the context of medical negligence; it was argued in *Sidaway v Board of Governors of the Bethlem Royal Hospital* (1985) that a patient who was not fully informed as to the risks associated with the operation she was to undergo should be able to succeed against the doctor when one of those risks did materialise. However, it was found that so long as the doctor had acted in accordance with practice accepted as proper by a body of medical practitioners (the test deriving from *Bolam v Friern HMC* (1957)) with regard to disclosure of risks, the action must fail.

It may be argued that this stance fails to accord sufficient weight to the personal autonomy of the patient. Where a number of choices of treatment lie before a patient, how far would it be expected that he or she should participate in the decision making process? For example, if a patient had a serious cancerous condition, there might be two main options: radical treatment which would be disfiguring, but might prolong life, or conservative treatment, which would not prolong life, but would not disfigure. Length of life would have to be weighed against quality of life. It might appear that only the patient who knows intimately which of the options fits with his or her own aspirations and lifestyle and who must live for the rest of his or her life with the decision taken can make it and must be fully informed as to the options in order to do so.

The law has not, however, recognised any general right to autonomy. The *Sidaway* case concerned an operation which would not be termed elective, in that it was aimed at pain relief, but where a purely elective operation was in question in *Gold v Haringey Health Authority* (1987), the same principles applied. Clearly, in order that a patient can exercise self-determination, he or she must know of the options for treatment and of the likely outcome in each instance. The patient can then give or withhold consent to the proposed course of treatment and, further, can question it. However, the test to be applied as to whether a doctor has been negligent in failing to inform the patient of certain possibilities – the *Bolam* test – does not lay a heavy burden upon doctors in terms of the amount of information which must be given. This test may be acceptable in respect of decisions as to diagnosis and treatment (although it may be argued that it puts the claimant in medical negligence cases in an extremely difficult position), but, arguably, it is unacceptable in respect of the duty to disclose information so that the patient can give an informed consent to the treatment proposed. It appears that judges have put their fear of defensive medicine and a flood of medical litigation before the need to uphold the right of the patient to control over his or her own body.[1]

Self-determination as regards the body in areas relating to sexuality may be regarded as a related interest, because it raises questions as to the extent to which individuals have the power of choice in relation to the expression of sexuality. At present, sexual freedom is restricted by the criminal law, which prohibits certain acts between consenting participants. The rationale for such prohibition seems to depend partly on use of the criminal law as the means of affirming and upholding a certain moral standard, and partly on the need to prevent certain specific harms. The debate as to whether or not the proper function of the criminal law is to interfere in the private lives of citizens in order to enforce a particular pattern of behaviour where no clear harm will arise from the prohibited behaviour remains unresolved. However, if the criminal law is to be used to uphold a certain moral standard, it should be clear that a general standard can be discerned; if it cannot, the law may be said to be in danger of enshrining and perpetuating prejudice.

The offence of buggery consists at common law of intercourse *per anum* by a man with a man or woman and intercourse *per anum* or *vaginum* with an animal. An exception is provided by s 12 of the Sexual Offences Act 1967, as amended, which permits consensual buggery between people both of whom are 18 or over, done in private. However, this relaxation on the banning of homosexual acts was not applicable to Ireland or Scotland and might not now be universal in the UK if the ECHR had not accepted that restriction of sexual freedom may be a violation of Art 8. *Dudgeon v UK* (1981) challenged the law in Northern Ireland (the Offences Against the Person Act 1861) which made buggery between consenting males of any age a crime. Dudgeon, who was suspected of homosexual activities, was arrested on that basis and questioned, but the police decided not to prosecute. He applied to the ECHR, claiming a breach of the right to privacy under Art 8. The ECHR held that the legislation in question constituted a continuing interference with his private life, which included his sexual life. He was forced either to abstain from sexual relations completely or to commit a crime.

However, the court considered that some regulation of homosexual activity was acceptable; the question was what was necessary in a democratic society. The court took into account the doctrine of the margin of appreciation (the discretion of Member State government as to what is necessary) as considered in the *Handyside* case (1976), where it was held that State authorities were in the best position to judge the requirements of morals. However, the court found that the instant case concerned a very intimate aspect of private life. A restriction on a Convention right cannot be regarded as necessary, unless it is proportionate to the aim pursued. In the instant case, there was a grave detrimental interference with the applicant's private life and, on the other hand, there was little evidence of damage to morals. The law had not been enforced and no evidence had been adduced to show that this had been harmful to moral standards. So, the aim of the restriction was *not proportional* to the damage to the applicants' privacy and, therefore, the invasion of privacy went beyond what was needed.

In response to this ruling, Northern Irish law was changed under the Homosexual Offences (NI) Order 1982. *Dudgeon* demonstrates that the European Court is prepared to uphold the right of the individual to choose to indulge in homosexual practices and suggests that the term 'private life' in Art 8 may be used to cover a wide range of situations where bodily or sexual privacy is in question.[2]

Some types of sado-masochistic behaviour are held to be unlawful whether or not the participants consent to it. The level of behaviour which will be unlawful despite consent is of a surprisingly minor nature; in *Donovan* (1934), it was defined as 'any hurt of injury calculated to interfere with health or comfort ... it need not be permanent, but must be more than merely transient or trifling'. However, such interference may be justified as in the public interest, thus exempting blows given in the course of friendly athletic contests which, following the ruling in *Coney* (1882), are seen as being for 'good reason'.

In *Brown* (1993), a group of sado-masochistic homosexuals had regularly, over 10 years, willingly participated in acts of violence against each other for the sexual pleasure engendered in the giving and receiving of pain. It was found that the inflicting of injuries amounting to actual bodily harm could not fall within the category of 'good reason' and, therefore, despite the consent of all the participants, the defendants were convicted of actual bodily harm under the Offences Against the Person Act 1861. After the House of Lords upheld their conviction, the men appealed to the ECHR (*Laskey, Jaggard and Brown v UK* (1997)). The Court unanimously found that there has been no violation of Art 8, since it was within the State's competence to regard the convictions as necessary for the protection of health within Art 8(2).

This decision may be criticised for its subjectivity; it is unclear why it is acceptable that boxing contests may be carried out which can result in serious permanent injury or even death, while activities such as those in *Brown* are criminalised, although they may result in a lesser degree of harm. The activities in question were carried on privately and there was no suggestion that any of the 'victims' were coerced into consenting to them: all had chosen freely to participate and none seemed to be in a more powerful position than the others. The inescapable inference appears to be that while boxing is regarded as a 'manly' sport, homosexual activity, although legal, is barely tolerated. Further, the domestic law appears to discriminate in favour of married couples (*Wilson*

(1997), where a man branding his wife on the bottom was not a serious assault due to her consent). Such discrimination should be difficult to continue to justify now that Art 14 of the European Convention is to be read into UK criminal law; the results remain to be seen. Other areas for concern include transsexual rights (which have not been upheld regularly under the ECHR – see *Rees* (1987)) – and gender rights in general (which have been enforced more successfully under the ECHR – see *Lustig-Prean v UK* (1999), where army recruits' sexual orientation had been investigated intrusively and those found to be homosexual had been dismissed; this breached Arts 8 and 13).

It is concluded that the law fails to give sufficient weight to the interest in bodily and sexual privacy and that this area of privacy may be said to be in its infancy as far as legal protection is concerned, especially when compared to the protection for personal information which is available or currently under consideration. In particular, the decision in *Brown* has curtailed severely the sexual activities which individuals might wish to engage in. The House of Lords may have considered that it was reflecting a general moral standard, but whether there is general support for interfering in such activities when carried out in private is unclear.

## Notes

1  It could be noted that medical consent forms are now, however, more detailed than they were 10 years ago, which suggests that respect for patient wishes is now seen as a priority.

2  It could be pointed out that although the age of consent for homosexual sex is now 18 under s 145 of the Criminal Justice and Public Order Act 1994, that provision still differentiates between homosexual and heterosexual acts, thereby curtailing choice for a certain group of citizens. This was challenged in *Sutherland v UK* (1998) and found to be discriminatory in relation to sexuality and the right to respect for private life under Art 8; however, attempts to change domestic law have so far failed at late stages.

# Question 23

Consider the extent to which UK law maintains a reasonable balance between the freedom from infringement of privacy by agents of the State and the need to maintain internal security.

## Answer plan

This is clearly quite a general and wide ranging essay which requires knowledge of a number of different areas. It is mainly concerned with the power of the agents of the State to enter private property or to interfere with private property in furtherance of crime control and national security. The following areas should be considered:

- the Security Services Act 1989, the Intelligence Services Act 1994, the Police Act 1997, the Interception of Communications Act 1985 and the Regulation of Investigatory Powers Act 2000 – safeguards against unreasonable intrusion;
- the influence of the European Court of Human Rights (ECHR) in this area;
- ss 17 and 18 of the Police and Criminal Evidence Act 1984 – safeguards in respect of the search and seizure power;
- Code of Practice B made under the Police and Criminal Evidence Act;
- comparison between powers of the security services to enter premises and those of police officers.

## Answer

Before addressing this question, it is necessary to consider what is meant by 'infringement of privacy' by State agents. It should not merely connote physical intrusion, but could clearly occur in a number of ways. Apart from entry to property, search and seizure, it could include the use of long range surveillance devices, telephone tapping, and the planting of surveillance devices on property. It would seem to include any form of violation of the privacy of the home. A number of private persons, such as reporters, might wish to undertake such intrusion, but the concern here is with intrusion by the agents of the State, with the aim of promoting internal security. Such an aim is clearly legitimate; the question is whether the safeguards against unreasonable intrusion are adequate.

The first point to be made is that the citizen may not even be aware that intrusion is taking place. This is particularly true of telephone tapping and the use of surveillance devices. Public awareness of the use of such devices is severely curtailed by the operation of the Official Secrets Act 1989, the Interception of Communications Act, the Security Services Act 1989 and the Regulation of Investigatory Powers Act 2000. In addition to preventing information as to the operation of the security services reaching the public domain, these statutes provide wide grounds on which the powers of the security service and the power to tap can be invoked.

The Interception of Communications Act 1985 came into being after the decision of the ECHR in the *Malone* case (1984), which found that the tapping of Mr Malone's telephone constituted a breach of Art 8, which protects the right to privacy. However, the decision only required the UK Government to introduce legislation to regulate the circumstances in which the power to tap could be used, rather than giving guidance as to what would be acceptable limits on the right to privacy. The response of the government in the Interception of Communications Act was to provide very wide grounds on which warrants for the purposes of interception could be authorised by the Home Secretary. The regime introduced by this Act is now governed by the Regulation of Investigatory Powers Act 2000, which has largely replaced the 1985 Act. The purposes for which warrants may be issued are, however, the same and include warrants necessary 'in the interests of national security' and 'for the purpose of safeguarding the economic well being of the UK'. These seem to be significantly wider than the old Home Office guidelines previously relied on in respect of the authorising of warrants. In one respect, however, the 2000 Act has restricted the powers, in that the Secretary of State 'shall not' issue an interception warrant unless he believes that the conduct it authorises 'is proportionate to what is sought to be achieved'. This acknowledges the approach of the European Convention case law, which has emphasised the need for 'proportionality' when States seek, on legitimate grounds, to restrict the freedoms protected by the Convention.

As under the 1985 Act, complaints can be made only to a tribunal set up under the Act with no possibility of scrutiny by a court. Tribunal decisions are not published and, although an annual report giving some information on the number of intercept warrants issued must be made available, it is first subject to censorship by the Prime Minister. Interestingly, in 1986, CND brought a High Court action challenging the decision to tap the phones of its members (*Secretary of State for Home Affairs ex p Ruddock* (1987)) on the ground that the Government had aroused a legitimate expectation through published statements that it would not use tapping for party political purposes.

The action failed, but did establish the principle that the courts were entitled to review unfair actions by government arising from failure to live up to legitimate expectations created in this way. The judge, Taylor J, also stated that the jurisdiction of the court to look into such a complaint against a minister should not be totally ousted. It had been argued on behalf of the Crown that the court should not entertain the action, because to do so would be detrimental to national security. Taylor J, however, ruled that such ousting of the courts' jurisdiction in a field where the citizen could have no right to be consulted would be a 'dangerous and draconian step indeed'. That case was the last time such statements would be heard publicly in respect of telephone tapping: s 9 of the 1985 Act then precluded the possibility of their repetition and, of course, brought about the danger Taylor J wanted to avert.

Similarly, the Security Services Act 1989 came into being largely as a response to the finding of the ECHR that a complaint against MI5 was admissible (*Harman and Hewitt v UK* (1986)). The case was brought by two former NCCL officers, Patricia Hewitt and Harriet Harman, who were complaining of their classification as 'subversive' by MI5, which had placed them under surveillance. Part of their complaint concerned a breach of Art 13 on the basis that no effective remedy for complainants existed. The Security Services Act placed MI5 on a statutory basis, but prevented almost all effective scrutiny of its operations. If a member of the public has a grievance concerning its operations complaint to a court is not possible: under s 5 of the Act, complaint can only be made to a tribunal and, under s 5(4), the decisions of the tribunal are not questionable in any court of law.

Citizens may often be unaware that surveillance is taking place; service personnel who feel that they have been required to act improperly in bugging or searching a person's property are not permitted to complain to the tribunal. Furthermore, the Act provides for no real form of parliamentary oversight of the security service. This Act provided a model for the Intelligence Services Act 1994, which places MI6 and GCHQ on a statutory basis. The 1994 Act sets up, under s 10, a Parliamentary Committee to oversee the administration and policy of MI5, MI6 and GCHQ. However, since the Committee is not a Select Committee, its powers will be limited; therefore, although this is a welcome move, the oversight may have in practice little impact on the services.

Given the width of the powers conferred on members of the security services under this legislation, this lack of accountability is disturbing. Any private individual can have surveillance devices placed on his or her premises, or can be subject to a search of the premises, even though engaged in lawful political activity which is not intended to serve any foreign interest. An amendment to the Security Services Bill was put forward which would have exempted such a person from the operation of the legislation, but it was rejected by the Government. If the security services wish to enter property, the Home Secretary can issue a warrant under the 1989 Act authorising the 'taking of any such action as is specified in the warrant in respect of any property so specified'. In other words, members of MI5 can interfere in any way with property, so long as it appears that they are doing so in order to discharge any of their functions. These functions are set out in s 1 of the Act and include 'the protection of national security and, in particular, its protection from ... actions intended to overthrow or undermine parliamentary democracy by political industrial or violent means'. Under s 5 of the 1994 Act, a warrant will be issued by a minister if the action it covers 'would be of substantial value in assisting the services to carry out their functions'. It is apparent that such wording covers a very large number of circumstances.

The ease with which warrants may be obtained and the concomitant disregard for individual privacy may be contrasted with the position in Canada regarding the powers of the Canadian Security Intelligence Service (CSIS). The CSIS can only be granted warrants on the authorisation of a judge, thus ensuring a measure of independent oversight. Moreover, the warrant will not be issued unless the facts relied on to justify the belief that a warrant is necessary to investigate a threat to national security are set out in a sworn statement. Clearly, the Canadian system places greater emphasis on the privacy of the citizen and therefore appears to strike a fairer balance between privacy on the one hand and the security of the State on the other.

The two statutes mentioned will work in tandem with the Official Secrets Act 1989, s 1 of which prevents members or former members of the security services disclosing anything at all about the operation of those services. All such members come under a lifelong duty to keep silent, even though their information might reveal serious abuse of power by the security services. These provisions also apply to anyone who is notified that he or she is subject to the provisions of the sub-section. Similarly, s 4(3) of the Act prohibits disclosure of information obtained by or relating to the issue of a warrant under the Interception of Communications Act 1985 or the Security Services Act 1989. The wide grounds on which intrusion may be authorised, the secrecy surrounding the issuing of intercept warrants and burgling warrants, and the lack of an effective complaints procedure suggest that the balance has tipped too far away from concern for the privacy of the individual.

In contrast, as one would expect, the other State body with the power to enter private property – the police – may only enter premises in certain carefully defined circumstances and must follow a procedure once there designed to allow the citizen a reasonable chance of making a complaint if he or she wishes to do so. The procedure is regulated in Code of Practice B made under the Police and Criminal Evidence Act 1984. Code B has recently been revised with a view to improving the procedures to be followed and thereby goes some way towards ensuring that police officers will be accountable in respect of searches undertaken, especially consensual ones.

First, the power to enter premises conferred by ss 17 and 18 of the Police and Criminal Evidence Act is balanced by limitations on its exercise; it can be exercised either where an officer wants to arrest a person suspected of an arrestable offence or where a person has been so arrested and the intention is to search the person's premises immediately after arrest. Thus, the power arises only in respect of a limited range of offences; it does not arise in respect of an arrest under s 25. Searching of premises other than under ss 17 and 18 can only occur if a search warrant is issued by a magistrate. A warrant will only be issued if there are reasonable grounds for believing that a serious arrestable offence has been committed and where the material is likely to be of substantial value to the investigation of the offence. The warrant must identify the articles to be sought, although once the officer is on the premises, other articles may be seized under s 19 if they appear to relate to any other offence. Further, the warrant authorises entry to premises on one occasion only.

Secondly, under paras 4 and 5 of Code B, the subjects of all searches, regardless of the status of the search, must receive information about the search in the form of a Notice of Powers and Rights and, under para 5.8, where a consensual search has taken place but the occupier is absent, the Notice should be endorsed with the name, number and station of the officer concerned.[1] Oddly enough, it is not stated expressly that this information must be added to the Notice where the subject of a consensual search is *present*.[2] Paragraph 5.5 provides that officers must identify themselves, except in the case of inquiries linked to terrorism, but this provision appears to apply only to non-consensual searches due to the heading of that section. It might be thought that a person who voluntarily allows police officers to come onto his or her premises does not need the information mentioned, but this is to ignore the possibility that such a person might wish to withdraw consent during the search, but might feel too intimidated to do so.[3]

These provisions suggest some determination to strike a reasonable balance between the perceived need to confer on the police a general power to search property and the need to protect the citizen. If the powers are exceeded, an action for trespass will lie. However, it may be argued that although the provisions governing the power to enter premises show a respect for privacy, the provisions governing seizure come too close to allowing a general ransacking of the premises once a lawful entry has been effected. But one further aspect of police activity in this field is not so well regulated. The Police Act 1997 put bugging and surveillance (other than searches) on a statutory footing for the first time. A warrant in respect of private premises can only be granted if the independent Commissioner has been consulted first. But the Act allows unauthorised surveillance to be admitted as evidence in a later trial and, hence, has attracted much negative criticism.

The Regulation of Investigatory Powers Act 2000 has extended the Police Act approach to 'directed' and 'intrusive' surveillance by the police and the security services. An example of directed surveillance would be where a 'bugging' device is placed in the hallway of a block of flats, thus providing information of a lesser quality than if the device was inside one of the flats. Intrusive surveillance would occur, for example, where a bugging device is placed in a car parked near a private house, thus providing information of the same quality as if the device was inside the house. The difference between the two types of surveillance is also indicated by the level of authority required to authorise it. As far as the police are concerned, for example, directed surveillance must generally be authorised by a superintendent; intrusive surveillance, on the other hand, must generally be authorised by the Chief Constable. Moreover, unless the case is urgent, approval for intrusive surveillance must generally be obtained in advance from an independent Surveillance Commissioner. It has been argued that this 'twin-track' approach to the different types of surveillance is unsatisfactory – and, in particular, that the scheme for directed surveillance demonstrates little respect for individual privacy.

In conclusion, although it is to be welcomed that the statutory controls over surveillance now encompass both the police and the security services, it is not clear that the balance between personal privacy and the needs of internal security has been struck in the right place. There may well be challenges to the operation of these powers under the HRA 1998. The record of the European Court of Human Rights in applying Art 8 of the Convention to this area has not been particularly strong, however. Provided that there is a statutory scheme and that the question of the 'proportionality' of any action is addressed (both of which are dealt with by the RIPA), the ECHR has been prepared to allow intrusive actions by the police and security services. There is no reason, of course, why the British courts should not take a stronger line than the ECHR. The likelihood is, however, that they will not do so. The conclusion must be that the balance in this area is still in favour of the police and security services as opposed to the privacy of the individual.

## Notes

1   The information to be conveyed under the Notice of Powers and Rights includes specification of the type of search in question, a summary of the powers of search and seizure arising under the Act and the rights of the subjects of searches.

2   The issue of consent could be considered further: a search of premises can take place with the consent of the occupier, but the consent should be in writing. Paragraph 4.3 provides that the search must cease if the consent is withdrawn during it, and also contains an express provision against using duress to obtain consent.

3   It could be noted that once an officer is lawfully on the premises, he or she has a wide power of seizure under s 19, which extends beyond items relating to the offence for which the suspect has been arrested. This wide power of seizure is balanced to some extent under Code B, which requires that the owner of property seized must be informed as to what has been seized within a reasonable time.

# Question 24

'The current law adequately protects privacy: further measures are unnecessary and undesirable.' Discuss.

## Answer plan

A reasonably straightforward essay question which, ideally, requires consideration of means of developing the current law so that there are no gaps in the protection offered to privacy. Since the essay is so wide ranging, it is necessary to be selective in the coverage of topics; otherwise, it will be too superficial. Since protection of personal information is seen as such a key privacy issue, at present, the coverage below has concentrated largely on that area.

Essentially, the following areas should be considered:

- breach of confidence;
- defamation and malicious falsehood;
- trespass and nuisance;
- development of existing remedies;
- proposals for the new tort of invasion of privacy.

# Answer

Privacy may be said to encompass two broad interests which may be termed: control over intrusions and control over personal information. In the past, UK law recognised no general right to privacy, although there is some evidence, as will be seen, that judges considered this to be an evil which should be remedied. It can be argued that various areas of tort or equity such as trespass, breach of confidence, copyright and defamation are instances of a general right to privacy, but it is reasonably clear from judicial pronouncements in cases such as *Kaye v Robertson* (1991) that these areas and others were treated as covering specific and distinct interests which only incidentally offered protection to privacy – despite the fact that the term 'privacy' is used in a number of the rulings. Thus, it will be argued that UK law has offered a somewhat piecemeal protection to privacy and, therefore, a number of privacy interests have been largely unprotected. Whether the above analysis is still accurate, however, depends on how our courts react to the HRA 1998 and the fact that Art 8 of the Convention, guaranteeing respect for private and family life, must now be given proper consideration in all appropriate cases. The recent decision of the Court of Appeal in *Douglas v Hello!* (2001), which will be discussed further below, suggests that a common law recognition of privacy may be on the point of development. Before considering this, however, the traditional approach will be explored in a little more detail.

Traditionally, the law has viewed intrusions on property as being less serious than physical intrusion on the body and, therefore, remedies are found in the civil, as opposed to the criminal law. A number of private persons, such as reporters, as well as agents of the State, might wish to undertake such intrusion and, therefore, the right to be left alone to enjoy one's property may impose positive obligations or negative obligations on the State. The term 'intrusion' as used here is being given a wide meaning; it is intended to connote not just physical intrusion, but any activity which results in diminishing the privacy of the home. In this sense, many methods of invasion of the home may be seen as intrusion: trespassing, harassing, photographing, watching or lurking, or snooping using long range electronic surveillance devices. Many sophisticated devices are now available to someone who wants to place a person's home under surveillance and, therefore, at the present time, there is no need for the snooper or watcher to actually invade the territory as in the past. However, it is apparent that a law which grew up before the possibility of using such technology became available has not caught up with it. Although the use of surveillance by the police and security services is now governed by the Police Act 1997 and the Regulation of Investigatory Powers Act 2000, it may be significant that the new tort created by the latter Act deals only with unauthorised interception of communications.

The main common law protection from such physical intrusion is afforded by actions for the torts of trespass or nuisance, but it may be argued that the protection offered is limited. Trespass is defined as entering onto land in the possession of another without lawful justification. It is confined to instances in which there is some physical entry; prying with binoculars is not covered and, obviously, nor is electronic eavesdropping. The limitations of the law have been determined by a certain group of cases. In *Hickman v Maisey* (1900), the defendant who was on the highway was watching the plaintiff's land. It was found that the plaintiff owned the land under the highway and that the defendant was entitled to make ordinary and reasonable use of it. Such watching was held not to be reasonable; the defendant had gone outside the accepted use and therefore had trespassed. Thus, it was made clear that intention in such instances is all important, but that, unless behaviour could be linked to some kind of physical presence on land, trespass would not provide a remedy.

This case can be contrasted with that of *Bernstein v Skyviews & General Ltd* (1978), in order to determine the limits of trespass. The defendants flew over the plaintiff's land in an aircraft to take photographs of it, and the question arose whether the plaintiff had a right in trespass to prevent such intrusion. It was held that either he had no rights of ownership over the air space to that height or, alternatively, if he did have such rights, s 40 of the Civil Aviation Act 1942 exempted reasonable flights from liability. The court was not prepared to find that the taking of one photograph was unreasonable and a remedy could not be based solely on invasion of privacy as, of course, there is no such tort. The distinction between this decision and that in *Hickman* arises because the plaintiff could not show that he had an interest in what was violated – the air space – and so he fell outside the ambit of trespass.

How far can nuisance provide a means of protecting privacy? Nuisance involves disturbing a person in the enjoyment of his or her land to an extent that the law regards as unreasonable. There is a dearth of authority on the issue of surveillance but, in an Australian case (*Victoria Park Racing Co v Taylor* (1937)), where a platform was erected in order to gain a view of a racecourse which diminished the value of the plaintiff's business, no remedy in nuisance was available. The activity was held not to affect the use and enjoyment of the land, but *dicta* in the case suggested that there would, in general, be no remedy in nuisance for looking over another's premises. However, *dicta* in *Bernstein* favoured the possibility that grossly invasive, embarrassing surveillance would amount to a nuisance and that possibility was followed up, though not explicitly, in somewhat different circumstances in *Khorasandijan v Bush* (1993). An injunction was granted against the defendant restraining him from using violence to, harassing, pestering or communicating with the plaintiff, the child of the owner of the property in question.

In *Hunter v Canary Wharf* (1997), however, the House of Lords overruled the Court of Appeal's decision in *Khorasandjian v Bush*, to the extent that it gave a right in nuisance to a person who had no proprietary interest. A potential route for the development of a broad privacy right was thereby cut off. The House of Lords were partly influenced by the fact that it saw 'harassing' behaviour of the kind which occurred in *Bush* as being dealt with by the new

Protection from Harassment Act 1997. Since Parliament had intervened in the area, there was no need for the common law to develop its own remedies. The 1997 Act, however, although used quite frequently, does not appear to be providing any general protection against intrusive behaviour. The first reported cases of its use concerned the activities of animal rights protesters (*Huntingdon Life Sciences v Curtin* (1997); *DPP v Mosely* (1999)). It is still fair to conclude that trespass and nuisance offer only limited protection in this area from the crudest forms of invasions of privacy.[1]

It may be noted that in 1972, the Younger Committee recommended that there should be a crime of unlawful surveillance by surreptitious means and also a new tort covering this area. It seems to be clear that a measure specifically aimed at privacy is needed, rather than trying to force trespass and nuisance to fulfil a role they were not intended to fulfil. The Calcutt Committee also recommended certain specific criminal offences aimed at the means of *collecting* information. These included the placing of surveillance devices on private property and the taking of photographs or recording the voice of a person on private property without their consent by the use of long and short range surveillance devices, with the intention of publishing the information gained. As far as long range devices are concerned, this would plug a complete gap in the law. As regards short range devices, it would strengthen trespass to land as a remedy.

Intrusion on property may be undertaken with a view to obtaining and then publishing personal information. Various areas of the law exist aimed specifically at the dual invasion of privacy which is involved in such activity and, therefore, they control, to an extent, the activity of the media in obtaining information regarding an individual's private life and then publishing the details, possibly in exaggerated, lurid terms. These controls may affect both the publication of the information and the *methods* used to obtain it. Control over the publication of personal information is to be found in the laws of confidence, copyright, defamation and malicious falsehood. The potential for the development of these areas as protections for privacy will now be considered.

The law of defamation is often thought to be closely linked to the protection of privacy. The difficulty with the use of defamation, however, is that the defence of justification means that it will not usually affect the situation where true facts are revealed. Moreover, the interest protected by defamation – the interest in preserving reputation – is not synonymous with the interest in preserving privacy. A reputation may not suffer, but private facts may nevertheless be spread abroad, which is, in itself, hurtful for the individual affected.

In *Corelli v Wall* (1906), the defendants had published, without the plaintiff's permission, postcards depicting imaginary events in her life. This was held not to be libellous and no remedy was available. *Kaye v Robertson and Another* (1990), which was of a similar nature, may be said to have made clear the inadequacy of defamation as a remedy for invasions of privacy. Mr Kaye, a well known actor, was involved in a car accident and suffered severe injuries to his head and brain. While he was lying in hospital, two journalists got into his room, photographed him and interviewed him. Due to his injuries, he did not object to their presence and shortly after the incident had no recollection of it.

The resultant article gave the impression that Mr Kaye had consented to the interview. His advisers sought and obtained an injunction restraining the defendants from publishing the photographs and the interview. On appeal by the defendants, the Court of Appeal ruled that the plaintiff's claim could not be based on a right to privacy, as such a right is unknown to English law. His true grievance lay in the 'monstrous invasion of privacy' which he had suffered, but he would have to look to other rights of action in order to obtain a remedy, namely libel and malicious falsehood. The basis of the defamation claim was that the article's implication that Mr Kaye had consented to a first 'exclusive' interview for a 'lurid and sensational' newspaper would lower him in the esteem of right thinking people. The Court of Appeal held that this claim might well succeed, but that, as such a conclusion was not inevitable, it could not warrant grant of an interim injunction.

An injunction founded on malicious falsehood, restraining the defendants until trial from publishing anything which suggested that the plaintiff had given an informed consent to the interview or the taking of the photographs, was substituted for the original order. However, this was a limited injunction, which allowed publication of the story with a certain number of the photographs. Thus, it seemed that no effective remedy was available for the plaintiff.

The final possibility as a candidate for the development of a common law remedy for privacy is breach of confidence. This will protect some confidential communications, and its breadth has supported the view that it could provide a general means of protecting personal information. The Younger Committee, which reported on the legal protection of privacy in 1972, considered that confidence was the area of the law which offered the most effective protection of privacy. It has a wider ambit than defamation, in that it prevents truthful communications and appears to protect confidential communications, whether or not their unauthorised disclosure causes detriment to the reputation of any person. But it must be remembered that confidence, while quite closely associated with it, is protecting a somewhat different interest from that of privacy; it is concerned with the preservation of confidentiality and, therefore, is not apt to cover all possible circumstances in which private life is laid bare.

At one time, it was thought that aside from commercial secrets breach of confidence is relevant only where a formal relationship could be identified. In *Stephens v Avery* (1988), however, which concerned information communicated within a close friendship, it was not found necessary to identify a formal relationship between the parties at the time when the information was communicated, thus suggesting that the confidential nature of the information was the important factor: 'It is unconscionable for a person who has received information on the basis that it is confidential subsequently to reveal that information. No particular pre-existing relationship is needed.' These comments might appear to cover a communication of confidential information by one complete stranger to another, so long as the communicator informed the recipient that the information was confidential. If so, this ruling points the way to a broader use of breach of confidence as a means of protecting privacy.

Further possibilities for development in this area where illustrated by the obiter comments of Laws J of *Hellewell v Chief Constable of Derbyshire* (1995). The case concerned photographs taken of a man in police custody. Local shopkeepers had sought copies as part of their attempts to reduce shoplifting. The plaintiff sought an injunction to restrain such distribution. Although it was held that a public interest defence would, on these facts, be bound to succeed at trial, Laws J was clearly of the view that apart from this, the law should recognise a right of privacy in the distribution of an unauthorised photograph, if, for example, it was taken with a telephoto lens and was of a 'private act'.

As has been noted earlier, the HRA 1998 has been seen as possibly providing the catalyst for further development in this area, and this seems to have occurred with the decision of the Court of Appeal in *Douglas v Hello!* (2001), which, like *Hellewell*, was concerned with unauthorised photographs. The situation was that the film stars Michael Douglas and Catherine Zeta-Jones had entered into an exclusive contract with the magazine *OK!* for the publication of photographs of their wedding. A rival magazine, *Hello!* obtained photographs of the event (it is unclear how) and proposed to publish them. Douglas and Zeta-Jones sought and obtained an interim injunction restraining such publication. On appeal, the Court of Appeal had to consider whether there was any basis for such an action. In finding that there was, the Court of Appeal, clearly spurred on by the HRA 1998, gave considerable impetus to the argument that the law of breach of confidence has the potential to develop into a full right of privacy. The strongest statements of this kind were made by Sedley LJ. He suggested that *Kaye v Robertson* (1991) might well be decided differently if it recurred, and referring to the *obiter dicta* in *Hellewell*, expressed the view that English law would now protect all those who find themselves subjected to an unwanted intrusion into their private lives. The other members of the Court of Appeal did not go quite so far, but accepted that the claimants had an arguable case for breach of confidence. The interim injunctions were lifted, however, on the basis either of s 12 of the HRA 1998 (which requires freedom of expression to be given particular consideration when injunctive relief is being considered), or because on the normal 'balance of convenience' test from *American Cyanamid v Ethicon* (1975), the more harm would be caused to the defendants by refusing to allow publication than to the claimants by letting it proceed. In coming to this conclusion, the court was clearly influenced by the fact that the claimants were not seeking to keep their wedding secret, in that they had already sold photographic rights to another magazine.

The decision in this case has clearly pointed the way for the development of privacy rights via the concept of breach of confidence. Whether this is pursued will have to await later cases, and, in particular, the full trial of the action between Michael Douglas and *Hello!* (assuming that it is not settled beforehand). It is significant, however, that in the subsequent case of *Venables v News Group Newspapers* (2001), the Court of Appeal's decision in *Douglas v Hello!* was referred to in a rather different context. In this case, two young men who were in serving sentences for the murder of a young boy sought injunctions restraining the media from revealing information which would enable them to be identified once they were released from prison and given new identities. Granting the injunctions on the basis of confidentiality, the judge made specific reference to the *Douglas* case. She also considered directly the extent to which it was possible to justify such an injunction in the light of Art 10. She felt that it was, because it fell within the restrictions on freedom of expression allowed by Art 10(2). The claimants' lives might be at risk if their identities were revealed, so the injunction had the effect of protecting their right to life under Art 2 of the Convention.

It seems, therefore, that the common law is showing itself capable of developing at least a partial right of privacy, and it is arguable that this presents less of a threat to freedom of expression than would adoption of a broad statutory tort as proposed in the 1993 Green Paper with narrow defences.[2]

In conclusion, although it seems that there are some gaps in the protection offered to privacy by the common law, it does not follow that broad statutory measures to protect it should be adopted. Further development of the common law may be the safest way forward. The main difficulty will be to ensure that such measures do not cover private information relating to the public lives of public figures in a way which might keep matters of public interest from the press. It will be important that courts continue to give full effect to s 12 of the HRA 1998, and only restrict publication where it is clearly necessary to protect the rights of individuals, and where there is no countervailing public interest favouring disclosure.

## Notes

1   It could further be noted that various statutes afford piecemeal protection from certain specified types of intrusion. Intrusion by creditors is regulated under s 40 of the Administration of Justice Act 1970 and by landlords under s 30 of the Rent Act 1965. Obscene phone calls are prohibited under s 66 of the Post Office Act 1953, as are unsolicited obscene publications under s 4 of the Unsolicited Goods and Services Act 1971.

2   It could be pointed out that the defences would offer reasonable protection to journalists if an honest belief in the factor in question was required. If a reasonable belief was required, this might stifle investigative journalism since, at an early stage in the investigation, such a belief could not be formed.

# Question 25

You have been asked to research whether the UK requires a new privacy law in order to comply with the its obligations under the Human Rights Act 1998. Present the findings of your research.

## Answer plan

A slightly more inventive way of presenting a reasonably straightforward essay question which requires consideration of the current law of privacy and of means of developing it to ensure that there are no gaps in its protection of the right to privacy. Since the essay is so wide ranging, it will be necessary to be selective in the coverage of topics; otherwise, it will be too superficial. Since protection of personal information is seen as a key privacy issue at present, the coverage below has largely concentrated on that area.

Essentially, the following areas should be considered:

• breach of confidence;

• defamation and malicious falsehood;

• trespass and nuisance;

• development of existing remedies;

- possible incompatibility with the European Convention on Human Rights;
- proposals for a new tort of invasion of privacy;
- recent controversial legislation such as the Regulation of Investigatory Powers Act 2000.

# Answer

Since the European Convention on Human Rights (the Convention) has been incorporated into UK law, a right to respect for private and family life has for the first time become part of domestic law due to Art 8. It should be noted that this is not, strictly speaking, a right to privacy, but merely a right to 'respect', which is a lesser measure. Further, UK law by no means ignores privacy rights, but rather has a strange, sketchy and complicated way of protecting them.Thus, in order to decide whether and how reform is necessary, the present law must first be considered and then compared with relevant European Court of Human Rights (ECHR) case law.

Privacy may be said to encompass two broad interests which may be termed control over intrusions and control over personal information. At present, UK law recognises no general rights to privacy, although there is some evidence, as will be seen, that judges consider it to be an evil which should be remedied. It can be argued that the various heads of tort or equity such as trespass, breach of confidence, copyright and defamation are instances of a general right to privacy, but it is reasonably clear from judicial pronouncements in cases such as *Kaye v Robertson* (1991) that these areas and others must be treated as covering specific and distinct interests which may only incidentally offer protection to privacy – despite the fact that the term 'privacy' is used in a number of the judgments. In such instances, it will be found that a recognised interest such as property actually formed the basis of the ruling. Thus, it will be argued that UK law currently offers a somewhat piecemeal protection to privacy and, therefore, a number of privacy interests are largely unprotected. It will further be argued, however, that this finding does not necessarily lead to the conclusion that further measures to protect privacy are needed.

Traditionally, the law has regarded intrusions on property as being less serious than physical intrusion on the body and, therefore, remedies are found in the civil, rather than the criminal law. A number of private persons, such as reporters, as well as agents of the State, might wish to undertake such intrusion and, therefore, the right to be left alone to enjoy one's property may impose positive obligations upon the State. The term 'intrusion' as used here is being given a wide meaning; it is intended to connote not just physical intrusion, but any activity which results in diminishing the privacy of the home. In this sense, many methods of invasion of the home may be seen as intrusion: trespassing, harassing, photographing, watching or lurking, or snooping using long range electronic surveillance devices. Many sophisticated devices are now available to someone who wants to place a person's home under surveillance and, therefore, at the present time, there is no need for the snooper or watcher to actually invade the territory, as in the past. However, it can be argued that a law which grew up before the possibility of using such technology became available has not caught up with it. The use of surveillance devices was not covered by the Interception of Communications Act 1985, and is not prevented by the Regulation of Investigatory Powers Act 2000.

The main protection from such intrusion is afforded by actions for the torts of trespass or nuisance, but it may be argued that the protection offered is limited. Trespass is defined as entering onto land in the possession of another without lawful justification. It is confined to instances in which there is some physical entry; prying with binoculars is not covered and, obviously, nor is electronic eavesdropping. The limitations of the law have been determined by a certain group of cases. In *Hickman v Massey* (1900), the defendant, who was on the highway, was watching the plaintiff's land. It was found that the plaintiff owned the land under the highway and that the defendant was entitled to make ordinary and reasonable use of it. Watching was held not to be reasonable; the defendant had gone outside the accepted use and therefore had trespassed. Thus, it was made clear that intention in such instances is all-important, but that, unless behaviour could be linked to some kind of physical presence on land, trespass would not provide a remedy.

This case can be contrasted with that of *Bernstein v Skyviews* (1976), in order to determine the limits of trespass. The defendants flew over the plaintiff's land in an aircraft to take photographs of it, and the question arose whether the plaintiff had a right in trespass to prevent such intrusion. It was held that either he had no rights of ownership over the air space to that height or, alternatively, if he did have such rights, s 40 of the Civil Aviation Act 1942 exempted reasonable flights from liability. The court was not prepared to find that the taking of one photograph was unreasonable and a remedy could not be based solely on invasion of privacy as, of course, there is no such tort. The distinction between this decision and that in *Hickman* arises because the plaintiff could not show that he had an interest in what was violated – the air space – and so he fell outside the ambit of trespass.

How far can nuisance provide a means of protecting privacy? Nuisance involves disturbing a person in the enjoyment of his or her land to an extent that the law regards as unreasonable. There is a dearth of authority on the issue of surveillance but, in an Australian case (*Victoria Park Racing Co v Taylor* (1937)), where a platform had been erected in order to gain a view of a racecourse and diminished the value of the plaintiff's business, no remedy in nuisance was available. The activity was held not to affect the use and enjoyment of the land, but *dicta* in the case suggested that there would, in general, be no remedy in nuisance for looking over another's premises. However, *dicta* in *Bernstein* favoured the possibility that grossly invasive, embarrassing surveillance would amount to a nuisance. That possibility was followed up by the Court of Appeal in *Khorasandijan v Bush* (1993), where it was held that harassment could amount to nuisance, independent of any proprietary interest of the claimant. This aspect of the decision was, however, overruled by the House of Lords in *Hunter v Canary Wharf* (1997). A potential route for the development of a broad privacy right was thereby cut off. The House of Lords was partly influenced by the fact that it saw 'harassing' behaviour of the kind which occurred in *Bush* as being dealt with by the new Protection from Harassment Act 1997. Since Parliament had intervened in the area, there was no need for the common law to develop its own remedies. The 1997 Act makes it an offence to pursue a course of conduct which amounts to harassment of another, where the harasser knows or ought to know that this will be its effect. It also provides for a civil remedy in the form or damages or a restraining order. The primary target of this legislation was 'stalking', however, and it has severe limitations as a general weapon against intrusion on privacy. Most significant is the requirement of a 'course of conduct', which means that a single intrusion would not engage the Act's provisions (see *Sai Lau v DPP* (2000)). Although the Act has been used quite frequently since coming into force, the first reported cases concerned the activities of animal rights protesters (*Huntingdon Life Sciences v Curtin* (1997); *DPP v Mosely* (1999)).

It is probably fair to conclude that the common law actions in trespass and nuisance offer only limited protection in this area from the crudest forms of invasion of privacy. Since 1972, there have been repeated recommendations that surveillance would become a crime when surreptitious and that information collected by these means should be banned from publication. These reforms would clearly plug a gap in the law and strengthen its existing protection of privacy.

Intrusion on property may be with a view to obtaining and then publishing personal information. Various areas of the law exist aimed specifically at the dual invasion of privacy which is involved in such activity and, therefore, they control, to a extent, the activity of the media in obtaining information regarding an individual's private life and the publishing the details, possibly in exaggerated terms. These controls may affect both the publication of information and the methods used to obtain it. Control over the publication of personal information is to be found in the laws of confidence, copyright, defamation and malicious falsehood. However, it will be argued that these controls are limited in scope and are aimed at the protection of other interests, making them ill suited to the protection of privacy.

The law of defamation is often thought to be closely linked to the protection of privacy. The difficulty with the use of defamation, however, is that the defence of justification means that it will not usually affect the situation where true facts are revealed. Moreover, the interest protected by defamation – the interest in preserving reputation – is not synonymous with the interest in preserving privacy. A reputation may not suffer, but private facts may nevertheless be spread abroad, which is, in itself, hurtful for the individual affected.

*Kaye v Robertson and Another* (1990) clearly illustrates the inadequacy of defamation as a remedy for invasions of privacy. Mr Kaye, a well known actor, was involved in a car accident and suffered severe injuries to his head and brain. While he was lying in hospital, two journalists got into his room, photographed him and interviewed him. Due to his injuries, he did not object to their presence and shortly after the incident had no recollection of it.

The resultant article gave the impression that Mr Kaye had consented to the interview. His advisers sought and obtained an injunction restraining the defendants from publishing the photographs and the interview. On appeal by the defendants, the Court of Appeal ruled that the plaintiff's claim could not be based on a right to privacy, as such a right is unknown to English law. His true grievance lay in the 'monstrous invasion of privacy' which he had suffered, but he would have to look to other rights of action in order to obtain a remedy, namely libel and malicious falsehood. The basis of the defamation claim was that the article's implication that Mr Kaye had consented to a first 'exclusive' interview for a 'lurid and sensational' newspaper would lower him in the esteem of right thinking people. The Court of Appeal held that this claim might well succeed, but that, as such a conclusion was not inevitable, it could not warrant grant of an interim injunction.

An injunction founded on malicious falsehood, restraining the defendants until trial from publishing anything which suggested that the plaintiff had given an informed consent to the interview or the taking of the photographs, was substituted for the original order. However, this was a limited injunction, which allowed publication of the story with a certain number of the photographs. Thus, it seemed that no effective remedy was available for the plaintiff.

A further possible candidate for the development of a common law remedy for privacy is breach of confidence. This will protect some confidential communications, and its breadth has supported the view that it could afford a general means of protecting personal information. The Younger Committee, which reported in the legal protection of privacy in 1972, considered that confidence was the area of law which offered the most effective protection of privacy. It has a wider ambit than defamation, in that it prevents truthful communications and appears to protect confidential communications, whether or not their unauthorised disclosure causes detriment to the reputation of any person. But it must be remembered that confidence, while quite closely associated with it, is, strictly speaking, protecting a somewhat different interest to that of privacy; it is concerned with the preservation of confidentiality and, therefore, may not be apt to cover all possible circumstances in which private life is laid bare.

At one time, it was thought that, aside from commercial secrets breach of confidence is relevant only where a formal relationship could be identified. In *Stephens v Avery* (1988), however, which concerned information communicated within a close friendship, it was not found necessary to identify a formal relationship between the parties at the time when the information was communicated, thus suggesting that the confidential nature of the information was the important factor: 'It is unconscionable for a person who has received information on the basis that it is confidential subsequently to reveal that information. No particular pre-existing relationship is needed.' These comments seem to cover a communication of confidential information by one complete stranger to another, so long as the communicator informed the recipient of the information that it was confidential. If so, this ruling pointed the way to a broader use of breach of confidence as a means of protecting privacy.

Further possibilities for development in this area where illustrated by the *obiter* comments of Laws J in *Hellewell v Chief Constable of Derbyshire* (1995). The case concerned photographs taken of a man in police custody. Local shopkeepers had sought copies as part of their attempts to reduce shoplifting. The plaintiff sought an injunction to restrain such distribution. Although it was held that a public interest defence would on these facts be bound to succeed at trial, Laws J was clearly of the view that apart from this, the law should recognise a right of privacy in the distribution of an unauthorised photograph, if for example it was taken with a telephoto lens and was of a 'private act'.

As has been noted earlier, the HRA 1998 has been seen as possibly providing the catalyst for further development in this area, and this seems to have occurred with the decision of the

Court of Appeal in *Douglas v Hello!* (2001), which, like *Hellewell*, was concerned with unauthorised photographs. The situation was that the film stars Michael Douglas and Catherine Zeta-Jones had entered into an exclusive contract with the magazine *OK!* for the publication of photographs of their wedding. A rival magazine, *Hello!* obtained photographs of the event (it is unclear how) and proposed to publish them. Douglas and Zeta-Jones sought and obtained an interim injunction restraining such publication. On appeal, the Court of Appeal had to consider whether there was any basis for such an action. In finding that there was, the Court of Appeal, clearly spurred on by the HRA 1998, gave considerable impetus to the argument that the law of breach of confidence has the potential to develop into a full right of privacy. The strongest statements of this kind were made by Sedley LJ. He suggested that *Kaye v Robertson* (1991) might well be decided differently if it recurred, and referring to the *obiter dicta* in *Hellewell*, expressed the view that English law would now protect all those who find themselves subjected to an unwanted intrusion into their private lives. The other members of the Court of Appeal did not go quite so far, but accepted that the claimants had an arguable case for breach of confidence. The interim injunctions were lifted, however, on the basis either of s 12 of the HRA 1998 (which requires freedom of expression to be given particular consideration when injunctive relief is being considered), or because on the normal 'balance of convenience' test from *American Cyanamid v Ethicon* (1975), the more harm would be caused to the defendants by refusing to allow publication, than to the claimants by letting it proceed. In coming to this conclusion, the court was clearly influenced by the fact that the claimants were not seeking to keep their wedding secret, in that they had already sold photographic rights to another magazine.

The decision in this case has clearly pointed the way for the development of privacy rights via the concept of breach of confidence. Whether this is pursued will have to await later cases, and, in particular, the full trial of the action between Michael Douglas and *Hello!* (assuming that it is not settled beforehand). It is significant, however, that in the subsequent case of *Venables v News Group Newspapers* (2001), the Court of Appeal's decision in *Douglas v Hello!* was referred to in a rather different context. In this case, two young men who were in serving sentences for the murder of a young boy sought injunctions restraining the media from revealing information which would enable them to be identified once they were released from prison and given new identities. Granting the injunctions on the basis of confidentiality, the judge made specific reference to the *Douglas* case. She also considered directly the extent to which it was possible to justify such an injunction in the light of Art 10. She felt that it was, because it fell within the restrictions on freedom of expression allowed by Art 10(2). The claimants' lives might be at risk if their identities were revealed, so the injunction had the effect of protecting their right to life under Art 2 of the Convention.

The law of breach of confidence is thus providing the best possibility for the development of a common law right of privacy. Whether this is the best way forward will be considered further below. First, however, some recent statutory developments require discussion.

Two recent statutes have trodden into the field of privacy, that is, the Freedom of Information Act 2000 and the Regulation of Investigatory Powers Act 2000. Little judgment can be made of these statutes until it has been seen how they operate in practice and how they are interpreted by courts and public authorities, but some general comments must be made. The Freedom of Information Act 2000 creates a right of access to government information, but requires consideration of the interests of private individuals in keeping such information private when any request is made. The Regulation of Investigatory Powers Act 2000 has already been the subject of much controversy since, rather than aiming merely to regulate the exercise of police-type powers such as surveillance and interception of communications, it actually extends them in some cases and allows (for example) employers to copy, intercept and read the contents of communications made by their employees at work, whether by telephone, letter or email, unless the communication is clearly labelled as 'private' and security cameras may be trained on employees constantly. Likely consequences of this include that a remarkable amount of emails will be entitled 'private' and hence an employer will risk court action if they are intercepted, but the messages being sent by this statute show a contradictory attitude towards privacy rights.

In conclusion, then, it seems that the common law currently offers only a partial protection of privacy. The most likely future development, as we have seen, is that the HRA 1998 will encourage further expansion of the concept of breach of confidence, as indicated by *Douglas v Hello!* (2001). Would such a development of a general privacy right based on Art 8 of the European Convention be the most satisfactory way forward? Article 8 gives each individual a right to respect for his private and family life, and the ECHR has developed these rights fairly broadly. For example, the State has a positive duty to ensure respect for individuals' private and family lives (*X and Y v The Netherlands* (1986)); searches of the home or office are open to special scrutiny (*Niemietz v Germany* (1993)); there is a right to peaceful enjoyment of the home (*Sporrong and Lonnroth v Sweden* (1982), *Powell and Rayner v UK* (1990)); and surveillance of the home by police or others is at least open to question (*Khan v UK* (2000)). However, there are problems with envisaging Art 8 as a perfect way to provide for protection of privacy in the UK. Art 8(2) allows public authorities to invade or limit privacy in the interests of national security, public safety, the economic well being of the country, to prevent disorder or crime, to protect health and morals or to protect the rights and freedoms of others. These exceptions could be interpreted broadly by any court reluctant to create any privacy-related rights, and the ECHR has been particularly cautious in cases related to personal information (see *Leander v Sweden* (1988)). Thus, much depends upon the attitude taken by future courts and governments. In order to remove the complexity, confusion and gaps in the present situation, a tort of invasion of privacy would be a short term and quick solution, but it appears to be politically unpopular. There also seems to be great difficulty in drafting any new tort to balance the press' right of access to information of public interest against the rights of public figures to some degree of privacy in their lives.

# CHAPTER 5

# POLICE POWERS

## Introduction

Examiners often set problem questions in this area, as the detailed rules of the Police and Criminal Evidence Act (PACE) 1984 and the Codes of Practice made under it lend themselves to such a format. The questions usually concern a number of stages from first contact between police and suspect in the street up to the charge. This allows consideration of the rules governing stop and search, arrest, searching of premises, seizure of articles, detention, treatment in the police station and interviewing. (It must be borne in mind that interviews do not invariably take place in the police station; an important area in the question may concern an interview of the suspect which takes place in the street or in the police car.) You need to be aware of ss 34–37 of the Criminal Justice and Public Order Act 1994, which curtail the right to silence and therefore affect police interviewing. You should also be aware of the extension of police powers in the public order context contained in Pt V of the 1994 Act.

The rules governing obstruction and assault on a police officer in the execution of his duty under s 89 of the Police Act 1996 may be relevant as necessitating analysis of the legality of police conduct in order to determine whether or not a police officer was in the execution of his or her duty. Finally, the question may call for an analysis of the forms of redress available to the suspect in respect of any misuse of police power. If essay questions are set, they often tend to place an emphasis on the balance struck by PACE between suspect's rights and police powers.

Students must be familiar with the following areas:

- provisions under PACE and the Codes of Practice which affect the areas mentioned above;
- provisions under the Criminal Justice and Public Order Act 1994 relevant to police powers, especially ss 34, 36, 37 and 60;
- obstruction and assault on a police officer in the execution of his duty under s 89 of the Police Act 1996;

- issues raised by the revisions to the Codes of Practice made under the PACE;
- the PACE rules governing exclusion of evidence, particularly s 78;
- relevant European Court of Human Rights (ECHR) cases;
- relevant tortious remedies;
- the police complaints mechanism.

# Question 26

Jane is standing on a street corner at 2.00 am on Sunday when she is approached by two police officers in uniform, Andy and Beryl. Andy and Beryl ask her to turn out her pockets. She does so and produces a small quantity of cannabis. Andy tells her to get into the police car; once she is in it, he questions her about the cannabis. After some time, Jane says 'Yes, I've been selling it'. Andy then says, 'I'm arresting you for drug dealing' and cautions her.

Arriving at the police station at 2.30 am, Jane is received by the custody officer, re-cautioned and informed of her rights under Code C. Jane asks if she can see her solicitor and ring her mother. She is told that she can do both in the morning. She is then questioned for one hour, during which she repeats the admission made in the police car. A record of this interview is made and Jane signs it. At 6.00 am on Sunday, she is charged with supplying drugs and allowed home on bail.

Jane now alleges that her confession was untrue; she says she only confessed because she was frightened and upset and wanted to get home.

Advise her on the legality of the police conduct and on whether her confession and the cannabis found will be admissible in evidence against her.

## Answer plan

This is a fairly tricky problem question, since it involves two interviews which may each be tainted by breaches of PACE. It must first be established that breaches of PACE have occurred and then determined whether or not they are likely to lead to exclusion of admissions made during the interviews affected. Note that the question does not call for consideration of forms of redress available to Jane *other than* exclusion of evidence. Essentially, the following points should be considered:

- the lawfulness of Jane's arrest under s 24 of PACE, bearing in mind provisions of the Misuse of Drugs Act 1971;
- the legality of the stop and search under s 1 of PACE and Code of Practice A;
- the applicability of the prohibition on interviews outside the police station under para 11.1 of Code C;
- assuming that the interview outside the police station was unlawful, the likelihood that it will be excluded from evidence;
- possible breaches of ss 58 and 56 affecting the second interview;
- assuming such breaches are established, the likelihood that the second interview will be excluded from evidence (taking into account ss 34–37 of the Criminal Justice and Public Order Act 1994);
- the likelihood that the cannabis will be excluded from evidence – this will depend in part on the conclusion reached as to the second issue above.

## Answer

Confessions may be excluded from evidence under s 78 or 76 of the PACE, but other evidence can be excluded only under s 78. A first step in the direction of exclusion from evidence of the cannabis and the admissions made by Jane is to demonstrate that substantial and significant breaches of PACE or the Codes have occurred.

The facts of the instant case may support an argument that Jane was unlawfully arrested. If the arrest was unlawful, the subsequent detention would probably also be unlawful, as her detention is dependent on the power to detain for questioning under s 37(2) of PACE, which is, in turn, dependent on an 'arrest', not an unlawful arrest. Jane is arrested for supplying cannabis, an offence arising under s 5(3) of the Misuse of Drugs Act 1971. This is an arrestable offence under s 24(1)(b) of PACE, as it carries a sentence of five years or more (Sched 4 of the Misuse of Drugs Act). In order to arrest under s 24, it is necessary to show that Andy and Beryl had reasonable grounds for suspecting that Jane was in possession of the cannabis with intent to supply it. Her possession of the cannabis, coupled with the admission she makes, is sufficient to give rise to the necessary suspicion, which is described in paras 1.6 and 1.7 of Code A.

However, the cannabis is discovered during the course of a stop and search which, at first sight, appears to be of doubtful legality. It may appear strange that an illegal stop and search could provide the reasonable suspicion necessary to found a lawful arrest. This point need not be determined, because it may be argued that the stop and search was consensual and therefore lawful (it will be assumed that Jane does not fall within a category of persons exempt from consensual searches under Code A, Note 1E). Although it is not clear that Jane gave consent to the search, Andy and Beryl were under a duty only to seek her co-operation, not her express consent (Code A, Note 1D(b)) and, on that basis, as Jane accedes to the request made, could be said to have fulfilled the requirements of Code A in respect of consensual searches. Thus far, the necessary reasonable suspicion was properly arrived at – on that basis, the arrest and, therefore, the subsequent detention were lawful.[1]

The next question to consider is whether, by questioning Jane in the police car, Andy and Beryl breached the prohibition on interviews outside the police station under para 11.1 of Code C. If para 11.1 is to apply, two conditions must be satisfied: the questioning must constitute an interview under Code C, Note 11.1A, and the decision to arrest must have been made before the interview took place. It is apparent that the first of these conditions has been met, as questions were put to Jane which concerned her suspected involvement in drug dealing. The second is less clearly satisfied: the police might argue that until Jane admitted that she had been selling drugs, the level of suspicion was not high enough to justify an arrest; however, the stronger argument is that the available facts gave rise to a level of suspicion sufficient to justify an arrest (for possession of cannabis, which is also an arrestable offence, given the penalty of five years' imprisonment available under the Misuse of Drugs Act 1971) even before the admission in question was made. Therefore, the questioning falls within para 11.1 and should not have taken place at all until the police station was reached.[2]

Paragraph 11.1 was included in the revised Code C as a means of preventing the police circumventing the various safeguards available only in the police station, in particular, tape recording under Code E and access to legal advice under s 58 and para 6.6 of Code C. Could it be argued that the interview should be excluded from evidence under s 76, as it took place outside the police station without those safeguards?

Under s 76(2)(a), the prosecution must prove beyond reasonable doubt that Jane's confession was not obtained by oppression. According to the Court of Appeal in *Fulling* (1987), 'oppression' should be given its dictionary definition: 'The exercise of authority or power in a burdensome, harsh or wrongful manner.' The breach of para 11.1 could fall within this definition on the basis that the police acted in a wrongful manner. However, the Court of Appeal in *Hughes* (1988) ruled that oppression could not arise in the absence of 'misconduct' on the part of the police; in the context of the case, 'misconduct' appeared to mean bad faith. On that basis, and assuming that Andy and Beryl merely misinterpreted the level of suspicion connoted by the wording of para 11.1, the holding of the interview in the police car could not be termed oppressive.

Under s 76(2)(b), it is necessary to show that something was said or done in the first interview in circumstances conducive of unreliability. Following the rulings of the Court of Appeal in *Delaney* (1989) and *Barry* (1991), it is essential under this head to identify some special factor in the situation (such as the mental state of the defendant or an offer made to him) which make it crucial that the interview should be properly conducted and recorded. In other words, a breach of PACE cannot amount to both 'circumstances' and 'something said or done' under s 76(2)(b). As the only special circumstance in the situation is the breach of para 11.1, a strong argument for exclusion of the interview under this head of s 76 cannot be put forward.

However, even if the first interview is admissible under s 76, the trial judge will still have a discretion to exclude it from evidence under s 78 if, due to the circumstances in which it was obtained, its admission would have a significantly adverse effect on the fairness of the trial. A number of possible arguments can be put forward under s 78. The view could be taken that although suspects need not be informed of the right to legal advice until the police station is reached, questioning a person away from the station is, in effect, depriving him or her of that right. If this assumption is accepted, the next stage of the argument may be based on that successfully put forward in *Samuel* (1988): admissions causally related to an improper denial of access to legal advice can be excluded under s 78. Two tests must be satisfied if this argument is to succeed: first, according to the rulings of the Court of Appeal in *Mathews* (1990) and *Pall* (1991), the breach of para 11.1 must be shown to be substantial and significant. This can be established on the basis that para 11.1 is concerned with ensuring that important safeguards for the suspect are secured, such as access to legal advice.[3]

Secondly, it must be shown that the breach of para 11.1 is causally related to the admissions made by Jane in the police car. The chain of causation would be fairly long, but could be established as follows: had Jane been taken to the police station to be interviewed, as she should have been under para 11.1, she would have been notified of her right to legal advice; had she been so notified, she would have asked for advice; had she received advice, she would not have made the admissions in question, because her solicitor might have advised her to remain silent. This last link in the chain is not easy to establish in the light of s 36 of the Criminal Justice and Public Order Act 1994, since it provides that a failure to account for possession of a substance (in this instance, the cannabis) means that inferences may be drawn at trial from that failure. However, s 36 applies after arrest and, at the point in question, Jane had not been arrested. On the other hand, had she been taken to the police station as she should have been, she would have been arrested *before* the interview occurred, in which case, s 36 would have applied. Presumably, in that case, the solicitor might have been unlikely to advise her to refuse to account for the presence of the cannabis. Thus, it is concluded that the causal relationship in question has not clearly been established. In *Bailey v DPP* (1998), it was held that an interview occurs whenever the purpose of questioning is to get D to incriminate himself, and thus a caution must be given in all such situations. Jane should have been cautioned before *any* questions (other than names, etc) were asked.

It might further be argued that as Jane failed in fact to receive advice at the police station, it would have made no difference to the situation had she been taken there as she should have been. This argument raises the question of impropriety at the police station and it is submitted that the police cannot use their own impropriety to found an argument that the chain of causation in question was broken. It will be assumed at this point that the police did act improperly in failing to afford Jane advice at the police station, but it cannot be further assumed that, had she had advice, she would not have made the admissions in question. Both these points will be considered below in relation to the second interview. On this analysis, there has been a breach of para 11.1 which is not, however, causally related to the admissions made in the police car. Therefore, it would seem that they will not be excluded from evidence. The ECHR takes a slightly different perspective: in *Khan* (2000) and *Condron* (2000), it was held that the only question is whether the proceedings as a whole, including the way in which the evidence was obtained, were fair. So, any evidence obtained improperly or in breach of PACE Codes may be excluded on the basis that it may prejudice the fairness of the trial.

Can it also be argued further under s 78 that the first interview should be excluded from evidence as unreliable as it should have taken place at the police station where it would have been tape recorded under the provisions of Code E or contemporaneously recorded under para 11.5 of Code C? Jane should at least have been offered the notes of the interview to sign under para 11.13 of Code C and *Bailey v DPP* (1998). Against this, it may be argued that Jane is not alleging that she did not make the admissions in question, but that they are untrue. Thus, the failure to tape record the interview could be said to be irrelevant. This argument could also apply to the second interview which was not contemporaneously recorded or tape recorded in breach of paras 11.5 and 11.10 of Code C or of Code E. The police appear to have recorded it in accordance with the provisions of para 11.13 of Code C; that provision, however, applies to comments made outside the context of an interview; clearly the recording was defective.[4] A similar situation arose in *Keenan* (1989) – the Court of Appeal held that the admissions in question should have been excluded under s 78. This is probably the stronger argument.

Can an argument also be advanced that the second interview should be excluded from evidence under s 76? As noted above, unless it can be shown that the custody officer acted in bad faith in failing to allow Jane access to a solicitor, it seems that s 76(2)(a) will not apply. However, it could be argued under s 76(2)(b) that Jane was in a vulnerable position in the second interview, since she had already been interviewed unlawfully in the police car and had made admissions then: in those circumstances, the interview should have been conducted with particular propriety; the failure to afford her legal advice could be said in that context to amount to something conducive of unreliability. Some support for this view comes from the case of *Delaney* and perhaps from the ruling of the Court of Appeal in *Ismail* (1990) that subsequent interviews may be tainted with illegality affecting earlier interviews, although that case was concerned with the operation of s 76(2)(a) and s 78.

It will now be considered whether a further argument for the exclusion from evidence of the second interview under s 78 can be advanced on the basis that the police should have complied with Jane's request for legal advice. Following the ruling in *Samuel* (1988), a breach of s 58 which entitles the suspect to legal advice will occur if the suspect is denied advice, unless one of the exceptions under s 58(8) can be invoked. In the instant case, the police have not expressly invoked an exception, but, in any event, the exceptions will only apply if, *inter alia*,[5] some quality about the particular solicitor in question could found a reasonable belief that he or she would bring about one of the contingencies envisaged in s 58(8) if contacted. There is nothing to suggest that the police considered this possibility and, therefore, s 58 has been breached. This strict view of s 58 accords with the prominence given to legal advice in the PACE scheme.[6] It is given additional weight by the importance attached to access to legal advice by the European Court of Human Rights in cases such as *Murray (John) v UK* (1996) and *Averill v UK* (2000). The HRA 1998 means that these decisions will need to be taken into account in considering this area.

Following the above argument under s 58, it appears that s 56, which affords detainees the right to have someone informed of the arrest, has also been breached. However, such a breach would not appear to be causally related to the admissions made and, therefore, will not contribute to the argument for their exclusion under s 78. Is the breach of s 58 causally related to the admissions made in the second interview? It may be that Jane decided to make the admissions and would have done so had she had advice. This argument succeeded in *Dunford* (1990) and *Alladice* (1988), on the basis that the appellants in those cases were experienced criminals, aware of their rights. Jane may be an inexperienced suspect; however, she may consider that she should say something to account for the presence of the cannabis in the light of s 31 of the 1994 Act. On the other hand, the solicitor, weighing up the situation, might have considered that she should remain silent, despite the adverse inferences which would later be drawn. On this analysis, the requisite causal relationship may not exist and the second interview will probably not be excluded from evidence under s 78.

Will the cannabis be excluded from evidence under s 78? According to the analysis above, the stop and search could be characterised as consensual; no breach of Code A therefore took place.[7] In any event, according to *Thomas* (1990) and *Effick* (1992), real evidence will be excluded only if obtained with deliberate illegality.

In conclusion, it appears that both the first and second interviews may be excluded from evidence, the first under s 78 and the second under s 78 or s 76(2)(b). The finding of the cannabis will, however, be admissible in evidence. Further, the risk of an unfair trial, in breach of Art 6 of the European Convention, may lead a domestic court to exclude any of the evidence because of the manner in which it was obtained, since the ECHR views the proceedings as a whole, rather than separately inspecting the legality or fairness of each event.

## Notes

1  However, it could be argued that the arrest for supplying drugs as opposed to merely possessing drugs is based on reasonable suspicion deriving from an unlawful interview (the

question of the unlawfulness of the interview is considered below) and is therefore an unlawful arrest. Against this, it may be argued that the prohibition on interviewing outside the police station was aimed at ensuring that all the proper safeguards were available; therefore, a breach of the prohibition is relevant in evidential terms, but cannot render an otherwise lawful arrest unlawful.

2   The exception under para 11.1(b) does not apply, as the questions were not directed to determining the whereabouts of other persons involved in drug dealing. Urgent interviewing is allowed under this provision only with the object of preventing the contingency envisaged in it arising.

3   This argument could be supported by the ruling of the Court of Appeal in *Absolam* (1988), in which it was held that the suspect must be notified of his or her entitlement to legal advice before any questioning can take place.

4   If Jane later testifies that she did make the admissions which were improperly recorded, no dispute over the content of the admissions will arise. Jane will merely be seeking to show that the circumstances were such that they were likely to be untrue. However, if, at trial, the particular unfairness likely to arise from the improper recording is not specified, but the breaches of the recording provisions affecting both interviews are pointed out, it may appear that the interviews cannot be relied on and they will then be excluded from evidence under s 78.

5   A further condition is that Jane is being detained in respect of a serious arrestable offence. She is in detention in respect of an arrestable offence: her arrest took place under s 24, as opposed to s 25; whether or not the offence can be termed a serious arrestable offence depends on the provisions of s 116. The section as amended includes as serious arrestable offences under sub-s (2)(a) 'offences mentioned in paras (a) to (f) of s 1(3) of the Drug Trafficking Act 1994'. Thus, this condition is fulfilled.

6   The police might argue that the failure to contact a solicitor arose only due to the lateness of the hour. However, if such an argument were to prevail, s 58 would be rendered almost worthless. The police could have tried to obtain the services of the duty solicitor or could have postponed the interview until

Jane's own solicitor arrived. This argument could be supported by the provision of para 6.4 of Code C that no attempt must be made to persuade the suspect to forego advice: a failure to make efforts to obtain advice could be characterised as part of such an attempt, in the sense that it might have the effect of persuading the detainee to forego advice. It is also supported by the strict approach to the legal advice provisions taken in *Beycan* (1990) by the Court of Appeal.

7   Had the search been non-consensual, it might have been possible to argue, following *Edward Fennelly* (1989), that the products of the search should be excluded from evidence on the basis that there was no power to search in the circumstances: the fact that Jane was standing on a street corner in the early hours of the morning would not be enough to give rise to the reasonable suspicion that drugs were being carried required by s 23(2) of the Misuse of Drugs Act 1971, which provides a power of stop and search. This power will be interpreted in the same way as that arising under paras 1.6 and 1.7 of Code A.

# Question 27

Albert and Bill, two policemen in uniform and driving a police car, see Colin outside a factory gate at 11.30 pm on a Saturday. Albert and Bill know that Colin has a conviction for burglary. Colin looks nervous and is looking repeatedly at his watch. Bearing in mind a spate of burglaries in the area, Albert and Bill ask Colin what he is doing. Colin replies that he is waiting for a friend. Dissatisfied with this response, Bill tells Colin to turn out his pockets, which he does. Bill seizes a bunch of keys which Colin produces and, still suspicious, asks Colin to accompany them to the police station. Colin then becomes abusive and when Bill takes hold of him to restrain him, Colin hits Bill in the mouth. Albert and Bill then bundle Colin into the police car and tell him he is being arrested for 'assaulting a police officer in the execution of his duty'. They then proceed to Colin's flat and search it, despite his protests. They discover nothing relating to a burglary, but do discover a small amount of cannabis, which they seize.

Albert and Bill then take Colin to the police station, arriving at 12.20 am. He is cautioned, informed of his rights under Code C by the Custody Officer and told that he is suspected of dealing in cannabis. Colin asks if he can see a solicitor, but his request is refused 'for the time being'. Colin is then questioned for two hours, but makes no reply to the questions. He then has a short break; when the interview recommences, he is re-cautioned and reminded of his right to legal advice. After another two hours, he admits to supplying cannabis. All the interviews are tape recorded. He is then charged with supplying cannabis and with assaulting a police officer in the execution of his duty.

Advise Colin.

## Answer plan

This is a reasonably straightforward question, but it does cover a wide range of issues. The most straightforward approach is probably to consider the legality of the police conduct at every point. Once this issue has been determined at each point, the applicability of the possible forms of redress can be considered. It should be noted that the examinee is merely asked to 'advise Colin'; therefore, all relevant possibilities should be discussed. Essentially, the following issues should be considered:

- legality of the search under ss 1 and 2 of the Police and Criminal Evidence Act (PACE) 1984 and Code of Practice A;
- assaulting a police officer in the execution of his duty under s 89(1) of the Police Act 1996;
- the legality of the arrest under s 25 of PACE;
- the legality of the search of premises and the seizure of the cannabis under ss 18 and 19 of PACE;
- access to legal advice under s 58 of PACE – legality of the refusal of advice;
- exclusion of evidence under ss 76 and 78 of PACE – relevance of s 36 of the Criminal Justice and Public Order Act 1994;

- relevant tortious remedies;
- police complaints procedure;
- relevant European Court of Human Rights (ECHR) cases.

# Answer

The legality of the police conduct in this instance will be considered first; any possible forms of redress open to Colin will then be examined.

The first contact between the police officers and Colin appears to be of a voluntary nature: the officers are, of course, entitled to ask questions, which Colin may answer if he wishes to (*Rice v Connolly* (1966)). It is not therefore necessary to ask whether Albert and Bill are invoking powers of stop and search under s 1 of PACE at this stage. When Colin is asked to turn out his pockets, this appears to be a request which he could refuse. It may therefore be characterised as part of a voluntary search. Although it is not clear that Colin consented to the search, Albert and Bill were under a duty only to explain that he may withhold consent (Code A, Note 1D(b)) and, on that basis, as Colin accedes to the request made, could be said to have fulfilled the requirements of Code A in respect of consensual searches.

However, the seizure of the keys does not appear to be done with Colin's consent and therefore will only be lawful if it is part of a lawful stop and search. Thus, it must be shown that the police officers complied with the provisions of ss 1 and 2 of PACE and of Code A. Under s 1(2), a police officer may search for stolen or prohibited articles if he has reasonable grounds (s 1(3)) for believing that he will find such articles. The necessary reasonable suspicion is defined in paras 1.6 and 1.7 of Code A. There must be some objective basis for it which will relate to the nature of the article suspected of being carried. Various factors are mentioned in para 1.6 which may be taken into account in arriving at the necessary reasonable suspicion. These include the time and place, the behaviour of the person concerned and the carrying of certain articles in an area which has recently experienced a number of burglaries. In the instant situation, the lateness of the hour and the fact that Colin is outside a factory in an area which has recently experienced burglaries, coupled with his nervous behaviour, might give rise to a generalised suspicion, but it may be argued that the suspicion does not relate specifically enough to a particular article, since there is very little to suggest that Colin is carrying any particular article. Following this argument, no power to stop and search arises; the seizure of the keys is therefore unlawful. In any event, if reasonable suspicion is present, the search and seizure is unlawful, since the procedural requirements of s 2 are breached.[1]

The request made to come to the police station appears to assume that Colin will come on a voluntary basis; therefore, it is not necessary at this point to consider whether a power to arrest arises. However, after Colin becomes abusive, Bill takes hold of him to restrain him. If this restraining is not part of a lawful arrest and therefore lawful under s 117, it could be characterised as an assault on Colin. Have Albert and Bill a power to arrest at this point? Any such power would have to concern an arrest on suspicion of participation in burglary and therefore would arise under s 24, as burglary is an arrestable offence. However, in order to invoke the power under s 24, Albert and Bill would have to show reasonable suspicion that Colin is involved in burglary and, as already considered under s 1, no such suspicion arises on the facts; Colin's abusiveness could not be said to add anything to the suspicion already present. Therefore, no power to arrest arises; the restraint of Colin is unlawful. In any event, it seems that the restraint may not have been an integral part of an arrest; if not, following *Kenlin v Gardner* (1967), it was clearly unlawful. Either argument obviously produces the same result.

Albert and Bill then arrest Colin for assault on a police officer in the execution of his duty, an offence arising under s 89(1) of the Police Act 1996. Is this arrest lawful? There is no power to arrest under s 89 of the Police Act 1996 and the offence in question is not an arrestable offence under s 24. Therefore, the arrest power must arise, if it arises at all, under s 25 or at common law, on the basis that the assault amounted to a breach of the peace. If it is to arise under s 25, two tests must be satisfied. First, it must be shown that one of the general arrest conditions under s 25(3) was fulfilled. It may be argued that the arrest was necessary to prevent Colin causing further physical harm to Bill; in that case, the condition under s 25(3)(d)(i) would be satisfied. Secondly, Albert and Bill must have reasonable suspicion that the assault has been perpetrated. It can be argued that Bill was not at that point in the execution of his duty, as he had laid hands on Colin unlawfully; therefore, can Albert and Bill be said to have reasonable suspicion as to that aspect of the offence? It can be argued that the reason given for the arrest, following *Christie v Leachinsky* (1947), and receiving some support from *Abassy v Metropolitan Police Commissioner* (1990), must ensure that the arrested person knows which act he has been arrested for, but that there is no need to be more precise than that. The reason given in the instant case conveyed the fact that the arrest was for striking Bill; arguably, this was sufficient; the necessary reasonable suspicion is therefore established. But, more recently, in *Mullady v DPP* (1997), where the arrest reasons were given as 'obstruction' (which is also not arrestable), it was held that where the reasons given to a suspect for his arrest are invalid or the wrong reasons, then the arrest itself is unlawful.

However, it may be argued, following *Marsden* (1868) and *Fennell* (1970), that, since Bill had exceeded his authority in restraining Colin, Colin was entitled to resist by way of reasonable force; any such resistance would be lawful and, therefore, could not amount to an assault. Assuming that Colin's action amounted to no more than reasonable force, he has not committed an assault. Thus, it appears that no power to arrest arises; the arrest therefore appears to be unlawful. When Colin is bundled into the car, Albert and Bill are not therefore entitled to use reasonable force under s 117, as they are not in the exercise of an arrest power. Thus, the subsequent detention is presumably also unlawful.

The search of Colin's flat also appears to be unlawful. Under s 18, a power to enter and search premises after arrest arises, but only in instances when the arrest is for an arrestable offence. As the arrest has been effected under s 25, this condition is not satisfied. It follows from this that the power of seizure under s 19(2) does not arise, as it may only be exercised under s 19(1) by a constable lawfully on the premises. The seizure of the cannabis is therefore unlawful.

At the police station, Colin is denied access to legal advice. Delay in affording such access will be lawful if one of the contingencies envisaged under s 58(8) will arise if a solicitor is contacted. Following *Samuel* (1988), the police must have a clear basis for this belief. In this instance, the police made no effort to invoke one of the exceptions and have therefore breached s 58 and para 6 of Code C, which provides that, once a suspect has requested advice, he must not be interviewed until he has received it.

Having identified a series of illegal acts on the part of the police, it will now be necessary to consider the redress available to Colin in respect of them. The first such act was the unlawful seizure of the keys. The appropriate cause of action in this instance will be trespass to goods; damages will, however, be minimal.

In taking hold of Colin outside the context of a lawful arrest, Bill commits assault and battery and breaches Art 5 of the European Convention on Human Rights (the Convention). The facts of the instant case closely resemble those of *Collins v Willcock* (1984) or *Kenlin v Gardner* (1967), which established this principle. Further, the unlawful arrest and the subsequent unlawful detention will support a claim of false imprisonment. The entry of the flat was unlawful, as was the seizure of the cannabis; Colin could therefore sue the police authority for trespass to land and to goods.

Further, Colin may hope that the cannabis will be excluded from evidence under s 78, as it was found during the course of an unlawful search. However, according to *Thomas* (1990) and *Effick* (1992), real evidence will be excluded only if obtained with deliberate illegality. The first instance decision in *Edward Fennelly* (1989), in which a failure to give the reason for a stop and search led to exclusion of the search, appears then to be out of line with the other authorities. It may be that Albert and Bill merely misconstrued their powers in thinking that a power of entry to premises arose in the circumstances, rather than deliberately perpetrating an illegal stop and search. In any event, it may be very hard to show that they acted in bad faith. If so, it appears that no strong argument for exclusion of the cannabis from evidence arises.

Can a reasonable argument be advanced that Colin's admissions might be excluded from evidence under s 76? Following *Alladice* (1988) and *Hughes* (1988), unless it can be shown that the custody officer acted in bad faith in failing to allow Colin access to a solicitor, it seems that s 76(2)(a) will not apply.

Following *Delaney* (1989), it is necessary to show under s 76(2)(b) that the defendant was in some particularly difficult or vulnerable position, making the breach of PACE of special significance. Since this does not appear to be the case here, it seems that s 76(2)(b) cannot be invoked.

On the other hand, Colin's admissions may be excluded from evidence under s 78 on the basis that the police breached s 58. If so, following *Samuel* (1988), it must be shown that the breach of s 58 was causally related to the admissions made in the second interview. It may be that Colin was aware that he could keep silent (although he was aware that this might disadvantage him at trial), but decided to make admissions and would have done so had he had advice. This argument succeeded in *Dunford* (1990) and *Alladice* (1988), on the basis that the appellants in those cases were experienced criminals, aware of their rights. It appears that Colin did remain silent for some time; possibly, therefore, he would have made the admissions in any event. It might be argued that access to legal advice would have added nothing to his ability to weigh up the situation.[2] On this analysis, the requisite causal relationship does not exist and the admissions might not, therefore, be excluded from evidence under s 78.

On the other hand, the ECHR has placed considerable importance on the right of access to legal advice in cases such as *Murray (John) v UK* (1996) and *Averill v UK* (2000). It has held that delay in access can amount to a breach of Art 6 of the Convention. This might make the court more willing to exclude evidence obtained while access to legal advice was refused. It also raises the possibility of Colin being able to bring an action against the police under s 7 of the HRA 1998, claiming infringement of his Art 6 rights.

A further possibility is that the actions of the police could be the subject of a complaint, as could the other unlawful actions mentioned. Under s 84, the complaint would go in the first instance to the chief officer of police of the force Albert and Bill belong to.

Finally, Colin may want to know whether the charge of assaulting a police officer in the execution of his duty will succeed. Clearly, it will fail on the argument that Colin's actions did not amount to an assault, as he was entitled to resist Bill. Moreover, it has been determined that Bill was outside the execution of his duty.

Thus, in conclusion, a number of tort actions are available to Colin, as well as the possibility of an HRA 1998 action, or of making a complaint in respect of Albert and Bill's behaviour. It further seems that the charge of assaulting a police officer will be unsuccessful. However, it remains in doubt whether Colin's admissions and the cannabis found will be admissible in evidence against him.

### Notes

1   Had it been found that the stop and search was lawful, the seizure of the keys could nevertheless be unlawful on the basis that the keys do not fall into the category of 'stolen or prohibited articles' which may be seized if discovered under s 1(6). Thus, on three separate grounds, the seizure of the keys is unlawful.

2   This argument could be explored in more detail. It could be argued that, despite his conviction, Colin may not be well equipped to withstand questioning. Possibly, had his solicitor been present, he or she might have been able to help Colin to keep silent (if that appeared to be in his best interests, despite the provision of s 36 of the Criminal Justice and Public Order Act 1994 that a failure to account for having a substance in his possession might lead to the drawing of adverse inferences at trial) even after the prolonged questioning.

# Question 28

At midnight on Saturday night, Carl and Bert, two policemen in uniform and driving a police car, see Ali, a black youth, hurrying through the street. Bearing in mind a knife attack perpetrated at 11.50 pm by black youths in the area, they approach Ali and ask him where he has just been. He refuses to answer their questions and they ask him to get into the police car. Bert then says, 'We're going to search you. OK?'. Ali does not reply, but makes no resistance to the search. Carl and Bert then search him and discover a knife. Carl then questions Ali as to the whereabouts of the others involved in the attack; Ali does not reply, but does admit that he was with some other youths in the street where the attack took place at 11.50 pm. Bert cautions Ali and informs him that he is under arrest for wounding.

They arrive at the police station at 12.35 am. Ali is re-cautioned and informed of his rights under Code C by the custody officer, Doris. He makes a request to contact his solicitor, but Eileen, the investigating officer, is unable to contact the solicitor. Eileen then asks Ali whether he is prepared to go ahead with the interview without a solicitor and he reluctantly agrees to do so. He is then questioned for two hours, but refuses to answer the questions. After a break, a further interview is begun and he is re-cautioned and reminded of his right to free legal advice (both interviews are tape recorded). After half an hour, he admits that he participated in the knife attack, although he says that he acted in self-defence. He is asked to sign the notes of the interview in the police car and does so.

At 8.00 am on Sunday morning, he is charged with wounding and is remanded in custody.

Ali (who has no previous convictions, but was cautioned for theft two years previously when he was 16) now alleges that his confession was untrue, that he knew nothing of the attack until informed of it by the police and was merely carrying the knife as a precaution. He says 'I only confessed because I was desperate to get home, as I knew my family would be out of their minds with worry. I wasn't even there; I only said I was because I was scared of them'.

Advise Ali as to whether the three interviews and the finding of the knife will be admissible in evidence against him.

## Answer plan

This is a fairly tricky problem question, since it involves police behaviour which is close to rule bending, as opposed to rule breaking. It must first be established that breaches of the Police and Criminal Evidence Act (PACE) 1984 have occurred and then asked whether or not they are likely to lead to exclusion of admissions made during any interview affected. Note that the question does not call for consideration of forms of redress available to Ali other than exclusion of evidence. Essentially, the following matters should be considered:

- the lawfulness of Ali's arrest under s 24 of PACE;
- the legality of the stop and search;
- the applicability of the prohibition on interviews outside the police station under para 11.1 of Code C, bearing in mind the exception under para 11.1(b);
- a possible breach of para 11.5 of Code C in respect of the first interview (in the police car) – impracticability of contemporaneous recording?;
- a possible breach of para 6 of Code C affecting the third interview;
- assuming such a breach is established, the likelihood that the third interview will be excluded from evidence – relevance of s 36 of the Criminal Justice and Public Order Act 1994;
- inferences to be drawn from the second interview at trial under ss 34 and 36 of the Criminal Justice and Public Order Act – admissibility of the second interview;
- the likelihood that the knife will be excluded from evidence under s 78.

# Answer

Confessions may be excluded from evidence under s 78 or s 76 of PACE. A first step in the direction of exclusion from evidence of the admissions made by Ali is to demonstrate that substantial and significant breaches of PACE or the Codes have occurred.

The facts of the instant case may support an argument that Ali was unlawfully arrested. If the arrest was unlawful, the subsequent detention would also be unlawful, as his detention is dependent on the power to detain for questioning under s 37(2) of PACE which is, in turn, dependent on an 'arrest', not an unlawful arrest. Ali is arrested for wounding, an offence arising under s 18 or 20 of the Offences Against the Person Act 1861. Both offences are arrestable offences under s 24(1)(b) of PACE. In order to arrest under the section, it is necessary to show that Carl and Bert had reasonable grounds for suspecting that Ali had committed the wounding. Ali's proximity in time and place to the offence coupled with his possession of the knife are, it is submitted, sufficient to give rise to the necessary suspicion which is described in paras 1.6 and 1.7 of Code A.

However, the knife is discovered during the course of a stop and search of doubtful legality. It would be strange if an illegal stop and search could provide the reasonable suspicion necessary to found a lawful arrest. This point need not be determined, because it may be argued that the stop and search was consensual and therefore lawful (since Ali is 18, he does not fall within a category of persons exempt from consensual searches under Code A, Note 1E). It is not clear that Ali gave consent to the search; Carl and Bert were under a duty to seek his consent (Code A, Note 1D(b)) and to explain that he may withhold consent – if this is done, they could be said to have fulfilled the requirements of Code A in respect of consensual searches. Thus, the necessary reasonable suspicion was properly arrived at: the arrest and, therefore, subsequent detention were probably lawful.

The next question to consider is whether, by questioning Ali in the police car, Carl and Bert breached the prohibition on interviews outside the police station under para 11.1 of Code C. If para 11.1 is to apply, two conditions must be satisfied: the questioning must constitute an interview under Code C, Note 11.1A; and the decision to arrest must have been made at the point when the questioning took place. It is apparent that the first of these conditions has been met, as questions were put to Ali which concerned his suspected involvement in the wounding. The second is less clearly satisfied: the police might argue that, until Ali admitted that he was in the street when the wounding took place, the level of suspicion was not high enough to justify an arrest; however, the stronger argument is that the other factors present (the finding of the knife, his proximity to the offence already observed by the officers) gave rise to a level of suspicion sufficient to justify an arrest even before the admission in question was made. Therefore, the questioning falls within para 11.1 and should not have taken place at all until the police station was reached, unless the exception under para 11.1(b) can apply. The exception may be invoked if a delay in interviewing would be likely to 'lead to the alerting of other persons suspected of having committed an offence, but not yet arrested for it'. The questions were directed to determining the whereabouts of the other youths involved in the attack who might be alerted by the news of Ali's arrest. It is only necessary to show a likelihood that such a contingency might arise, not a reasonable suspicion; therefore, it appears that this exception may be invoked. No breach of para 11.1 has therefore occurred. But, in *Bailey* (1998), it was held that an 'interview' exists whenever the purpose of the questioning is for D to incriminate himself, and so a caution should have been given *before* the question.

If an interview takes place outside the police station, but falls outside the para 11.1 prohibition, the verifying and recording provisions under paras 11.10 and 11.5 will apply, with the proviso that contemporaneous recording may be impracticable. The mere fact that an interview is conducted in the street or in a police car, as here, may not be enough to support an assertion that it could not be contemporaneously recorded. This seems to follow from the decision in *Fogah* (1989). What is impracticable does not connote something that is extremely difficult, but must involve more than mere inconvenience (*Parchment* (1989)). Note-taking while the suspect was dressing and showing the officers round his flat was held to be impracticable. However, Carl and Bert are in the police car at the time and Ali has shown no sign of violence. Whilst it might have been inconvenient to record the interview in the police car, it would not have been difficult. It appears, then, that para 11.5 has been breached. It should be noted that Carl and Bert assumed wrongly that the minimum level of protection provided by para 11.13 for comments made outside the context of an interview applied: a written record was made of the interview and the notes were offered to Ali to sign.

Could it be argued that the interview should be excluded under s 76, as it was not contemporaneously recorded? Under s 76(2)(a), the prosecution must prove beyond reasonable doubt that Ali's confession was not obtained by oppression. According to the Court of Appeal in *Fulling* (1987), 'oppression' should be given its dictionary definition: 'The exercise of authority or power in a burdensome, harsh or wrongful manner.' The breach of para 11.5 could fall within this definition on the basis that the police acted in a wrongful manner. However, the Court of Appeal in *Hughes* (1988) ruled that oppression could not arise in the absence of 'misconduct' on the part of the police; in the context of the case, 'misconduct' clearly meant bad faith. On that basis, and assuming that Carl and Bert merely misinterpreted the level of suspicion connoted by the wording of para 11.1, the holding of the interview in the police car could not be termed oppressive.

Under s 76(2)(b), it is necessary to show that something was said or done in the first interview in circumstances conducive of unreliability. Following the rulings of the Court of Appeal in *Delaney* (1989) and *Barry* (1991), it is essential under this head to identify some special factor in the situation (such as the mental state of the defendant or an offer made to him) which make it crucial that the interview should be properly recorded. In other words, a breach of PACE cannot amount to both 'circumstances' and 'something said or done' under s 76(2)(b).

However, even if the first interview is admissible under s 76, the trial judge will still have a discretion to exclude it from evidence under s 78 if, due to the circumstances in which it was obtained, its admission would have a significantly adverse effect on the fairness of the trial. Can it be argued under s 78 that the first interview should be excluded from evidence as unreliable, due to the lack of contemporaneous recording? Ali is not alleging that he did not make the admissions in question, but that they are untrue. Presumably, he signed the interview record as a means of indicating his acceptance that he had made the admissions, although he intended to allege that he had lied out of fear. Thus, admission of the first interview which was not recorded contemporaneously may not have the necessary adverse affect on the fairness of the trial: its recording under para 11.13 may be sufficient and therefore will not lead to its exclusion under s 78.[1] However, the standard under Art 6 of the Convention appears to differ; evidence should be excluded whenever the proceedings as a whole, including the methods by which evidence was obtained, were *unfair* (rather than having a *significant adverse effect* on the trial's fairness). Thus, a court might now use *Khan* (2000) to exclude any of the interviews.

It will now be considered whether the third interview would be excluded from evidence under s 76, on the basis that Ali's consent to be interviewed without legal advice must be treated as vitiated, due to the failure to advise him of the duty solicitor scheme (this argument is considered fully below in relation to s 78). Unless it can be shown that Eileen acted in bad faith in failing to inform Ali of the duty solicitor scheme (which, as argued below, does not appear to be the case), s 76(2)(a) will not apply. As noted above, if argument under s 76(2)(b) is to succeed, it would have to be shown that Ali was in a vulnerable position in the third interview. No specific factor can be identified which might support such an argument. The courts appear to take the view (see *Canale* (1990)) that when a defendant of ordinary ability to withstand questioning is interviewed in breach of one of the PACE provisions, s 78 should be considered, rather than s 76(2)(b). Therefore, although it could be argued that the failure to afford him legal advice could amount to 'something said or done' conducive of unreliability, some special circumstance as identified in *Delaney* is missing.

It will now be considered whether a reasonable argument for the exclusion from evidence of the third interview under s 78 can be advanced. Again, it will be necessary to identify some impropriety occurring in the police station. It will be argued that insufficient effort was made to comply with Ali's request for legal advice. Under para 6.6(d) of Code C, a suspect who has requested advice can change his mind and consent to the commencement of the interview, even though he has not obtained it. However, it can be argued that the suspect should not be misled into giving such consent. Once she had failed in her effort to contact Ali's solicitor, Eileen failed to inform him that he could obtain the services of the duty solicitor; it could therefore be argued that his consent was vitiated as based on the misapprehension that unless he obtained advice from his own solicitor, he could not obtain it at all. However, in the case of *Hughes* (1988), the Court of Appeal considered that a consent to go ahead with an interview after a suspect had been led to believe that the duty solicitor was unavailable could be treated as a genuine consent. The police had given this information in good faith, although the duty solicitor was in fact available. In principle, there is little difference between leading a suspect to believe that the duty solicitor is unavailable and failing to inform the suspect of the duty solicitor scheme. Thus, following *Hughes,* Ali's consent to go ahead with the interview could be treated as genuine; on this analysis, para 6.6 has not been breached.[2] But *Condron* (2000) and *Murray* (1996) show that the ECHR values access to legal advice very highly, especially during interviews, and so courts may now decide that this situation breaches Art 6.

On the other hand, even if Eileen acted in good faith, it could be argued that a requirement to inform of the duty solicitor scheme is implied in para 6 (rather than arising only from Note 6B, which is not a Code provision according to para 1.3 of Code C) and that, therefore, the instant situation is not analogous to that in *Hughes*. It is submitted that this is the better view, since it accords with the prominence given to legal advice in the PACE scheme. This view is supported by the provision of para 6.4 of Code C that no attempt must be made to persuade the suspect to forego advice: a failure to provide the requisite information could be characterised as part of such an attempt, in the sense that it might have the effect of persuading the detainee to forego advice. It is also supported by the first instance decision of *Vernon* (1988), which concerned a situation almost exactly in point with that of the instant case, and by the strict approach to the legal advice provisions taken in *Beycan* (1990) by the Court of Appeal.

On this argument, a breach of para 6.6 has occurred. However, this breach may not be causally related to the admissions made in the third interview. It may be that Ali would have made the admissions had he had advice. This is suggested since the solicitor would be aware that under s 34 of the Criminal Justice and Public Order Act 1994, it is disadvantageous to a defendant to hold back a defence. On the other hand, his confession in the third interview may suggest that he gave in eventually to pressure to confess and that the 'defence' he puts forward is just part of a false confession. A solicitor who believed him would probably still have advised him to remain silent. On this analysis, it is hard to be sure that the requisite causal relationship exists, and the third interview may therefore be admissible in evidence under s 78, although possibly not under Art 6 of the Convention. It follows that the second interview, which may be said to be causally related to the breach of para 6.6, may be so excluded, since had Ali had legal advice, he might *not* have decided to remain silent. The solicitor, weighing up the situation, might well have decided that he should offer his explanation of the facts, rather than allow an adverse inference to be drawn at trial from a failure to do so. This would be in accordance with s 34 of the Criminal Justice and Public Order Act 1994, which provides that where a person fails to mention a fact which he subsequently relies on in his defence, adverse inferences can be drawn from such a failure. The solicitor might also have advised him to account for the presence of the knife since, under s 36 of the 1994 Act, an adverse inference can be drawn from a failure to so account.

Will the knife be excluded from evidence under s 78? According to the analysis above, the stop and search could be characterised as consensual; no breach of Code A or s 1 of PACE therefore took place. Had the search been non-consensual, it might have been possible to argue, following *Edward Fennelly* (1989), that the products of the search should be excluded from evidence on the basis that there was no power to search in the circumstances: the fact that Ali was black and was hurrying through the street near the scene of the attack only 15 minutes after it had taken place would probably not be enough to give rise to the reasonable suspicion that weapons were being carried required by paras 1.6 and 1.7 of Code A.[3] According to *Thomas* (1990) and *Effick* (1992), however, physical evidence will be excluded only if obtained with deliberate illegality. Therefore, had a breach of Code A occurred, it would still seem that the knife would not be excluded from evidence.

In conclusion, the stronger argument seems to be that the second interview only will be excluded from evidence under s 78. The other two interviews and the finding of the knife might be excluded under Art 6 of the Convention as incompatible with a fair trial, due to the manner in which they were obtained.

## Notes

1   There are two arguments which could be used to escape from this conclusion. One is set out above – the other is indicated here. It might be possible to show that Eileen deliberately failed to mention the duty solicitor scheme in order to obtain a confession from Ali more readily. In *Hughes*, the consent in question would have been treated as vitiated had the police acted in bad faith. However, it may be that the failure to advise Ali of the duty solicitor scheme arose because Eileen mistakenly believed that he did not need to be specifically advised of it again after the notification of rights by Doris and the reminder before the third interview that advice was

available. Eileen is not specifically required to remind a suspect unable to obtain advice from his own solicitor of the duty solicitor scheme before he gives consent to be interviewed, although this can perhaps be implied from the wording of Note 6B.

2    However, if, at trial, the particular unfairness likely to arise from the improper recording is not specified, but the breaches of the recording provisions affecting this interview are pointed out, it may appear that it cannot be relied on; it will then be excluded from evidence under s 78. A similar situation arose in *Keenan* (1989); the Court of Appeal held that the admissions in question should have been excluded under s 78. In *Canale* (1990), the importance of contemporaneous recording was stressed. However, in those instances, the defendant had not signed the interview record. Thus, although these points might be raised, the conclusion will remain the same.

3    The question of the meaning of reasonable suspicion could be considered in more detail at this point, bearing in mind the provision of para 1.7 of Code A states that reasonable suspicion cannot be supported on the basis of personal factors (including colour) alone.

# Question 29

Toby, who has a history of mental disorder and has two convictions for possessing cannabis, is standing on a street corner at 2.00 am on Sunday when he is seen by two police officers in uniform, Andy and Beryl. Andy says: 'What are you up to now, Toby? Let's have look in your pockets.' Toby does not reply, but turns out his pockets and produces a small quantity of cannabis. Andy and Beryl then ask Toby to come to the police station; he agrees to do so.

They arrive at the police station at 2.20 am. Toby is cautioned, informed of his rights under Code C by the Custody Officer and told that he is suspected of dealing in cannabis. He asks if he can see a solicitor, but his request is refused by Superintendent Smith, on the ground that this will lead to the alerting of others whom the police suspect are involved. Toby is then questioned for two hours, but makes no reply to the questions. He then has a short break; when the interview recommences, he is re-cautioned and reminded of his right to legal advice. After another hour, he admits to supplying cannabis. All the interviews are tape recorded. He is then charged with supplying cannabis.

Toby now says that he only confessed because he thought he had to in order to get home.

Advise Toby as to any means of redress available to him.

## Answer plan

This question is fairly demanding and quite tricky, since it covers the problem of apparently voluntary compliance with police requests and the particular difficulty created when the police are dealing with a mentally disordered person. The most straightforward approach is probably to consider the legality of the police conduct at every point. Once this has been done, the applicability of the possible forms of redress in respect of each possible breach can be considered. As special problems arise in respect of each, they should be looked at separately. It should be noted that the examinee is merely asked to 'advise Toby as to any means of redress'; therefore, all relevant possibilities should be discussed. Essentially, the following issues should be considered:

- legality of the search under s 23(2) of the Misuse of Drugs Act 1971 and Code A of the Police and Criminal Evidence Act (PACE) 1984 – relevance of Note 1E;

- a voluntary detention or an arrest under s 24 PACE? Legality of the arrest?;

- access to legal advice under s 58 of PACE – exceptions under s 58(8) – legality of the refusal of advice;

- failure to ensure that an appropriate adult was present during the interview as required under para 11.14 of Code C;

- exclusion of evidence under ss 76 and 78 of PACE – relevance of s 36 of the Criminal Justice and Public Order Act 1994;

- relevant tortious remedies;

- police complaints and disciplinary action – s 67(8) of PACE;

- *Khan* (2000) – the European Court of Human Rights (ECHR).

# Answer

The legality of the police conduct in this instance will be considered first; any possible forms of redress open to Toby will then be examined.

The first contact between the police officers and Toby appears to be of a voluntary nature: the officers are entitled to ask questions; equally, Toby can refuse to answer them (*Rice v Connolly* (1966)). When Toby is asked to turn out his pockets, this appears to be a request which he could refuse. It may therefore be characterised as part of a voluntary search. Although it is not clear that Toby gave consent to the search, Andy and Beryl were under a duty only to explain that he could withhold consent and to seek his consent (Code A, Note 1D(b) of PACE) and, on that basis, as Toby accedes to the request made, could be said to have fulfilled the requirements of Code A in respect of consensual searches. However, he is mentally disordered and so belongs to one of the vulnerable groups who may not be subject to a voluntary search at all under Code A, Note 1E. As the police know him, they may be aware of this fact. Even if they are not aware that he has a specific mental disorder, they may recognise him as a person incapable of giving an informed consent to the search; if so, the Note 1E provisions will still apply.

Thus, the search should not have taken place unless the police officers can show reasonable suspicion as the basis for the exercise of the power. In order to do so, it must be shown that the police officers complied with the provisions of s 23(2) of the Misuse of Drugs Act 1971 and of Code A. Under s 23(2), a police officer may search for controlled drugs if he has reasonable grounds for believing that he will find such articles. The necessary reasonable suspicion is defined in paras 1.6 and 1.7 of Code A. There must be some objective basis for it, which might include various factors which are mentioned in para 1.6, including the time and place and the behaviour of the person concerned. In the instant situation, the lateness of the hour might give rise to some suspicion, but it is apparent that the suspicion does not relate specifically enough to the possibility that Toby is in possession of drugs. Following this argument, no power to stop and search arises; the seizure of the cannabis is therefore unlawful. It should further be noted that the procedural requirements of s 2 are breached.

The request made to come to the police station appears to assume that Toby will come on a voluntary basis; however, it might be argued that if Toby is deemed incapable of giving consent to a stop and search, he cannot be capable of consenting to a voluntary detention. If this assumption is correct, it is necessary to consider whether a power to arrest arises. Toby is presumably arrested for possessing cannabis, an offence arising under s 5(3) of the Misuse of Drugs Act 1971. It is an arrestable offence under s 24(1)(b) of PACE, as it carries a sentence of five years or more (Sched 4 to the Misuse of Drugs Act). In order to arrest under s 24, it is necessary to show that Andy and Beryl had reasonable grounds for suspecting that Toby was in possession of the cannabis. Clearly, this is the case. However, the cannabis is discovered during the course of an illegal stop and search. It may appear strange that an illegal stop and search could provide the reasonable suspicion necessary to found a lawful arrest. However, the leading case on reasonable suspicion (*Castorina v Chief Constable of Surrey* (1988)) gives no guidance on the point. In any event, it need not be determined, because the 'arrest' (if it may be characterised as such) is clearly unlawful due to the failure to state the fact of the arrest and the reason for it as required under s 28.

At the police station, Toby is denied access to legal advice. Delay in affording such access will be lawful if one of the contingencies envisaged under s 58(8) will arise if a solicitor is contacted. In this instance, the police will wish to rely on the exception under s 58(8)(b) allowing delay where contacting the solicitor will lead to the alerting of others suspected of the offence. Leaving aside the lack of any substantial evidence that others are involved at all, it will be necessary for the police to show, following *Samuel* (1988), that some quality about the particular solicitor in question could found a reasonable belief that he or she would bring about one of the contingencies envisaged if contacted. There is nothing to suggest that the police have any basis for this belief, especially as Toby has not specified the solicitor he wishes to contact. He may well wish to contact the duty solicitor. A further condition for the operation of s 58(8) is that Toby is being detained in respect of a serious arrestable offence. He is in detention at this point in respect of possession of cannabis. This is an arrestable offence under s 24, although he has not been arrested for it. Whether or not the offence can be termed a serious arrestable offence depends on the provisions of s 116. The section as amended includes as serious arrestable offences under sub-s (2)(a) 'offence mentioned in paras (a) to (f) of s 1(3) of the Drug Trafficking Act 1994'. As supplying cannabis is included in this section, this condition is fulfilled. However, the lack of any basis for the necessary reasonable belief under s 58(8) means that there has been a breach of s 58.

Since Toby is mentally disordered, he should not have been interviewed except in the presence of an 'appropriate adult' as required under para 11.14 of Code C. Therefore, a further breach of PACE has occurred, unless it could be argued that the officers were not aware of his disorder; if so, following *Raymond Maurice Clarke* (1989), no breach of the Code provision occurred. The behaviour of Andy suggests, however, that the officers were aware of Toby's condition.[1]

Having identified a series of illegal acts on the part of the police, it will now be necessary to consider any redress available to Toby in respect of them. The first such act was the unlawful seizure of the cannabis.[2] The appropriate cause of action in this instance will be trespass to goods; damages will, however, be minimal.

Will the cannabis be excluded from evidence under s 78? According to the analysis above, the stop and search could perhaps be characterised as consensual but, even if this is the case, a breach of Code A, Note 1E took place. However, this provision is only a Note for Guidance and, therefore, it does not have the same legal status as Code provisions. If a court was prepared to have regard to the breach at all, the view might be taken that the decision to include the provision concerned only as a Note should be respected: it should be treated as general guidance only and no consequences adverse to the prosecution should flow from its breach. However, in *DPP v Blake* (1989), the Divisional Court impliedly accepted that breach of a Note for Guidance will be considered and, on this basis, s 78 might be invoked. It would then be possible to argue, following *Edward Fennelly* (1989) that the products of the search should be excluded from evidence on the basis that there was no power to search in the circumstances. According to *Thomas* (1990) and *Effick* (1992), however, physical evidence will be excluded only if obtained with deliberate illegality; the pre-PACE ruling of the House of Lords in *Fox* (1986) would also lend support to this contention. It may be concluded that the cannabis would not be excluded from evidence.

Toby could make a complaint in respect of the illegal seizure of the cannabis if it could be characterised as resulting from a non-consensual search in breach of s 23(2) of the Misuse of Drugs Act 1971 and of Code A. However, assuming that it was consensual, the only breach which occurred was that of Code A, Note 1E. Breach of a Note is not a breach of the police disciplinary Code under s 67(8) of PACE, although breach of a Code provision would be (Code A Notes are not part of Code A under para 1.2).

Assuming that the arrest was unlawful (which cannot be determined with certainty), Toby could bring an action for false imprisonment for the whole period of his detention. There is also the possibility of taking action under s 7 of the HRA 1998 based on the infringement of his rights under Art 5 of the Convention. A further option might be to make a complaint in respect of the failure to observe the provisions of s 28 of PACE.

Can a reasonable argument be advanced that the admissions made by Toby will be excluded from evidence under s 76? Following *Alladice* and *Hughes* (1988), unless it can be shown that the custody officer acted in bad faith in failing to allow Toby access to a solicitor, it seems that s 76(2)(a) will not apply. However, following *Delaney* (1989), which was concerned with the operation of s 76(2)(b), if the defendant was in some particularly difficult or vulnerable position, the breach of PACE may be of special significance. Toby may be said to be in such a position due to the fact that he is mentally disordered. On this basis, it seems that s 76(2)(b) may be invoked to exclude the admissions from evidence.

The admissions may also be excluded from evidence under s 78, on the basis that the police breached s 58. If so, following *Samuel* (1988), it must be shown that the breach of s 58 was causally related to the admissions made in the second interview. It may be that Toby would have made admissions had he had advice. The advisor might have considered that he should make admissions, since a failure to account for the cannabis would be commented on adversely in court under s 36 of the Criminal Justice and Public Order Act 1994. On the other hand, the advisor might have considered that this risk should be taken. This seems the stronger argument, bearing in mind Toby's mental disorder. It appears that Toby may have needed such advice. This argument failed in *Dunford* (1990) and *Alladice* (1988) on the basis that the appellants in those cases were experienced criminals, aware of their rights. It appears that Toby did remain silent for some time; possibly, therefore, he would have made the admissions in any event. As he has convictions, he will be aware of police procedures and know that he can keep silent. It might be argued that access to legal advice would have added nothing to his understanding of the situation. On the other hand, given his mental condition, it is unlikely that he would fully understand the implications of silence; he was obviously more vulnerable than the appellant in *Dunford*. On this analysis, the requisite causal relationship exists and the admissions may also be excluded from evidence under s 78. This approach is given additional weight by the importance attached to access to legal advice by the ECHR in cases such as *Murray (John) v UK* (1996) and *Averill v UK* (2000). The HRA 1998 means that these decisions will need to be taken into account in considering whether the evidence should be excluded.

It has further been argued that a breach of para 11.14 of Code C occurred, in that Toby was interviewed, although no appropriate adult was present.[3] Following *DPP v Blake* (1989), the judge would therefore be likely to use his discretion to exclude the interview under s 78 on the basis that it may be unreliable or because Toby would not have made the admissions at all had the adult been present.[4]

The breach of s 58 could also be the subject of a complaint, as could the breach of para 11.14 of Code C.

## Notes

1 This point is strengthened by the provisions of Code C, Note 11B in respect of the likelihood that mentally disordered persons might make an unreliable confession.

2 It could be noted that under s 67(10) of PACE, no civil liability can arise from a breach of the Codes and, therefore, *a fortiori* from a breach of a Note for Guidance (in this case, Note 1E). If the search is voluntary, so, presumably, is the seizure; the only

illegality might therefore arise from the breach of the Note. Assuming then that the search is voluntary, it would appear that no cause of action will arise.

3   The breach of para 11.14 could also be considered under s 76 but, if so, the argument would not differ from that in respect of the breach of s 58. Note that since Toby is mentally disordered as opposed to mentally handicapped, the special provisions of s 77 in respect of the mentally handicapped do not apply. Nevertheless, as in *Delaney,* courts will be particularly vigilant when determining whether to exclude confessions of the mentally disordered under either s 76 or s 78. The ruling in *Mckenzie* (1992) supports this point.

4   It could be pointed out that if the police deliberately failed to afford Toby access to an appropriate adult, s 76(2)(a) might be invoked to exclude the admissions; alternatively (following *Alladice* (1988)), s 78 would be invoked without needing to discuss the question of reliability or of the requisite causal relationship between the breach and the confession.

# Question 30

'The Police and Criminal Evidence Act 1984 provides important safeguards for the suspect during interviews in the police station, but no adequate means of redress is available if the police do not comply with them.' Discuss.

## Answer plan

A reasonably straightforward essay question which is quite often set on the Police and Criminal Evidence Act (PACE) 1984. It is important to take the provisions of the Criminal Justice and Public Order Act 1994 into account and to bear in mind the changes consequent to Code C. It should be noted that it is only concerned with the interviewing scheme and its applicability inside the police station. Essentially, the following matters should be considered:

• the nature of the safeguards available under Pts IV and V of PACE and Codes of Practice C and E;

- relevant tortious remedies;
- the efficacy of the police complaints mechanism;
- the nature of the PACE scheme for exclusion of evidence;
- relevance of ss 34–37 of the Criminal Justice and Public Order Act 1994;
- the value of exclusion of evidence as a form of redress;
- new possibilities under the Human Rights Act (HRA) 1998.

# Answer

It is generally accepted that the safeguards for interviews introduced by PACE, particularly access to legal advice and tape recording, can reduce the likelihood that an interview will be unreliable. However, it will be argued that the forms of redress available in respect of breaches of these provisions are inadequate, either as a means of encouraging the police to comply with them or as a means of compensating the detainee if they do not.

The most important safeguards available inside the police station include contemporaneous recording under para 11.5 of Code C or tape recording under para 3 of Code E, the ability to read over, verify and sign the notes of the interview as a correct record under para 11.10 of Code C, notification of the right to legal advice under s 58 and para 3.1 of Code C, the option of having the adviser present under para 6.6 and, where appropriate, the presence of an adult under para 11.14. The right to silence, encapsulated in the old Code C caution, has been viewed as a valuable safeguard, but it has now been greatly curtailed by ss 34–37 of the Criminal Justice and Public Order Act 1994. These provisions were reflected in the new and much more complex caution introduced in the 1995 revision of Code C.

The interpretation given to these provisions by the courts has meant that the circumstances in which non compliance with a provision will be lawful have been narrowed down. For example, in *Samuel* (1988), the Court of Appeal had to consider s 58(8), which provides that access to legal advice may be delayed where, *inter alia*, allowing such access might alert others involved in the offence. It was determined that s 58(8) could not be fulfilled by an unsubstantiated assertion that this contingency would materialise if a solicitor was contacted. After this ruling, in order to fulfil s 58(8), the police must be able to demonstrate a reasonable belief in some particular quality of naivety or corruption possessed by the solicitor in question.

Equally, the courts have been not been willing to accept that compliance with PACE was impracticable even in informal situations. In *Absolam* (1988), the Custody Officer questioned the detainee in the heat of the moment, without first advising him of his right to legal advice. At first instance, it was determined that the detainee was only entitled to his right to consult a solicitor as soon as it was practicable under para 3.1 of Code C and, further, that the questions and answers did not constitute an interview; therefore, para 3.1 did not apply. The Court of Appeal, however, held that the questions and answers did not constitute a formal interview, but were nevertheless an interview within the purview of para 6.3. Since the appellant's situation was precisely the type of situation in which the Code's provisions were most significant, there could be no question of waiving them. Paragraph 3.1 of Code C had been breached.

However, although the courts may be quick to find that a breach of PACE has occurred, this does not mean that redress will automatically be available to the detainee who has thereby been disadvantaged. What form of redress might such a detainee seek?

Tort damages will be available in respect of some breaches of PACE. For example, if a police officer arrests a citizen where no reasonable suspicion arises under s 24 or 25 of PACE, an action for false imprisonment will be available. Equally, such a remedy would be available if the Pt IV provisions governing time limits on detention were breached. However, tortious remedies are inapplicable to the provisions of the Codes under s 67(10) and may not be available in respect of the most significant statutory interviewing provision, the entitlement to legal advice. There is no tort of denial of access to legal advice: the only possible tortious action would be for breach of statutory duty. Whether such an action would lie is a question of policy in relation to any particular statutory provision.[1] At present, the application of this remedy must be purely conjectural. Theoretically, an action for false imprisonment might lie; an argument could be advanced that where gross breaches of the questioning provisions had taken place, such as interviewing a person unlawfully held incommunicado, a detention in itself lawful might thereby be rendered unlawful. However, although the ruling in *Middleweek v Chief Constable of Merseyside* (1985) gave some encouragement to such argument, it now seems to be ruled out due to the decision in *Weldon v Home Office* (1991) in the context of lawful detention in a prison. It seems likely, therefore, that access to legal advice, like the rest of the safeguards for interviewing, will continue to be unaffected by the availability of tortious remedies.

The police complaints mechanism covers any breaches of PACE, including breaches of the Codes under s 67(8), but it is generally agreed that it is defective as a means of redress. It does not allow for compensation to the victim or for the victim to attend any disciplinary proceedings. In any event, most complaints do not result in disciplinary proceedings and it appears that no disciplinary proceedings have been brought in respect of breaches of the Codes. The suspect concerned might, in many instances, be unaware that a breach of the Codes had occurred and while, theoretically, another officer could make a complaint leading to disciplinary proceedings for such a breach, in practice, this appears to be highly unlikely. Furthermore, despite the involvement (albeit limited) of the Police Complaints Authority, the complaints procedure tends to be perceived as being administered by the police themselves: under s 84, a complaint will go in the first instance to the Chief Officer of Police of the force in question, who must determine by reference to the section whether or not he or she is the appropriate person to deal with it. In *Khan* (2000), the European Court of Human Rights (ECHR) found a violation of Art 13 of the European Convention, since the Police Complaints Authority is not a sufficient means of redress for Convention breaches; since complaints can be handled internally, the Chief Constable of the area is able to appoint from his own force to carry out an investigation; and since the Secretary of State is involved in appointments to the Police Complaints Authority, it was found to be insufficiently independent as a remedial procedure. Thus, reform is necessary. However, the HRA 1998 will divert many complaints to the courts and so limit this problem.

The context in which breaches of Code C and of the entitlement to legal advice have been considered is, of course, that of exclusion of evidence. It must be borne in mind that the PACE mechanism for exclusion of evidence provides a means of redress for breach of the interviewing provisions only in one circumstance – that the case is pursued to trial and the defendant pleads not guilty. In this one instance it can be of great value in that the defendant may be placed in the position he would have been in had the breach not occurred (the approach taken in *Absolam* (1988)) and the police may seem to be 'punished' for their non compliance with the rules by being prevented from profiting from their own breach.

The Act contains three separate tests which may be considered after a breach of the interviewing rules has been shown and, in theory, all three could be considered in a particular instance. Under the 'oppression' test (s 76(2)(a)), once the defence has advanced a reasonable argument (*Liverpool Juvenile Court ex p R* (1987)) that the confession was obtained by oppression, it will not be admitted in evidence unless the prosecution can prove that it was not so obtained.[2] In *Fulling* (1987), the Court of Appeal proffered its own definition of oppression: 'The exercise of authority or power in a burdensome, harsh or wrongful manner'. The terms 'wrongful' and 'improper' used in this test could cover any unlawful action on the part of the police and would therefore mean that any breach of the Act or Codes could constitute oppression. This wide possibility has been pursued at first instance (in *Davison* (1988)), but the Court of Appeal in *Hughes* (1988) held that a denial of legal advice due, not to bad faith on the part of the police, but to a misunderstanding, could not amount to oppression. In *Alladice* (1988), the Court of Appeal also took this view in suggesting, *obiter*, that an improper denial of legal advice, if accompanied by bad faith on the part of the police would certainly amount to 'unfairness' under s 78 and probably also to 'oppression'.

The test for oppression then does not appear to depend entirely on the nature of the impropriety, but rather on whether it was perpetrated deliberately. Thus, bad faith seems to be a necessary, but not sufficient condition for the operation of s 76(2)(a), whereas it seems that it will automatically render a confession inadmissible under s 78.

The test under s 76(2)(b), the 'reliability' test, is concerned with objective reliability: the judge must consider the situation at the time the confession was made and ask whether the confession would be likely to be unreliable, not whether it *is* unreliable. It is not necessary, under this test, to show that there has been any misconduct on the part of the police.[3] In *Delaney* (1989), the defendant was 17, had an IQ of 80 and, according to an educational psychologist, was subject to emotional arousal which would lead him to wish to bring a police interview to an end as quickly as possible. These were circumstances in which it was important to ensure that the interrogation was conducted with all propriety. In fact, the officers offered some inducement to the defendant to confess by playing down the gravity of the offence and by suggesting that, if he confessed, he would get the psychiatric help he needed. They also failed to make an accurate, contemporaneous record of the interview in breach of para 11.5 of Code C. Failing to make the proper record was of indirect relevance to the question of reliability, since it meant that the court could not assess the full extent of the suggestions held out to the defendant. Thus, in the circumstances existing at the time (the mental state of the defendant), the police impropriety did have the necessary special significance necessary.

Thus, it appears that the 'circumstances existing at the time' may be circumstances created by the police in breaching the interviewing rules; equally, following *Mathias* (1989), such a breach may amount to something said or done. However, a single breach of the interviewing rules, such as a denial of legal advice in ordinary circumstances, would not, it seems, fulfil both limbs of the test.

Due to the need to find some special factor in the situation in order to invoke either head of s 76, breaches of the interviewing rules unaccompanied by any such factor are usually considered under s 78. The idea behind the section was that the function of exclusion of evidence after police misconduct must not be disciplinary, but must be to safeguard the fairness of the trial. The first question to be asked under s 78 is whether a breach of the rules has occurred at all and then whether it is significant and substantial (*Keenan* (1988)). Once such a breach is found, the next question to be asked will be whether admission of the confession gained during the improperly conducted interview will render the trial unfair. This might occur if, for example, as in *Canale* (1990), there has been a failure to make contemporaneous notes of the

235

interview in breach of para 11.5 of Code C. The defence may then challenge the interview record on the basis that the police have fabricated all or part of it or may allege that something adverse to the detainee happened during the interview which has not been recorded. The court then has no means of knowing which version is true, precisely the situation which Code C was designed to prevent. In such a situation, a judge may well exclude the confession on the basis that it would be unfair to allow evidence of doubtful reliability to go before the jury.[4]

Breaches of the recording provisions will normally be considered under s 78 as opposed to s 76(2). Allegedly fabricated confessions cannot fall within s 76(2), due to its requirement that something has happened to the defendant which causes him to confess; its terms are not therefore fulfilled if the defence alleges that no confession made by the defendant exists. Secondly, s 76(2)(b) requires that something is said or done in special circumstances; a breach of the recording provisions could amount to something said or done in the *Delaney* sense (see above), but unless special circumstances, such as the particular vulnerability of the defendant exist, the other test under the section is unsatisfied. In *Canale* (1990), the police breached the recording provisions and allegedly played a trick on the appellant in order to obtain the confession. Ruling that the confession should have been excluded under s 78, the Court of Appeal took into account the fact that the appellant could not be said to be weak minded; it was therefore thought inappropriate to invoke s 76(2)(b). Equally, such instances would not normally fall within s 76(2)(a), because it may not be apparent that the police deliberately breached the recording provisions. On the other hand, if the defence alleges that the police made threats or *deliberately* tricked the detainee into confessing, the prosecution might not be able to prove beyond reasonable doubt that the police had in fact behaved properly, due to the breach of the recording provisions. This line of argument could have been considered in *Canale*.

Moreover, a significant and substantial breach of the interviewing rules, although unaccompanied by bad faith, may have caused the defendant to confess and, on that basis, admission of the confession could be said to render the trial unfair, even though it appears that the confession is reliable. The difficulty here lies in determining whether the defendant confessed for other reasons. In *Samuel* (1988), the Court of Appeal determined that the police impropriety – a failure to allow the appellant access to legal advice – was causally linked to the confession: the appellant was not a sophisticated, hardened criminal able to handle the interview without advice. Conversely, in *Dunford* (1990), the Court of Appeal determined that the criminally experienced appellant had made his own assessment of the situation in deciding to make certain admissions and legal advice would not have affected his decision; the failure to allow legal advice was not therefore causally linked to the confession. Curtailment of the right to silence under ss 34–37 of the Criminal Justice and Public Order Act 1994 means that legal advisers are less likely to advise silence and, therefore, the causal relationship in question will be more difficult to establish. Section 78 may therefore become less effective as a means of providing a form of redress where there is a failure to comply with the PACE provisions.[5] On the other hand, the importance attached to access to legal advice by the ECHR in cases such as *Murray (John) v UK* (1996) and *Averill v UK* (2000) may encourage greater use of s 78, since the HRA 1998 means that these decisions will need to be taken into account in considering whether the evidence should be excluded.

In conclusion, it is apparent that the courts are concerned to uphold the safeguards created by the PACE interviewing rules, but it must be questioned whether exclusion of evidence is an adequate or appropriate method of doing so. The majority of defendants plead guilty. Thus, the police have an incentive to break the rules by, for example, refusing a request for legal advice in the hope of obtaining admissions and a guilty plea. If, in such circumstances, a defendant does plead guilty, he or she has suffered denial of a fundamental right with no hope of redress, apart from that offered by a complaint. Whilst not a direct remedy for breaches of PACE and its Codes, the incorporation of the Convention by the HRA 1998 has provided a separate method of redress for many situations which involve a PACE breach; if the proceedings before and during the trial are unfair, viewed as a whole, then there will be an Art 5 or 6 issue, for which any domestic court may provide any available remedy (s 8 of the HRA 1998).

## Notes

1 The tone of the only relevant case (a 1985 unreported application to prevent a breach of s 58) was unpropitious: '... were I to make the order sought it would be unreasonable, a hindrance to police inquiries may be caused.'

2 The meaning of oppression could be considered in more detail. The only evidence given in the Act as to the its meaning is the non-exhaustive definition contained in s 76(8): 'In this section, "oppression" includes torture, inhuman or degrading treatment, and the use or threat of violence (whether or not amounting to torture).' The word 'includes' ought to be given its literal meaning according to the Court of Appeal in *Fulling* (1987). Therefore, the concept of oppression may be fairly wide: the question is whether it could encompass breaches of the interviewing scheme unaccompanied by any other impropriety.

3 There are two limbs to the test as *Harvey* (1988) illustrates: the defendant, a mentally ill woman of low intelligence, may have been induced to confess to murder by hearing her lover's confession; the 'something said or done' (the first limb) was the confession of the lover, while the 'circumstances' (the second limb) were the defendant's emotional state, low intelligence and mental illness.

4 The question of any other available evidence as to what occurred could be pursued further at this point. In *Dunn* (1990), the defence had an independent witness to what occurred – a legal representative – and the judge admitted the confession as the defence had therefore a proper basis from which to challenge the police evidence.

5 For completeness, s 82(3), which preserves the whole of the common law discretion to exclude evidence could be mentioned at this point, although it should be noted that, in practice, its role in relation to breaches of the interviewing rules is largely insignificant, due to the width of s 78.

# Question 31

How far would it be fair to say that the Police and Criminal Act 1984 and the Codes of Practice made under it strike a reasonable balance between increased police powers and greater safeguards for the suspect?

## Answer plan

A reasonably straightforward essay question which is commonly set on PACE. It is clearly much more wide ranging than the previous one and therefore needs care in planning in order to cover provisions relating to all the main stages in the investigation. Essentially, the following points should be considered:

- the arrest provision under s 25;
- stop and search provision under s 1 and Code of Practice A and the efficacy of the procedural safeguards;
- powers of entry to premises under ss 17 and 18 and Code B – information to be conveyed to owners of property to be searched;
- detention provisions under Pt IV;
- safeguards for interviews under Pt V and Codes C and E – relevance of ss 34–37 under the Criminal Justice and Public Order Act 1994;
- identification procedures under Code D;
- brief overview of redress available for breaches of these provisions – tortious remedies, the police complaints mechanism, exclusion of evidence;
- European Court of Human Rights (ECHR) criticism.

# Answer

It will be argued that although the Police and Criminal Evidence Act (PACE) 1984 and the Codes of Practice contain provisions capable of achieving a reasonable balance between increasing the power of the police to detain and question and providing safeguards for the suspect, that balance is not maintained in practice. This failure arguably arises partly because many of the safeguards can be evaded quite readily and partly because there is no effective sanction available for their breach.

Before the inception of PACE, the police had no general and clear powers of arrest, stop and search or entry to premises. They wanted such powers put on a clear statutory basis, so that they could exercise them where they felt it was their duty to do so, without laying themselves open to the possibility of a civil action. In s 1, a general power to stop and search persons is conferred on the police if reasonable suspicion arises that stolen goods or prohibited articles may be found. This general power is balanced in two ways. First, the concept of reasonable suspicion, which is defined in paras 1.6 and 1.7 of Code A, allows it to be exercised only when quite a high level of suspicion exists. Secondly, the police must give the person to be searched certain information, including the object of the search and the name of the police station to which the officer in question is attached. However, these safeguards can be evaded if the search is made on an apparently voluntary basis, although certain restrictions on voluntary searches under Code A go some way towards addressing this problem.[1] It should be pointed out that s 1 of PACE may be undermined in any event by s 60 of the Criminal Justice and Public Order Act 1994, which, in certain circumstances, allows stop and search without reasonable suspicion if authorisation to do so has been given by a superintendent.

The police also acquired a general power of arrest under s 25. However, this power does not merely allow an officer to arrest for any offence so long as reasonable suspicion can be shown. Such a power would probably have been viewed as too draconian. It is balanced by what are known as the general arrest conditions which must also be fulfilled. One of these conditions (s 25(3)(c)) consists of a failure to furnish a satisfactory name or address, so that the service of a summons later on would be impracticable. The others concern the immediate need to remove the suspect from the street. The inclusion of these provisions implies that the infringement of civil liberties represented by an arrest should be resorted to only where no other alternative exists. The concept of reasonable suspicion, which should ensure that the arrest takes place at quite a late stage in the investigation, also limits the use of this power.

The power to enter premises conferred by ss 17 and 18 is balanced in a manner similar to the method employed in respect of stop and search. The power can be exercised either where an officer wants to arrest a person suspected of an arrestable offence or where a person has been so arrested and the intention is to search the person's premises immediately after arrest. Thus, the power arises only in respect of a limited range of offences; it does not arise in respect of an arrest under s 25. It is further balanced by the need to convey certain information to the subject of the search in question, thereby rendering officers (at least theoretically) accountable for searches carried out.[2]

Searching of premises other than under ss 17 and 18 can only occur if a search warrant is issued under s 8 of PACE by a magistrate. A warrant will only be issued if there are reasonable grounds for believing that a serious arrestable offence has been committed and where the material is likely to be of substantial value to the investigation of the offence. Further safeguards are set out in ss 15 and 16. The warrant must identify the articles to be sought although, once the officer is on the premises, other articles may be seized under s 19 if they appear to relate to any other offence. Further, the warrant authorises entry to premises on one occasion only.

Prior to PACE, the police had no clear power to hold a person for questioning. Such a power has now been put on a clear statutory basis under s 41 and it is made clear under s 37(2) that the purpose of the detention is to obtain a confession. The detention can be for up to 24 hours. In the case of a person in police custody for a serious arrestable offence (defined in s 116), it can extend to 36 hours with the permission of a police officer of the rank of superintendent or above, and may extend to 96 hours under s 44 after an application to a magistrate's court. These are very significant new powers. However, they are supposed to be balanced by all the safeguards created by Pt V of PACE and by Codes C and E.

The most important safeguards available inside the police station include contemporaneous recording under para 11.5 of Code C, tape recording under para 3 of Code E, the ability to read over, verify and sign the notes of the interview as a correct record under para 11.10 of Code C, notification of the right to legal advice under s 58 and para 3.1, the option of having the adviser present under para 6.6 and, where appropriate, the presence of an adult under para 11.14.

However, there are methods of avoiding these safeguards without actually breaking the rules. For example, in *Hughes* (1988), the detainee, disappointed of obtaining advice from his own solicitor, inquired about the duty solicitor scheme, but was informed, erroneously (but apparently in good faith) that no solicitor was available. Under this misapprehension, he gave consent to be interviewed and the Court of Appeal took the view that his consent was not thereby vitiated.

Further, access to legal advice and tape recording can be evaded and rendered worthless if the suspect is interviewed outside the police station. There has been an attempt to address the problem of such evasion: under para 11.1 as revised, such interviewing can no longer occur unless the decision to arrest the person being interviewed has not been taken or the exchanges do not amount to 'the questioning of a person regarding his involvement or suspected involvement in a criminal offence or offences' (Note for Guidance 11.1A); or urgent interviewing is necessary to prevent various contingencies arising. Thus, if, in the result, most suspects are taken to the police station to be questioned, this will help to maintain the balance between the increase in detention powers and the safeguards for suspects in detention, but the number and width of the express or implied exceptions to the prohibition may lessen its impact.

Obtaining a confession from the suspect is clearly a crucial stage in the investigation, but obtaining a positive identification of him or her may be of almost equal importance. Thus, it is essential that the most reliable means of obtaining such evidence is made available. The provision for various methods of identification of suspects under Code D, including a confrontation between suspect and witness, is balanced by the need to hold an identification parade if practicable, on the basis that a parade provides the most sure safeguard for the suspect against unreliability in the identification procedure. The courts have attempted to ensure that the police do not accept that a parade was impracticable too readily. In *Ladlow, Moss, Green and Jackson* (1989), 20 suspects had been arrested and the confrontation method of identification was used, since, otherwise, it would allegedly have been necessary to hold 221 separate parades. Despite this, it was ruled that evidence derived from the parades would be excluded. Thus, it appears likely that the police will have to go to great lengths to find persons to stand in a parade before one can be said to be impracticable.[3] The approach that an identification parade should always be the preferred method was confirmed by the House of Lords in *Forbes* (2001). When identification is made, it must be on a concrete basis and not on 'non-detailed descriptions'. Any informal identification is vulnerable to exclusion under s 78 of PACE: see *Hickin* (1996).

It may therefore appear that throughout PACE, a reasonable balance has been struck between safeguards and increased police powers. However, one of the safeguards originally included in the PACE scheme, under Code C, the right to silence, has now been severely curtailed by ss 34–37 of the Criminal Justice and Public Order Act 1994, thereby disturbing the 'balance' which was originally created. Also, as has been pointed out, the safeguards may be evaded, even though the powers may, of course, be used to their full. Further, where it is clear that evasion or breach of the safeguards has occurred, thereby destroying the balance, there will not always be an effective remedy available which could go some way towards restoring it.

Damages will be available at common law in respect of some breaches of PACE. For example, if a police officer arrests a citizen where no reasonable suspicion arises under s 24 or 25 of PACE, an action for false imprisonment might arise. Equally, such a remedy would be available if the provisions governing time limits on detention were breached. The question whether damages are available in respect of property unlawfully seized was considered in *Chief Constable of Lancashire ex p Parker and McGrath* (1993). It was argued on behalf of the police that s 22(2)(a) of PACE, which allows the retention of 'anything seized for the purposes of a criminal investigation', would be superfluous, unless denoting a general power to retain unlawfully seized material. It was held, however, that the sub-section could not bear the weight sought to be placed upon it: it was merely intended to give examples of matters falling within the general provision of s 22(1). Therefore, the police were not entitled to retain the material seized. This decision re-affirmed the need to retain the balance between safeguards for the subject of the search and the police power to search, which might have been disturbed had the various issues been resolved differently.

However, tortious remedies were inapplicable to the provisions of the Codes under s 67(10) and seem to be inapplicable to the most significant statutory interviewing provision, the entitlement to legal advice. There was no tort of denial of access to legal advice: the only possible tortious action was for breach of statutory duty. Whether this tort would lie was a question of policy in relation to any particular statutory provision, and so, until the HRA 1998, the application of this remedy was purely conjectural.[4]

The police complaints mechanism covers any breaches of PACE, including breaches of the Codes under s 67(8), but it is generally agreed that it is defective as a means of redress. It does not allow for compensation to the victim or for the victim to attend any disciplinary proceedings. In any event, most complaints do not result in disciplinary proceedings and it appears that no disciplinary proceedings have been brought in respect of breaches of the Codes. The suspect concerned might, in many instances, be unaware that a breach of the Codes had occurred and while, theoretically, another officer could make a complaint leading to disciplinary proceedings for such a breach, in practice, this appears to be highly unlikely. Furthermore, despite the involvement (albeit limited) of the Police Complaints Authority, the complaints procedure tends to be perceived as being administered by the police themselves: under s 84, a complaint will go in the first instance to the Chief Officer of Police of the force in question, who must determine by reference to the section whether or not he is the appropriate person to deal with it. The Police Complaints Authority has been found to be an insufficient remedy for Convention breaches, under Art 13, in *Khan* (2000), which criticised both its lack of independence and its lack of real remedies. The HRA 1998 has gone a long way towards redressing this problem by allowing Convention-related issues, including Art 5 and 6 complaints against police, to be raised in ordinary courts and receive the normal range of remedies.

The context in which many breaches of PACE have been considered is that of exclusion of evidence. Confessions may be excluded under s 76 if obtained by oppression or in circumstances conducive of unreliability. Any evidence may be excluded under s 78 if its admission would be likely to render the trial unfair. It must be borne in mind that the PACE mechanism for exclusion of evidence provides a means of redress for such breaches only in one circumstance – that the case is pursued to trial and the defendant pleads not guilty. In this one instance, they can be of great value, in that the defendant may be placed in the position he would have been in had the breach not occurred and the police may seem to be 'punished' for their non-compliance with the rules by being prevented from profiting from their own breach. In this sense, exclusion of evidence does provide an effective means of redress. For example, in *Canale* (1990), the police failed to record an interview contemporaneously in breach of para 11.3 of Code C; it was excluded as possibly unreliable under s 78. In *Samuel* (1988), the police unlawfully denied the appellant access to legal advice; the court took the view that if a breach of s 58 had taken place which was causally linked to the confession, s 78 should be invoked. It could be said that in *Samuel*, the court succeeded in restoring the balance between the police power to detain and question, which had been used fully in the case, and the safeguards the detainee should have had, in the sense that the outcome was what it would have been had the proper safeguards been in place. However, the provisions of ss 34–37 of the Criminal Justice Act and Public Order Act 1994, reflected in the new caution introduced under the 1995 revision of Code C, make it less likely that advisers will advise silence, since adverse inferences may be drawn at trial from silence. Thus, it may be more difficult to establish the causal relationship in question relying on the method used in *Samuel*. Section 78 may become less effective as a means of maintaining the balance between police powers and suspects' rights.

Theoretically, the *Samuel* argument as to the causal relationship between an impropriety and a confession could be applied to non-confession evidence but, in practice, it appears that it will not be. According to *Thomas* (1990) and *Effick* (1992), physical evidence will be excluded only if obtained with deliberate illegality; the pre-PACE ruling of the House of Lords in *Fox* (1986) would also lend support to this contention.[5]

Thus, although exclusion of evidence can provide a means of redress when police have not complied with one of the PACE safeguards, it may be unavailable where the evidence obtained due to the breach is physical evidence. It may be unavailable in any event: first, even where a clear breach of PACE has occurred, the evidence may, nevertheless, be admissible; secondly, exclusion of evidence is irrelevant to the majority of defendants who plead guilty. Thus, the police had an incentive to break the rules by, for example, refusing a request for legal advice in the hope of obtaining admissions and a guilty plea. If, in such circumstances, a defendant did plead guilty, he or she had suffered denial of a fundamental right with no hope of redress apart from that offered by a complaint. Now, however, the HRA 1998 will enable any person who believes his arrest or trial have been unfair due to the behaviour of police will be able to argue breaches of, *inter alia*, Art 5 or 6; and *Khan* (2000) makes it clear that any effect on the fairness of proceedings, viewed as a whole, will create a breach of Art 6. Thus courts will be able to monitor and sanction police powers to a far greater extent, and the remedies for most PACE breaches will be greatly expanded. Thus, in conclusion, it appears that the balance between safeguards and police powers has not always been maintained, due to the ease with which certain of the domestic safeguards may be evaded or ignored. Clearly, if safeguards are not observed, the justification for increasing police powers to stop, arrest, search premises, detain and question is lost. It is hoped that courts will use the HRA and the Convention to create stronger protection in these areas for individual rights.

## Notes

1   The problem of voluntary searches and provision for them could be considered in more detail. Note for Guidance 1E provides that certain persons – juveniles, the mentally handicapped or mentally disordered and any person who appears incapable of giving an informed consent – should not be subject to a voluntary search at all. However, this provision is contained only in a Note for Guidance and may therefore be even more likely to be disregarded than an ordinary Code provision. Of course, if an apparently voluntary search takes place, but its subject feels intimidated during it, he or she will

find it hard to make a complaint, as the requisite information will not have been given. Persons who do not fall within the groups mentioned may be subject to a voluntary search under Note 1D(b), but the officer should 'always make it clear that he is seeking the co-operation of the person concerned'.

2    Under the original Code B, before police officers entered a person's property in order to conduct a non-consensual search, they had to inform the person of their identity, the purpose of the search and the grounds for undertaking it. Now, the subjects of all searches must receive further information by means of a standard form – the Notice of Powers and Rights. This form was introduced by para 5.7; the information to be conveyed includes specification of the type of search in question, a summary of the powers of search and seizure arising under the Act and the rights of the subjects of searches.

3    It could be mentioned that a similar caution was shown in the introduction of video identification as an alternative to a parade or a group identification; it was accompanied by various new safeguards: under para 2.15 of Code D, the suspect must be reminded that free legal advice is available before taking part in the identification procedure and, under the new para 2.16, the identification procedure and the consequences if consent to taking part is not forthcoming must be explained in a written notice which the suspect must be given reasonable time to read.

4    Theoretically, use of a false imprisonment claim might be available; argument could be advanced at this point that where gross breaches of the questioning provisions had taken place, such as interviewing a person unlawfully held incommunicado, a detention in itself lawful might thereby be rendered unlawful. However, although the ruling in *Middleweek v Chief Constable of Merseyside* (1985) gave some encouragement to such argument, it now seems to be ruled out, due to the decision in *Weldon v Home Office* (1991) in the context of lawful detention in a prison. It seems likely, therefore, that access to legal advice will continue to be unaffected by the availability of tortious remedies.

5    This important issue could be considered further. The first instance decision in *Edward Fennelly* (1989), in which a failure

to give the reason for a stop and search led to exclusion of the search, appears, then, to be on the wrong track. Furthermore, even if the principles developed under s 78 with respect to confession evidence could properly be applied to other evidence, *Edward Fennelly* would still be a doubtful decision, as no causal relationship could exist between the impropriety in question and the evidence obtained.

# Question 32

Critically evaluate the current scheme under which a citizen can be arrested.

## Answer plan

A fairly difficult question, since it asks you to concentrate only on the arrest scheme. Moreover, it is no good merely writing down everything you know about arrest: you need to probe the weaknesses in the scheme and the areas of uncertainty.

Essentially, the following matters should be considered:

- arrest under common law powers;
- arrest under ss 24 and 25 of the Police and Criminal Evidence Act (PACE) 1984;
- arrest under the Prevention of Terrorism Act and subsequent legislation;
- procedural elements of a valid arrest;
- Art 5 of the European Convention on Human Rights (the Convention) and relevant cases.

# Answer

An arrest may often be the first formal stage in the criminal process. However, any arrest represents a serious curtailment of liberty; therefore, use of the arrest power requires careful regulation. An arrest is seen as *prima facie* illegal, necessitating justification under a specific legal power. If an arrest is effected where no arrest power arises, a civil action for false imprisonment may lie. Despite the need for clarity and precision, such powers were, until relatively recently, granted piecemeal, with the result that, prior to PACE, they were contained in a mass of common law and statutory provisions. No consistent rationale could be discerned and there were a number of gaps and anomalies.[1] The powers are now contained largely in PACE, but common law powers remain, while some statutes create a specific power of arrest which may overlap with the PACE powers.

PACE has not affected the power to arrest which arises at common law for breach of the peace. Factors present in a situation in which breach of the peace occurs may also give rise to arrest powers under PACE, but may extend further than they do due to the wide definition of breach of the peace. The leading case is *Howell* (1981), in which it was found that breach of the peace will arise if violence to persons or property either actual or apprehended occurs. Threatening words are not in themselves a breach of the peace, but they may lead a police officer to apprehend that a breach will arise. A police officer or any other person may arrest if a breach of the peace is in being or apprehended, but not when it has been terminated, unless there is reason to believe that it may be renewed.

PACE contains two separate powers of arrest without warrant, one arising under s 24 and the other under s 25. Broadly speaking, s 24 provides a power of arrest in respect of more serious offences, while s 25 covers all offences, however trivial (including, for example, dropping litter), if certain conditions are satisfied apart from suspicion that the offence in question has been committed. Thus, s 25 operates to cover persons suspected of offences falling outside s 24. Obviously, had s 25 not contained special conditions, there would have been no need for s 24. The difference between s 24 and s 25 is quite important, because, once a person has been arrested under s 24, he or she is said to have been arrested for 'an arrestable offence' and this may have an effect on his or her treatment later on. An 'arrestable offence' is, therefore, one for which a person can be arrested if the necessary reasonable suspicion is present, without a need to show any other ingredients in the situation at the time of arrest.

A police officer can arrest for one of the offences covered by s 24 if he or she has reasonable grounds to suspect that the offence is about to be, is being, or has been committed. An ordinary citizen can arrest under s 24 in the same way, with the omission of the possibility of arresting where the offence is about to be committed. Offences for which a person can be arrested under s 24 may also be classified as 'serious arrestable offences' under s 116.

The police acquired the general power of arrest under s 25 which they had lacked previously. However, this power does not merely allow an officer to arrest for any offence so long as reasonable suspicion can be shown. Such a power would have been viewed as too draconian and a very severe threat to civil liberties. It is balanced by what are known as the 'general arrest conditions', which must also be fulfilled. Therefore, in order to arrest under s 25, two steps must be taken: first, there must be reasonable suspicion relating to the offence in question; and, secondly, one of the arrest conditions must be fulfilled. The need for the officer to have suspicion of the offence in question and the general arrest conditions was emphasised in *Edwards v DPP* (1993). A police constable (but not an ordinary citizen) can arrest if he or she has reasonable grounds to suspect the person of having committed or having attempted to commit the offence or of being in the course of committing or attempting to commit it.

The general arrest conditions divide into two groups: those in which there is or appears to be a failure to furnish a satisfactory name or address so that the service of a summons later on would be impracticable; and those which concern the immediate need to remove the suspect from the street, which would make it inappropriate to serve a summons later. The inclusion of these provisions implies that the infringement of civil liberties represented by an arrest should be resorted to only where no other alternative exists.

Sections 24 and 25 both depend on the concept of reasonable suspicion; the idea behind it is that an arrest should take place at quite a late stage in the investigation. This limits the number of arrests, thereby ensuring that liberty is infringed only where there is a fairly pressing reason to justify the infringement; it also makes it less likely that a person will be wrongfully arrested. It seems likely that the concept of reasonable suspicion will be interpreted in accordance with the provisions as to reasonable suspicion under Code A.

However, Annex B, para 4 of the original Code A stated that the level of suspicion for a stop would be 'no less' than that needed for arrest. Although this provision is omitted from the revised Code A, it would seem that, in principle, the Code A provisions should be relevant to arrests if the Codes and statute are to be treated as a harmonious whole. Moreover, it would appear strange if a more rigorous test could be applied to the reasonable suspicion necessary to effect a stop than that necessary to effect an arrest. If this is correct, it would seem that certain matters, such as an individual's racial group, could never be factors which could support a finding of reasonable suspicion.

The objective nature of suspicion required under Code A is echoed in various decisions on the suspicion needed for an arrest. In *Dallison v Caffrey* (1965), Lord Diplock said the test was whether 'a reasonable man assumed to know the law and possessed of the information which in fact was possessed by the defendant would believe there were [reasonable grounds]'. Thus, it is not enough for a police officer to have a hunch that a person has committed or is about to commit an offence; there must be a concrete basis for this suspicion which relates to the particular person in question and could be evaluated by an objective observer. If an officer only has a hunch – mere suspicion as opposed to reasonable suspicion – he or she might continue to observe the person in question, but could not arrest until the suspicion had increased and could be termed 'reasonable suspicion'.[2]

However, this still leaves a great deal of leeway to officers to arrest where suspicion relating to the particular person is at a low level, but they want to further the investigation by gathering information. At present, the courts seem prepared to allow police such leeway, and it should be noted that PACE endorses a reasonably low level of suspicion due to the distinction it maintains between belief and suspicion, suspicion probably being the lower standard. In *Ward v Chief Constable of Somerset and Avon Constabulary* (1986), for example, the grounds for suspicion were fairly flimsy and might have warranted further inquiries before arresting. Similarly, the Court of Appeal in *Castorina v Chief Constable of Surrey* (1988) appeared reluctant to take a rigorous approach to the question of reasonable suspicion. Detectives were investigating a burglary of a company's premises and, on reasonable grounds, came to the conclusion that it was an 'inside job'. The managing director told them that a certain employee had recently been dismissed and that the documents taken would be useful to someone with a grudge. However, she also said that she would not have expected the particular employee to commit a burglary. The detectives then arrested the employee, having found that she had no previous criminal record. She was detained for nearly four hours and then released without charge. She claimed damages for false imprisonment and was awarded £4,500. The judge considered that it was necessary to find that the detectives had had 'an honest belief founded on a reasonable suspicion leading an ordinary cautious man to the conclusion that the person arrested was guilty of the offence'.

However, the Court of Appeal overturned the award on the basis that the test applied by the judge had been too severe. It was held that the question of honest belief was irrelevant; the issue of reasonable suspicion had nothing to do with the officer's subjective state of mind. The question was whether there was reasonable cause to suspect the plaintiff of burglary. Given that certain factors could be identified, including inside knowledge of the company's affairs and the motive of the plaintiff, it appeared that there was sufficient basis for the detectives to have reasonable grounds for suspicion. Purchas J ruled that, once reasonable suspicion arises, officers have discretion as to whether to arrest or do something else, such as making further inquiries. This discretion can be attacked on *Wednesbury* principles: an arrest will be found to be unlawful if no reasonable person looking at the circumstances could have considered that an arrest should be affected, if the decision is based on irrelevant considerations and if it is not made in good faith and for a proper purpose. It was found that no breach of these principles had occurred and, as reasonable grounds for making the arrest were found, the first instance judge had erred in ruling that further inquiries should have been made before the arrest.

Thus, the need to make further inquiries would be relevant to the first stage – arriving at reasonable suspicion – but not to the second – determining whether to make an arrest. That it must be relevant to the first is axiomatic: an investigation passes through many stages, from the first, in which a vague suspicion relating to a particular person arises, up until the point when it is proved – if it is – that that person's guilt can be shown beyond reasonable doubt. At some point in that process, reasonable suspicion giving rise to a direction as to whether to effect an arrest arises; thus, there must be a point in the early stages at which it is possible to say that more inquiries should have been made, more evidence gathered, before the arrest could lawfully take place. As the courts appear prepared to accept that arrest at quite an early stage in this process may be said to be based on reasonable grounds, and that the application of *Wednesbury* principle leaves little leeway for challenge to the decision to arrest, it may be said that the interest of the citizen in his or her personal liberty is not being accorded sufficient weight under the current tests.[3]

The power of arrest with warrant does not arise under PACE. There are a large number of statutory provisions allowing an arrest warrant to be issued of which the most significant is that arising under s 1 of the Magistrates Court Act 1980. Under this power, a warrant may be issued if a person aged at least 17 is suspected of an offence which is indictable or punishable with imprisonment, or where no satisfactory address is known allowing a summons to be served. This provision therefore limits the circumstances under which a warrant will be sought, as opposed to using the non-warrant powers under PACE and, as the police now have such broad powers of arrest under ss 24 and 25, it seems that arrest in reliance on a warrant will be used even less under PACE than it was previously.

If a statute creates an offence which is a serious offence falling within s 24, then, obviously, the arrest power under s 24 is applicable. If a statute creates a more minor offence, then, equally, the arrest power under s 25 is applicable, so long as one or more of the general arrest conditions are satisfied. Section 11 of the Public Order Act 1986 and s 51 of the Police Act 1964 provide examples of such offences. However, certain statutes expressly create specific powers of arrest which are not dependent on s 24 or 25, such as s 155 of the Criminal Justice and Public Order Act 1994. In such cases, the procedure under s 28 which will be considered below will still apply.

Almost all the indictable offences under the Prevention of (Temporary Provisions) Terrorism Act 1989 and the Terrorism Act 2000, which replaces it, carry a penalty of at least five years' imprisonment and are, therefore, arrestable offences under s 24 of

PACE. There is also a power of arrest under the Acts themselves. This power has two limbs. The first empowers a constable to arrest for certain specified offences under the Terrorism Act 2000. As these offences are arrestable offences in any event, this power would seem to overlap with that under s 24. However, if an arrest is effected under the Terrorism Act as opposed to s 24 of PACE, this has an effect on the length of detention, as will be seen below. The second limb provides a completely separate power from the PACE power; it allows arrest without needing to show suspicion relating to a particular offence.

Instead, the constable needs to have reasonable grounds for suspecting that a person is concerned in the preparation or instigation of acts of terrorism. This arrest is not for an offence but, in practice, for investigation, questioning and general intelligence gathering which may be conducted for the purpose, as Lowry puts it, of 'isolating and identifying the urban guerillas and then detaching them from the supportive or ambivalent community'. Thus, this power represents a clear departure from the principle that liberty should be curtailed only on clear and specific grounds which connect the actions of the suspect with a specific offence under criminal law.

For an arrest to be made validly, not only must the power of arrest exist, whatever its source, but the procedural elements must be complied with. The fact that a power of arrest arises will not alone make the arrest lawful. These elements are of crucial importance, due to the consequences which may flow from a lawful arrest which will not flow from an unlawful one. Such consequences include the right of the officer to use force in making an arrest if necessary and the loss of liberty inherent in an arrest. If an arrest has not occurred, the citizen is free to go wherever he or she will and any attempt to prevent him or her doing so will be unlawful. It is therefore important to convey the fact of the arrest to the arrestee and to mark the point at which the arrest comes into being and general liberty ceases.

At common law, there had to be a physical detention or a touching of the arrestee to convey the fact of detention, unless he or she made this unnecessary by submitting to it; the fact of arrest had to be made clear (*Alderson v Booth* (1969)) and the reason for it had to be made known (*Christie v Leachinsky* (1947)). The common law safeguards have been modified and strengthened by s 28 of PACE. Under s 28, both the fact of and the reason for the arrest must be made known at the time or as soon as practicable afterwards. However, an ordinary citizen is not under this duty if the fact of the arrest and the reason for it are obvious. Conveying the fact of the arrest does not involve using a particular form of words, but it may be that reasonable detail must be given so that the arrestee will be in a position to give a convincing denial and therefore be more speedily released from detention. Given the infringement of liberty represented by an arrest and the need, therefore, to restore liberty as soon as possible, consistent with the needs of the investigation, it is unfortunate that s 28 did not make it clear that a reasonable degree of detail should be given.

However, the reason for the arrest need only be made known as soon as practicable. The meaning and implications of this provision were considered in *DPP v Hawkins* (1988). A police officer took hold of the defendant to arrest him, but did not give the reason. The youth struggled and was therefore later charged with assaulting an officer in the execution of his duty. The question which arose was whether the officer was in the execution of his duty, as he had failed to give the reason for the arrest. If the arrest was thereby rendered invalid, he could not be in the execution of his duty, as it could not include effecting an unlawful arrest. It was determined in the Court of Appeal that the arrest became unlawful when the time came at which it was practicable to inform the defendant of the reason, but he was not so informed. This occurred at the police station or perhaps in the police car, but did not occur earlier, due to the defendant's behaviour. However, the arrest did not become retrospectively unlawful and, therefore, did not affect acts done before its unlawfulness came into being, which thus remained acts done in the execution of duty.

Thus, the police have a certain leeway as to informing the arrestee; the arrest will not be affected and nor will other acts arising from it, until the time when it would be practicable to inform of the reason for it has come and gone. However, if there was nothing in the behaviour of the arrestee to make informing him or her impracticable, then the arrest will be unlawful from its inception. Following this decision, what can be said as to the status of the suspect before the time came and passed at which the requisite words should have been spoken? Was he or was he or not under arrest at that time? In *Murray v Ministry of Defence* (1988), soldiers occupied a woman's house, thus clearly taking her into detention, but did not inform her of the fact of arrest for half an hour. The question arose whether she was falsely imprisoned during that half hour. The House of Lords found that delay in giving the requisite information was acceptable due to the alarm which the fact of arrest, if known, might have aroused in the particular circumstances – the unsettled situation in Northern Ireland.

If a false arrest occurs, a remedy will be available. Where the procedural elements are not complied with, but no good reason for such failure arises, or if no power to arrest arose in the first place, the arrestee would have grounds for bringing an action for false imprisonment. Further, if a false arrest occurs and, subsequently, physical evidence is discovered or the defendant makes a confession, the defence may argue that the evidence should be excluded due to the false arrest. However, Murray has rendered the concept of a false arrest less clear cut.

It seems that an arrest which does not comply with all the procedural requirements will still be an arrest, as far as all the consequences arising from it are concerned, for a period of time. It is therefore in a more precarious position than an arrest which, from its inception, complies with all the requirements, because it will cease to be an arrest at an uncertain point. Therefore, some departure has occurred from the principle that there should be a clear demarcation between the point at which the citizen is at liberty and the point at which his or her liberty is restrained.

A new dimension needs to be added to these comments: the cases which have interpreted Art 5 of the Convention in relation to UK law. It remains to be seen whether UK courts will demand or create changes to the current statutory arrest conditions and rules, but some reform or, at least, clarification appears necessary. *Brogan v UK* (1988) established that detention of terrorism suspects for prolonged periods was unlawful and so breached Art 5. *Murray* (1994) shows that Art 5 takes an objective approach to whether an arrest was justified by reasonable grounds. *Fox, Campbell and Hartley v UK* (1990) shows that 'reasonable suspicion' varies according to the circumstances of the alleged offence; 'honest suspicion' is, however, not enough, unless it is also reasonable to an objective view. Thus, the subjective approach taken in some UK cases is wrong, and the decision in *Castorina* (1988) is endorsed. In future, the remedies available for wrongful arrest, whatever the statutory basis of the arrest, will be the same and arise from the HRA 1998 and the courts' future interpretation of Art 5.

## Notes

1   For example, the Criminal Law Act 1967 gave a power of arrest without warrant where the offence in question arose under statute and carried a sentence of five years. Thus, no power of arrest arose in respect of common law offences carrying such a sentence. This situation was detrimental to civil liberties, due to the uncertainty of the powers, but it was also detrimental to the maintenance of law and order, as officers may have been deterred from effecting an arrest where one was necessary.

2   It would seem that a future revision of the Codes might usefully state that the concept of reasonable suspicion in Code A applies to arrest as well; if so, it would at least be clear that certain factors can never support reasonable suspicion.

3   Under s 24, it is not always necessary to show that reasonable suspicion exists. If an arrestable offence is, in fact, being committed, or has been committed, or is about to be committed, a constable can arrest, even if he or she is just acting on an hunch which luckily turns out to be justified. Of course, if an officer arrests without reasonable suspicion, he or she is taking a risk. These provisions were included because it might seem strange if a person could found an action for false imprisonment on the basis that, although they were committing an offence, they should not have been arrested for it. However, if it cannot be established that the offence was committed or was about to be committed, it is not enough to show that reasonable grounds for suspicion did, in fact, exist, although the officer did not know of them. In *Siddiqui v Swain* (1979), the Divisional Court held that the words 'reasonable grounds to suspect' used in s 8(5) of the Road Traffic Act 1972 include the requirement that the officer should actually suspect. This approach was also adopted in *Chapman v DPP* (1988).

# Question 33

'The interviewing scheme under the Police and Criminal Evidence Act 1984 is wholly inadequate as a means of preventing miscarriages of justice.' Do you agree?

## Answer plan

It should be noted that the question is only concerned with the interviewing scheme under the Police and Criminal Evidence Act (PACE) 1984, not with other methods of addressing the problem of miscarriages of justice. Essentially, the following matters should be considered:

- the nature of the safeguards available under Pts IV and V of PACE and Codes of Practice C and E;
- the provisions determining when the safeguards come into play – definition of an 'interview' – interviewing inside or outside the police station;
- the legal advice provisions;
- the recording provisions;
- the value of exclusion of evidence as a form of redress for breaches of the interviewing scheme – the relevance of ss 34–37 of the Criminal Justice and Public Order Act 1994;
- the scope for miscarriages of justice which remains.

# Answer

Our criminal justice process relies heavily on the use of confession evidence but, at the same time, is wedded to a system in which a suspect is interviewed by a body, the police, who have a strong interest in securing a conviction, under conditions which are entirely under police control. In such circumstances, what can be done to ensure that a confession so acquired can be relied on by a court?

A body of rules can be devised, intended first to alter the balance of power between interviewers and interviewee, reducing the vulnerability of the interviewee and, secondly, to create confidence in the evidence of what was said, putting the jury as far as possible in the position they would have been in had they been there. Such rules will, however, tend to run counter to the concerns of those expected to apply them and, therefore, may not be observed or, more subtly, weaknesses and loopholes will be discovered and explored. Further rules may then be created to eradicate the loopholes. However, the pressure to find loopholes will remain unchanged and may become greater as the unwieldiness and complexity of the scheme creates greater frustration with it.

This process began in this country with the Judges' Rules, which were replaced by the more complex interviewing scheme under PACE and Code C which was, in turn, modified by the revision of Code C and the introduction of tape recording under Code E. A more sophisticated scheme still is in view, centring around video taping of interviews. Nevertheless, the pressure which originally led the police to circumvent the rules is still unchanged.

Is it possible in this situation to prevent such evasion? Some might argue that it is not and that the system will always be flawed until its central weakness is addressed. However, before coming to such a conclusion, it seems worth considering the latest attempt to create a sound set of rules for interviewing. The rules were aimed at certain specific loopholes which had become apparent in Code C – suspects could be encouraged out of having legal advice and suspects could be interviewed outside the police station, thereby evading the safeguards available within it. An inquiry into the means used to eradicate these loopholes and the likely impact in terms of confessions admitted may say something about the general use of rules in this situation.

These changes represent an attempt to obtain greater control of the interviewing process, to address the inherent limitations of police interviews. If an interview is conducted in compliance with sound interviewing rules it should be possible to feel confident that a conviction based on it will be safe and therefore miscarriages of justice should be less likely. Of course, it is possible that a confession obtained after adherence to all the provisions of the interviewing scheme will nevertheless be excluded from evidence. Evidence of compliance with the interviewing scheme without more will not preclude exclusion of the confession. It will be assumed only that a sound interviewing scheme is capable of taking the necessary first step towards ensuring the reliability of admissions obtained and the integrity of a resultant conviction.

It may be worth pausing here for a moment to consider the general nature of the interviewing scheme which PACE brought into being in order to place the changes in their context. It consists of a web of provisions which derive from three sources of differing legal status: the Act itself, Codes C and E made under it and the Notes for Guidance accompanying the Codes. The Notes were apparently included as a means of helping police officers to apply the Code provisions; they are not part of the Codes, except in a physical sense. In this context, the nature of the safeguards surrounding interviews will be indicated, but the important issue will be the question when they come into play. It will be argued that there is still too great a variation in the levels of protection available. The safeguards available are intended to ensure either that the suspect is not at an undue disadvantage in comparison with the interviewers or to protect the integrity of the interview, so that it can be used later on as evidence against the suspect if necessary. Of course, these functions are not entirely distinct; in a sense, each one flows from the other. In what follows, both functions are in question where levels of protection for interviews are referred to. It should be pointed out at this stage that under the Code C scheme as revised, the safeguards available were reasonably adequate if they were all in place. However, a radical change to that scheme has been made by curtailment of the right to silence under ss 34–37 of the Criminal Justice and Public Order Act 1994 and this is reflected in the new and complex caution introduced under the 1995 revision of Code C. This means that, at present, even where all the safeguards are in place, there may be great pressure on the suspect to speak, bearing in mind the disadvantage which silence may create, and this may result in an increase in the number of false confessions. However, the ECHR cases make it clear that a suspect must not be compelled to speak (*Funke v France* (1993), *Murray v UK* (1996)) and that inferences may not be drawn from silence *unless* that silence 'could only sensibly be attributed to their having no answer or none that would stand up to cross-examination', as to the question originally asked (*Condron v UK* (2000)). So, any silence which can later be explained plausibly should no longer trigger inferences or Art 6 will be breached.

The correct interpretation of the term 'interview' used in Code C as originally drafted was a matter of great importance, because the relevant safeguards only came into play once an exchange between police officer and suspect was designated an interview. The term 'interview' therefore tended to be given a wide interpretation and, eventually, the definition given to it by the Court of Appeal in *Mathews* (1990), 'any discussion or talk between suspect and police officer', brought within its ambit many exchanges far removed from formal interviews.

However, assuming that an exchange could be called an interview, the safeguards applying to it differed quite markedly, depending on where it took place. Those available *inside* the police station included contemporaneous recording or tape recording; the ability to read over, verify and sign the notes of the interview as a correct record; notification of the right to legal advice; the option of having legal advice and of having the adviser present and, where appropriate, the presence of an adult.[1] In 'the field', however, it was only necessary to ensure that an accurate record of the interview was made and, where appropriate, an adult was present. In other words, a minimum level of protection only was available, thus creating greater scope for impropriety, including fabrication of confessions, in such circumstances. The arbitrary dividing line thus drawn between those suspects interviewed in or out of the police station was one of the main deficiencies of Code C.

At present, classifying an exchange as an interview will not be quite as crucial under the new scheme as it was previously because, under para 11.13, as revised, any comments relevant to the offence made by a suspected person outside the context of an interview must be accurately recorded and then verified and signed by the suspect. However, such classification will still be important, because it remains the first, although not the only, step towards ensuring that the other safeguards mentioned above are available. A definition of the term 'interview' is now contained in para 11.1A, which reads:

An interview is the questioning of a person regarding his involvement or suspected involvement in a criminal offence or offences, which, by virtue of paragraph 10.1 of Code C, is required to be carried out under caution.

Paragraph 10.1 of Code C requires a caution to be given where the answers to questions (or the suspect's failure to answer questions) may be given in evidence to a court in a prosecution. Questioning which is simply to establish a person's identity, or the ownership of a vehicle, or to assist in the conduct of a search of a person or property, will not, therefore, constitute an 'interview'.

The previous definition, which the one given above replaced in 1995, had tried to draw a distinction between questioning about a criminal offence (an interview), and questioning in order to obtain information or an explanation of facts, or 'in the ordinary course of the officer's duties' (not an interview). This proved problematic, and was criticised by the Court of Appeal in *Cox* (1992), leading to the revised version being introduced.

The hallmark of an interview is 'questioning', so if the conversation is instigated by the suspect, this may not be an interview (*Menard* (1995)). The current definition is in line with the approach taken in *Absolam* (1989), where an interview was defined as a questions directed by the police to a suspect, and in *Maguire* (1989), where an invitation to the suspect to explain himself was not treated as amounting to an interview.

Once an exchange can be designated an interview, it will be of significance whether it takes place inside or outside the police station but, due to certain new provisions, the significance will not be as great as it was under the original scheme. Paragraph 11 now contains provisions in sub-para 11.10 for giving the suspect the record of the interview to verify and sign. This provision was previously contained in para 12 which applied only to interviews in police stations due to its heading and was not, therefore, available to the suspect being interviewed outside it. Further, under new para 11.5, the interview must be recorded contemporaneously wherever it takes place unless, in the investigating officer's view, this would not be practicable or would interfere with its conduct. Thus, where an exchange is an interview, the new provisions do go beyond para 11.13. However, there is no change as far as notification of the right to legal advice is concerned. It is also, at present, unlikely that the interview would be tape recorded: Code E on tape recording does not envisage recording taking place anywhere but inside the police station. Thus, an unsatisfactory distinction between suspects interviewed in or out of the police station is still preserved.

However, the scheme, as revised, appeared to address itself to this problem in a radical way by means of a prohibition under para 11.1 on interviewing outside the police station except in exceptional circumstances. It is, of course, only 'interviews' which must not occur outside the police station; other exchanges can take place because, in general, the need for them to be subject to the level of protection available inside it will not be so pressing. Any comments made relevant to an offence would be subject only to the provisions of new para 11.13. However, courts have recently interpreted *any* questioning designed to incriminate the suspect as an 'interview': see *Bailey v DPP* (1998).

Even if an interview is taking place, para 11.1 will not apply if the decision to arrest has not yet been taken. Paragraph 11.1 requires a police officer to categorise a person either as someone who may possibly be involved in an offence or as someone who will clearly be arrested. Presumably, the para 11.1 prohibition was aimed at ensuring that suspects being interviewed were afforded the safeguards available once they were in the police station. It is therefore anomalous that persons suspected of an offence can be questioned away from it. This anomaly is created by the difference between the levels of suspicion denoted by para 11.1A and 11.1: the level under para 11.1A appears to be the lower, giving scope for the argument that the decision to arrest had not yet been made because the level of suspicion was not high enough. This loophole could have been closed had the words 'suspected involvement' in an offence also been used in para 11.1 to determine the point at which an exchange would become an interview. The police may find it difficult where there are very strong grounds for suspicion to support a claim that interviewing could continue, because the decision to arrest had not been taken, but, otherwise, it will be difficult to be certain, in retrospect, on this point.

Under para 11.1(a), (b) and (c), interviewing can occur outside the station in order to avert certain specified risks. The first exception under para 11.1(a), allowing interviewing to take place at once where delay might lead to interference with evidence, could be interpreted very broadly and could apply whenever there was some likelihood that evidence connected with any offence, but not immediately obtainable, was in existence.[2]

It is clear that there is continuing variation in levels of protection for interviews; the change brought about by para 11.1 is far less radical than may at first appear. Wide, but uncertain scope for interviewing outside the police station still remains. Thus, things stand as they did under the original Code: in order to bring certain safeguards into play, it must first be found that an exchange constitutes an interview and then that it took place within the police station. Taking access to legal advice, tape recording and the provision for interviews under paras 11 and 12 as the main safeguards, it becomes apparent that there are three levels of protection available which depend on the category into which the exchange falls.

Inside the police station, if the person in question is an arrestee or a volunteer under caution and the exchange is an interview, all the available safeguards will apply. If an interview takes place outside the police station, but falls outside the para 11.1 prohibition, the same verifying and recording provisions will apply, with the proviso that contemporaneous recording (and, at present, tape recording) is likely to be impracticable. The most important difference is that no notification of the right to legal advice need be given.

If the person is suspected of involvement in an offence, but the level of suspicion is below that which would warrant a caution or *a fortiori* an arrest and the interview takes place in the police station, the lower level of protection described above will apply, but the person also has the right to have legal advice and, possibly, due to the provision of new para 11.2, to be told of this right. The paragraph requires a reminder to be given of the entitlement to free legal advice before any interview in a police station. This provision may apply to the situation envisaged, although it could be argued that the use of the word 'remind' suggests that that was not the intention behind it, because the person in question will not already be aware of the right. Utterances relevant to the offence outside the context of an interview made by a suspected person (who could obviously be an arrestee or a volunteer under caution) are subject only to the basic level of protection which obtains under para 11.13.

The main objection to this scheme is that an arbitrary dividing line is still being drawn between suspects interviewed inside or outside the police station, although, admittedly, interviewing outside it should now occur less frequently. The arbitrariness of this division is most clearly apparent in the distinction drawn between suspects who fall just outside and just inside the category of those who will clearly be arrested. Further, even where, formally speaking, all the safeguards should be in place, there may still be methods of evading them. As research conducted by Sanders in 1989 showed, the police have developed a number of means of subverting the legal advice scheme, with a view to discouraging suspects from obtaining access to legal advice.

Disputes over the admissibility of confessions under s 78 will continue, because it will be necessary to put exchanges between suspect and police into the categories mentioned above; having done so, if one of the safeguards applicable to that category has not been made available, the confession may be inadmissible. The other category of confessions which may be inadmissible will be those which should not have taken place at all, because they occurred outside the police station, but fell within the para 11.1 prohibition. If one of the aims of new para 11.1 was to reduce the scope for such disputes, it appears unlikely to fulfil it. Moreover, the scheme is unlikely to prevent miscarriages of justice, because it leaves open scope for evading certain of the key safeguards including tape recording and access to legal advice. Confessions obtained without such safeguards will only be subject to the s 78 test if the suspect pleads not guilty. Further, evasion of the rules must usually be characterised as a breach of the scheme in order to trigger off use of s 78. However, it may not appear that a breach has occurred, again leaving open the possibility that a potential miscarriage of justice will go unrecognised. But it is hoped that the regeneration of case law and renewed discussion of these issues in the HRA 1998-based cases on Art 6 of the Convention will result in clarification of the existing rules and give the courts the ability to provide comprehensive remedies for all police abuses, whatever their PACE classification, since the focus has shifted from the legality or illegality of the police actions towards an evaluation of the fairness of the trial and pre-trial behaviour, viewed as a whole.

## Notes

1 If the interview took place on 'other premises', all the safeguards outlined above would apply apart from the requirements to *inform* of the right to legal advice and to allow the suspect to verify and sign the record of the interview.

2 In support of this, it could be pointed out that, even if there were no others involved in the offence who had not been apprehended, it could be argued that the evidence was at risk from the moment of arrest, because news of the arrest might become known to persons with a motive for concealing it. This argument could also apply to the exception under (c) in respect of hindering the recovery of property obtained in consequence of the commission of any offence, with the proviso that (c) will obviously apply to a narrower range of offences.

# Question 34

Marcus, a journalist, is seen at 3 am outside a nightclub by two police officers who are responding to report that a violent disturbance is occurring. He appears to be angry and hostile. The police officers stop Marcus, search his pockets and question him. They find a weapon which they believe has been used in an assault earlier that night. At this point, Marcus becomes angry and swears at the officers, then repeatedly kicks the police car. While Marcus is being taken to the police station, an officer visits Marcus' home and searches there for evidence related to the earlier assault. They find items which they believe are related to several other serious offences. Advise Marcus of his rights and the likelihood of any successful prosecution against him.

## Answer plan

This is a reasonably straightforward, if broad ranging, problem question which encompasses almost all of a defendant's rights under the Police and Criminal Evidence Act (PACE) 1984. Students should demonstrate detailed knowledge of PACE, the Codes and the relevant Notes. Case law should also be considered.

The key issues are:

- were the officers entitled to stop and search Marcus?;
- at which point were there sufficient grounds for arrest?;
- was the evidence found at Marcus' house obtained properly, and so is it admissible?

# Answer

The first issue to be addressed is whether the officers were originally entitled to stop and search Marcus, and on which basis. Section 1 of PACE 1984 allows a valid stop and search of a person only when a number of conditions have been met. The search must be for stolen or prohibited articles, or offensive weapons, and the officer must be able to show that he had reasonable grounds for suspicion that any such article would be found. It is not clear why the decision to stop and search Marcus was made: it could have been on suspicion that he had been involved in the violent disturbance, or because he was on the street late at night, or because he fits the description of the man wanted for the earlier assault, or because the officers believe that he may have an offensive weapon.

Not all of these possibilities will fall within those acceptable under PACE. There is no general power to stop and search Marcus; it is only if there are reasonable grounds for suspicion that he has a weapon or stolen property on his person that the search is justifiable under s 1. The further conditions are in s 2 and include that the officer must identify himself as such, state the grounds and reasons for the search and, where practicable, keep a record of the search. If more than outer clothing is to be removed, then the suspect must be taken out of public view and the search must be conducted by a person of the same sex as the suspect. If the PACE rules are not followed, then any evidence found may be inadmissible and any later arrest may be groundless; hence, the safeguards have great importance. It is not known whether the officers have any reasonable grounds for suspicion that Marcus has a prohibited article on his person; if they were simply lucky in finding the weapon, then the search will not be justified under PACE. The reasonable grounds must exist prior to the search: in

*King v Gardiner* (1979), it was held that officer must be able to demonstrate that he believed that here were reasonable grounds at the time of the search, and that 'reasonableness' is an objective term. Hence, the officers who carried out the search need to provide information as to the reasons why Marcus was searched and to demonstrate that they complied with Code A of PACE.

However, it is likely that those officers will argue that the search fell outside PACE, since it was carried out 'by consent'. Under such a search, there is no need to demonstrate reasonable grounds for suspicion; mere curiosity is enough. There seem to be many such 'consensual' searches where the suspect disputes ever having given his consent. The Notes For Guidance do state that a search by consent should only occur where the officer has made it clear that he is seeking the consent of the person to be searched and has told that person that he need not consent and can refuse to be searched (Note 1D(b)).

The second issue is whether and when there were sufficient grounds to justify arresting Marcus and whether he has been correctly cautioned. Once Marcus became angry and then kicked the police car, there is more than one basis on which to justify arresting him. Any arrest is unlawful unless justified at common law or under the two PACE methods: with or without a warrant. It is not clear whether Marcus was arrested at this stage, if at all. It is possible that he attends the police station voluntarily to 'help police with their inquiries'; however, it is more likely that he has been arrested, since it is hard to argue voluntary attendance by a man in an angry and violent state of mind.

There are three methods by which an arrest may validly be made: at common law for breach of the peace; or by two separate PACE methods, which will be discussed below. According to the leading case of *Howell* (1981), arrest at common law may be carried out where the constable (or other person) has actually witnessed a breach of the peace by the arrestee; or where, although no breach of the peace has occurred, the person making the arrest reasonably believes that one is imminent; or where a breach of the peace has already been committed by the person being arrested and the person making the arrest now has a reasonable belief that a further breach of the peace will occur. Any of these could be argued on the present facts, and so a common law arrest is justifiable from the moment that Marcus became angry and kicked the car.

If however Marcus has been arrested under either of the PACE methods, then matters are less straightforward. The first PACE method is under s 24 – without a warrant, where an arrestable offence is being, or has been, committed by the suspect. Depending upon the injuries inflicted in the earlier assault, that offence might justify arrest without warrant in this way, or the kicking of the car could be criminal damage. Swearing at the police officers is not, in itself, arrestable; however, it might justify arrest under the s 25 General Arrest Conditions, since it can be argued that Marcus' current state of mind makes him likely to injure another or damage property (s 25(3)(d)). Under PACE, the question of whether the arresting officer had reasonable grounds for his belief arises again. In *Castorina v Chief Constable of Surrey* (1988), it was stated that it is not necessary 'for the officer to conclude that the person was guilty of the offence; it was enough that a reasonable man would suspect that that was so'.

The third method of arrest is by warrant, which is not practicable or likely on the present facts, due to the time delay which would be involved.

Whichever the method of and grounds for arrest, Marcus must now be cautioned and informed of the reasons for his arrest (Code C, para 10.1; s 28(3) of PACE). The arrest will be unlawful if these safeguards are not carried out.

The next issue is whether the evidence found at his house was obtained properly and, hence, whether it is admissible in court against him. It does not appear that Marcus has given his consent to the search of his premises. Therefore, one of the two relevant PACE provisions must have been complied with: either s 8 (entry and search with a warrant) or s 18 (entry and search without a warrant after arrest). Under s 8, magistrates may issue warrants to enter premises to search them for evidence of serious arrestable offences if satisfied that there are reasonable grounds for belief that all five following grounds exist:

- that a serious arrestable offence has been committed;
- that there is material on the premises which is likely to be of substantial value to the investigation of that offence;

- that the material is likely to be relevant evidence;
- that the material is not subject to legal privilege (s 10), is not excluded material (s 11) or special procedure material (s 14); and
- that one of the conditions in s 8(3) applies, for example, it is not practicable to obtain consent of any person to the entry onto the premises, or that the purposes of the search might be frustrated unless entry is immediate.

Further, the safeguards for search warrants in s 15 of PACE and Code B, para 2 must be complied with. The warrant must specify which material is to be sought, and the entry and search of the premises will be unlawful if the terms of the warrant are not complied with, for example, if the police have conducted a 'fishing expedition' and the material which they have taken was not what they were looking for.

Under s 18, police may, after arresting a person for an arrestable offence, enter and search premises occupied or controlled by the arrestee if they have reasonable grounds to suspect that evidence may be found there which relates to that offence; and any such evidence found may be seized under s 18(2). Since it appears that the evidence taken, or at least some of it, does not relate to the offence for which Marcus has been arrested, but to other serious offences, there is a problem here for the police in justifying its removal. In *Jeffrey v Black* (1978), a search was held to be unlawful, since the offence of arrest and the items found did not match. For s 18, written authorisation must have been given to the searching constable by an inspector. Again, s 32 allows searches of premises which an arrestee has left shortly before being arrested, but only for evidence related to the offence of arrest. The seizure of articles found in any of these manners is covered by s 19 and Code B, para 6; a constable who is lawfully on premises may seize any items found on the premises if he or she has reasonable grounds for belief that they were obtained through the offence, that they would otherwise be destroyed or disposed of, or that they are evidence relating to *any* offence *and* it is necessary to seize them in order to prevent them being disposed of (even if they are excluded material). The crucial question, then, is whether the entry was lawful in the first place, since, otherwise, the seizure cannot be justified. Marcus is a journalist; hence, some of the material at his house is likely to be excluded material under s 11(1)(c), and so cannot be taken from the premises unless it was intended for publication or the s 19 power is used. In any case, the material must be returned as soon as is practicable.

Thus, every aspect of Marcus' treatment before, during and after arrest must be scrutinised and found to comply with PACE and its Codes if the evidence so produced is to be used against him at his later trial, especially in the light of the Human Rights Act 1998 and the subsequent likely use of the Art 6 right to a fair trial to exclude evidence which might otherwise have been admissible under s 78 of PACE.

# CHAPTER 6

# PRISONERS' RIGHTS

## Introduction

Examiners tend to set both problem and essay questions in this area. Problem questions often concern the use of judicial review by prisoners to challenge disciplinary hearings which appear to have fallen below the standards demanded by natural justice. Essay questions often concern the use of judicial review and Arts 6 and 8 of the European Convention on Human Rights to uphold prisoners' rights.

Students should be familiar with the following areas:

- Arts 6 and 8 of the European Convention on Human Rights (the Convention);

- key decisions of the European Court of Human Rights on privacy, access to a court and standards in disciplinary hearings;

- use of judicial review in this area, particularly the application of the principles of natural justice;

- key provisions of the Prison Rules 1999 (which incorporate and amend the earlier versions) and the Prison Amendment Rules (Nos 1 and 2) 2000;

- the Woolf proposals and Ramsbottom Reports;

- influence of private law remedies

- proposals for prison reform, including potential privatisation

## Question 35

'Enjoyment of civil liberties no longer stops at the prison gates. Nevertheless, despite the influence of the European Convention on Human Rights, prisoners' rights are still in their infancy.' Discuss.

## Answer plan

A reasonably straightforward essay question. It is necessary to identify the areas in which improvement has occurred and to consider how far the Convention has influenced those areas. It is also necessary to ask whether in certain instances the domestic courts have gone further in protecting prisoners' rights than the European Court of Human Rights (ECHR). It should be asked in relation to the fundamental right to freedom from inhuman and degrading treatment whether reliance on the ECHR is the best method of improving basic living standards in UK prisons. The extent to which, in the various areas, improvement is still needed should be considered. Essentially, the following matters should be considered:

- key decisions of the ECHR on privacy, access to a court and standards in disciplinary hearings;
- use of judicial review in this area, particularly the application of the principles of natural justice: general influence of the ECHR;
- *Deputy Governor of Parkhurst Prison ex p Hague, Weldon v Home Office* (1991);
- limitations of the ECHR, particularly in relation to improving basic living standards in UK prisons.

# Answer

During the late 1970s and 1980s, there was an increasing recognition that certain fundamental rights of prisoners should receive legal protection, even though the Prison Rules themselves allowed them to be unjustifiably infringe or seemed to provide only basic protection. It will be argued that greater protection has been achieved partly, but not solely, due to the influence of the Convention; improvement has also come about through the application of the principles of natural justice in judicial review proceedings. Of course, in some instances, UK judges may have been influenced by an expected ruling of the ECHR while, in others, UK judges may have set out to ensure that UK law was in conformity with the Convention. However, use of the Convention may be of limited impact, in view of the application of the doctrine of the margin of appreciation; a particularly broad margin will tend to be allowed where positive obligations would be placed upon a State party by a decision under the Convention. It will be argued that although in certain areas, such as the right to a fair hearing, progress has been made, prisoners' rights can be said to be in their infancy as regards the right to freedom from degrading and cruel treatment.

Article 6 of the Convention has been invoked as a means of improving the standards of prison disciplinary hearings. However, improvement has come about largely, it is suggested, due to the reliance on the principles of natural justice. Until recently, a prisoner could receive a substantial loss of remission after a hearing of the Board of Visitors in which he was not allowed to call witnesses or cross-examine prison officers. However, gradually, in judicial review proceedings, prisoners established the right to a fair hearing before punishment could be awarded.

Natural justice includes two principles. First, there should be a fair hearing of the accused's case, in the sense that the proper procedural elements are in place and, secondly, there should be no bias.[1] Prison Rule 54 provides that the prisoner must be given a full opportunity of hearing the allegations against him and of presenting his own case and thus is clearly declaratory of natural justice, but it was uncertain, what consequences would follow if it was breached, and, in any event, it did not detail the requirements of a fair hearing.

In *Board of Visitors of Hull Prison ex p St Germain (No 1)* (1979), certain prisoners complained that the disciplinary proceedings which followed the Hull prison riots were not conducted in accordance with the principles of natural justice. The Court of Appeal, in the first such ruling since *Ridge v Baldwin* (1964), held that prisoners only lose those liberties expressly denied them by Parliament – otherwise, they retain their rights under the law. There was nothing in the Prison Act 1952 or the Prison Rules made under it to take away the jurisdiction of the courts, and the Board of Visitors was discharging a quasi-judicial function. Thus, it was found that the decision in question must be open to review and that Boards of Visitors must act in accordance with the rules of natural justice. In *Board of Visitors of Hull Prison ex p St Germain (No 2)* (1979), it was held that a Board of Visitors must be able to exercise a discretion to refuse a prisoner's request for witnesses, but that mere administrative inconvenience would not support a decision to refuse such a request.[2]

In *Fraser v Mudge* (1975), the Court of Appeal determined that a prisoner had no right to legal representation. However, in *Secretary of State for the Home Department ex p Tarrant* (1985), it was ruled that a Board of Visitors must exercise a discretion as to its grant. This decision may have been influenced by the expected outcome in *Campbell and Fell v UK* (1984) in the ECHR, which found that Art 6 of the Convention had been breached by a failure to allow legal representation to a prisoner in a disciplinary hearing. Breaches were found of Art 6(3)(b) and (c) concerning time and facilities to prepare a defence and availability of legal assistance; the applicants had had no assistance before the hearing or representation at it.[3]

After *Campbell,* as far as especially grave offences were concerned, legal advice became mandatory under new Home Office guidelines to that effect. However, that category of offences was abolished by the Prisons Amendment Rules 1989. 'Mutiny' was replaced by a number of lesser offences which carry with them lesser punishments. Generally speaking, therefore, the decision in *Campbell* has not had much impact. The House of Lords considered the issue afresh in *Board of Visitors of HM Prison, the Maze ex p Hone* (1988), but determined that legal representation in prison disciplinary hearings would remain discretionary.

The courts have viewed the disciplinary function exercised by the Governor of the prison and the disciplinary function administered by Boards of Visitors as two separate processes because the punishments available for each differ in degree of seriousness. There are far more governors' hearings, and it was thought that no possibility of judicial review could arise in respect of such hearings due to the administrative inconvenience which review might entail. The cases already considered did not address the question whether Governors' hearings should be open to review (apart from *dicta* in *St Germain*).

The House of Lords in *Deputy Governor of Parkhurst Prison ex p Leech, Deputy Governor of Long Lartin Prison ex p Prevot* (1988) had to determine whether prison governors' decisions should be open to judicial review, bearing in mind the recent recognition that Boards of Visitors' hearings should be so open.[4] Could the two types of hearing be properly distinguished? Governors could also affect the rights of prisoners, in that they could award loss of remission; it had already been accepted that prisoners had a legitimate expectation of receiving remission. Moreover, the Governor had a duty to act in accordance with natural justice which was spelt out in the Prison Rules (r 49). Thus, it was hard to find a logical distinction between the two disciplinary functions. The House of Lords was not prepared to find a distinction on policy grounds. It was concluded that hearings before governors should be conducted in accordance with the principles of natural justice. Once the principle is accepted that natural justice applies in proceedings before a governor as well as before a Board of Visitors, it follows that all the aspects of a fair hearing already considered may apply in governors' hearings, although in such hearings administrative inconvenience is likely to be allowed much more weight. In any event, it seems to be clear that the prisoner must be allowed the opportunity of seeing a full statement of the allegations in accordance with the provision under r 54 of the Prison Rules to this effect. If r 54 is declaratory of the principles of natural justice, it may be said to represent in that respect a minimum standard.

Despite improvements the conduct of governors' hearings is still a matter for concern. In 1988, the Chief Inspector of Prisons reported that 'Governor's adjudications were not always being carried out in accordance with appropriate standards of justice'. Now that such hearings are open to review, further improvement may come about, but it is unlikely to be very far reaching. This is of particular concern because none of the Government's proposals for reform have any real impact on governors' hearings. Serious criminal offences will be considered by the ordinary courts, but governors will still consider the majority of disciplinary offences. The Board of Visitors' disciplinary jurisdiction was abolished in 1992. There may be a case for arguing that all adjudication of offences above a certain level (not only those which constitute serious criminal offences) should be placed in the hands of an independent body, such as a Prison Tribunal.

Improvement has also occurred in relation to respect for the prisoner's right to privacy and to access to a court. Cases brought under Art 6 of the Convention have led to protection for the right of free access to the court while cases brought under Art 8 have ensure privacy of correspondence generally. Under r 34 of the Prison Rules, which relates to correspondence, the Home Secretary's permission was required before a prisoner could contact a solicitor. This provision was challenged in *Golder* (1975) in the ECHR, the applicant alleging a violation of Art 8, which guarantees respect for privacy, expressly mentioning correspondence, and of Art 6, which governs the right to a fair hearing. The Court considered whether there were implied limitations on access to a court for detainees. The court took a rather cautious stance on this point and did not rule that prisoners have an absolute right of access to court. It ruled that, in this particular instance, given all the factors in the situation including the fact that unpleasant consequence had already arisen from the alleged libel, Golder should have been able to go before a court. Thus, a breach of Art 6 had occurred.

In *Secretary of State for Home Department ex p Anderson* (1984), the domestic court went further in finding that requiring prisoners to register a complaint internally before contacting a solicitor was *ultra vires*, because it conflicted with the fundamental right of access to a court – a right so fundamental that it could only be taken away by express language. *Anderson* is an interesting decision because it provides an instance of a domestic decision going beyond the rights provided by the Convention, and the same may be said of *Secretary of State for the Home Department ex p Leech (No 2)* (1993), in which the Court of Appeal found that it was a principle of great importance that every citizen had an unimpeded right of access to a court and that this was buttressed by the principle of legal professional privilege. A common law privilege of this nature could openly be taken away by subordinate legislation only where that was expressly authorised by the enabling legislation. See, also, *R v Secretary of State for the Home Department ex p O'Brien and Simms* (1999). The latest version of the Rules, the Prison Rules 1999, allows access to a lawyer and to legal action (rr 38 and 39).

The improvement which has come about in relation to privacy of correspondence (see *Silver v UK* (1983)), the right of access to a court and in the standards of prison disciplinary proceedings may be contrasted with the failure of prisoners to use the courts to prevent cruel and degrading treatment in prisons. Once a prisoner is inside a prison, he or she may be subject to various punishments such as solitary confinement or withdrawal of privileges. Where formal punishment is not ordered, a decision may nevertheless be taken which subjects a prisoner to unpleasant conditions or even to violence from other prisoners. However, in contrast to their intervention in disciplinary hearings, the courts have not shown much willingness to provide remedies where prisoners complain of punishment or of conditions on prison.

In *Secretary of State for Home Department ex p Herbage (No 2)* (1987), the applicant was of sound mind, but was detained in the prison near mentally disturbed inmates. He complained that by his detention he was subjected to a 'cruel and unusual' punishment contrary to the Bill of Rights 1688. He sought, by way of judicial review, an order of mandamus, directing the Secretary of State and the prison governor to detain him according to law; the Court of Appeal found that he was entitled to leave to apply for judicial review and to order discovery in the proceedings for judicial review. This ruling provided a contrast to the finding in *Williams v Home Office (No 2)* (1982) that detention in the control unit at Wakefield prison which involved denial of association with other prisoners, little exercise, and constant surveillance and searches was not a breach of the Bill of Rights' prohibition of cruel and unusual punishment. It was found that a punishment had to be both cruel and unusual and that the control unit regime did not fall within either head: it was not cruel, because it did not fall below the minimum standard below which treatment would always be cruel, and it was not unusual, as a similar regime could be found in a number of prisons. This ruling did not leave much scope for invocation of the Bill of Rights' prohibition or create much incentive to raise standards in prisons, because even if a punishment was found to be cruel, it might not be unusual if conditions were equally poor in a number of prisons. Perhaps the courts might interpret this differently under s 3 of the HRA and, in any case, prisoners might bring direct actions under s 7 of the Act, claiming a violation of Art 3. It was found that the then r 43(2) of the Prison Rules had been breached, in that the segregation had not been reviewed at monthly intervals, but that a claim of false imprisonment or breach of statutory duty would not lie in respect of a breach of the Prison Rules.

The question as to how far, if at all, a prisoner could use private law remedies to challenge the use of certain punishments due to their particular nature or to their application in breach of the Prison Rules was considered by the House of Lords in *Deputy Governor of Parkhurst Prison ex p Hague, Weldon v Home Office* (1991). The Deputy Governor of Parkhurst prison ordered Hague to be transferred to another prison as a troublemaker and segregated there for 28 days under r 43 of the Prison Rules. He therefore lost normal privileges during that time. It was found in the House of Lords that r 43 had not been complied with in determining the segregation. However, Hague's claim of damages for breach of statutory duty failed, because, as a matter of interpretation, Lord Bridge found that r 43 was not intended to confer a right of action on an individual prisoner.

In relation to the claim of false imprisonment put forward by both Hague and Weldon, the question was whether treatment within a prison, rather than the imprisonment itself, could amount to false imprisonment. Hague argued that prisoners, despite their confinement, possess a residual liberty which can only be infringed by lawful order. Weldon argued that he had been subjected to intolerable conditions in respect of confinement in a strip cell and that he had therefore been deprived of his residual liberty. This claim failed, because it was found that the notion of a species of freedom of movement within the prison enjoyed as a legal right which prison authorities cannot lawfully restrain is illusory: the prisoner is lawfully restrained by the fact of imprisonment; if he is segregated as opposed to being allowed into the company of other prisoners, this is merely the substitution of one form of restraint for another. In *Toumia v Evans* (1999), the Court of Appeal held that a prisoner could proceed with an action against a prisoner officer (the head of the Prison Service trade union) in an action for false imprisonment (when, due to industrial action, the prisoners were kept in their cells for longer periods).

This ruling, which confines private law remedies to assault, negligence and misfeasance in public office, may be contrasted with the development in the public law field which is considered above. Obviously, allowing prisoners a substantive cause of action against prisoner officers would be controversial, as it would alter the balance of power between the two parties. In contrast, insisting on procedural fairness is less contentious. However, it has not worsened the position of prisoners in private law terms, although it has closed off two possible avenues of argument. It means that a prisoner may be subjected to solitary confinement without any lawful basis and will have no remedy unless the prison authorities have acted with malice, in which case, the tort of malfeasance in public office applies.[5]

Lord Bridge differed from Lord Goff in contemplating that liability for negligence might sometimes be appropriate even where no physical harm had occurred, a possibility which would of course represent a departure from the traditional stance as to what may be termed harm within the meaning of damage in negligence. However, although this might be the case where intolerable conditions had been imposed, it would not be in the case in respect of r 45 treatment in itself according to the Court of Appeal in *H v The Home Office* (1992). A prisoner who had been placed on r 45 due to the carelessness of the prison authorities in allowing his sexual offences to become known had therefore suffered assaults from other prisoners as well as loss of association and earnings. However, damages in negligence were available only in respect of the assaults. The Home Office has subsequently amended the procedure for transferring and segregating allegedly subversive prisoners.

At present, it seems that the problems of overcrowding in prisons and of general conditions of sanitation are unlikely to be solved in the near future despite repeated critical reports from Her Majesty's Inspectorate of Prisons and the Government's controversial proposals for privatisation of some prisons where conditions have been declared unacceptable. The implementation of the Woolf Inquiry's recommendations and the establishment of the Criminal Justice Consultative Council have created some improvements. However, it is likely that the 1999 Prison Rules will face ECHR challenges under the HRA 1998 and declarations of incompatibility under s 4 could be issued. Likely challenges include: the continued interceptions and censorship of mail; the parole process; the allocation of inmates to particular prisons; the legality of adjudications of disciplinary charges; and the status of the Prisons Ombudsman, who may need a new statutory footing and extended powers to compel the prison service to comply with his recommendations. At this stage, the end result of such litigation can only belabelled as uncertain.

## Notes

1   In *Ridge v Baldwin* (1964), the House of Lords held that when an administrative body takes a decision affecting the rights or legitimate expectations of citizens, that exercise of power is open to review by the courts. If there has been a failure to follow the principles of natural justice (procedural impropriety), a court can make an order under Ord 53 of the Rules of the Supreme Court Act 1981 – usually certiorari – which renders the decision void.

2   This point could be developed: it might be noted that these principles were confirmed in *Board of Visitors for Nottingham Prison* (1981); it was held that if it were established that a prisoner had asked for and been refused permission to call witnesses, that would, *prima facie*, be unfair. The refusal of witnesses and of cross-examination led to the quashing of six convictions in *St Germain (No 2)*.

3   This decision is not, of course, binding on UK domestic courts, but, although it might be expected that decisions in such courts would be in harmony with it, it will only affect a narrow band of cases due to the implied finding that not all disciplinary charges which have equivalents in criminal law can fall within Art 6; probably only those of a very grave nature would do so.

4   In *Deputy Governor of Camphill Prison ex p King* (1985), the Court of Appeal took the view that although the Deputy Governor had misconstrued a prison rule and interpreted it out of line with the general principles of criminal law, it had no jurisdiction to entertain an application for judicial review of the Prison Governor's adjudication on the prisoner.

5   It might be further argued that prison represents a deprivation of liberty, but not a complete deprivation, due to a degree of freedom in moving about within the prison. The curtailment of that remaining freedom is part of the essence of the punishment represented by segregation. Such deprivation of remaining freedom might be acceptable if it were within that

which the relevant statute allows, but, otherwise, it is arguable that it should be tortious.

# Question 36

Prisoners at Burham prison occupy the roof in an attempt to air their grievances. After the disturbance has been brought under control, Abel and Bert, two of the prisoners, are charged with various offences against discipline as laid down in the Prison Rules 1999. Abel is charged with attempting to assault an officer by throwing a slate from the prison roof and is sentenced by the governor to the forfeiture of 20 days' remission. Bert is charged with intentionally obstructing an officer in the execution of his duty. He is dealt with by the governor, who imposes a punishment of 14 days' forfeiture of privileges and 28 days' stoppage of earnings.

Both Abel and Bert are allowed to appear in person at their respective hearings, but both are refused legal representation on the ground that the hearings must be dealt with swiftly. Abel is permitted to call one witness in his defence, but two others are refused on the ground that they have been dispersed to other prisons. Bert's request to call a witness is refused. Abel is allowed to remain present during his hearing while a prison officer gives evidence against him, but is refused permission to cross-examine him. The governor gives Bert a summary of the allegations made against him by a prison officer, but refuses to allow him to see the full statement. Bert is surprised by the content of the allegations, which appear to be more extensive than those appearing in the statement of charges given to him prior to the hearing. Despite this, the governor refuses to give him time to consider them.

Advise Abel and Bert as to any redress they might have.

## Answer plan

This is a very straightforward question on the principles of natural justice. At the outset, it is very important to bear in mind that what is meant by a fair hearing will vary from hearing to hearing, and that the more serious the penalty, the higher should be the standards observed. Thus, it is probably a good idea to deal with both hearings separately. It must first be shown that the courts are prepared to review the decision in question on the ground of want of natural justice, and, secondly, in relation to each hearing separately, that a breach (or breaches) of natural justice have taken place. Although one serious breach might lead to the quashing of the decision, you should strengthen your argument by considering as many as possible.

Essentially, the following matters should be discussed:

- the courts are prepared to review prison disciplinary decisions on the ground of want of natural justice (*St Germain* (1979);
- the courts are prepared to review decisions of governors in prison disciplinary hearings on the ground of want of natural justice (*Leech v Deputy Governor of Parkhurst Prison; Prevot v Deputy Governor of Parkhurst Prison* (1988));
- the discretion to allow the calling of witnesses;
- the discretion to allow cross-examination;
- the discretion to allow legal representation which was established in Boards of Visitors' hearings;
- the right of a prisoner to a full opportunity of hearing the allegations against him and to present his case (r 54) and Art 6 of the European Convention on Human Rights (the Convention).

# Answer

Both Abel and Bert will wish to show that these decisions were made in breach of the principles of natural justice. First, it must be determined whether the rules of natural justice apply to the process in question. As Abel and Bert are involved in two separate hearings and the consequences for each differ in degree of seriousness, their cases will be considered separately.

It was determined in *Board of Visitors of Hull Prison ex p St Germain (No 1)* (1979) that prison disciplinary hearings were subject to the principles of natural justice. Certain prisoners complained that the disciplinary proceedings which followed the Hull prison riots were not conducted in accordance with the principles of natural justice. The Court of Appeal, in the first such ruling since *Ridge v Baldwin* (1964), held that prisoners only lose those liberties expressly denied them by Parliament – otherwise they retain their rights under the law. 'The rights of the citizen, however, circumscribed by penal sentence or otherwise must always be the concern of the courts unless their jurisdiction is expressly excluded by statute' (Shaw LJ). This ruling was confined to Board of Visitors' hearings, however, and did not apply to those of governors, because it was thought that Boards of Visitors were more like an independent tribunal, that they conducted their proceedings more formally and, importantly, dealt with more serious matters and could award serious punishments.

However, following *Leech v Deputy Governor of Parkhurst Prison; Prevot v Deputy Governor of Long Lartin Prison* (1988), it is clear that the principles developed in relation to Boards of Visitors' hearings can be applied to those of governors on the basis that it is not possible to distinguish between the disciplinary function of the Board of Visitors and that of governors. Both should be conducted in accordance with the principles of natural justice. *Dicta* in *St German (No 1)*, already mentioned, pointed the way to this conclusion. Shaw LJ said, 'I do not find it easy, if at all possible to distinguish between disciplinary proceedings conducted by a Board of Visitors and those carried out by a prison Governor ... the essential nature of the proceedings ... is the same. So in nature if not in degree are the consequences to a prisoner'. It does follow, however, that principles developed in relation to Boards of Visitors' hearings must be applied with caution to those of governors', since governors cannot award such serious punishments.

The rules of natural justice will therefore apply in Abel's case; however, can it be said that they have been breached? One of the two main principles of natural justice is the right to a fair hearing: the *audi alteram partem* rule. The question, therefore, is whether a disciplinary hearing requires the calling of all or any of the witnesses requested by the prisoner, cross-examination of witnesses or legal representation in order to be fair. These matters will be looked at in turn.

In *Board of Visitors of Hull Prison ex p St Germain (No 2)* (1979), it was held that Boards of Visitors must be able to exercise a discretion to refuse a prisoner's request for witnesses if they feel that he is purposely trying to obstruct or subvert the proceedings by calling large numbers of witnesses or if, where the request is made in good faith, they feel that the calling of large numbers of witnesses is unnecessary. However, mere administrative inconvenience would not support a decision to refuse such a request. In the instant case, it appears that the only reason for the refusal was the inconvenience involved in recalling the witnesses from other prisons. It seems, therefore, that the governor took into account a factor he should have disregarded. It does not appear that Abel requested three witnesses with a view to subverting the proceedings. Furthermore, given the fact that Abel was allegedly merely one of a group of prisoners on the roof, it would seem essential that he should be able to challenge evidence that he was present, that he threw the slate and that, in doing so, he was attempting to assault a prison officer. It seems unlikely that the case was so straightforward as to require only one witness for the defence. Therefore, if Abel can demonstrate that calling more than one witness was necessary due to the nature of his defence, it would follow that he should have been allowed to call them.[1] The refusal to allow him to do so would amount to a breach of the *Audi* rule.

It was determined in *St Germain (No 2)* that cross-examination of hearsay evidence should be made possible if it appertains to the central question of guilt or innocence. In this instance, hearsay evidence is not being presented; nevertheless, many of the arguments used in *St Germain* as to the desirability of allowing cross-examination where hearsay evidence is presented are equally applicable where it is not. Further, in *Board of Visitors of Gartree Prison ex p Mealy* (1985), it was held that the accused should have been allowed to ask questions of a defence witness. On this basis, it may be argued that Abel should have been allowed to cross-examine prison officers.

Abel's final ground of complaint is that he received no legal representation. Does a fair hearing before a governor include the right to legal representation? In *Fraser v Mudge* (1975), the Court of Appeal determined that a prisoner had no such right, while in *Maynard v Osmond* (1977), it was held that it would not be normal to have such a right, although a friend or helper might be permitted to be present. However, in *Secretary of State for the Home Department ex p Tarrant* (1985), although it was accepted, following

*Fraser v Mudge,* that a prisoner could not claim a right to legal representation, it was ruled that a Board of Visitors must exercise a discretion as to its grant. The court then suggested certain factors which a Board could properly take into account. These included the seriousness of the charge and of the penalty, the likelihood that points of law might be likely to arise, the ability of the prisoner to conduct his own case and the need for speed in making the adjudication.[2] The House of Lords in *Board of Visitors of HM Prison, the Maze ex p Hone* (1988) considered the issue afresh, but determined that no absolute right to legal representation in prison disciplinary hearings could be created; the position would remain as in *Tarrant.* In *Hone,* the House of Lords was eager to deny that a right to legal advice, as opposed to a discretion to award it, existed, on the basis that otherwise it would be hard to deny such a right in governors' hearings. It therefore follows that a discretion to award legal advice does exist in governors' hearings, although it is likely that it will rarely appear necessary to grant it. Also, in *Secretary of State for the Home Department ex p Whyte* (2000), the court rejected the prisoner's claim for legal representation. Furthermore, this state of affairs may be in breach of Art 6 (*Campbell and Fell v UK*) and that two prisoners are challenging their disciplinary awards on this basis – *Ezeh v UK* (App No 39665/98) and *Connors v UK* (App No 40086/98).

On this basis, given that the request for legal advice in the instant case was refused due to the need for expedition, can it be argued that a governor who had properly exercised discretion would have granted it? The charge is fairly serious and it carries a serious penalty. Points of law might well arise; Abel might wish to argue that he did not possess the requisite *mens rea* for attempted assault. This is probably the strongest argument for the grant of legal representation, but, possibly, it is outweighed by the particular need for speedy adjudication due to the tense situation in the prison. It may be concluded that the governor did exercise his or her discretion properly.

Thus, proceedings in Abel's case seem to have breached the *Audi* rule, in that he was not allowed witnesses and probably in that he was not allowed an opportunity for cross-examination.

The requirements of a fair hearing in Bert's case will differ from those in Abel's, because the consequences for Bert are less serious than for Abel: he is losing privileges and earnings, rather than remission. In *Aston University ex p Rothy* (1969), it was held that natural justice would apply, although there was no kind of legal right in the question; it was necessary to look at all the circumstances – the expectation of a fair hearing and the serious consequences which would follow from the decision. Possibly, the loss of privileges might not alone be sufficiently serious to warrant the application of the principles of natural justice, but may be so coupled with the loss of earnings – deprivation of a legal right – and on this ground natural justice may apply. On this argument, *Leech v Deputy Governor of Parkhurst Prison; Prevot v Deputy Governor of Long Lartin Prison* (1988) applies to Bert's hearing, which should therefore have been conducted in accordance with the principles of natural justice.

Was the *Audi* rule breached in Bert's case? He has four grounds of complaint: he was not allowed to call witnesses; have legal representation; see a full statement of the allegations against him; and it seemed that the allegations had been added to since he saw the statement of charges against him prior to the inquiry.

Once the principle is accepted that natural justice applies in proceedings before a governor as well as before a Board of Visitors, it follows that all the aspects of a fair hearing considered in decisions relating to Boards of Visitors' hearings may apply in governors' hearings, although, in such hearings, administrative inconvenience is likely to be allowed much more weight, especially where loss of remission is not in question. The tests from *Tarrant* may be applied in the instant case; it may then be argued that the triviality of the penalty involved, coupled with the need for speed in making the adjudication outweigh other factors, such as the need to deal with points of law and therefore do not warrant the grant of legal representation.

However, it may be urged that the governor should have exercised his discretion in favour of allowing Bert to call a witness (and perhaps allowing cross-examination of the prison officer whose evidence is presented). The test from *St Germain (No 2)* seems to be satisfied: Bert appears to be making the request in good faith and there seems no sufficient reason for refusing it. The administrative inconvenience involved would be minor since the witness is presumably present in the prison.

Furthermore, Bert is denied the opportunity to see a full statement of the allegations. Rule 54 of the Prison Rules 1999 provides that a prisoner shall have a full opportunity of hearing what is alleged against him. It may be said that r 54 is declaratory of the principles of natural justice and indeed may represent, in that respect, a minimum standard. It was determined in *Tarrant* that a prisoner should be given sufficient time to understand what is alleged against him and prepare a defence. Clearly, if somebody is unaware of the extent of the charges against him, he will be unable to answer them; the inconvenience involved would have been very minor.

In *Board of Visitors of Gartree Prison ex p Mealy* (1985), Mealy alleged unfairness, because, when he came to answer the charges against him, he found that the order of the proceedings had been changed. This took him by surprise and, he believed, adversely affected his ability to defend himself. The Divisional Court found that Chairmen of Boards of Visitors should guide prisoners through the proceedings and not surprise them by sudden changes of format. This could apply to the instant case as Bert was upset by additional allegations which he had not expected. Of course, *Mealy's* case was in the context of proceedings before a Board of Visitors. However, in principle, the rule from *Mealy* could apply in governors' hearings; although the procedure is obviously more informal, it is still necessary to give the accused time to consider how to answer the charges. This is supported by the requirement under r 54 that prisoners should be given a full opportunity of presenting their case.

Although, in general, what is required for a fair hearing will differ as between governors and Boards of Visitors and, clearly, the latter will be expected to adhere to a higher standard, a reasonable standard must be observed in governors' hearings, even where loss of liberty is not in question, which does not appear to be the case here. Therefore, Bert may be able to show that the *Audi* rule has been breached with regard to all his complaints, apart from denial of legal representation.

Thus, since both Abel and Bert are able to show breaches of the principles of natural justice,[3] the decisions will be void. (In *The Anismnic* (1979), the House of Lords held that a decision which breached the principles of natural justice would be void, not voidable.) Under the Civil Procedure Rules 1998, quashing orders will be issued to quash the decision in each instance.

## Notes

1   A further case could be mentioned at this point: in *Board of Visitors for Nottingham Prison* (1981), it was held that, if it were established that a prisoner had asked for and been refused permission to call witnesses, this would, *prima facie*, be unfair.

2   This decision was influenced by the expected outcome in *Campbell and Fell v UK* (1984) in the ECHR, which found that Art 6 of the Convention had been breached by a failure to allow legal representation to a prisoner in a disciplinary hearing. This decision is now, of course, binding on UK domestic courts. Article 6 applies to criminal charges; the European Court therefore had to equate a disciplinary charge with a criminal charge and this was done on the basis that the charge in question had equivalents in domestic criminal law and, further, was of a very grave nature. It was made reasonably clear that not all disciplinary charges which had equivalents in criminal law would fall within Art 6. See, also, *Ezeh v UK* and *Connors v UK*.

3   Bert might argue that there has been a breach of the rule against bias – that no man should be a judge in his own cause. In a sense, the governor of the prison is the prosecution, but he is also the judge. At first sight, this seems to be a breach of the *nemo judex in causa sua* rule, and urges that an independent body should have charge of discipline in prisons. However, the whole statutory context must be considered because the doctrine of natural justice depends on implying principles into enabling Acts. The rule against bias would run contrary to the enabling Act governing the power of prison governors and, therefore, it is submitted, could not afford relief in this situation.

# Question 37

'Recent developments have made it apparent that prisoners must look to the European Convention on Human Rights in order to uphold their basic rights to privacy and to access to a court.' Do you agree?

**Answer plan**

This is a reasonably straightforward essay question. It should be noted that it is confined to two particular areas of prisoners' rights. Clearly, it is necessary to consider the general influence of the Convention, not merely the decided cases. It is also necessary to ask whether in certain instances the domestic courts have gone further in protecting prisoners' rights than the European Court of Human Rights (ECHR). Finally, it might be asked whether domestic courts are now taking a more activist stance in these areas.

Essentially, the following areas should be considered:

- key provisions of the Prison Rules relating to correspondence;
- Arts 8 and 6 of the European Convention on Human Rights (the Convention);
- key decisions of the ECHR on privacy and access to a court;
- use of judicial review in this area – general influence of the ECHR.

# Answer

It is an inevitable concomitant of imprisonment that certain basic rights, such as freedom of movement, are removed from prisoners, while others are curtailed. Privacy is clearly curtailed, but this does not mean that a prisoner enjoys no privacy, while, on the other hand, the fundamental right of access to a court need not be abrogated at all. Articles 8 and 6 of the European Convention have been used successfully by prisoners to protect these fundamental liberties and recently the domestic courts have, it will be argued, adopted a more activist stance in these areas. Now that the Human Rights Act (HRA) 1998 is in force, domestic opportunities for challenges of the Prison Rules 1999 have become far greater, and they may well be subject to a s 4 declaration of incompatibility in the near future.

Cases brought under Art 6 of the Convention have led to greater protection for the right of free access to the court. Under r 34 of the Prison Rules, which related to correspondence (now r 39), the Home Secretary's permission was required before a prisoner could contact a solicitor. This provision was challenged in *Golder* (1975) in the ECHR. The applicant, at the time a prisoner, had wished to bring a libel action against a prison officer who had wrongly accused him of assault. The assault charges were eventually dropped but, for a time, the fact that he had been charged with an offence against discipline was on his prison record and it prevented him obtaining parole. Golder therefore wished to communicate with his solicitor but, under r 34 of the Prison Rules, had to obtain the Home Secretary's permission to do so. He asked for permission, but was refused it and, therefore, could not initiate the action. When he was released from prison, he applied to the Commission, alleging a violation of Art 8, which guarantees respect for privacy, expressly mentioning correspondence, and of Art 6, which governs the right to a fair hearing. The Commission declared the application admissible, gave its opinion that it should succeed and referred it to the court.

Golder's claim that he had been denied the right to a hearing could be considered only if Art 6 included a substantive right of access to a court, rather than merely providing guarantees of fairness once the hearing was in being.[1] It was held that Art 6(1) could not be narrowed only to include procedural guarantees, because it would not be possible to benefit from such guarantees if access to a court itself could be denied. Thus, it was found that access to a court must be inherent in Art 6(1).

The court considered whether there were implied limitations on such access for detainees; it took a rather cautious stance on this point and did not rule that prisoners have an absolute right of access to court. It ruled that, in this particular instance, given all the factors in the situation, including the fact that unpleasant consequence had already arisen from the alleged libel, Golder should have been able to go before a court. Thus, a breach of Art 6 had occurred. In responding to this finding, the Government modified r 34 of the Prison Rules, but in a fairly minimal fashion – only to the extent that prisoners could communicate with their solicitors freely, but complaints about the inner workings of the prison could not be communicated, unless the internal complaints machinery had first been exhausted. This was known as the prior ventilation rule and it was clearly still likely to inhibit access to a court.

However, in the *Silver* case (1983), an application was made to the Commission in respect of a number of interferences with correspondence alleging breaches of Arts 6 and 8. Part of the judgment in the court concerned the prior ventilation rule, which was found to be an unwarranted curb on correspondence. Prison orders regarding correspondence were again modified, so that a solicitor could be contacted with matter relating to a complaint as soon as the complaint had been registered internally.

This rule, known as the simultaneous ventilation rule, was itself challenged successfully in the domestic courts. In *Secretary of State for Home Department ex p Anderson* (1984), the prisoner applicant was refused a visit from his solicitor to discuss an action he wanted to bring, because the simultaneous ventilation rule had not been complied with. He sought judicial review of the decision to refuse permission. The court considered *Golder* and applied *Raymond v Honey* (1983), which had determined that a prisoner still retained a basic right of access to a court. According to *Golder*, this right included as an integral part access to a solicitor. It was found that if prisoners had to register a complaint internally before communicating with a solicitor, this would constitute an impediment; an inmate might hesitate to make an internal complaint, because he could lay himself open to a disciplinary charge. The court held that the restriction placed on him by the simultaneous ventilation rule was *ultra vires*, because it conflicted with this fundamental right – a right so fundamental that it could only be taken away by express language.

*Anderson* is an interesting decision, because it provides an instance of a domestic decision going beyond the rights provided by the Convention, and the same may be said of *Secretary of State for the Home Department ex p Leech (No 2)* (1993), in which the Court of Appeal found that it was a principle of great importance that every citizen had an unimpeded right of access to a court, and that this was buttressed by the principle of legal professional privilege. A common law privilege of this nature could openly be taken away by subordinate legislation only where that was expressly authorised by the enabling legislation (s 47 of the Prison Act 1952). Section 47 might authorise some screening of correspondence, but it must be strictly construed in accordance with the presumption against statutory interference with common law rights. Thus, it could not authorise an unrestricted right to read correspondence or a broad right to stop a letter on grounds of prolixity or objectionability. This application of r 33(3) was therefore *ultra vires* s 47. This ruling, it is suggested, represents an example of judicial activism in using the common law to demonstrate that reliance on the European Convention is not always necessary. See, also, *Secretary of State for the Home Department ex p O'Brien and Simms.*

The area in which the ECHR, as opposed to the domestic courts, has had a particular influence is that of privacy of correspondence under Art 8. In *Golder,* it was found that prisoners' privacy of correspondence must be upheld; implied limitations on it due to detention were rejected. *Silver* was also concerned with privacy of correspondence generally; certain letters unconcerned with legal proceedings, including communications with journalists, had also been stopped. It was found that such interference with correspondence was in breach of Art 8, and certain changes were therefore made to standing orders in prisons. Prisoners were freer as to the contents of letters; previously, they could not make criticism of persons in public life or make complaints about the prison. They were also allowed greater freedom in their choice of correspondents; they were not confined to relatives or friends, but could correspond with others, including journalists.

However, under r 33(3), all letters at non-'open' establishments could be routinely read, except for correspondence relating to legal proceedings to which the inmate was a party. Such correspondence could not be read or stopped under r 37A1 unless the governor had reason to suppose that it contained matter not relating to the proceedings. However, other correspondence with a solicitor, including that in respect of proceedings to which the inmate was not already a party, could be read and stopped if objectionable. The latter rule was challenged successfully in *Campbell v UK* (1992) under Art 8, the applicant alleging that correspondence with his solicitor and with the European Commission had been opened. The Government's argument that this was necessary in order to prevent disorder or crime was rejected on the basis that the risk that correspondence might contain an illicit enclosure did not justify routinely allowing such correspondence to be opened. There had been nothing to suggest that the solicitor in question would not comply with the rules of his profession; where such a suggestion was made, correspondence could be opened, but not read in the presence of the prisoner. The Prison Rules 1999 have extended the scope of the confidentiality of prisoners' correspondence to all such correspondence with a legal adviser, whether or not legal proceedings have been commenced.

Although letters unrelated to legal proceedings may still be opened, read and stopped, routine censorship of correspondence generally has been abolished in open prisons and, in 1988, it was reduced at category C prisons and many closed Young Offender Establishments. Following the Woolf Report, the Home Secretary announced the end of routine censorship of most prisoners' letters. Thus, the categories of letters which may be routinely subject to restrictions and interference have steadily been reduced, while the categories of possible correspondents and of contents of correspondence has been widened. However, such correspondence may still be opened under r 39 if the governor has reasonable cause to believe its contents to be illicit, illegal or a threat to security. Personal letters were, until recently, subject to serious restrictions: under the Prison rules 1999, r 35 allowed only unconvicted prisoners the right to send and receive unlimited letters and r 34 allowed interference with prisoners' communications on far wider grounds than would seem permissible under the ECHR cases. The recent Prison Amendment Rules (No 2) 2000 has replaced r 34 of the 1999 Rules (to make it more compatible with the HRA 1998) and add new provisions to r 35 of the 1999 Rules regarding monitoring of prisoners' correspondence and activities.

It may be concluded that the ECHR has provided the impetus needed to ensure that these particular fundamental freedoms are upheld. However, greater protection for privacy and the right of access to a court has not come about solely due to decisions under the European Convention; improvement has also come about through the application of the principles of natural justice in judicial review proceedings. Of course, in some instances, UK judges were influenced by an expected ruling of the ECHR, while, in others, UK judges may have set out to ensure that UK law was in conformity with the Convention. There are signs, particularly in relation to access to a court, that domestic judges considered that fundamental common law principles must be used to protect this fundamental right in default of enactment of the Convention into UK law. It is to be hoped that courts will use their post-enactment powers to improve prisoners' human rights in line with the spirit of the Convention and the HRA 1998.

## Note

1   This point could be explained more fully. The Home Secretary had not formally denied Golder access to a court, but had done so in practice by preventing him contacting his solicitor – an essential step, as he was a prisoner.

# Question 38

Evaluate the recent proposals for reform of UK prisons and the government response to them. Is further reform needed?

### Answer plan

This is a reasonably straightforward question, assuming that you are aware of the main proposals. You do need to keep specifically to the recent reforms and resist the temptation to write down everything about changes in prisoners' rights which you have revised.

Essentially, the following matters should be discussed:

- the Prior Report – main proposals;
- the Woolf Report;
- the White Paper;
- a Code of Standards in prisons;
- limitations of the government response, particularly in relation to improving basic living standards in UK prisons.

# Answer

Reform in prisons has concentrated on improving the quality of prison disciplinary hearings and on improving basic living standards. In particular, standards have required improvement in relation to over-crowding and sanitation. It will be suggested that despite various proposals response in terms of the changes in prison disciplinary hearings does not go far enough, while the government response to proposals to improve standards is still too minimal.

Before the cases of *Leech v Deputy Governor of Parkhurst Prison* (1988) and *Prevot v Deputy Governor of Long Lartin Prison* (1988), which allowed judicial review of the disciplinary function of prison governors, the Home Secretary had ordered a report into prison discipline under Mr Prior, which was published in 1987. It recommended leaving Governors' disciplinary proceedings unaffected, but transferring the disciplinary function of Boards of Visitors to a new prison disciplinary tribunal, thereby creating a new independent tier of adjudication which would be more court-like and would contain greater safeguards for the accused. Legislation was anticipated but, in 1987, the Home Office announced that, for the time being, the Prior Report would not be implemented.

The prison riots in 1990 were followed by an inquiry which led to the Woolf Report in 1991. Its recommendations were, in principle, similar to those of the Prior Report; governors should retain jurisdiction over minor offences, but the more serious should be dealt with by the ordinary courts, a proposal which would cost less to implement than the Prior proposals. It is argued that the Woolf proposals created, on the whole, a sensible method of dealing with the situation. First, the Board of Visitors was increasingly being perceived as insufficiently independent of the prison administration and as conducting hearings in which proper procedural safeguards were not in place, despite decisions improving their quality. For example, it was still the case, despite decisions such as *Tarrant* (1985), that legal representation was very rarely granted. Unfair decisions may have contributed to unrest in prisons. Secondly, the disciplinary function of Boards of Visitors was perceived as incompatible with their other function as prison 'watchdog'. Boards of Visitors are meant to provide an outlet and a remedy for prisoners' grievances. Increasingly, they could not fulfil this central role, because they were distrusted by prisoners. Again, this perception of the nature of Boards of Visitors may have contributed to unrest: prisoners may have perceived that a sufficient legitimate outlet for grievances was lacking.

The Government published a White Paper, *Custody, Care and Justice*, in 1991, dealing with the Woolf proposals, in which it accepted the suggestion that the disciplinary function of Boards of Visitors should be removed. It proposed that governors should retain their current disciplinary function and should be able to award 28 days' loss of remission with the possibility of 28 added days, and that 'serious criminal offences' should be referred to the police with a view to prosecution.

The determination as to remission differed from the Woolf proposals which were based on reducing and eventually abolishing the use of loss of remission as a punishment, and increasingly substituting loss of facilities and opportunities. Moreover, Woolf proposed that offences which are also *prima facie* criminal offences considered too serious for a governor to deal with should be referred to the police. Such a formulation is not necessarily synonymous with 'serious criminal offences'. The danger may be that the governors' disciplinary jurisdiction may merely extend to cover a part of that of the Board of Visitors', while only a small percentage of offences will be dealt with in court. Given that procedural safeguards in governors' hearings are of a far more basic nature than those in Board of Visitors' hearings (and legal representation is unheard of), this may be a retrograde step. Woolf would have minimised this danger in proposing that loss of remission would eventually be abolished as a punishment; this would have provided the incentive for governors to refer cases to the police, which may be lacking under the White Paper proposals. Arguably, both Woolf and the White Paper focused too exclusively on the deficiencies of Board of Visitors' hearings to the exclusion of concern with those of governors'.

The conduct of governors' hearings is a matter for concern. In 1988, the Chief Inspector of Prisons reported that 'Governor's adjudications were not always being carried out in accordance with the appropriate standard of justice'. Now that such hearings are open to judicial review, some improvement may come about, but it is unlikely to be very far reaching. This is particularly a matter of concern, because the Government's proposals for reform in prisons will have little impact on governors' hearings. There may be a case for arguing that all adjudication of offences above a certain level (not only those which constitute serious criminal offences) should be placed in the hands of an independent body.

Arguably, second tier adjudication need not have been completely swept away, but should instead have been made entirely independent of the prison administration by entrusting it to Prison Tribunal, which could sometimes meet externally to the prison or, where appropriate, could convene within it, and which would conduct its proceedings in a court-like fashion with a duty solicitor always on hand to conduct the defence. As things stand, more serious disciplinary offences (equivalent to criminal offences) which previously would have been considered by the Board of Visitors may be considered in future either by the Governor or by a court.

It appears that the Governor will make the decision whether to refer the case to the police; if so, he or she may weigh up the need for the higher penalty available in court against the trouble caused by the police investigation, the delay before a penalty will be imposed, the possibility that the prisoner will be acquitted due to the procedural safeguards the court will observe, the possibility of exclusion of evidence under ss 78 and 76 of the Police and Criminal Evidence Act 1984 and the need to prove the offence beyond reasonable doubt. In practice, these safeguards may not be in place in a governors' hearing; therefore, in some instances, except where very serious offences are in question, the balance may come down in favour of expeditious and certain punishment in a governor's hearing.

This danger, and the general problem of procedural deficiency in governors' hearings, has been addressed to some extent by the proposal in the White Paper that prisoners should be able to appeal against governors' decisions to the Area Manager and from there to an independent body. This is an improvement on the current arrangements, but it is not yet clear how wide the appellate function of the Manager or independent body will be.

The Woolf Report also recommended that a Code of Standards in Prisons should be promulgated influenced by the European Prison Rules 1987 and the United Nations Standard Minimum Rules for the Treatment of Offenders. This proposal is accepted in the White Paper with a view to providing 'humane and decent standards' in relation to such matters as accommodation, heating and lighting, basic necessaries such as the provision of food and clothing and hygiene arrangements; visits and other contacts with families are also included.

This step is to be greatly welcomed; however, it is not proposed that the Code should be legally enforceable: presumably, it may contain a form of words similar to that contained in the police Codes of Practice. There is some evidence that the Police Codes which are not legally enforceable might sometimes have been accorded little respect in practice had it not been that decisions excluding evidence where breaches of Code C were shown began to be handed down. This may suggest that a Prison Code of Practice would not always be adhered to. On the other hand, there is no evidence available that provisions of Code C which specifically govern the conditions of detention (such as the provision of meals at certain times) are routinely breached, despite the fact that they have not generally been affected by decisions as to exclusion of evidence.

The decision to allow appeal against decisions in response to complaints to be considered by the same independent body as will hear appeals from disciplinary decisions would strengthen the Code safeguards if such a body were given jurisdiction to hear complaints specifically relating to Prison Code provisions. The White Paper does not make this clear and, by dealing with the Code in Chapter 6 and the independent body in Chapter 8, may suggest that the jurisdiction of the body will be confined to complaints against particular decisions and against members of staff rather than covering complaints as to conditions. The Government only envisages in the White Paper that compliance with the standards would be monitored by the Inspector of Prisons and possibly by the Board of Visitors.

Generally speaking, the White Paper leaves a number of issues uncertain and the timetable for implementation of the Woolf proposals is particularly vague. Although a Code of Standards is a clear improvement on present practice, even if its implementation is patchy and slow, the likely effect of the other proposals may not be as positive as their reception would seem to suggest, although, of course, this will not be entirely clear until the legislation is in place. It is suggested that unless the improvements in standards and in other practices such as provision for visits and other contact with families is made legally enforceable, the UK may be unlikely to achieve the goal of providing the minimum standards set out in the United Nations Standard Minimum Rules for the Treatment of Offenders.[1]

## Note

1   It could be argued further that Art 3 of the European Convention might be used to improve minimum standards in prisons, but that recourse to Strasbourg should not be seen as a substitute for government action. The European Court of Human Rights should not be placed in the position of having to determine domestic spending priorities. The Prison Reform Trust has produced a paper, *Strangeways – Ten Years On*, which is a retrospective of the last 10 years of prison reform in the light of the Woolf proposals.

# CHAPTER 7

# FREEDOM OF MOVEMENT

## Introduction

Examiners usually set essay questions in this area, although a problem question on the effect of the European Court of Human Rights on asylum and immigration law is becoming more common. The emphasis is usually on the degree to which a balance is struck between the interest of the State in national security and the individual's basic freedom to enter, move about within and leave the UK. Students should be aware that this is an area in which there have been repeated and relatively major changes recently; for example, the former power to make an exclusion order from the UK or Northern Ireland lapsed in 1998 and is not included in the new permanent Terrorism Act 2000, which also repeals and replaces the Prevention of Terrorism (Temporary Provisions) Act 1989 and related legislation.

Students should be familiar with the following areas:

- relevant provisions of the European Convention on Human Rights;

- deportation and administrative removal provisions under the Immigration Act 1971, as amended, and the Immigration and Asylum Act 1999;

- the Geneva Convention of 1951 as amended by the 1967 Protocol;

- key provisions of the Asylum and Immigration Act 1996 and the Immigration and Asylum Act 1999 relating to asylum seekers;

- the appeals procedure under the Immigration and Asylum Act 1999;

- the contents and effects of the Asylum and Immigration Act 1996 and the Immigration and Asylum Act 1999.

# Question 39

'The law governing deportation is in need of further reform in order to create a fairer balance between individual civil liberties and the right of a Sovereign State to determine who should come within its boundaries.' Do you agree?

## Answer plan

In answering this question, it will be necessary not only to identify substantive and procedural aspects of the deportation procedure which have an adverse impact on civil liberties, but also to suggest what might be meant by a 'fairer' balance.

Essentially, the following matters should be discussed:

- deportation and administrative removal provisions under the Immigration Act 1971, as amended, and the Immigration and Asylum Act 1999;
- the relevant provisions under the Immigration Rules 2000;
- procedure followed in making the decision to deport/remove;
- the impact on terrorism;
- infringement of civil liberties;
- the relevance of the European Court of Human Rights (ECHR).

## Answer

Deportation and its close relative 'administrative removal' represent the clearest infringement of freedom of movement and therefore should be used only where there is clear justification and where there are mechanisms allowing careful scrutiny of the decision to deport. Broadly speaking, a person who is not a UK citizen with rights of residence is liable to deportation only if the Secretary of State deems that person's removal to be conducive to the common good, or where a court has recommended it after a conviction for a serious offence, or for national security reasons or where the person is a relative of someone deported on one of those grounds (ss 3(5)(b) and 3(6) of the Immigration Act 1971).

However, the Immigration and Asylum Act 1999 also allows 'administrative removal' of a person who did originally have leave to enter or remain, but has failed to observe the conditions attached to his leave, overstayed or obtained leave by deception (s 10). 'Administrative removal' is a controversial term which is practically indistinguishable from deportation and formerly was a procedure which only applied to illegal entrants. An overstayer may apply for leave to remain under the new arrangements in s 9 of the 1999 Act and, if refused, may appeal to the Immigration Appellate Authority; as soon as he has applied for leave to remain, he cannot be subject to administrative removal, but may be deported if his application and any appeal fail.

The deportation of family members of a deportee has caused concern, since the practice has been discriminatory: a wife is normally deported with her husband, but a husband often remains when his wife is deported. The wife will not, however, automatically be deported; r 367 of the Immigration Rules 2000 provides that various circumstances should be taken into account, including her own wishes and her ability to maintain herself, but the bland assumption that all husbands, whatever their actual circumstances, can be treated differently from all wives is unjustifiable, particularly after ECHR cases such as *Abdulaziz* (1985).

In considering the decision to deport or administratively remove, r 364 provides guidance as to the factors to be taken into account: these include balancing the public interest against any compassionate circumstances of the case. While each case will be considered in the light of the particular circumstances, the aim is an exercise of the power to deport or remove which is consistent and fair as between one person and another, although one case will rarely be identical with another in all material respects. However, as will be seen, the Human Rights Act (HRA) 1998 will complicate the situation somewhat, since the leading relevant cases have been decided on the basis of what is fair on those particular facts, rather than a scrutiny of the rules and procedures themselves.

Deportation due to conviction of a criminal offence is fairly readily resorted to, but, as the Court of Appeal held in *Nazari* (1980), no court should 'make an order recommending deportation without full inquiry into all the circumstances. It should not be done, as has sometimes happened in the past ... as if by an afterthought at the end of observations about any sentence of imprisonment'. A number of factors were identified which a court might bear in mind when considering deportation: the long criminal record of the accused; the seriousness of the offence, bearing in mind the circumstances surrounding it, not merely its nature;[1] the effect that an order recommending deportation (or now removal) will have on others who are not before the court and who are innocent persons, in terms of hardship and breaking up of families. The court should take into account the nature of the regime to which the deportee will return. This last point should be compared with relevant ECHR cases.

In *Serry* (1980), a single offence of shoplifting was found insufficiently serious, presumably because there were no particular aggravating circumstances. An important circumstance will be the likelihood of the repetition of the offence; where this factor is present, it may aggravate an otherwise trivial offence; where it is absent, it may have a mitigating effect on a serious offence. *B v Secretary of State* (2000) (below) confirms the latter point and makes it likely that a proportionality test will be applied in future, with far greater regard to all the individual circumstances of the case. In *Aramide v Secretary of State for the Home Department* (2000), the Court of Appeal also held that the seriousness of the criminal offence (to be judged by the sentence actually given, not in a general manner) must be carefully balanced against the applicant's family ties.

The 'conducive to public good' ground for deportation can be used where a person is convicted of an offence, but the court does not recommend deportation in respect of persons who have engaged in criminal activity abroad (*Martinez-Tobon v IAT* (1988)). The use of this power to exclude people on political rather than criminal grounds has attracted the most criticism. For example, the former militant student leader, Rudi Deutschke, was deported back to West Germany in 1969, thereby terminating his studies at Cambridge, on the basis that he might 'become a focus for student unrest'. Similarly, the journalists Agee and Hosenball were deported on national security grounds, Agee presumably due to the damage he might have done to the CIA in writing books exposing certain of their activities (*Secretary of State for the Home Department ex p Hosenball* (1977)). Rather flimsy grounds were also, it seems, relied upon in making the decision to deport a number of Iraqi or Kuwaiti residents during the Gulf War in 1991.

The purpose of deportation on this ground would seem to be clear: that removal of the deportee is necessary for the public good; even if this is not the only purpose, then it should be the primary one. However, in a number of rulings, courts have not applied a 'dominant purpose' test in considering the relevance of other purposes which may have influenced the Secretary of State's decision to deport.

In *Brixton Prison Governor ex p Soblen* (1963), a deportation order was challenged on the grounds that the Secretary of State had acted for an improper purpose – allegedly in order to comply with a request from the US for S's return, made in order to circumvent the non-availability of extradition proceedings which were not possible due to the nature of S's alleged offences (conspiracy to commit espionage). The Court of Appeal upheld the deportation order on the basis that the Secretary of State could act for a plurality of purposes. The fact that this might be termed extradition by the back door did not affect the validity of the order. The court considered that the need to serve the public good by the removal of S need not be the dominant motive in making of the order, although the Minister must have a genuine belief that removal was necessary on that basis. It did not matter if the Minister's main motive for acting might have been to comply with the request from the US. Since the Home Secretary had (and still has) an unfettered discretion regarding where to deport a person to, he did not need to consider deporting S to Czechoslovakia (which was willing to take him).

The danger in this approach is clearly that the individual circumstances of the person in question may become much less significant than the political expediency of falling in with the wishes of particular governments. However, there have been indications that such an approach is no longer justifiable. As early as *Lewisham London Borough Council ex p Shell UK Ltd* (1988), it was accepted that there may be a 'plurality of purposes', but that it should be shown that the same decision would have been reached even in the absence of consideration of the 'improper' purpose.

Now that European Convention rights (particularly Arts 8, 3 and 5) must always be considered in relation to any proposed deportation, it is likely that individual circumstances will gain far greater weight in judgments. For example, in *B v Secretary of State for the Home Department* (2000), a deportation order was issued against B, an Italian citizen, after he had served prison sentences in the UK for child abuse. The deportation order relied on the 'conducive to public good' ground. The Court of Appeal held that, in the new rights-aware legal culture, deportation must be a proportionate measure in all the circumstances, whether the applicant is an EC citizen (and so entitled to freedom of movement within the EC) or not. Thus the applicant's rights to both freedom of movement and family life were found to outweigh any pressing social need to deport him. A crucial issue was the perceived lack of likelihood that he would re-offend, coupled with his real and substantial ties to the UK; hence, deportation would be a disproportionate measure.

The 'public good' head of deportation can cover a number of widely different factors, but it seems reasonably clear that the decision to deport should be based on all the circumstances relevant to the particular evil in question and the likely consequences flowing from any deportation. Thus, in *IAT ex p (Mahmud) Khan* (1983), the applicant successfully challenged the IAT's dismissal of his appeal against deportation, on the ground that the tribunal's reason for its decision – that he had entered into a marriage of convenience – failed to show that it had properly considered whether the couple did intend to live as man and wife. In other words, grounds which might raise an inference that the marriage was merely one of convenience were not examined to see whether this was actually the case. Similarly, it is not enough to show that a person has behaved in an anti-social manner in the past; it must be considered whether future wrongdoing is likely (*IAT ex p Ullah* (1983)).

In considering consequences flowing from the deportation, it would appear that detriment flowing from it to the public or part of the public as well as the good may be considered: the two may be balanced against each other. Thus, in *Singh v IAT* (1986), the House of Lords held that the immigration adjudicatory authorities ought to have taken into account the detrimental effect on the Sikh community in the UK which deportation of the applicant would have. The applicant was a valued member of that community by virtue of his religious, charitable and cultural activities.

In *Rehman v Secretary of State for the Home Department* (2000), the first case to be appealed from a decision of the Special Immigration Appeals Commission (SIAC), the Court of Appeal considered when deportation could be justified on the basis of national security grounds. The applicant had been refused indefinite leave to remain and a deportation order had been issued by the Home Secretary. The SIAC found that the Home Secretary had defined 'national security' too widely and stated that a person could be said to have offended against national security if he had engaged in, promoted or encouraged violent activity which was affected the security of the UK or its nationals, wherever they might be. Applying the test of a 'high civil balance of probabilities', the SIAC then found that the Secretary of State had not shown that the applicant was a threat to national security. On appeal, the Court of Appeal found that the security of all States is intertwined and so a threat against State B may justify a person's deportation from State A. The SIAC's approach had been too narrow: if a person had been engaged in violent activity which involved a real possibility of either direct or indirect adverse repercussions upon the security of the UK, then deportation was justified. It does not have to be shown to a high standard of probability that the person in question has performed any individual act which would justify the conclusion that he was a threat to national security.

One major recent change is in the availability and consistency of rights of appeal. The Immigration and Asylum Act 1999 and subsequent Rules, coupled with the application of the HRA 1998, have created a unified right of appeal on immigration, asylum and deportation matters. A person against whom a deportation order is to be issued may appeal to an adjudicator under s 63; whilst any right to appeal subsists, a deportation or removal order cannot be carried out. One change is that a person to be removed on 'public good' grounds does now have this right to appeal rather than the previous '*ex gratia*' arrangements; this is a move to be welcomed. But s 64 contains an exemption: if a threatened deportation is based on national security or other political grounds, then there is no right to appeal. Once a deportation order had been made, there is no appeal against a refusal to revoke it if that refusal is certified by the Secretary of State to be on the basis that removal is 'conducive to the public good'. But every person threatened with deportation is now able to use an additional method of appeal; if any human rights issue is arguable on the facts, then s 65 of the Immigration and Asylum Act 1999 allows him to appeal to an adjudicator or the tribunal. Thus, it is likely that issues will be raised in future deportation cases as to Arts 3, 5 and, particularly, 8; further, challenges are likely to be made to the validity of the 'national security' exception from appeal rights, since it is difficult to think of a situation where a person could be deported on national security grounds, yet not have any arguable ECHR right.[2]

### Notes

1   The ruling in *Caird* (1970) would also support this point.

2   If space allowed it, far more consideration could be given to relevant ECHR cases such as *Chahal v UK* (1996); *D v UK* (1997); and *Ahmed v Austria* (1996).

# Question 40

The current arrangements for considering the claims of asylum seekers suggest that the UK respects the letter of the Geneva Convention, but not its spirit. Do you agree?

### Answer plan

This is a relatively straightforward essay question. It is particularly topical at a time when the number of asylum seekers is rapidly increasing, and there has been a great deal of recent statutory and case law on the subject.

Essentially, the following matters should be discussed:

* the Geneva Convention of 1951, as amended by the 1967 Protocol;

* key provisions of the Asylum and Immigration Act 1996 and the Immigration and Asylum Act 1999 and of the Immigration Rules relating to asylum seekers;

* the appeals procedure under the 1999 Act and 2000 Rules.

# Answer

The UK accepts certain international obligations in respect of asylum seekers under the Geneva Convention of 1951, as amended by the 1967 Protocol relating to the Status of Refugees,[1] and this is reflected in the Immigration Rules and the Immigration Appeals Act 1993, although neither the Convention nor the Protocol have been enacted directly into the law of the UK. Rule 334 of the Immigration Rules provides that immigrants:

> ... will be granted asylum in the UK if the Secretary of State is satisfied that ... refusing his application would result in his being required to go (whether immediately or after the time limited by an existing leave to enter or remain) in breach of the Convention and Protocol, to a country in which his life or freedom would be threatened on account of his race, religion, nationality, political opinion or membership of a particular social group.

Section 2 of the Immigration Appeals Act 1993 states that nothing shall be laid down in the immigration rules which would be contrary to the Geneva Convention.

The Convention and Protocol are concerned only with political asylum seekers and this is reflected in the ambit of r 334, so that those fleeing from famine or disaster are not covered. Sometimes, it may be hard to make this distinction when a person leaves a country which is in the middle of a civil war. The applicant must belong to a group which is likely to be persecuted and this will include a 'social group'. The meaning of this term of r 334 was considered in *Secretary of State for the Home Department ex p Binbasi* (1989): it was held to mean that a group of persons could be identified as sharing fundamental unchangeable characteristics or as sharing characteristics to which they had an overriding moral commitment on religious or other grounds. In *Islam v Secretary of State for the Home Department ex p Shah* (1999), the House of Lords found that a group of Pakistani women who had been falsely accused of adultery could claim refugee status under the Geneva Convention, since they were a group of people unprotected by their own State; there is no requirement of cohesiveness or indeed of minority status for persons to constitute a 'group'.

The obligation not to remove or return refugees will not apply if either of two circumstances is present: the refugee may be reasonably regarded as constituting a threat to the security of the country he is in; alternatively, he may represent a danger to the particular community in that country, a finding that will be made if the refugee has been convicted of a grave crime. It should be noted that, when the Terrorism Act 2000 is fully in force, the definition of 'threats to national security' may stretch far beyond terrorist activity and may encompass environmental and political agitation.

A duty to grant asylum is not directly imposed, but if no safe alternative destination can be found for the asylum seeker, the country in question will have to grant asylum. Under the Convention, the refugee must be given time to find a safe third country. If a person seeks asylum, the case must be referred by the immigration officer to the Home Office for decision, even though it appears that the claim is unjustified. The Home Office will consider the case in accordance with the provisions of the Convention and Protocol relating to the Status of Refugees and the claimant will not be removed until the Home Office has considered the case.

In making a decision, the Home Secretary may take into account guidance given by the advisory Executive Committee to the High Commissioner for Refugees, an office established in 1951 within the framework of the General Assembly of the united Nations, as to the interpretation of the Convention and Protocol (*Bugdaycay v Secretary of State* (1987); *IAT ex p Yassine* (1990)). If an interpretation of the Immigration Rules is adopted which does not conform with the Convention, the decision may be quashed for 'illegality' or 'irrationality' as happened in *Bugdaycay*; it may also now be quashed under s 2 of the 1993 Act. In *Bugdaycay*, the applicant was a Ugandan refugee whose father and cousins had been killed by the secret police and who therefore feared for his life if he should return to Uganda. He had lived in Kenya, and the Home Secretary, in rejecting his claim for asylum, determined to deport him there, regardless of the fact that Kenya had been known to return such refugees to Uganda.

The House of Lords found that when the Immigration Rules were interpreted in accordance with Art 33 of the Geneva Convention, it was found that the decision to deport him would be a breach; although deportation to Kenya would not directly threaten his life, it might lead to such a threat, due to the probability that Kenya would deport the applicant. The Court of Appeal in *Munongo v Secretary of State for the Home Department* (1991) confirmed that the courts would not interfere with the Home Secretary's decision as long as he had followed the correct procedure and his decision was not *Wednesbury* unreasonable – meaning tainted by illegality or irrationality. They would not, therefore, question the basic credibility of the Home Secretary's decision, as long as there was some evidence to support his findings. Now, of course, it would be profitable to make an additional human rights-based argument.

The term 'persecution' in Art 1(A) of the Convention has been interpreted fairly restrictively by the English courts as meaning 'to pursue with malignancy', 'to oppress for holding a heretical opinion or belief' (*IAT ex p Jonah* (1985)); under this strict interpretation, 'harassment' will not always be enough. The House of Lords in *Secretary of State for the Home Department ex p Sivakumaran* (1988) laid down the test for determining whether the fear of persecution is well founded. Once it appears that the applicant genuinely fears persecution, the Secretary of State is required to ask himself on the basis of all the available information whether there has been demonstrated a 'real likelihood' or, as in *Fernandez v Government of Singapore* (1971), a 'reasonable chance' of persecution.

The applicant has the burden of proving that there are grounds for thinking that persecution may occur. However, information may be taken into account of which he or she is unaware. Thus, the fear must be based on reasonable grounds, objectively assessed. It therefore appears that the question is not whether a person in possession of the information known to the applicant would have feared persecution, but whether such fear would have been felt by an objective observer in possession of all the available information.

The emphasis of this test differs from that put forward by the High Commission, which involves asking whether, subjectively, a real fear of persecution is present and then considering whether it is a fear no one would reasonably hold. The test put forward by the House of Lords therefore provided less protection for refugees and, moreover, the imprecise nature of expressions such as 'real likelihood' leaves considerable latitude for differences of opinion as to the severity of the risk of persecution.

The House of Lords' decision in the *Sivakumaran* case to uphold the Secretary of State in refusing asylum applications of the six applicant Tamils from Sri Lanka differed from that of the adjudicator who later heard the appeals of the Tamils from abroad and found that there was a sufficient risk of persecution based upon race, religion and political opinion (*IAT ex p Secretary of State for the Home Department* (1990)).

The fact that all the available information must be considered may, of course, work to the advantage of the applicant, as it will mean that a court cannot disregard any piece of information: this will include what has happened in the past which should be related to any current events, although the mere fact that an asylum seeker has been persecuted in the past will not raise a presumption in his favour that he is a refugee (*Secretary of State for the Home Department ex p Direk* (1992). It was found in *Secretary of State for the Home Department ex p Gulbache* (1991) that, in determining the well founded nature of the fear, the fact that the applicant has not been singled out for persecution will not be conclusive of the issue. But recent cases seem to be applying a new, lower threshold for asylum. In *Karanakaran v Secretary of State for the Home Department* (2000), the Court of Appeal held that, when considering whether there was a serious possibility of persecution if an asylum seeker were returned, or whether there was no such possibility in relation to that part of the country to which it was proposed that the asylum seeker be returned, it was wrong to exclude matter totally from consideration simply because the decision maker did not consider that they had been proved on the balance of probabilities. In asylum cases, no such burden or standard of proof arises; the relevant question is simply whether, taking all relevant matters into account, it would be unduly harsh to return the asylum seeker. Since K, a Tamil, had not been singled out for persecution, but rather had been among many victims of a general onslaught by government forces, the Immigration Appeal Tribunal had found that it would not be unduly harsh to remove him to another part of Sri Lanka. The Court of Appeal found that this had been a wrong decision; that opinions put forward by experts as to the likely effect for removal should not have been dismissed by the Tribunal as 'mere speculation'; and that the cumulative effect of several small factors could be sufficient to satisfy the 'unduly harsh' test.

In *Danian v Secretary of State for the Home Department* (1999), the Court of Appeal also held that a person will be protected under the Geneva Convention if he can establish that he has a well founded fear of persecution if returned to his home country, irrespective of whether the actions giving rise to the fear had been carried out in good or bad faith. No new exceptions are to be added to those under the Convention. Thus, even if the activities giving rise to the fear were carried out precisely so as to give grounds for a later asylum application, the protection of the Convention would still be triggered and must be afforded if its own requirements were satisfied.

One aspect of asylum claims which has come into greater prominence in recent years relates to the European Convention on Human Rights. Although refugees receive no direct protection under the main body of the Convention or under the Human Rights Act 1998, asylum seekers' rights have been considered under a variety of Articles. Thus Art 8, which imposes upon States an obligation to respect individuals' private and family life, might be used to show that family ties would be damaged by denial of an asylum claim when other members of the family are already within the UK. Most importantly, where an asylum claimant can show a risk of persecution or life-threatening conditions, the prohibition of torture and of inhuman or degrading treatment or punishment under Art 3 may arise. Thus, in *Hatami v Sweden* (1998), it was held that, although the right to political asylum is not within the scope of the Convention's protection, to remove an asylum claimant from the jurisdiction after finding his claim to be without foundation would constitute an Art 3 breach where substantial grounds have been shown that the claimant would face a real risk of being subjected to torture or inhuman or degrading treatment or punishment in the receiving country. In such circumstances, Art 3 includes an implied obligation not to expel the claimant to any such country. Further, the activities of the claimant cannot be a relevant consideration in a human rights claim, regardless of how undesirable or dangerous they may have been. *Soering v UK* (1989) and *Vilvarajah v UK* (1994) both confirm that the UK is covered by the implied obligation not to expel any person in such circumstances, although, in the latter case, the applicants, a group of Tamils, failed to show a breach of Art 3, since there was only a possibility that they might be detained and ill treated, rather than a substantial risk. Thus, it can be seen that, in some respects, the Convention is of weaker protection than the Geneva Convention, since the former requires greater likelihood of harm to the applicant.

Section 69 provides a right of appeal to an immigration adjudicator on the basis that the deportation or removal would be contrary to the UK's obligations under the 1951 Convention. The appellant must, however, have raised the issue of asylum prior to the decision of the Secretary of State (s 70). Section 15 provides that the appellant should not be deported until the claim has been determined. This is subject to a major exception, however, in that by virtue of ss 11 and 12, the Secretary of State is allowed to remove an asylum seeker to one of the Member States of the EU, all of which are deemed to be 'safe' under s 11(1). This runs counter to the decisions in *Besnik Gashi* (1999), *Lul Omar Adan* (1999) and *Aitseguer* (2000) that France and Germany were not 'safe' because they were not applying the Convention properly. Such an argument could now only be raised on the basis that the deportation would infringe the asylum seekers' rights under the HRA 1998. As regards non-EU countries, the Secretary of State may designate certain countries as generally 'safe', or certify that a particular country in relation to a particular application is 'safe'. In relation to this last category, there may be no removal until any appeal against the certification of 'safety' has been heard (s 71).

In most cases, therefore, the asylum seeker will be removed prior to the hearing of any appeal. The exception to this is where there is an appeal under s 65 that the removal is unlawful under s 6 of the HRA 1998. Even here, however, the Secretary of State can issue a certificate that the claim is 'manifestly unfounded' and this will remove the right to remain while the appeal is heard.

There is a further right of appeal under s 71 against the issue of certificates under s 11 or 12, but this does not give any additional right to remain in the UK while the appeal is heard.

There is also provision in ss 73 and 74 to ensure that all issues are heard in one appeal. If additional matters are raised after an initial appeal has been successful, s 74 allows the Secretary of State to certify that they could have been raised before, and that the purpose of the claim is to delay deportation. This will lead to the appeal being regarded as finally determined. It remains to be seen whether the 1999 Act and the Rules are interpreted entirely in line with the Geneva Convention, although the Act intends this to be the case; and whether existing safeguards and appeals mechanisms will shift the balance in favour of the applicant.

## Note

1   It may be noted that the Protocol removed restrictions on refugee status: it allowed the Convention to apply to those who became refugees due to events occurring after 1 January 1951.

# Question 41

Miss Shia is a trained specialist gynaecological nurse. In the past, she resided and worked in Entriastan (a non-European Union State), where she assisted in the carrying out of abortions. Whilst she was resident there, she was under repeated threats from religious fundamentalists opposed to abortion. When the fundamentalists came to power in a coup, she fled to France. From France, she entered the UK illegally, but is seeking political asylum. Her brother is a student at a UK university and intends to begin a PhD after he has completed his undergraduate studies. Miss Shia is under threat of being sent back to France, but is terrified that other fundamentalist groups unconnected with the Entriastan Government may threaten her there. She is also worried that threatened health care cuts in Entriastan would not only cost her a job, but would limit her access to drugs which control her serious asthma. Advise Miss Shia of her chances of being allowed to remain in the UK.

## Answer plan

This problem question deals with a variety of issues relating to the grant of political asylum. Students must be aware of not only the relevant domestic law and practice, but also the Geneva Convention, as amended and a number of key decisions of the

European Court of Human Rights (ECHR). Essentially, students should discuss the following issues:

- is Miss Shia a political refugee entitled to asylum under the Geneva Convention 1951?;

- is she a member of a 'particular social group' (*Ouanes* (1998), *Islam* (1999))?;

- is France a 'safe third country' under the Dublin Convention 1990?;

- will ECHR decisions as to Arts 8 and 3 give her a better chance of asylum or a right to remain in the UK?

# Answer

The first question which must be answered is whether Miss Shia is in fact a political asylum seeker. In order to assess this, we must look to the definitions given in the Geneva Convention 1951, which is adopted into domestic law by the Immigration and Asylum Act 1999. The Convention provides that a person is an asylum seeker when he or she is:

> ... owing to a well founded fear of being persecuted for reasons of race, religion, nationality, membership of a particular social group or political opinion, is outside the country of his nationality and is unable or, owing to such fear, is unwilling to avail himself of that protection of that country; or who, not having a nationality and being outside the country of his former habitual residence or as a result of such events, is unable or, owing to such fear, is unwilling to return to it.

Hence, the key relevant elements of the test are a well founded fear of persecution, and that the persecution feared must be on relevant grounds. Miss Shia may try to argue that she has a well founded fear of persecution, either on a personal level due to any acts from which she had already suffered before she left Entriastan, or as a member of a 'particular social group'. In relation to the former, she is unlikely to succeed, particularly if Entriastan is now a violent country where human rights violations are likely to occur: see *Ward v Secretary of State for the Home Department* (1997), where an individual's torture was found to be 'nothing more than the sort of random difficulties faced by many thousands of people in Peru'. Further, 'solitary individuals do not exhibit cohesiveness, co-operation or interdependence', which were seen to be the requirements for a social group by Lord Justice Staughton in *Islam* (1998). But the fact that the threats which she suffered came from anti-abortion fundamentalists is not in itself a problem, since the persecution need not come from a State source: *R v Secretary of State for the Home Department ex p Bouheraoua and Kerkeb* (2000); the Convention provides protection from persecution by non-State agents if the authorities of the State in question are unwilling or unable to give effective protection. Thus, whether the present Government in Entriastan supports the anti-abortion fundamentalists' activities or not, Miss Shia has an arguable claim of fear of persecution. She may argue that she is a 'member of a particular social group' and fears persecution on that basis. There is some debate as to the correct approach on which to determine this issue. In *Ouanes v Secretary of State for the Home Department* (1998), the claimant was an Algerian citizen who worked as a midwife for the Ministry of Health. Her job included providing contraceptive advice. She had received threats for not wearing a veil in public, and there had been incidents where other midwives similarly employed had been killed by fundamentalists. The Tribunal found that she was a member of a group, that is, government-employed midwives, and that she had a well founded fear of persecution, because the fundamentalists were opposed to her duty to provide contraceptive advice and the State was unable to provide effective protection. However, on appeal, the House of Lords found that 'government-employed midwives' lacked the degree of cohesiveness required in the earlier case of *Shah* (1997), and that the expression 'particular social group' does not ordinarily cover a body of people linked only by the work that they do. The characteristic which defines a 'particular social group' must be one which members should not be required to change, since it is fundamental to their 'individual identities or conscience'. Thus, the original decision was reversed. So, if *Ouanes* is followed, Miss Shia would have great trouble in showing that she is a member of a 'particular social group'. However, there is also the rival approach adopted by the House of Lords in *Islam* and *Shah* (1999), where Pakistani women were found to be a 'particular social group' within the meaning of Art 1A(2) of the

Geneva Convention. The women claimants had both been falsely accused of adultery in Pakistan and feared that if they were returned, they would face criminal proceedings for sexual immorality and could be sentenced to either flogging or stoning to death. The House of Lords found that, although the general low status of women in Pakistan and the high level of violence against women in that society would not, in themselves, give rise to a claim to refugee status, the fact that the State tolerated and partly sanctioned discrimination against women, coupled with the fact that they were not granted the same rights as men, meant that they were a particular social group and so the claimants could satisfy the Geneva Convention test. There was not found to be any requirement of cohesiveness of a 'particular social group'. Hence, these two House of Lords' authorities appear to conflict, and it is difficult to choose which would be followed in Miss Shia's case. Unfortunately, the consequences would be greatly different for her depending on which is followed.

Assuming that she is found to be a member of a relevant particular social group, the next issue to be determined is whether there is a 'safe third country' to which she may be returned under the Dublin Convention 1990. The 1990 Convention provides that the European country in which an asylum seeker first arrived should be the country to determine his application unless, under the 1951 Geneva Convention, that country would not be considered to be a safe third country. Since Miss Shia has travelled to the UK via France, we need to decide whether France could be considered to be a safe third country. In *Secretary of State ex p Aitseguer* (2000), the House of Lords held that France could not automatically be treated as 'safe' because it was not interpreting the 1951 Convention properly. In particular, it did not recognise that the threat of persecution could come from source other than the State itself. This ruling has, however, effectively been overturned by s 11 of the Immigration and Asylum Act 1999. This deems all member countries of the European Union to be 'safe' for the purposes of dealing with asylum applications.

The only possibility of assistance to Miss Shia in this situation, therefore, comes from the European Convention on Human Rights and Fundamental Freedoms, and the Human Rights Act 1998. Although there is no direct or implied right of asylum in either the Convention or the Act, a number of other Articles of the

Convention have been employed in certain situations where the removal of an asylum seeker from the jurisdiction would cause exceptional hardship in his personal circumstances, or would show a lack of respect for his family or private life, or would risk him being tortured or otherwise ill treated on return to his home country or to a 'safe' third country. Miss Shia has potential arguments based on each of these lines. First, she might argue under Art 3 that to return her to her home country or to France would risk torture, inhuman or degrading treatment or punishment contrary to Art 3. Cases such as *Soering v UK* (1989) and *Hatami v Sweden* (1998) have shown that where there are substantial grounds for believing that there is a real risk that the asylum seeker will be subjected to torture or inhuman or degrading treatment or punishment in the receiving country, then the State who currently has the asylum seeker within its jurisdiction falls under a positive obligation not to expel that person. Secondly, under Art 8, there must be respect for the claimant's right to a private and family life. Since Miss Shia has a brother at university in the UK who intends to be there for an extended period as a postgraduate student, it is arguable that she may have strong family ties within the UK which might be upheld under Art 8. This is variable in its success: see *Ahmut v the Netherlands* (1996), where the argument failed, but *C v Belgium* (1996), where it succeeded. Finally, an argument might be made along the lines of *D v UK* (1997) that the claimant's medical condition and the lack of access to adequate long term treatment and comfort in her home country might violate Art 3 if she were removed (although this would not work, of course, if France were deemed to be a safe third country, since France has adequate medical treatment for asthma). Physical distress caused by untreated illness can be 'inhuman treatment'.

Thus, the relevant laws and its interpretation are in such an uncertain state that it is difficult to give a finite decision as to whether Miss Shia is likely to receive leave to remain; however, on any appeal, the new appeals procedures under the 1999 Act and 2000 Rules give greater priority to, and expedite, human rights-based claims, and so the final paragraph has been thrown into sharper focus.

# Question 42

In what ways can a person faced with an order for deportation from the UK challenge that decision? To what extent does the law in this area comply with the UK's international obligations?

## Answer plan

The first part of this question requires you to explain the various procedures for appeal that exist at common law or under the immigration legislation. In particular, you will need to deal with:

* habeas corpus;
* judicial review;
* appeal under the Immigration and Asylum Act 1999, and the Special Immigration Appeals Commission Act 1997;
* challenge under the Human Rights Act 1998.

As far as appeals under the immigration legislation are concerned, the special provisions relating to asylum seekers will need to be noted.

In relation to the second part of the question, the most obvious international obligations arise under:

* the Geneva Convention on the Status of Refugees 1951;
* the European Convention on Human Rights (the Convention).

The first of these is particularly relevant to the way in which appeals for asylum are treated; the Convention is, of course, more generally relevant, and the discussion of this area will obviously be closely linked to the section of your answer to the first part of the question which deals with the HRA 1998.

# Answer

All those who do not have a 'right of abode' in the UK, as defined by the Immigration Act 1971, are liable to deportation. The grounds on which such deportation can be ordered are to be found in s 3 of the 1971 Act, as amended by the Immigration and

Asylum Act (IAA) 1999. They include being convicted of a criminal offence (this only applies to adults), having a family member who is subject to a deportation order, or where the Secretary of State deems that the deportation would be 'conducive to the public good'. Slightly more restricted grounds apply to citizens of Member States of the European Economic Area in order to give recognition to the rights of free movement within that area.

Once a decision to deport has been made, how can it be challenged? There are four possible methods which need to be considered – habeas corpus, judicial review, appeal under provisions contained in the immigration legislation and challenge under the HRA 1998.

Where a person is being detained prior to deportation, then the action for the writ of habeas corpus might be used. This is the traditional common law remedy by which a person's release from detention by the executive can be achieved. It is sought by means of an application to the High Court, which takes precedence over all other actions. It is only concerned with jurisdiction, however, rather than the substance of a decision, so its use is limited. In *Secretary of State ex p Cheblak* (1991). for example, it was held that the Secretary of State did not need to give reasons for a decision that deportation would benefit 'national security'. Further, in *Secretary of State ex p Rahman* (1997), it was held that the Home Secretary was, in making his decision, entitled to rely on evidence which in ordinary legal proceedings would clearly amount to hearsay, and therefore would be inadmissible. Other methods of challenge rather than habeas corpus are therefore more likely to be effective.

A second possible route of challenge is by judicial review. The decision to deport and the procedures which have led to it are clearly administrative acts which are susceptible to such challenge. The very broad wording of the statutory powers, however, means that the applicant would generally have to establish bad faith, or *Wednesbury* unreasonableness to have any chance of success. Linking the application with a challenge on HRA 1998 grounds might raise more chance of success, and this is considered further below. The restrictive approach which the courts have traditionally taken to judicial review in this area is illustrated by *Secretary of State ex p Hosenball* (1977), where the

Court of Appeal refused to look behind the Home Secretary's assertion of national security grounds for his decision, and expressed a surprising confidence that the executive would never act against the freedom of an individual unless it was absolutely necessary. It may be that a more sceptical approach is indicated by the recent case of *Mullen* (1999). This was concerned with a deportation from Zimbabwe to the UK. There was evidence of unlawful action by the British and Zimbabwean authorities and that the deportation had been used to circumvent extradition procedures (which involves a judicial rather than administrative process). The Court of Appeal overturned Mullen's subsequent conviction in this country on the basis of the abuse of process in the pre-trial procedures. If this approach were taken in relation to deportation decisions by the UK authorities, then it might suggest a greater scope for using judicial review in this area.

The main route of appeal, however, will be to use the procedures set out in the immigration legislation. The IAA 1999 gives a right of appeal to an immigration adjudicator and thence to the Immigration Appeal Tribunal (IAT). This does not apply, however, where the decision follows a recommendation of a court before which the applicant has been convicted of an offence (an appeal through the criminal process being the appropriate remedy), or where the decision is to deport on the basis that this would be conducive to the public good on grounds of national security (this being subject to a special procedure, outlined below). The adjudicator or the IAT can review the facts, the legality of the decision, and the way in which any discretion has been exercised. In other words, it is a full reconsideration of the substance of the decision, and not simply a review of the process (as with judicial review). The decisions of the adjudicator or IAT (unless appealed) are binding on the Secretary of State.

Until 1997, there was no proper appeal process where the decision to deport was said to be based on national security grounds. The deportee could make representations to the three 'advisers' appointed by the Home Secretary, but there was no proper hearing, and the Home Secretary was not obliged to follow the advisers' advice (which, in any case, was not disclosed). These procedures were strongly criticised by the European Court in *Chahal v UK* (1997). Such appeals now go to the Special Immigration Appeals Commission (SIAC), under the Special

Immigration Appeals Commission Act (SIACA) 1997. The SIAC has three members, including a judge and an experienced immigration adjudicator. The appellant may be excluded from seeing some evidence or being present at part of the proceedings on public interest grounds. If this happens, a 'special advocate' will be appointed by the Attorney General to represent the appellant's interests. The SIAC has full binding power to review and overturn the deportation decision. An appeal on a point of law may be taken by either side to the Court of Appeal. In *Secretary of State for the Home Department v Rehman* (2000), the Court of Appeal took a broader view than the SIAC of what could be prejudicial to national security, holding that it could cover international terrorism which had no direct impact on the UK. The decision to deport was restored.

Special procedures also apply under the IAA 1999 where a person against whom a deportation order has been made seeks to claim political asylum. Section 69 gives a right of appeal to an immigration adjudicator on the ground that the deportation would be contrary to the UK's obligations under the Geneva Convention on the Status of Refugees 1951 (the 1951 Convention), provided that the asylum issue has previously been raised prior to the decision to deport. Once such an appeal has been made, s 15 of the IAA provides that the person should not be removed from the UK until the claim is determined. This is subject to very wide exceptions, however, in that it does not apply where the removal is to a 'safe' country, and all Member States of the European Union are deemed to be 'safe'. This is despite the fact that the English courts have recently ruled when applying earlier provisions that France and Germany were not applying the 1951 Convention properly, and were not therefore 'safe' (see *Besnik Gashi* (1999), *Lul Omar Adan* (1999) and *Aitseguer* (2000)). A right to remain will also arise where there is a HRA 1998 claim pending, unless the Home Secretary certifies that such a claim is 'manifestly unfounded'.

There are also provisions in the IAA 1999 to ensure that consecutive appeals are not allowed. Section 74 requires a person in relation to whom a decision to deport has been made to state all grounds for wishing to remain in the UK. This will prevent a person waiting until an appeal on one ground has been heard, and then raising another.

The fourth basis for an appeal against deportation would be by means of a direct challenge under s 7 of the HRA 1998. The most likely Articles on which to rely would be Art 3 or Art 8. These are discussed further below. More generally, however, it is likely that HRA 1998 arguments will be raised in connection with an application for judicial review, or an appeal under the IAA or SIACA. As has been noted, however, the IAA 1999 places some restrictions on the way in which human rights claims can be raised. The question of whether these are compatible with the UK's obligations under the ECHR is considered below.

Turning to the UK's international obligations in this area, there are two relevant treaties – the 1951 Convention and the European Convention. The obligation under the 1951 Convention is that a person should not be returned to a country where there is a well founded fear that he or she would face 'persecution' for reasons of, for example, race, nationality, political opinion, or membership of a particular social group. 'Persecution' is a strong word meaning more than harassment or discrimination. As far as 'social group' is concerned, it was held in *Islam v Secretary of State for the Home Department* (1999) that 'women' could constitute a 'social group' in the context of their potential return to Pakistan, because of the institutionalised State-sanctioned discrimination against them which might lead to their being flogged or stoned to death for adultery under Sharia law. The current UK law on immigration clearly does pay attention to this obligation, as indicated by ss 1 and 2 of the Asylum and Immigration Appeals Act 1993. As we have seen, special provisions exist to deal with the claims of asylum seekers. What must be open to question, however, are the current rules on what amounts to a 'safe' country to which to return an asylum seeker. As has been noted, under the IAA 1999, all Member States of the European Union are deemed to be safe, despite the fact that there have been very recent court decisions holding that various of them are failing to implement the 1951 Convention properly, and that individuals deported to them would be at risk of being further deported to a country where they might face persecution. There is already a very low success rate of appeals in relation to asylum (the 1997 figure was less than 1%) and these changes will do nothing to alter that.

A broader set of obligations is placed on the UK by the Convention, and these must, of course, now be taken into account by our courts under the HRA 1998. The Articles which are most relevant to this area are Arts 3, 6 and 8. In *Chahal v UK* (1997), for example, a decision to deport was held to involve breaches of Arts 3 and 6. The applicant was a Sikh activist who had been ordered to be deported to India. It was held that there was sufficient evidence of the risk that the applicant would suffer treatment falling within Art 3 ('torture or inhuman or degrading treatment') to find that his deportation to that country would be contrary to his rights under the Convention. Moreover, the failure at that time to provide a proper route of appeal when the deportation was on grounds of national security was a breach of the right to a fair trial under Art 6 (this defect was the reason for the introduction of the SIAC, discussed above). In *D v UK* (1997), it was held that deporting a person suffering from AIDS to a country which had no proper facilities for treatment could amount to a breach of Art 3.

There is also the obligation under Art 8 to respect private and family life. Deporting someone who has lived in the UK for a long time and who is dependent on family here could amount to a breach of this Article. It must be remembered that Art 8, unlike Art 3, is qualified, in that certain legitimate grounds for infringement are recognised in Art 8.2. It may well be possible, therefore, for a deportation to be argued to be necessary in the interests of, for example, national security, or preventing crime.

Immigration officials, immigration adjudicators, the courts and the Home Secretary will, since they are all 'public bodies' for the purposes of the HRA 1998, have to keep the above Articles in mind when dealing with deportation decisions. To that extent, the UK does now give proper attention to its obligations under the Convention. What is more difficult to justify is that although the IAA 1999 specifically recognises the right to challenge decisions on the HRA, this is hedged around with controls, some of which are based on the discretion of the Secretary of State There must be doubts, for example, as to whether the power of a member of the executive to declare a human rights claim 'manifestly unfounded' is compatible with Art 6. Similarly, the same Article may cast doubt on the requirement that deportees should, in many cases, pursue their appeals from outside the jurisdiction. For example, the difficulty of communicating with legal advisers in such a situation must raise doubts as to whether a fair trial is being guaranteed.

In conclusion, there are various routes for appeal against deportation, and the current UK laws pay at least some attention to the international obligations under the 1951 Convention and the European Convention. In various areas, however, as has been indicated they are open to criticism, and it may be expected that there will be further challenges to certain aspects of the system, either in the UK courts or, failing that, in Strasbourg.

# Question 43

'A political refugee has a far greater chance of success in avoiding deportation under the European Convention on Human Rights 1950 than under existing domestic law.'

Discuss.

## Answer plan

This question requires discussion of a variety of issues relating to the grant of political asylum. Students must be aware of not only the relevant domestic law and practice, but also the Geneva Convention as amended and a number of key decisions of the European Court of Human Rights (ECHR). Essentially, students should discuss the following issues:

- when is a political refugee entitled to asylum under the Geneva Convention 1951?;
- the definition of 'particular social group' (*Ouanes* (1998); *Islam* (1999));
- the relevance of a 'safe third country' under the Dublin Convention 1990;
- will ECHR decisions as to Art 8 and Art 3 give a better chance of asylum or a right to remain in the UK?

# Answer

In any application for asylum, the first question (and, hopefully, an obvious one) which must be answered is whether the applicant in fact falls within the definition of a political asylum seeker. In order to assess this, we must look to the definitions given in the Geneva Convention 1951, which is adopted into domestic law by the Immigration and Asylum Act 1999. The Convention provides that a person is an asylum seeker when he is: '... owing to a well founded fear of being persecuted for reasons of race, religion, nationality, membership of a particular social group or political opinion, is outside the country of his nationality and is unable or, owing to such fear, is unwilling to avail himself of that protection of that country; or who, not having a nationality and being outside the country of his former habitual residence or as a result of such events, is unable or, owing to such fear, is unwilling to return to it.'

Hence, the key relevant elements of the test are a well founded fear of persecution and that the persecution feared must be on relevant grounds. It is not sufficient that the applicant has a well founded fear of persecution on a personal level due to any acts from which he or she has already suffered before he left his or her home State, particularly if that State is now a violent country where human rights violations are likely to occur: see *Ward v Secretary of State for the Home Department* (1997), where an individual's torture was found to be 'nothing more than the sort of random difficulties faced by many thousands of people in Peru'. It is, rather, required that he is likely to suffer persecution as a member of a 'particular social group'. Further, 'solitary individuals do not exhibit cohesiveness, co-operation or interdependence', which were seen to be the requirements for a social group by Staughton LJ in *Islam* (1998). The persecution need not come from a State source (*R v Secretary of State for the Home Department ex p Bouheraoua and Kerkeb* (2000)); the Convention provides protection from persecution by non-State agents if the authorities of the State in question are unwilling or unable to give effective protection. There is some debate as to the correct approach on which to determine the issue of what constitutes a 'particular social group'. In *Ouanes v Secretary of State for the Home Department* (1998), the plaintiff was an Algerian citizen who worked as a midwife for the Ministry of Health. Her job included providing contraceptive advice. She had received threats for not wearing a veil in public and there had been incidents where other midwives similarly employed had been killed by fundamentalists. The tribunal found that she was a member of a group, that is, government-employed midwives, and that she had a well founded fear of persecution, because the fundamentalists were opposed to her duty to provide contraceptive advice and the State was unable to provide effective protection. However, on appeal, the House of Lords found that 'government-employed midwives' lacked the degree of cohesiveness required in the earlier case of *Shah* (1997), and that the expression 'particular social group' does not ordinarily cover a body of people linked only by the work that they do. The characteristic which defines a 'particular social group' must be one which members should not be required to change, since it is fundamental to their 'individual identities or conscience'. Thus, the original decision was reversed. So, if *Ouanes* is followed, any applicant is likely to face great difficulty in showing that he or she is a member of a 'particular social group'. However, there is also the rival approach adopted by the House of Lords in *Islam and Shah* (1999), where Pakistani women were found to be a 'particular social group' within the meaning of Art 1A(2) of the Geneva Convention. The women claimants had both been falsely accused of adultery in Pakistan and feared that if they were returned, they would face criminal proceedings for sexual immorality and could be sentenced to either flogging or stoning to death. The House of Lords found that, although the general low status of women in Pakistan and the high level of violence against women in that society would not, in themselves, give rise to a claim to refugee status, the fact that the State tolerated and partly sanctioned discrimination against women, coupled with the fact that they were not granted the same rights as men, meant that they were a particular social group, and so the claimants could satisfy the Geneva Convention test. There was not found to be any requirement of cohesiveness of a 'particular social group'. Hence, these two House of Lords authorities appear to conflict and it is difficult to choose which would be followed in any future case. Unfortunately, the consequences would be greatly different for an applicant, depending on which is followed.

Assuming that the applicant is found to be a member of a relevant particular social group, the next issue to be determined is whether there is a 'safe third country' to which he or she may be returned under the Dublin Convention 1990. The 1990 Convention provides that the European country in which an asylum seeker first arrived should be the country to determine his application unless, under the Geneva Convention, that country would not be considered to be a safe third country. As far as Member States of the European Union are concerned, that issue is now determined by s 11 of the Immigration and Asylum Act 1999, which deems all of them to be 'safe' for these purposes. This runs counter to the decisions in *Besnik Gashi* (1999), *Lul Omar Adan* (1999) and *Aitseguer* (2000) that France and Germany were not 'safe' because they were not applying the Convention properly. As regards States which are not members of the EU, a judgment must be made in each case. The test will be whether the country will deal with the asylum seeker in accordance with the requirements of the 1951 Geneva Convention.

The final possibility of aid to a political asylum seeker comes from the European Convention on Human Rights and Fundamental Freedoms, and the Human Rights Act 1998. Although there is no direct or implied right of asylum in either the Convention or the Act, a number of other Articles of the Convention have been employed in certain situations where the removal of an asylum seeker from the jurisdiction would cause exceptional hardship in his or her personal circumstances, or would show a lack of respect for his or her family or private life, or would risk him or her being tortured or otherwise ill treated on return to his or her home country or to a 'safe' third country.

The potential arguments based on each of these lines include the following. First, he or she might argue under Art 3 that to return him or her to the home country or to France would risk torture, inhuman or degrading treatment or punishment contrary to Art 3. Cases such as *Soering v UK* (1989) and *Hatami v Sweden* (1998) have shown that where there are substantial grounds for believing that there is a real risk that the asylum seeker will be subjected to torture or inhuman or degrading treatment or punishment in the receiving country, then the State who currently has the asylum seeker within its jurisdiction falls under a positive obligation not to expel that person. Secondly, under Art 8, there must be respect for the claimant's right to a private and family life. If the applicant has strong family ties within the UK, then this is a 'family life' which might be upheld under Art 8. This is variable in its success: see *Ahmut v The Netherlands* (1996), where the argument failed, but *C v Belgium* (1996), where it succeeded. Finally, an argument might be made along the lines of *D v UK* (1997), that any medical condition or other personal circumstances of the applicant require treatment, facilities or opportunities which are not available in his or her home country; depending on the circumstances, there might thus be a violation of Art 3 if he or she were removed, although there will often be a safe third country, removal to which would allow the same facilities and opportunities as the UK. Physical distress caused by untreated illness can be 'inhuman treatment'.

Thus, the relevant laws and its interpretation are in such an uncertain state that it is difficult to give a finite decision as to whether any asylum seeker is likely to receive leave to remain; however, on any appeal, the new appeals procedures under the Immigration and Asylum Act 1999 and 2000 Rules give greater priority to, and expedite, human rights-based claims and so the final paragraph has been thrown into sharper focus. The Human Rights Act 1998 has indeed made Convention-based applications more likely to succeed, but the two sets of rules must now operate in tandem, which can only serve to add to the confusion facing asylum seekers and professional working in this field. Perhaps it is time for wide ranging reform so that the Geneva Convention and the ECHR case law can be given a better degree of fit in the UK.

# CHAPTER 8

# FREEDOM FROM DISCRIMINATION

## Introduction

Examiners tend to set essays in this area which focus not only on the provisions of the Sex Discrimination Act 1975, the Equal Pay Act 1970, as amended, and the Race Relations Act 1976, but also on the relevant EC provisions. However, at the present time, discrimination on grounds of sex and race is not the only concern; a question concerning legal provisions relating to discrimination on grounds of sexual orientation may also be asked. The emphasis in essay questions is usually on the extent to which anti-discrimination legislation has been successful in combatting discrimination.

Students should be familiar with the following areas:

- the Sex Discrimination Act 1975;
- the Equal Pay Act 1970, as amended;
- the Race Relations Act 1976 and Race Relations Remedies Act 1994;
- the Disability Discrimination Act 1995, as amended;
- Art 141 of the EC Treaty;
- the Equal Pay and Equal Treatment Directives;
- provisions in domestic law relevant to discrimination on grounds of sexual orientation;
- Art 14 of the European Convention on Human Rights.

# Question 44

'The remedies available in respect of an anti-discrimination claim in the UK are badly in need of reform, as is the procedure which must be used in bringing such a claim. An individual who attempts to gain redress under the legislation is entering a minefield.' Discuss.

## Answer plan

A fairly demanding essay question. It does not ask for a general survey of the substantive law, but for consideration of the procedure involved; therefore it is obviously important to ensure that your answer keeps firmly to its terms. Essentially, the following areas should be considered:

- remedies under the Race Relations Act 1976, the Sex Discrimination Act 1975, the Equal Pay Act 1970, as amended, and the Disability Discrimination Act 1995, as amended;
- influence of Art 141 of the EC Treaty, the Equal Pay and Equal Treatment Directives;
- tribunal procedure in discrimination cases;
- the Equal Opportunities Commission (EOC) and the Commission for Racial Equality (CRE) proposals for reform of the procedure;
- impact of the Convention.

# Answer

The various remedies available which are applicable in race, sex and disability discrimination cases are generally perceived as inadequate, as are the means of enforcing them. A tribunal can award a declaration which simply states the rights of the applicant and the respect in which the employer has breached the law. It can also award an action recommendation which will be intended to reduce the effect of the discrimination. However, the EAT in *British Gas plc v Sharma* (1991) held that this could not include a recommendation that the applicant be promoted to the next suitable vacancy, as this would amount to positive discrimination. It might, however, be argued that this would merely be putting the person in the position he or she should have been in, rather than giving them a special preference due to race or sex.

A tribunal can also award compensation which will be determined on the same basis as in other tort cases. It will be awarded for financial loss and injury to feelings; exemplary damages will not be available. Awards have tended to be low,[1] but they have risen since the decision in *Noone* (1988) that a consultant who was not appointed on grounds of race should be awarded £3,000 for injury to feelings. In *Alexander* (1988), it was held that awards for injury to feelings should not be minimal, because this would tend to trivialise the public policy to which the Act gives effect. On the other hand, it was found that they should be restrained and therefore should not be set at the same level as damages for defamation. On this basis, £500 was awarded for injured feelings due to racial discrimination.

However, the decision of the European Court of Justice (ECJ) in *Marshall (No 2)* (1993) has had a very significant impact on the level of awards. The ECJ found that the award of compensation in sex discrimination cases brought against organs of the State should be set at a level which would allow the loss sustained to be made good in full. It might even be possible for complainants bringing a case against private employers to sue the State in such instances under the principle in *Francovich v Italy* (1992).[2] In order to ensure, after *Marshall (No 2)*, that applicants in race discrimination cases were placed on the same footing as those in sex discrimination cases, the Race Relations Remedies Act 1994 was passed to remove the existing limits on the level of compensation. In the *Von Colson* case (1984), the ECJ held that any sanction must have a real deterrent effect. The EOC has recommended that equal pay and sex discrimination provisions should be combined in one statute and that the distinction between indirect and direct discrimination as regards compensation should be abolished. Thus, where a person had acted in an indirectly discriminatory fashion, although unmotivated by sexism, compensation would still be payable. This is desirable, because there is evidence that some employers have deliberately failed to conduct a review of working practices so as to be able to put forward a convincing argument that they did not appreciate the discriminatory affect of certain practices.

It seems fairly clear that awards at the levels set prior to *Marshall (No 2)* did not encourage claims, did not deter employers from discrimination and were unlikely to affect deeply rooted discriminatory ideologies in institutions. However, the *Marshall* decision has led to an improvement in the level of compensation payable in both race and sex discrimination cases, which may allow the legislation to have some real bite. There is now no statutory limit on the compensation awardable for unlawful discrimination.

It is fairly common for the defendant to fail to comply with the award. The applicant must then return to court in order to enforce it. If an action recommendation has not been complied with, the tribunal will award compensation, but only if compensation could have been awarded at the original hearing. As this is unlikely to be the case in an indirect discrimination claim, there will be no remedy available, except to apply to the CRE and the EOC, alleging persistent discrimination. However, an injunction may be awarded.

The number of applications began to decline from 1976 onwards, although there is evidence that it is beginning, in the 1990s, to rise again. Possibly, this is because the success rate is so low that applicants are deterred from ever bringing a claim in the first place. In other words, the number of applications may be self-limiting: only the very determined applicants will pursue cases all the way to a hearing. Of course, the decline in the rate of applications may be partly attributable to the initial rush to attack very blatant examples of sexism and racism which died away as employers and others began to ensure that policies enshrining such values were either abolished or made less overt.

Further, a number of aspects of the procedure which has to be used in bringing a discrimination claim may combine to deter applicants from engaging in it. Less than half of the applications are heard; there is obviously a strong tendency to give up a claim halfway through. There may be a number of reasons why cases are not brought, why they are abandoned and why the success rate is so low. Obviously, the applicant is in a very vulnerable position; the position of the parties is usually unequal, especially if an applicant is bringing the claim against his or her employer. The applicant will be afraid of being labelled a troublemaker, perhaps of being sacked or of losing promotion prospects. There may be continual pressure not only on the applicant, but on any workmates who have consented to act as witnesses in the claim, and they may withdraw their consent to act.

The weakness of the remedies is unlikely to encourage claims, and the complexity and technicality of the substantive law may also act as a deterrent. It may do so in any event but, coupled with the lack of legal aid, the task facing the applicant may appear overwhelming. These two factors are exacerbated by and also contribute to the lack of experience tribunal members have of discrimination cases. The procedure in respect of equal value claims in particular is so complex and involves so many hearings that the applicant is especially vulnerable to pressure to withdraw or settle the claim.

The applicant may be aided by the EOC, CRE or the new Disability Rights Commission, but these have to refuse the majority of applications due to their lack of funds. This leads to a poor quality of decision making and to the charge that the employers' lawyers may manipulate the members of the tribunal, due to their lack of experience in the area. Thus, a vicious circle is set up. The tribunals need more experience in these cases, but do not receive it, due to the factors mentioned here; when a tribunal does hear such a case, it may deal with it badly, thereby having the effect of deterring future applicants and ensuring that tribunals do not gain more experience. Indeed, it may be argued that the tribunal procedure is simply unsuitable for discrimination claims, given the current highly technical and complex nature of the substantive law.

The CRE has proposed that there should be a discrimination division of Employment Tribunals dealing only with discrimination claims. Such tribunals would gather expertise in this very specialist area and could be equipped with powers to order higher levels of compensation. Legal aid could be made available in this specialist division, even though it remained unavailable in respect of other tribunal cases. The EOC has recommended that equal pay and sex discrimination provisions should be combined in one statute; this would reduce the difficulty facing the lay applicant whose claim may appear to fall between the two statutes.

It may be concluded that individuals have not been able to use the legislation very effectively in practice in order to bring about change, although, possibly, this situation may improve as the influence of the ECJ increases. The EOC and CRE have proposed that they should be able to join in an individual's action in order to address institutionalised discrimination in an undertaking. This would both obviate to some extent the need for individuals to bring claims and would provide the support and expertise which is needed in order to allow individual claims to succeed. However, this would require a better level of funding from the Government; the level of funding these bodies receive at present suggests that there is a lack of commitment to ending discriminatory practices.

One possibly positive development is the Human Rights Act 1998, which will allow an Art 14 discrimination challenge to be brought in any case, in any UK court. However, this will, of course, only be possible where there is an arguable breach of any other Convention right, since Art 14 has no separate existence (see *Botta v Italy* (1998)).

### Notes

1   Gregory notes that, in 40% of the cases, the award was less than £200. Now, however, substantial awards are more common.

2   It might be pointed out that it was necessary for the same higher level of compensation to become available in race discrimination cases, since the 1975 and the 1976 Acts are intended to harmonise.

# Question 45

Evaluate the success of the Equal Opportunities Commission and the Commission for Racial Equality in curbing discrimination on grounds of race or sex in the UK.

## Answer plan

A reasonably straightforward essay question. It is important to view the powers of these two bodies in the context of the individual method of using the legislation which they are supposed to complement. Essentially, the following areas should be considered:

- power of the Equal Opportunities Commission (EOC) and the Commission for Racial Equality (CRE) to issue a non-discrimination notice;
- power to conduct a formal investigation;
- assistance to claimants;
- use of judicial review;
- limitations of the two bodies.

# Answer

Apart from the individual method of bringing about change, the Race Relations and Sex Discrimination Acts also contain an 'administrative method', which was included with the aim of relieving the burden on individual applicants. It may also represent a more coherent approach than the piecemeal method of bringing individual cases. The aim was to bring about general changes in discriminatory practices, rather than waiting for an individual to take on the risk and the burden of bringing a case. The new Disability Rights Commission will have similar rights, powers and lack of enforceable sanctions; this framework must therefore be one which appeals to the Government.

Both the CRE and the EOC have two main powers. They can assist claimants and they can issue a non-discrimination notice in respect of discriminatory practices where there may be no known victim who wants to bring a claim.[1] This may be because the company or institution has effectively deterred certain people from coming forward with applications for a job. If indications of race discrimination appear – if, for example, it appears that very few of a certain group are employed – then, first, a formal investigation will be conducted.

This decision might be taken if, for example, the workforce was only 1% Afro-Caribbean, although the company was in a racially mixed area in which that ethnic group comprised about 30% of the population. It may be that the recruiting policy is indirectly discriminatory; for example, it may largely be by word of mouth and, therefore, the existing workforce may tend to reproduce itself. However, the CRE has had the power to issue a non-discrimination notice curbed by the House of Lords' decision in *Prestige Group plc, CRE ex p Prestige Group* (1984). It was found that the CRE is not entitled to investigate a named person or company, unless it already has a strong reason to believe that discrimination has occurred.

Thus, after this decision, where the strong suspicion needed to bring a formal investigation is not already present (an investigation is needed in order to acquire it), the CRE and EOC can embark on a general investigation only. This means that their powers are more limited: they cannot subpoena witnesses or issue a non-discrimination notice.

Thus, the CRE and the EOC now tend to be confined to a reactive approach; they can only react to very blatant forms of discrimination. They cannot investigate more subtle and insidious instances of discrimination which may be the more pernicious, and this clearly represents a limitation of their role. After the *Prestige* decision, the CRE had to abandon a number of investigations which it had already begun. There has therefore been a tendency for subtle institutionalised racism and sexism to continue unchecked, although more blatant examples of racism and sexism, such as the phrase 'no blacks', which used to appear in advertisements, have now disappeared.

Although the investigative powers of the EOC have been curbed, it may be able to bring about general changes in discriminatory practices by seeking a direct change in the law. In *Secretary of State for Employment ex p EOC* (1994), it was found that the EOC can seek a declaration in judicial review proceedings to the effect that primary UK legislation is not in accord with EC equality legislation. Certain provisions of the Employment Protection (Consolidation) Act 1978 governed the right not to be unfairly dismissed, compensation for unfair dismissal and the right to statutory redundancy pay. These rights did not apply to workers who worked less than the specified number of hours a week. The EOC considered that since the majority of those working for less than the specified number of hours were women, the provisions operated to the disadvantage of women and were therefore discriminatory. The EOC accordingly wrote to the Secretary of State for Employment, expressing this view and arguing that, since the provisions in question were indirectly discriminatory, they were in breach of EC law.

The Secretary of State replied by letter that the conditions excluding part timers from the rights in question were justifiable and, therefore, not indirectly discriminatory. The EOC applied for judicial review of the Secretary of State's refusal to accept that the UK was in breach of its obligations under EC law. The application was amended to bring in an individual, Mrs Day, who worked part time and had been made redundant by her employers. It was found that Mrs Day's claim was a private law claim, which could not be advanced against the Secretary of State, who was not her employer and was not liable to meet the claim if it was successful.

The Secretary of State further argued that the EOC had no *locus standi* to bring the proceedings. However, the House of Lords found that since the EOC had a duty under s 53(1) of the Sex Discrimination Act to work for the elimination of discrimination, it was within its remit to try to secure a change in the provisions under consideration, and, therefore, the EOC had a sufficient interest to bring the proceedings and, hence, *locus standi*. The Secretary of State also argued that no decision or justiciable issue susceptible of judicial review existed. However, the House of Lords found that, although the letter itself was not a decision, the provisions themselves could be challenged in judicial review proceedings. In other words, the real question was whether judicial review was available for the purpose of securing a declaration that certain UK primary legislation was incompatible with EC law, and, following *Secretary of State for Transport ex p Factortame* (1992), it would appear that judicial review was so available.

As regards the substantive issue – whether the provisions in question, while admittedly discriminatory, could be justified – the House of Lords thought that, in certain special circumstances, an employer might be justified in differentiating between full and part time workers to the disadvantage of the latter, but that such differentiation, employed nationwide, could not be justified. Thus, the EOC, but not an individual applicant, was entitled to bring judicial review proceedings in order to secure a declaration that UK law was incompatible with EC law. Declarations were made that the conditions set out in the provisions in question were indeed incompatible with EC law.

This was a very far reaching decision: it means that where UK legislation is incompatible with EC law, a declaration can be obtained to that effect more rapidly than if it was necessary to wait for an individual affected to bring a case against the particular person or body who was acting within the terms of the UK legislation in question. The decision may not directly have an effect on race discrimination, but it opens the possibility that the EOC may challenge other provisions of UK law and, where such provisions have an equivalent under the Race Relations Act 1976, the end result may be that provisions relating to sex and race discrimination are brought into harmony with EC equality provisions, which tend to be more far reaching than domestic provisions.

The CRE and the EOC have made a number of proposals for reform which would strengthen the administrative method and allow it to work more closely in harmony with the individual method. The CRE wants to try to narrow the gap between individual cases and what can be achieved by a formal investigation and has proposed that, in order to do this, it should be able to join in the individual's case as a party to the action, so as to draw attention to the likelihood of further discrimination occurring. Thus, the individual would receive the remedy, but the general effect of discrimination in the defendant company would be addressed by issuing a non-discrimination notice at the same time. This may be supported on the ground that if one individual brings a successful case against an employer, it is probable that discrimination in that concern is quite widespread.[2] Both the EOC and the CRE want legislation to reverse the *Prestige* decision. They want to be able to launch investigations into a named person or company, even when there is no initial strong evidence of discrimination.

It may be argued in conclusion that both bodies have been set a task – the curbing of discriminatory practices – which they were always ill fitted to undertake. Both have been subject to external pressures – lack of funding, lack of sympathy with their role evinced by the judiciary – which have undermined their purpose. Sacks argues that the EOC is also affected by its internal limitations, which spring from its status as a quango. She suggested that an internal contradiction inevitably arises from that status: it is supposed to have taken a stance independent of government and even in conflict with it, but it is at the same time at the mercy of government in terms of appointees to it and in terms of funding.

## Notes

1   Further, it might be pointed out that if a non-discrimination notice is issued, the CRE or EOC can apply for an injunction to enforce it under s 62(1).

2   If an individual in an undertaking has been the victim of discrimination, it is likely that discrimination may be institutionalised within it and may recur in future if the remedy is confined to the individual applicant only.

# Question 46

Evaluate the case for bringing homosexuals within the scope of anti-discrimination legislation in the UK.

## Answer plan

This question seems reasonably straightforward, but it should be borne in mind that examiners will tend to be looking for the more perceptive answers which ask not only whether there is strong case for adopting anti-discrimination measures applying to homosexuals, but also whether the existing scheme is the best model available. Possibly, the situation of homosexuals places them in a different position in terms of discriminatory practices than that of women and members of certain ethnic groups.

The following matters should be considered:

- unfair dismissal provisions of the Employment Rights Act 1996;
- provisions relating to homosexuality in the armed forces and recent European Court of Human Rights (ECHR) cases;
- s 28 of the Local Government Act 1988;
- s 1 of the Sexual Offences Act 1967, as amended – homosexual age of consent;
- s 32 of the Sexual Offences Act 1956;
- directions of reform;
- ECHR authorities.

# Answer

At present, a person who is refused promotion, dismissed from a job or refused an offer of housing on grounds of sexual orientation is in the same position as a woman so treated on the ground of sex would have been before 1975. If a lesbian or homosexual has been employed for at least one year before dismissal, the law of unfair dismissal under the Employment Rights Act 1996 may offer some protection, although a dismissal will be fair if it is for 'some other substantial reason of a kind to justify dismissal', provided that the employer acts reasonably.

Where dismissal is on grounds of sexual orientation, it seems that a wide interpretation will be given to the meaning of 'reasonable'. In *Saunders v Scottish National Camps* (1981), the applicant, who was employed as a maintenance handyman at a boy's camp, was dismissed on the grounds of homosexuality, although his duties did not ordinarily bring him into contact with the boys. His dismissal was, nevertheless, held to be fair on the ground that many other employers would have responded in the same way. The decision is clearly open to attack on the ground that had his duties brought him into contact with the boys there would have been no more reason to believe that they would have been in danger from him than would girls from a male heterosexual. Similarly, it was found in *Director of GCHQ ex p Hodges* (1988) that the dismissal of a homosexual from the Government Communications Headquarters (GCHQ) as a threat to national security was not unreasonable.

In the UK, homosexuals were, until recently, barred from the merchant navy and the armed forces, where homosexual acts were classed as 'disgraceful conduct' (s 66 of the Army Act 1955; s 1(2) and (5) of the Sexual Offences Act 1967)), although the armed forces in Belgium, Denmark, France, the Netherlands and Spain are all open to homosexuals. The European Commission on Human Rights at first rejected a challenge to the provision relating to the army as inadmissible on the argument that there is a special need to prevent disorder in the armed forces (*B v UK* (1983)). However, a sudden turnaround occurred in the case of *Lustig-Prean v UK* (1999). All four applicants were homosexual members of the armed forces, who were discharged on that sole ground after Ministry of Defence inquiries. They argued that the investigations into their sexual orientation and their subsequent discharges violated Arts 8, 3 and 14, amongst others. The Court found that the investigations had been exceptionally intrusive and that the ban on homosexuals was unjustified. Hence, there were breaches of both Art 8 and Art 13, the latter because judicial review was only available if the policy was 'irrational'.

Discrimination against homosexuals in the field of education is enshrined in s 28 of the Local Government Act 1988; it prohibits the promotion of homosexuality or the teaching of 'the acceptability of homosexuality as a pretended family relationship'. Thus, local authorities may still fund certain groups, so long as this is aimed at benefitting the group, rather than at promoting homosexuality. Robertson argues that s 28 should not have a significant effect in schools, since local authorities do not directly control the curriculum (and this is particularly the case under Local Management of Schools). However, s 28 may serve to ratify and legitimise intolerance of homosexuals in education and outside it. At the time of writing, the debate continues as to whether s 28 will be repealed.

The criminal law also enshrines overt direct discrimination. Until 1967, homosexual intercourse between males was prohibited under the common law offence of buggery, which was incorporated in s 12(1) of the Sexual Offences Act 1956. Relaxation of the prohibition was effected by s 1 of the Sexual Offences Act 1967, which permitted homosexual acts, including buggery, between consenting males, both of whom are 21 or over (the highest age of consent for homosexual intercourse in the EC), which took place in private. The limited nature of this exception obviously placed the sexual freedom of homosexuals on an entirely unequal footing with that of heterosexuals and such lack of equality is reflected in the area of liability which still remains to catch homosexual acts. After the case of *Sutherland* (1998), a campaign has continued to reduce the homosexual age of consent from its present 18 to that for heterosexuals, 16. But, in spite of the finding in that case that the difference of treatment was discriminatory and breached Art 8 in conjunction with Art 14, repeated attempts at legislative change failed. Thus, it remains uncertain when this factual difference of treatment on grounds of sexuality will be removed.

A homosexual act which takes place in 'public' will be an offence and this will include any place where anyone apart from the two parties is present. Thus, a homosexual act occurring in a house owned by one of the parties (known either as the 'agent' or the 'patient') would be criminalised if another person was in the same room, although unaware of what was occurring. If there is uncertainty as to whether a place is private or public, it must be resolved by reference to all the facts, including the likelihood of a third person coming on the scene (*Reakes* (1974)).

It is an offence under s 4 of the 1967 Act to procure another man to commit with a third man an act of buggery, while any agreement between two or more persons to facilitate homosexual activity may be caught by the common law offence of conspiracy to corrupt public morals. The existence of this offence was affirmed in *Knuller Ltd v DPP* (1972), in which Lord Reid made clear the policy of the law regarding homosexual acts: 'I read the (1967) Act as saying that, even though (buggery) may be corrupting, if people choose to corrupt themselves in this way, that is their affair and the law will not interfere. But no licence is given to others to encourage the practice.' He equated homosexual connection with prostitution, as an activity which was not in itself unlawful, but which was not 'lawful in the full sense'.

The legislation did not apply to Northern Ireland or Scotland and might not now be universal in the UK had not the ECHR accepted in *Dudgeon v UK* (1981) that restriction of sexual freedom may be a violation of Art 8. In response to this ruling, Northern Irish law was changed under the Homosexual Offences (NI) Order

1982. Thus, it is fair to say that the legalisation of homosexual acts was effected in almost the narrowest conceivable manner and suggested a bare toleration of them.

In the EC, Irish criminal law was, until recently, the most hostile to homosexuals and sexual acts between members of the same sex were outlawed in the Republic until June 1993, when the Irish Government introduced reform by lowering the age of consent for homosexual acts to 17, thus bringing it into line with the more progressive European countries. It was argued in *Dudgeon* that the age of consent should be lowered in order to ensure respect for the private life of homosexuals, but the ECHR accepted that it was within the Member States' margin or appreciation to fix the age of consent at a level which would seem to protect the rights of others.

It was recommended in 1984 by the Criminal Law Revision Committee that the age of consent should be lowered to 18, but this was not implemented. However, in 1994, the Criminal Justice and Public Order Act was passed to lower the homosexual age of consent to 18 under s 145, which amended s 1 of the 1967 Act. Parliament considered, but rejected a proposal to allow the ages of heterosexual and homosexual consent to be equalised. Thus, the criminal law will still demonstrate an acceptance of discrimination. If the issue returns to the ECHR, it might be prepared to reconsider its decision on the point in *Dudgeon*, on the basis that UK law will still be out of line with that of other Member States. The court tends to take the view that in sensitive matters of this nature, it should hold back until a clear European standard seems to be emerging; at the stage when a trend is clear, but no such standard has emerged, it will tend to invoke the margin of appreciation.

The UK Government takes the view, which it put forward in the *Dudgeon* case, that female homosexual activity does not present as great a danger to society and particularly to young persons as male homosexual activity. This may explain why the age of consent for lesbian acts remains the same as for heterosexual intercourse. That 16 is the age of consent is apparent on the basis that, although such acts may be capable of being indecent assaults under s 14 of the Sexual Offences Act 1956, they will normally be consented to and so will not be accounted assaults. However, a girl under 16 cannot give the relevant consent and so any homosexual act which takes place with a girl beneath that age would be unlawful, as would a heterosexual act. Discussion of this subject would not, however, support the reason given in *Dudgeon* for this apparent liberalism on behalf of the UK; Edwards argues that its true basis lies in a traditional belief in the sexual passivity of females.

Studies of discrimination against homosexuals in the criminal justice system have tended to concentrate on the investigation stage and methods of enforcing certain areas of the criminal law such as s 32 of the Sexual Offences Act 1956. This provides that it is an offence 'for a man to persistently solicit or importune in a public place for immoral purposes'. Research suggests that this section is used by police officers engaged in surveillance in public toilets to trap gay men into some behaviour which might be said to come within the terms of the section. It seems that almost any behaviour, 'any physical gesture or words' in context may fulfil its terms. Thus, homosexuals can be criminalised in respect of trivial behaviour, which would not have occurred had a police officer not trapped them into it. Prosecutions under this section, such as those undertaken in *Gray* (1981) and *Kirkup* (1992), reflect, it is suggested, the bare tolerance of homosexuality mentioned above.

The evidence of overt discrimination described here argues for an anti-discrimination scheme covering various contexts, including employment which would outlaw direct discrimination based on sexual orientation. Such a scheme could be modelled on the provisions of s 1(1) of the Sex Discrimination Act 1975, which requires the complainant to show that a comparable man would have been treated more favourably than she has been; in other words, the adverse treatment would not have occurred, but for the fact that she is a woman. A homosexual could be compared with a heterosexual of similar attributes in order to determine whether the adverse treatment was on grounds of homosexuality or due to neutral criteria, such as length of experience. The 1975 Act provides a defence of genuine occupational qualification, but, apart from that, it embodies the presumption that it can never be right to treat a woman adversely (in the contexts it covers) merely because she is a woman. In order to have any real impact, any equivalent statute protecting homosexuals from discrimination would also have to import such a presumption. However, although the provisions of the Sex Discrimination Act may provide a starting point, it is suggested that a wider ranging statute is needed which would provide protection for homosexuals from discrimination in a broad range of contexts.

At present, the political will to deal with this sensitive and contentious issue may not be apparent. However, there is some recognition in Europe that such discrimination amounts to a general problem, which should be addressed. A Report compiled for the Commission of the European Communities in May 1993 on discrimination against homosexuals found that the UK was one of the worst offenders and was one of only four Member States which provided no legal protection against discrimination. The Report also criticised the Commission, which has argued that homosexuality is a matter to be left to individual governments. It recommended that human rights for homosexuals should be enshrined in EC law.[1] Of course, adopting this course would be to further the social benefits of the single market in an instance in which the economic benefits of harmonisation of the law in the Member States was unclear.

Since the HRA 1998 came into force, the potential has existed for discrimination on the ground of sexuality to become illegal under UK law. Although Art 14 is limited by applying only where there is discrimination in relation to another Convention right, there are few situations where no such right is relevant. An obvious way in which this might be done is by linking the claim to Art 8, the right to respect for private life. Thus, improvements to UK discrimination law may shortly be made by courts, either by issuing declarations of incompatibility or by interpreting existing statutes and case authority, so that it does not conflict with Art 14.

## Note

1   The potential of Art 14 of the Convention could be considered here either as a source of general principles of EC law or as a means of improving the position of homosexuals in various contexts when read in conjunction with one of the other articles.

# CHAPTER 9

# THE HUMAN RIGHTS ACT 1998: A BILL OF RIGHTS FOR BRITAIN?

## Introduction

The first edition of this book dealt in considerable detail with the Bill of Rights debate, the advantages and disadvantages of a written human rights guarantee and the deficiencies of the European Convention on Human Rights then procedure as a human rights enforcement mechanism. The incorporation of the Convention into UK law via the Human Rights Act 1998 has rendered that debate largely defunct, but knowledge of the history of the Convention in the UK remains essential. Political and public support for some form of Bill of Rights grew overwhelming by the mid-1990s, but the resulting statute bears the marks of several compromises. The debate is now likely to centre upon the status of the Convention in UK law, its effectiveness as a human rights guarantee and the major improvements in domestic human rights which will result from incorporation and the gaps in both the Convention and the 1998 Act. The role of judges will now come under fresh scrutiny, since they hold an important new role as human rights watchdogs, yet lack the ultimate power of overriding legislation which breaches the Convention. Many different styles of essay question are possible on this large and wide ranging topic; the following questions cover most of the debate at the time of writing.

Students must be familiar with the following areas and their inter-relationships:

- the position before incorporation and the former difficulties of bringing a Convention action;
- the drive towards incorporation of the Convention;
- the doctrine of parliamentary sovereignty;

- the provisions of the Human Rights Act 1998 and the Convention;
- key case law on the Convention.

# Question 47

Critically examine the implications of the Human Rights Act 1998 as the UK's human rights guarantee.

## Answer plan

This is a straightforward essay question which is likely to be commonly set. However, it is important not to degenerate into a list of advantages and disadvantages of the Act and the Convention. The implications include the changed role of judges and the new dimension to all domestic legal cases.

# Answer

Until 1998, the precarious and disorderly state of civil liberties and human rights in the UK was a strong argument in favour of the adoption of some form of Bill of Rights. In certain areas of civil liberties, the existing statutory and case law safeguards against abuse of power were less comprehensive and, arguably, less effective than in many other democratic countries. Citizens of the UK did enjoy a reasonable level of tolerance of individual behaviour, but there were serious gaps and the tolerance itself, because it was not bolstered by a formal guarantee of rights, was fragile, especially in times of crisis. The law sought to protect certain values, such as the need to maintain public order but, in doing so, curtailed the exercise of certain freedoms because nothing prevented it from disregarding them. Thus, human rights had a precarious status, in that they only existed, by deduction, in the interstices of the law.

For example, the Public Order Act 1986 contains extensive provisions in ss 12 and 14 which allow stringent conditions to be imposed on marches and assemblies. Such conditions are intended to enhance the ability of the police to maintain public order, but they are not balanced by any provision in the Act which takes account of the need to protect freedom of assembly. Equally, the Official Secrets Act 1989 arguably provides a more efficient means of preventing the disclosure of official information than did its predecessor, but it was not intended to allow the release of any information at all to the public (although later statutes have done just that).

Not all statutes suggest the same reluctance to protect the freedom which their provisions may infringe; the Contempt of Court Act 1981, while primarily concerned with protecting the administration of justice, contains provisions in s 5 for allowing 'discussions in good faith of public affairs ... if the risk of prejudice to the particular legal proceedings is merely incidental to the discussion'. However, the Contempt of Court Act 1981 was, in fact, passed in response to the ruling by the European Court of Human Rights (ECHR) in the *Sunday Times* case (1979) that UK contempt law had infringed Art 10 of the Convention. The Contempt of Court Act may be contrasted with the Broadcasting Act passed in the same year, which allowed the Home Secretary to prohibit the broadcasting of 'any matter or class of matter'. This is typical of a number of provisions in domestic law which had the potential to undermine human rights very significantly and would have done so had not discretion been exercised in their interpretation and invocation. The Convention, as incorporated by the Human Rights Act (HRA) 1998, is surely a better safeguard than the previous reliance placed upon such forbearance.

In contrast to the previous situation, the HRA now represents a minimum guarantee of freedom. Certain fundamental values have been placed, theoretically and temporarily at least, out of the reach of any political majority. Citizens of the UK no longer have to rely upon the ruling party to ensure that its own legislation does not infringe freedoms. When laws are passed which conflict with some fundamental freedom, courts will now have to interpret such laws in the light of the Convention and consider to what extent the freedoms may legitimately be curtailed. This is in stark contrast to the prior situation, where the courts had no choice but to apply an Act of Parliament, no matter how much it might breach the Convention.

The HRA 1998 has therefore created a far more active judicial role in protecting basic rights and freedoms. If a court considers that either a new or existing statute which is under its consideration infringes the Convention rights or freedoms, then it may issue a Declaration of Incompatibility, upon which it is hoped the Government will act promptly. The interpretation of the US constitution illustrates what could happen in this country; vast edifices of civil rights have been constructed out of innocuous and ambiguous phrases. The generality of terms of the Convention means that its interpretation is likely to evolve in accordance with the UK's changing needs and social values; this is, in any case, one of the basic principles of Strasbourg-based Convention jurisprudence, since the Convention is intended to be a living document which is not bound by time or venue, but can develop to suit both in any jurisdiction. Thus, it is likely that, soon, there will be two versions of the Convention relevant to the UK: the domestic version as incorporated by the HRA; and the still-existing opportunity to take a persistent grievance to Strasbourg.

Incorporation has already had a number of advantages. Citizens may obtain redress for human rights breaches without needing, except as a last resort, to apply to the ECHR in Strasbourg. This saves a great deal of time and money for the citizen and thus greatly improves access to justice. The range of remedies available under the HRA 1998 is the same as in any ordinary UK court case, and so includes injunctions and specific performance where appropriate, rather than simply damages. British judges are presumably already making a greater contribution to the development of Convention rights jurisprudence in Strasbourg. But a major disadvantage, or at least a source of anxiety, is the doubt as to whether UK judges can be trusted to give a vigorous interpretation to the Convention. The British judiciary are, in general, highly regarded, but they are an elite group, drawn mainly from a certain stratum of society and, therefore, to varying degrees, out of touch with the working class. They have been trained in techniques of legal analysis which include deciding cases without the responsibility of considering their social repercussions; it is doubtful whether three days of human rights awareness training will have overturned years of this practice. The new role of the judiciary which is more important and, therefore, more overtly political might mean moves towards more political involvement in their appointments - a development which has taken place in the US. The interpretations given by judges to the Convention may greatly dilute its impact.

But, conversely, it may be argued, first, that UK judges have at times shown themselves capable of bearing in mind the public interest in, for example, freedom of speech. A clear example comes from Mr Justice Scott's ruling in *AG v Guardian (No 2)* (1988) (the *Spycatcher* case), which boldly rejected the argument that the need to maintain confidentiality outweighed the public interest in freedom of expression. Secondly, even if it may be conceded that Parliament, with its opportunities to receive expert advice and its mixture of members from various backgrounds, is better suited to consider the proper ambit of, for example, a right to privacy, the problem remains that Parliament is reluctant to legislate in these contentious areas: proposals that it should do so are elbowed aside by legislation furthering the ruling party's particular political programme. It is arguable that the whole of the law governing domestic human rights should be covered by a number of separate statutes, each covering one area. But it is notable just how few statutes have been passed (except since the HRA 1998 caused a dramatic rethink of some areas of law) which have as their sole purpose the protection of a particular liberty. The Contempt of Court Act 1981, Equal Pay legislation, Data Protection legislation and the Freedom of Information Act 2000 come to mind, but all of those except the last were, in fact, driven by European law. The UK still has no privacy legislation; the HRA 1998 appears to have a good chance of creating a far more comprehensive right to respect for private and family life than the patchy and piecemeal one currently protected under various other names in domestic law. At present, the Convention is incorporated into domestic law, but not entrenched; thus, it could be removed by the simple method of repeal of the HRA. It is submitted that this is a sensible situation at present, both in terms of the maintenance of parliamentary sovereignty and to avoid handing over too much power to the unelected judiciary.

In summary, the new scheme should allow the relatively fast, but incremental improvement of the UK's recognition and enforcement of domestic human rights. Certain weaknesses are identifiable[1] within the HRA 1998 and the Convention, but the method chosen is a reasonable compromise or first step towards a rights-based culture in UK law and society.

## Note

1   Obvious deficiencies of the HRA include the missing Art 13 (guarantee of a legal remedy for infringement of a Convention right); the exceptions made in the definition of 'public authority'; the fact that most of the ECHR rights which it incorporates are qualified, rather than absolute; and the lack of a direct power by which courts could strike down offending legislation. Each of these could be discussed in greater detail, as could the process of incorporation under the HRA 1998.

# Question 48

Which has the more advantageous results: the Human Rights Act 1998 or a tailor-made Bill of Rights for the UK?

## Answer plan

A fairly demanding question, which requires detailed knowledge of the European Convention on Human Rights (the Convention), the Human Rights Act (HRA) 1998 and key decisions on possible Convention breaches committed by the UK. Issues to be discussed include:

• the difficulties of constructing a tailor-made Bill of Rights;

• exceptions to the primary rights of the Convention;

• the effect of the margin of appreciation in certain ECHR decisions;

• general restrictions on Convention rights;

• deficiencies of the HRA 1998;

• weaknesses of some substantive Convention rights, for example, Art 14.

# Answer

Between 1976 and 1996, there were five major attempts to introduce a Human Rights Bill into UK law, and many attempts to at least raise the issue; the overwhelming majority of such attempts have advocated incorporation of the European Convention on Human Rights and Fundamental Freedoms into UK law using the mechanism of an ordinary Act of Parliament. (By incorporation of the Convention, such Bills have meant Arts 1–18 and the First Protocol.) The House of Lords Select Committee as long ago as 1978 was unanimous on this issue: 'To attempt to incorporate *de novo* a set of fundamental rights would be a fruitless exercise.' Starting from scratch and developing a Bill of Rights for the UK would almost inevitably have been a burdensome task, because the political parties (and the various pressure groups) would have had enormous difficulty in reaching agreement on it, while the process of hearing and considering all the representations made by interested parties would have been extremely lengthy. This is suggested by the experience of Austria, where a Commission was set up to draw up a code of fundamental rights. After 12 years, it had produced only alternative drafts of two rights. Apart from the cumbersome nature of the process, a Bill of Rights might have taken too much account of the interests of the government in power at the time when it was passed.

Although producing a tailor-made Bill of Rights would certainly have been difficult, it can be argued that the UK should nevertheless have attempted it, rather than incorporating the ready-made Convention, which is arguably defective in content. It is a cautious compromise document: it is not as open textured as the American Bill of Rights and it contains long lists of exceptions to most of the primary rights – exceptions, which suggest a strong respect for the institutions of the State. These exceptions have at times received a broad interpretation in the European Court of Human Rights (ECHR) and it is likely that the resulting case will will have a great influence on domestic courts when they come to apply the rights directly in the domestic arena for the first time. For example, Art 10, which protects freedom of expression, contains an exception in respect of the protection of morals. This was invoked in the *Handyside* case (1976) in respect of a booklet aimed at schoolchildren which was circulating freely in the rest of Europe. It was held that the UK Government was best placed to determine what was needed in its own country in order to protect morals, and so no breach of Art 10 had occurred. The decision in *Otto-Preminger Institut v Austria* (1994) was on very similar lines: the 'rights of others' exception could be invoked to allow suppression of a film which might cause offence to religious people since, in allowing such suppression, the State had not overstepped the margin of appreciation. A somewhat similar course was adopted in *The Observer and The Guardian v UK* (1991) (the *Spycatcher* case), which will be considered in some detail as an example of the readiness of the ECHR to afford a wide meaning to the exception provisions of the Convention.

The newspapers claimed that temporary injunctions granted to restrain publication of material from *Spycatcher* by Peter Wright violated the Art 10 guarantee of freedom of expression. The court found that, although the injunctions clearly constituted an interference with the newspapers' freedom of expression, those in force during the period before publication of the book in the US in July 1987 fell within the exception provided for by para 2 of Art 10 in respect of protecting national security. The injunctions had the aim of preventing publication of material which, according to evidence presented by the Attorney General, might have created a risk of detriment to MI5. The nature of the risk was uncertain, as the exact contents of *Spycatcher* were not known at that time, since it was still only in manuscript form. Further, the court ensured the preservation of the Attorney General's right to grant a permanent injunction; if *Spycatcher* material had been published before that claim could be heard, the subject matter of the action could have been damaged or destroyed. In the court's view, these factors established the existence of a pressing social need, which the injunctions answered.

The court then considered whether the actual restraints imposed were proportionate to the legitimate aims represented by the exceptions. It found that the injunctions did not prevent the papers from pursuing a campaign for an inquiry into the operation of the security services, and though preventing publication for a long time – over a year – the material in question could not be classified as urgent news. Thus, it was held that the interference complained of was proportionate to the ends in view. It is suggested that in this ruling, the court accepted very readily the view that the authority of the judiciary could best be preserved by allowing a claim of confidentiality, set up in the face of a strong competing public interest, to found an infringement of freedom of speech for over a year.[1]

In other areas, there has been an equal willingness to allow the exceptions a wide scope in curtailing the primary rights. In *CCSU v UK* (1988), the European Commission on Human Rights, in declaring the unions' application inadmissible, found that national security interests should prevail over freedom of association, even though the national security interest was weak, while the infringement of the primary right was very clear: an absolute ban on joining a trade union had been imposed. It is worth noting that the ILO Committee on Freedom of Association had earlier found that the ban breached the 1947 ILO Freedom of Association Convention.

However, these were all instances in which the doctrine of the 'margin of appreciation' had an influence on the decision in question. In other words, the view was taken that in certain particularly sensitive areas, such as the protection of morals or of national security, the domestic government had to be allowed a certain discretion in determining what was called for. In less sensitive areas, the ECHR has been more bold. In the *Sunday Times* case (1979), it determined that the exception to Art 10, allowing restraint of freedom of speech in order to protect the authority of the judiciary, was inapplicable in an instance where the litigation in question which could have been affected was dormant. The court has also been relatively bold in the area of prisoners' rights, holding in *Golder* (1975) and *Silver* (1983) that a prisoner's right to privacy of correspondence must be respected, and rejecting the UK Government's arguments that an express of implied exception to Art 8 could be invoked.

Apart from the exceptions to particular rights there are also general restrictions to the operation of the rights. All the Articles except Arts 3, 4(1), 6(2) and 7 are subject to certain restrictions, either because certain limitations are inherent in the formulation of the right itself, or because it is expressly stated that certain cases are not covered by the right in question. Even the right to life under Art 2 is far from absolute: 'unintentional' deprivations of life are not covered, and the use of necessary force is justified even where it results in death. Derogations and reservations also contributed to each State's ability to limit the extent to which it could be found to be in breach of Convention freedoms and rights, whilst maintaining the appearance of a rights guarantee in its domestic law. Some States did not even allow the right to individual petition of the Court, until it became compulsory under the 11th Protocol.

Now that the Convention has been incorporated and the interpretative jurisprudence of the Court is to be used in domestic cases as a guide, such exceptions and restrictions may, of course, offer judges a means of avoiding a controversial conflict with the Government and make it unlikely that a radical impact on UK law will exist in the long term; Woolf LCJ had made it clear that Convention rights should be argued only where they truly apply and that any sudden explosion of human rights arguments, where strictly unnecessary in UK courts, will not be supported. However, judges will have an important function in giving the language of rights primacy, even if, eventually, an exception to a particular right is allowed to prevail, rather than their previous position of merely applying the statute in question without any recognition to the freedoms it affects. This could be an important change for such statutes, as the Public Order Act 1986 and the Official Secrets Act 1989. In considering the effect of such statutes, their human rights dimension should at least, in future, be recognised.

An example of an area in which it is difficult to predict whether the Convention will have a strong effect on domestic law is that of discrimination. Article 14 prohibits discrimination on 'any ground such as sex, race, colour, language, religion', but only in relation to any other Convention right or freedom. It has been determined in a string of cases since *X v Federal Republic of Germany* (1970) that Art 14 has no separate existence, but that, nevertheless, a measure which is, in itself, in conformity with the requirement of the Convention right governing its field of law may, however, infringe that Article when it is read in conjunction with Art 14, for the reason that it is discriminatory in nature. In *Abdulaziz, Cabales and Balkandali v UK* (1985), it was held that although the application of Art 14 does not pre-suppose a breach of the substantive provisions of the Convention and is, therefore, to that extent, autonomous, it cannot be applied unless the facts in question fall within the ambit of one or more of the rights and freedoms. Thus, in one sense, Art 14 will be largely ineffective in strengthening the existing provisions of sex discrimination and race relations legislation which tends to be invoked in the context of employment, because general employment claims fall outside the ambit of the other rights and freedoms. Yet, conversely, Art 14 is almost certain to have an almost immediate and great impact on the forms of discrimination which will be unlawful in situations where another Convention right or freedom does apply, since Art 14 prohibits discrimination on any ground, not just the UK's current sex, race and disability. Case law exists on discrimination on the basis of sexuality and transsexuality, religion, lifestyle, political opinion, residence or wealth, which will all be argued in UK courts very soon and are likely to shake up the UK's narrow discrimination law considerably, at least as far as the activities of public authorities are concerned. Further, it should be remembered that the State bears a positive duty to prevent breaches of the Convention (*Abdulaziz v UK*) and that cases clearly state that discrimination on grounds of sex or race will almost never be justified (for example, *Schmidt v Germany* (1994)).

The Convention was never intended to be used as a domestic Bill of Rights. It has been argued that creation of such a new guarantee from scratch would be an incredibly difficult and complex task, and so it is understandable why the incorporation of the Convention has been chosen as a (comparatively) quick and easy 'fix'. But it may further be argued that due to the deficiencies of the Convention as a human rights guarantee for the UK, there should be a commitment towards creating a new Bill of Rights in the future, once it can be judged to what extent the HRA 1998 has been a success. The Convention has achieved some notable successes which may cause shock waves through UK courts and the Government; once these have dissipated, there will be room to consider whether further entrenched rights legislation is necessary and the form it should take. If such a course were taken in the UK, then it would be brought into line with the experience of most of the other European signatories. These States already possess codes of rights enshrined in their constitutions, but the majority also adhere to a general practice of incorporation of State Treaties into domestic law, either automatically, as in the case of Switzerland, or upon ratification, as in the case of Luxembourg. The dual system of the Convention rights and a domestic code of rights seems to operate well in these countries. Thus, the HRA could be an interim measure to secure the further protection of the rights provided by the Convention, in the hope that a domestic Bill of Rights would later cure the gaps, defects and inadequacies of the Convention. If a domestic Bill of Rights is ever created (in spite of the current Government's lack of will to do so, as evidenced in the White Paper, *Bringing Rights Home* (1997)), then the two documents could exist side by side in UK law and each could be invoked when its protection of rights on a point was stronger than the other.[2]

In conclusion, it is suggested that, whilst they have their deficiencies, both the Convention and the HRA 1998 which incorporates it are positive steps towards the greater priority and recognition of rights in the UK, particularly in courts. But the deficiencies do still leave room for argument that, at some stage, a supplementary and complementary Bill of Rights should be enacted in order to create a more tailor-made and comprehensive human rights guarantee for the UK.

## Notes

1 Further features of this decision could be considered: the court seems to have been readily pursuaded by the Attorney General's argument that a widely framed injunction was needed in July 1986, but it is arguable that it was wider than it needed to be to prevent a risk to national security. It could have required the newspapers to refrain from publishing Wright material which had not been previously published by others until (if) the action to prevent publication of the book was lost. Such wording would have taken care of any national security interest; therefore, wording going beyond that was disproportionate to that aim.

2 An example could be inserted here. Cyprus adopted a course similar to this when it became independent in 1960. It used the Convention as a drafting prototype for certain fundamental rights and freedoms which then became part of its new

constitution. The Convention itself was incorporated into the law of Cyprus and was then invoked before the Cypriot courts as a supplementary aid to interpreting corresponding articles of the constitution. This apparently circular method is not without success and does seem to highlight weaknesses in the constitution.

# Question 49

Critically evaluate the extent to which the Human Rights Act 1998 will force change in substantive UK law.

## Answer plan

This is likely to become an extremely common type of examination question, although it may appear in many forms. It is essential that students should be able to explain and evaluate cases on each of the rights within the European Convention on Human Rights (the Convention), and further to predict whether and how UK law will have to change in the coming years to reflect Convention jurisprudence. When a question is phrased as generally as this one, students should avoid the temptation to refer to a long list of instances where domestic law will be likely to be challenged; it is crucial to include some depth of argument and analysis of the case law. Examiners may also ask students to refer to one or more specific areas of domestic law, such as criminal law and evidence, or to refer to one or more Convention rights, such as privacy, expression, discrimination or torture. It is therefore essential that students have detailed knowledge of current issues concerning Convention rights and their status in domestic law. If the question is phrased generally, it will be necessary to be selective about the rights referred to in the answer.

The following matter must be considered:

- the impact of the Human Rights Act (HRA) 1998 on domestic law;
- leading European Court of Human Rights (ECHR) cases which raise issues about the UK's enforcement of human rights in key areas, for example, privacy, police powers, discrimination;

- role of domestic courts and Parliament in interpreting and giving effect to the new rights.

# Answer

Since October 2000, public authorities within the UK have been under a duty to act in compliance with the Convention. Since 'public authorities' includes the courts, all governmental organisations and the Press Complaints Commission (amongst many others), it is clear that there will be an immense effect on UK law, if only by necessitating checks that current procedures and rules are in compliance with the Convention rights. It is without doubt that all courts will be deluged with arguments based on the Convention, and so the existing case law of the ECHR will be a vital tool for interpretation purposes. Many statutes will be opened to rights-based scrutiny and may be vulnerable to declarations of incompatibility issued by a higher court under s 4 of the HRA 1998. A tide of legislation designed to ensure compliance is also underway, for example, the Regulation of Investigatory Powers Act 2000, which is discussed below. However, it remains to be seen to what extent new rights will be created in areas of the law where rights are, at present, weak; and whether the interpretation of Convention rights taken by the Government and the judiciary will similar to that taken by Strasbourg.

It should be remembered that neither the HRA 1998 nor the ECHR on which the latter is based give human rights free rein within domestic law; each has its own exceptions and limitations. The contents of the HRA show that it is a delicate political balance: the rights which it contains can only be upheld against public authorities except where there is a positive obligation upon the State; existing legislation which contravenes those rights is not automatically invalid, but remains in force until a declaration of incompatibility is made; and Art 13 of the Convention, the right to an effective remedy before a domestic court, has 'disappeared' from the text of the Act. It would be possible, although unlikely, for very little change to result from the whole exercise if courts and Parliament take a restrictive interpretation of the new rights.

The Convention was itself a compromise document which attempted to identify core values applicable in a range of very different signatory countries: it contains few economic and social rights; most of the rights it does contain have exceptions for such matters as national security and the prevention of crime, amongst others; the doctrine of the 'margin of appreciation' has traditionally allowed great leeway to States in the means and methods of upholding rights; and the rights and freedoms within the Convention often require balancing against each other in the same case, since one person's freedom of expression may infringe another's right to respect for his private life. In spite of these and other limitations, it is, however, possible to predict many fields of law which will require at least re-evaluate in the light of Convention rights. Since the potential areas of change are so many and varied, the likely impact on three will be examined here: privacy; police powers; and discrimination.

There is no substantive right to privacy in either domestic law or, strictly speaking, under the Convention. However, domestic law has long recognised a collection of disparate privacy-related rights, which fall within the scope of land law, tort, criminal law and a handful of statutes. Further, Art 8 of the Convention requires respect for family and private life, and it is this requirement which is likely to force change in domestic law now that the HRA 1998 is in force, with strong arguments now existing in favour of the introduction of one concrete right to privacy. But any such right would, of necessity, have limitations and exceptions to allow for the contrasting Convention rights to freedom of expression and freedom of information, for example, to be enforced; s 12 of the HRA 1998 makes it clear that freedom of expression usually takes primacy over the right to privacy where there is a conflict. This latter point's importance has been highlighted by the recent passing of the Freedom of Information Act 2000, which gives a citizen a qualified right of access to information held by public authorities, whether about himself or not.

The debate as to whether there should be a tort of invasion of privacy has raged since the Younger Committee reported in 1972; it is arguable that the time has now come to stop forcing all invasions of privacy into tortious remedies under nuisance, defamation, or trespass into equitable remedies for breach of confidence. Each of these actions, in any case, has limitations: for example, trespass is available only where the victim has an interest in a relevant piece of land; breach of confidence requires that the recipient of the information knew that it was confidential in nature; and defamation offers no protection against the malicious revelation or exploitation of information which is true and, further, has justificatory defences. The current domestic protection of privacy is complex, patchy and piecemeal, and these points in themselves form a strong argument towards declaratory statutory clarification.

Whilst the relevant ECHR cases are qualified and the European Court of Human Rights has arguably tended towards caution in its interpretation of Art 8, it is clear that both respect for private life and for family life require more clarity than they at present have in domestic law. The case of *X and Y v The Netherlands* (1986) held that the State is under a positive obligation to ensure respect for an individual's private and family life, even where the interference comes from a non-State source, such as another private individual. There is a right to peaceful enjoyment of the home (*Sporrong and Lonroth v Sweden* (1982), *Powell and Rayner v UK* (1990)). Invasions of the home or office, even when carried out under warrant by State officials, are open to special scrutiny (*Niemietz v Germany* (1993)). Covert surveillance must be carried out only in accordance with stringent safeguards and with an easily accessible method of appeal for an aggrieved party (*Khan v UK* (2000)); arguably, the Regulation of Investigatory Powers Act 2000 does nothing to ensure this, since it allows interception of all communications even by employers, save where they are clearly marked 'private'.

The right to respect for family life will probably have an impact not only on family law, but also on immigration law (see *Hatami v Sweden* (1998)). Paternal rights may also require reform (*Keegan v Ireland* (1994)). Whether or not any Art 8 violations are found in existing statutes or established case authority, it makes good sense that at least a tort of invasion of privacy should exist in order to ensure that there are no unjustifiable gaps or inconsistencies in domestic law. Since the domestic courts have stated that there is no such tort in cases such as *Khorasandjian v Bush* (1993), a new statutory tort would be the best and most straightforward method of achieving this.

# Question 50

The Eastern European democratic State of Mandislavia is considering how best to guarantee the human rights of its citizens. You have been employed by the Mandislavian Law Commission to draft a consultation paper detailing the options available to the government in this matter. Compare and contrast the main relevant methods of ensuring human rights.

### Answer plan

This is a new take on a standard question which requires consideration of a wide range of options in guaranteeing human rights. Essentially, the main options which must be discussed and evaluated are:

- becoming a signatory to the European Convention on Human Rights (the Convention) without incorporating it into domestic law;
- becoming a signatory to the Convention and incorporating it into domestic law;
- creating a free-standing declaratory Bill of Rights;
- creating a Bill of Rights enforced by a tailor-made court.

# Answer

The Mandislavian Government needs to decide to what extent it wishes to guarantee human rights within its jurisdiction and, hence, to what extent it needs to amend or overrule its existing law and legal system. Some of the available options are little more than window-dressing and would merely provide an additional legal remedy for a citizen who believes that his rights have been infringed; others would have a dramatic effect upon Mandislavian law and would override all existing and future contradictory provisions. There are essentially four main options available: becoming a signatory to the Convention without incorporating it into domestic law; becoming a signatory to the Convention and incorporating it into domestic law; creating a free-standing Bill of

Rights to perform a declaratory function; or creating a Bill of Rights with a Court to supervise and enforce it. Each of these options will be evaluated in turn.

The first option would put Mandislavia into broadly the same position as that held by the UK until the Human Rights Act (HRA) 1998 came into force on 2 October 2000. Until 1998, the precarious and disorderly state of civil liberties and human rights in the UK was a strong argument in favour of the adoption of some form of Bill of Rights. In certain areas of civil liberties, the existing statutory and case law safeguards against abuse of power were less comprehensive and, arguably, less effective than in many other democratic countries. Citizens of the UK did enjoy a reasonable level of tolerance of individual behaviour, but there were serious gaps and the tolerance itself, because it was not bolstered by a formal guarantee of rights, was fragile, especially in times of crisis. The law sought to protect certain values such as the need to maintain public order but, in doing so, curtailed the exercise of certain freedoms, because nothing prevented it from disregarding them. Thus, human rights had a precarious status, in that they only existed, by deduction, in the interstices of the law. Individual citizens who believed that their human rights had been violated had to either find an available domestic action and remedy or try to take a case to the European Court of Human Rights (ECHR) in Strasbourg. Although the Eleventh Protocol has recently speeded up the Strasbourg system and should reduce the cost of an application, it is still a slow and expensive process with a high chance of failure; average Mandislavian citizens might find their rights little more than illusory if this were the only guarantee given.

If the second option were to be taken, Mandislavia would find itself in a situation remarkably similar to that currently at play in the UK since the HRA 1998 came into force. In contrast to the previous situation, the HRA now represents a minimum guarantee of freedom. Certain fundamental values have been placed, theoretically and temporarily at least, out of the reach of any political majority. Citizens of the UK no longer have to rely upon the ruling party to ensure that its own legislation does not infringe freedoms. When laws are passed which conflict with some fundamental freedom, courts will now have to interpret such laws in the light of the Convention and consider to what extent the freedoms may legitimately be curtailed. This is in stark contrast to the prior situation, where the courts had no choice but to apply an Act of Parliament, no matter how much it might breach the Convention.

The HRA 1998 has therefore created a far more active judicial role in protecting basic rights and freedoms. If a court considers that either a new or existing statute which is under its consideration infringes the Convention rights or freedoms, then it may issue a Declaration of Incompatibility, upon which it is hoped the Government will act promptly. The interpretation of the US constitution illustrates what could happen in this country; vast edifices of civil rights have been constructed out of innocuous and ambiguous phrases. The generality of terms of the Convention means that its interpretation is likely to evolve in accordance with the UK's changing needs and social values; this is, in any case, one of the basic principles of Strasbourg-based Convention jurisprudence, since the Convention is intended to be a living document which is not bound by time or venue, but can develop to suit both in any jurisdiction. Thus, it is likely that soon there will be two versions of the Convention relevant to the UK: the domestic version as incorporated by the HRA; and the still-existing opportunity to take a persistent grievance to Strasbourg. Depending upon its political and legal systems and the degree of independence enjoyed by its judiciary, this option might be an attractive one for Mandislavia, albeit perhaps a first step towards a Bill of Rights tailored to the needs and mores of that State.

In the UK, incorporation has already had a number of advantages. Citizens may obtain redress for human rights breaches without needing, except as a last resort, to apply to the ECHR in Strasbourg. This saves a great deal of time and money for the citizen and thus greatly improves access to justice. The range of remedies available under the HRA is the same as in any ordinary UK court case, and so includes injunctions and specific performance where appropriate, rather than simply damages. British judges are presumably already making a greater contribution to the development of Convention rights jurisprudence in Strasbourg. But a major disadvantage, or at least a source of anxiety, is the doubt as to whether British judges can be trusted to give a vigorous interpretation to the Convention. The British judiciary are, in general, highly regarded, but they are an elite group, drawn mainly from a certain stratum of society and, therefore, to varying degrees, out of touch with the working class. They have been trained in techniques of legal analysis which include deciding cases without the responsibility of considering their social repercussions; it is doubtful whether three days of human rights awareness training will have overturned years of this practice. The new role of the judiciary which is more important and therefore more overtly political might mean moves towards more political involvement in their appointments – a development which has taken place in America. The interpretations given by judges to the Convention may greatly dilute its impact. The UK still has no privacy legislation; the HRA 1998 appears to have a good chance of creating a far more comprehensive right to respect for private and family life than the patchy and piecemeal one currently protected under various other names in domestic law. At present, the Convention is incorporated into domestic law, but not entrenched; thus it could be removed by the simple method of repeal of the HRA 1998. It is submitted that this is a sensible situation at present, both in terms of the maintenance of parliamentary sovereignty and to avoid handing over too much power to the unelected judiciary. Whether it is similarly sensible for Mandislavia depends upon information which is not provided in the question as to independence of the judiciary, the political system and the current status of human rights in that State. In summary, the new scheme should allow the relatively fast, but incremental improvement of the UK's recognition and enforcement of domestic human rights. Certain weaknesses are identifiable within the HRA and the Convention, but the method chosen is a reasonable compromise or first step towards a rights-based culture in UK law and society, and could serve the same function in another State.

The third option would be to create a Bill of Rights specific to Mandislavian needs. The UK has repeatedly rejected this option; perhaps the Mandislavian Government would have a more open approach to the question. The House of Lords Select Committee as long ago as 1978 was unanimous on this issue: 'To attempt to incorporate *de novo* a set of fundamental rights would be a fruitless exercise.'

Starting from scratch and developing a Bill of Rights for the UK would almost inevitably have been a burdensome task, because the political parties (and the various pressure groups) would have had enormous difficulty in reaching agreement on it, while the process of hearing and considering all the representations made by interested parties would have been extremely lengthy. This is suggested by the experience of Austria, where a Commission was set up to draw up a code of fundamental rights. After 12 years, it had produced only alternative drafts of two rights. Apart from the cumbersome nature of the process, a Bill of Rights might have taken too much account of the interests of the government in power at the time when it was passed. Again, without further information, it is difficult to guess whether Mandislavia would face such problems.

Although producing a tailor-made Bill of Rights would certainly have been difficult, it can be argued that the UK should nevertheless have attempted, it rather than incorporating the ready-made European Convention on Human Rights, which is arguably defective in content. It is a cautious compromise document: it is not as open textured as the American Bill of Rights and it contains long lists of exceptions to most of the primary rights, exceptions which suggest a strong respect for the institutions of the State. These exceptions have, at times, received a broad interpretation in the ECHR and it is likely that the resulting cases will have a great influence on domestic courts when they come to apply the rights directly in the domestic arena for the first time. For example, Art 10, which protects freedom of expression, contains an exception in respect of the protection of morals. This was invoked in the *Handyside* case (1976) in respect of a booklet aimed at schoolchildren which was circulating freely in the rest of Europe. It was held that the UK Government was best placed to determine what was needed in its own country in order to protect morals and so no breach of Art 10 had occurred. The Convention was never intended to be used as a domestic Bill of Rights. It has been argued that creation of such a new guarantee from scratch would be an incredibly difficult and complex task and so it is understandable why the incorporation of the Convention has been chosen as a (comparatively) quick and easy 'fix'.

However, it may further be argued that, due to the deficiencies of the Convention as a human rights guarantee for the UK, there should be a commitment towards creating a new Bill of Rights in the future, once it can be judged to what extent the HRA 1998 has been a success.

The Convention has achieved some notable successes which may cause shockwaves through UK courts and the Government; once these have dissipated, there will be room to consider whether further entrenched rights legislation is necessary and the form it should take. If such a course were taken in the UK, then it would be brought into line with the experience of most of the other European signatories. These States already possess codes of rights enshrined in their constitutions, but the majority also adhere to a general practice of incorporation of State treaties into domestic law, either automatically, as in the case of Switzerland, or upon ratification, as in the case of Luxembourg. The dual system of the Convention rights and a domestic code of rights seems to operate well in these countries. Thus, the Human Rights Act, and a Mandislavian equivalent, could be an interim measure to secure the further protection of the rights provided by the Convention, in the hope that a domestic Bill of Rights would later cure the gaps, defects and inadequacies of the Convention. If a domestic Bill of Rights is ever created (in spite of the current government's lack of will to do so, as evidenced in the White Paper, *Bringing Rights Home* (1997)), then the two documents could exist side by side in UK law and each could be invoked when its protection of rights on a point was stronger than the other.

Thus, the Convention and the HRA 1998 which incorporates it are positive steps towards the greater priority and recognition of rights in the UK, particularly in courts, and could be adapted to suit Mandislavian needs and culture.

The final, and by far the strongest and most radical solution for Mandislavia, would be to create a domestic Bill of Rights tailor-made to Mandislavian needs and mores, and supervised and enforced by a specific domestic Court. This would follow the model of many other European States and would be particularly apt if Mandislavia either already has a written constitution and a Constitutional Court or, alternatively, is willing to create both. This option has the advantages (*inter alia*) of clarity, supremacy of human rights over conflicting law and ease of access by citizens to their rights. However, much depends on the method of appointment of judges to the Court, since the American experience has demonstrated that political divisions can impede justice and that political neutrality may be difficult to maintain. However, the existence of such a strong declaration of rights, combined with a Court empowered to strike down legislation and overrule executive actions which infringe those rights, is a high ideal for which to aim and one which might well be apt for Mandislavia in future, if not under present conditions.

# Index